PANDEMIC ECONOMIC

Pandemic Economics applies economic theory to the Covid-19 era, exploring the micro and macro dimensions of the pre-pandemic, pandemic, and post-pandemic phases.

Using core economic tools such as marginal analysis, cost-benefit analysis, and opportunity cost, this book explores the breadth of economic outcomes from the pandemic. It shows that a tradeoff between public health and economic health led to widespread problems, including virus infections and unemployment. Taking an international and comparative approach, the book shows that because countries implemented different economic policies, interventions, and timelines during the crisis, outcomes varied with respect to the extent of recession, process of recovery, availability of medical equipment, public health, and additional waves of the virus.

Pedagogical features are weaved throughout the text, including country case studies, key terms, suggested further reading, and discussion questions for solo or group study. On top of this, the book offers online supplements comprising PowerPoint slides, test questions, extra case studies, and an instructor guide.

This textbook will be a valuable resource for advanced undergraduate and postgraduate courses on pandemic economics, macroeconomics, health economics, public policy, and related areas.

Thomas R. Sadler is Professor of Economics at Western Illinois University. He teaches courses on Pandemic Economics, Energy Economics, and Environmental Economics. His research focuses on environmental policy, professional sports leagues, and technological change.

PANDEMIC ECONOMICS

Thomas R. Sadler

Routledge
Taylor & Francis Group

LONDON AND NEW YORK

First published 2022
by Routledge
2 Park Square, Milton Park, Abingdon, Oxon OX14 4RN

and by Routledge
52 Vanderbilt Avenue, New York, NY 10017

Routledge is an imprint of the Taylor & Francis Group, an informa business

© 2022 Thomas R. Sadler

British Library Cataloguing-in-Publication Data
A catalogue record for this book is available from the British Library

Library of Congress Cataloging-in-Publication Data
Names: Sadler, Thomas R., author.
Title: Pandemic economics/Thomas R. Sadler.
Description: Milton Park, Abingdon, Oxon; New York, NY: Routledge, 2021. |
Includes bibliographical references and index. |
Identifiers: LCCN 2021003147 (print) | LCCN 2021003148 (ebook) |
ISBN 9780367679774 (hardback) | ISBN 9780367679040 (paperback) |
ISBN 9781003133629 (ebook)
Subjects: LCSH: COVID-19 (Disease)-Economic aspects. | Economic history–21st century.
Classification: LCC HC59.3 .S23 2021 (print) | LCC HC59.3 (ebook) |
DDC 330.9-dc23
LC record available at https://lccn.loc.gov/2021003147
LC ebook record available at https://lccn.loc.gov/2021003148

ISBN: 978-0-367-67977-4 (hbk)
ISBN: 978-0-367-67904-0 (pbk)
ISBN: 978-1-003-13362-9 (ebk)

Typeset in Interstate
by Deanta Global Publishing Services, Chennai, India

Visit the Support Material: www.routledge.com/9780367679040

BRIEF CONTENTS

DETAILED CONTENTS

PART I

INVESTIGATION AND RECOGNITION   21

FIGURES

TABLES

PREFACE

Everyone living during the coronavirus pandemic understood its magnitude. The crisis upended people's lives, leading to difficult health and economic outcomes. We learned about epidemic curves, deliberate recessions, and medical shortages. Overall, the pandemic led to a convergence of a health crisis and an economic crisis, creating challenging personal and collective choices. From an economics perspective, this book investigates the pandemic, arguing that choices involve tradeoffs and incentives matter. As the large number of examples in *Pandemic Economics* demonstrates, not only are policy measures and economic theories once restricted to economics courses now a part of our everyday discussions, but they make important differences in our lives.

ACKNOWLEDGMENTS

I would like to thank Routledge for publishing this book. At every stage of the process, it has been a pleasure to work with this company. In particular, I would like to thank Natalie Tomlinson, Editor in Economics, for her enthusiasm for the project and encouragement during the early stages of writing. I would also like to thank Chloe James, Senior Editorial Assistant, who guided the book to completion. I appreciate their professionalism and willingness to respond to queries. With copyediting, I would like to thank Sarah Fish for her work in ensuring the consistency and style of the chapters. With the final proofs and index, I would like to thank Kelly Cracknell. I have colleagues who encourage scholarship, schedule seminars, and maintain research agendas. I thank them for their ongoing support, especially Tara Feld, Jessica Harriger-Lin, Tej Kaul, J. Jobu Babin, Shankar Ghimire, Alla Melkumian, William Polley, Shane Sanders, Bhavneet Walia, Justin Ehrlich, and William Koch. Personally, I benefit from weekly conversations with family, particularly during the pandemic. I would like to thank Judy, Chris, Mark, and Fred for their willingness to discuss the book. Most importantly, I would like to thank Holly, Maya, and Mathew for love and support. This book, and all of my work, is for you.

AN OVERVIEW OF THE BOOK

The book is organized in three parts. Part I investigates the economics of optimal disease control (chapter 2) and the economics of global networks (chapter 3). Part II recognizes the connection between a country's confirmed cases and production of output. A pattern exists. Over time, confirmed cases accelerate, reach a peak, and decelerate. At the same time, output decreases during shutdown, reaches a minimum point during recession, and increases during recovery. Part II reflects this pattern. Chapter 4 develops theories of economic shutdown. Chapter 5 discusses recession, forecasting, and economic policy. Chapter 6 addresses economic recovery. Part III applies economic theory to pandemic outcomes, including healthcare economics (chapter 7), inequality of outcomes (chapter 8), economics of energy, the environment, and climate change (chapter 9), economics of education (chapter 10), economics of technology and innovation (chapter 11), international economic perspectives (chapter 12), new economic geography (chapter 13), game theory and mutual interdependence (chapter 14), and a trail of disruption (chapter 15). Instructors interested in specific topics may cover the chapters in part III in any order.

LEARNING OBJECTIVES

Each chapter lists learning objectives. By linking to chapter outlines and material, the learning objectives provide continuity. But the learning objectives also link to chapter takeaways at the end of each chapter. With this framework, students will understand chapter structure, the progression of ideas, and important points for review.

1 Introduction to pandemic economics

Learning objectives

After reading this chapter, you will be able to:

LO1   Describe the field of pandemic economics.
LO2   Discuss the economic approach and its application to the study of pandemics.
LO3   Analyze the origin of the coronavirus pandemic.
LO4   Assess the history and economic implications of previous pandemics.
LO5   Analyze the rules of pandemic economics.

Chapter outline

- Pandemic economics
- The economic approach
- A pandemic origin story
- Previous pandemics and economic history
- Rules of pandemic economics
- Summary

Pandemic economics

The disease Covid-19, which emerged in December 2019, is caused by severe acute respiratory syndrome coronavirus (SARS-CoV-2), named because of its genetic relationship to the virus responsible for the SARS outbreak in 2003. After emerging in China, Covid-19 quickly spread throughout Asia, Europe, North America, and the rest of the world. On March 11, 2020, the World Health Organization declared it a pandemic. The International Monetary Fund's Managing Director Kristalina Georgieva (2020) anticipated the "worst economic fallout since the Great Depression." Economic contagion spread from the developed world to low-income countries across Asia, Africa, and Latin America.

In response, federal governments implemented unprecedented controls, including household lockdowns, economic shutdowns, and quarantine orders. Government stimulus plans proved to be expensive palliatives, not cures. Exposures and deaths rose, while national economies fell. Anxious to get people back to work, countries experienced rising healthcare costs, social anxiety, and medical shortages. Economic sectors experienced supply shocks (mining and manufacturing), demand shocks (transportation and tourism), or both (restaurants). Unequal outcomes occurred. Members of marginalized communities with pre-existing health conditions, less access to medical care, and poor environmental quality experienced higher rates of morbidity and mortality. Gender inequalities existed with essential work, childcare, and employment (Sevilla and Smith, 2020). At the same time, people in high-income occupations, while implementing defensive measures to avoid the disease, were relatively immune from the economic downturn.

Urbanization and the growing connectivity among metropolitan centers contributed to the risk of contagion. The geographic spread of the disease affected the lives of hundreds of millions of people. The complexity of human mobility and the difficulty of containment strategies complicated the global response. Reacting to growing economic hardship, more than eighty countries sought help from the International Monetary Fund (Elliott, 2020a). As the pandemic progressed, many analysts wondered if the global economy would ever be the same. Writing in *Foreign Policy*, Adam Tooze (2020), director of the European Institute at Columbia University, argued that "There has never been a crash landing like this before. There is something new under the sun. And it is horrifying." With the disease spreading through global transmission networks, epidemiologists argued that humanity would struggle to contain future outbreaks. Economists warned that rising costs would cripple economies. At the intersection of these economic and health crises, the field of *pandemic economics* was born, the study of pandemics from an economics perspective.

The economic approach

The field of *economics* analyzes society's material wants under the condition of scarcity. To develop the area of pandemic economics, this book uses the economic approach, which combines assumptions of market equilibrium, maximizing behavior, and consumer preferences. To study individual topics, economists use their analytical toolboxes, filled with economic tools and concepts. In this book, readers will encounter economic methodology that is common in principles of economics courses.

Economic methodology

One example of economic methodology is cost-benefit analysis. After a disease outbreak becomes an epidemic and then a pandemic, most countries attempt to slow its transmission. Public sectors implement shutdown orders to shutter targeted segments of the economy. By reducing the risk of exposure, these policies create a public health benefit. Economic costs, however, include lost jobs and income. To determine the overall effect, a cost-benefit analysis balances the economic costs with the health benefits.

Another example of economic methodology is the concept of tradeoffs. The reason that economists think in terms of tradeoffs is we live in a world with limited resources. Tradeoffs result from the condition of *scarcity*–the state of being in short supply–which is the root of society's economic problems. During a pandemic, public sectors allocate resources to support public health, but then fewer resources are available to aid workers and businesses. Gordon Brown, former Prime Minister of Great Britain (2007–2010), when discussing the coronavirus pandemic, explained, "The more you intervene to deal with the medical emergency the more you put the economy at risk" (Elliott, 2020b). In this context, the opportunity cost of an extended economic shutdown means the value of the most desired but foregone alternative.

A potential tradeoff exists between *efficiency* and *equity*. Efficiency occurs when society receives the most it can from its scarce resources. Equity exists when those benefits are distributed fairly. That is, efficiency refers to the size of the economy while equity refers to how output or income is divided among members of society. But when the public sector implements economic or health policy, these goals may conflict. During a pandemic the public sector deems certain workers as "essential" or necessary to keep the most important segments of the economy operating, even when the disease is spreading. The problem with this approach is that many essential workers have lower-income status, pre-existing health conditions, and less access to healthcare systems. During a public health crisis, they face elevated risk to their physical well-being. Though achieving greater efficiency, this policy choice of keeping essential but compromised workers active leads to an inequality of health outcomes.

To analyze market effects, this book uses the model of supply and demand. This familiar framework provides a method to address several topics, including labor markets, shortages, unemployment, and public policy.

People respond to *incentives*, the policies, initiatives, and proclamations that induce responses among the human population. Implemented as reward or punishment, incentives are important in the field of economics. Higher prices, for example, provide the incentive for sellers to produce more output but for individuals to consume less output. Higher prices normally signal to economic agents how to react, which in turn provides the incentive for resource allocation.

Since the beginning of the coronavirus pandemic, economists have written many articles about the crisis, addressing such topics as the economic shutdown, recession, unemployment, recovery, policy intervention, economic costs of disease, inequality of outcomes, shortages, environmental and energy effects, innovation, geospatial impacts, mutual interdependence, international effects, and many others. This book draws on this growing body of research, arguing that the economics perspective provides an important method to analyze pandemics.

Economics and epidemiology

Pandemics create both economic costs and health consequences. Therefore, in addition to the research of economists, the field of pandemic economics includes research from *epidemiology*, the study of health that addresses the incidence, distribution, and control of diseases. The types of data gathered by epidemiologists studying pandemics include genetic strains, mutations, infectiousness, antibody tests, treatments, and the prevention of future outbreaks, topics addressed in this book. Because epidemiology plays a pre-eminent role in the study of pandemics, this book includes the epidemiological perspective. Epidemiology demonstrates that infectious diseases such as Covid-19 exist at the intersection of the environment, transmitting agents, and hosts (figure 1.1).

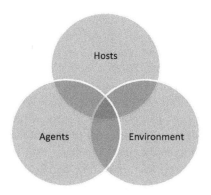

Figure 1.1 Infectious agents, hosts, and the environment.
Source: adapted from Morens and Fauci (2020), Figure 3

The strength of this comprehensive approach is that economics and epidemiology are both empirical fields. But in the following chapters, epidemiology is complementary: the book exists firmly in the field of economics. When we encounter topics from epidemiology, they are thoroughly explained. The book argues that, to study pandemic economics, the tools and empirical methods of both economics and epidemiology are important. Throughout the book, vital statistics provide the best method to understand trends in both the economy and public health.

From containment to recovery

The coronavirus pandemic inflicted multiple shocks on countries: the spread of disease, economic downturn, and reverberations from the rest of the world (World Bank, 2020a). During the pandemic, countries would follow a script, with few exceptions. To slow the spread of disease, shutdown interventions would first close segments of the economy, which would lead to recession. Changes in morbidity and mortality from the spread of disease would vary, depending on both the effectiveness of government interventions and behavioral responses. Eventually, when the disease was under control, economic recovery occurred. International outcomes included supply chain shortages, travel restrictions, and a decrease in direct foreign investment. The overall effect of the multiple shocks was to alter the economic conditions of countries (figure 1.2).

Economic costs of the downturn

The economic fallout crippled even the most resilient markets, leading to a global economic downturn. Before the pathogen completed its trip around the world, the coronavirus pandemic delivered an economic shock of "enormous magnitude," leading to widespread economic costs (World Bank, 2020b). Despite support from public sectors, the World Bank forecasted a 5 percent global economic contraction, the deepest global recession in 80 years. Countries with weak healthcare systems, fragile economies, and heavy reliance on global trade, tourism, and remittances from abroad experienced particularly severe downturns. The economic impact of the coronavirus pandemic included both direct and indirect

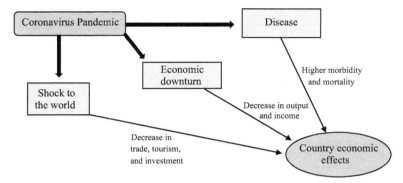

Figure 1.2 Multiple shocks from the pandemic.

Source: adapted from World Bank (2020a), Figure 1

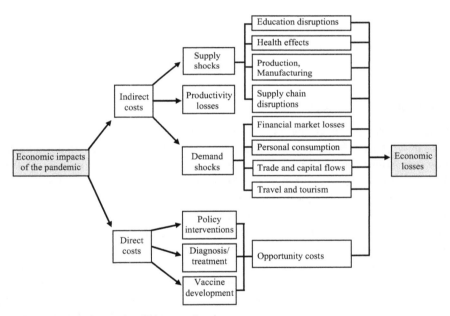

Figure 1.3 Economic impacts of the pandemic.

Source: adapted from Shretta (2020)

costs (Shretta, 2020). Direct costs entailed the costs of policy interventions; research, development, and deployment for a vaccine; and disease diagnosis and treatment in the healthcare industry. The indirect costs included productivity losses, supply shocks, and demand shocks (figure 1.3).

Confirmed cases

According to the World Health Organization, at the end of 2020, more than 65,000,000 confirmed cases and 1,500,000 deaths were recorded. The top-twelve countries experienced more than one million confirmed cases each (table 1.1). The United States, Spain, France, Argentina, and Brazil equaled or exceeded the 3 percent threshold of confirmed cases as

Table 1.1 Countries with the most confirmed cases at the end of 2020

Number	Country	Confirmed cases	Population	Confirmed cases as a percentage of population
1	United States	13,234,551	328,200,000	4.03%
2	India	9,462,809	1,353,000,000	0.69%
3	Brazil	6,314,740	209,500,000	3.01%
4	Russian Federation	2,295,654	144,500,000	1.58%
5	France	2,179,481	66,990,000	3.25%
6	Spain	1,628,208	46,940,000	3.46%
7	United Kingdom	1,617,331	66,650,000	2.42%
8	Italy	1,585,178	60,360,000	2.62%
9	Argentina	1,413,375	44,490,000	3.17%
10	Colombia	1,308,376	49,650,000	2.63%
11	Mexico	1,107,071	126,200,000	0.87%
12	Germany	1,053,869	83,020,000	1.26%

Source: World Health Organization, Covid19.who.int, accessed December 1, 2020

a percentage of the population. In economic terms, an increase in confirmed cases means greater resources necessary for policy, healthcare, and economic stimulus.

A pandemic origin story

Humanity's polarization from the natural world triggered the novel coronavirus pandemic. "Disease emergence reflects dynamic balances and imbalances, within complex globally distributed ecosystems comprising humans, animals, pathogens, and the environment" (Morens and Fauci, 2020). At some point in late 2019, the virus left a bat and found its way, either directly or through an intermediate host, into a human, and then more humans. Eventually the virus emerged in the Huanan seafood market in Wuhan, China and jumped from host to host in a superspreader event (Yong, 2020). Traveling with its human hosts, the virus made its way to other parts of China and eventually the rest of the world.

The novel coronavirus possessed three characteristics that created a historical assault on human health that required a lockdown on social interaction and economic activity. First, it was a virus that had never before infected humans in a sustained manner. Second, it possessed a high level of efficiency of transmission between humans. Third, it possessed a high level of morbidity and mortality. Taken together, these characteristics created a "perfect storm" for a new infectious disease (Morens and Fauci, 2020).

Zoonoses

Most infectious diseases are now classified as *zoonoses*, diseases transmitted to humans from animals (Jabr, 2020). Acquired Immune Deficiency Syndrome (AIDS), for example, crossed from chimpanzees to humans in the 1920s, leading to deadly outbreaks decades later. Although ancient, zoonoses increased during the twentieth century. Zoonotic *pathogens*—bacteria, viruses, and microorganisms that cause diseases—move between humans and animals when ecosystem reconfiguration (intensive agriculture, deforestation, and mining) increases the likelihood of transmission. Despite the existence of anti-poaching laws, the hunting of wild animals is common. If rural households have an insufficient supply of food, they may hunt wild animals.

Pathogens exist in *natural reservoirs*—environments in which infectious pathogens live—residing in species such as bats. Some diseases, however, may spill over to other species, depending on the frequency and severity of zoonotic outbreaks, networks of contagion, markets for exotic creatures, and methods of industrial agriculture. When humans transform ecosystems and reduce the world's biological diversity, diseases of animals may jump to humans. In this process, the excessive tracking, killing, and consumption of wildlife increases the probability of "cross-species infection" (Jabr, 2020). Once infection occurs, human transmission networks may transport a pathogen regionally via highways and railways and globally via airplanes. As David Quammen (2012) argues in his book, *Spillover: Animal Infections and the Next Human Pandemic*, "Human-caused ecological pressures and disruptions are bringing pathogens ever more into contact with human populations, while human technology and behavior are spreading those pathogens ever more widely and quickly."

The novel coronavirus may have passed to humans in one or several ways. A hunter of bats may have provided a new and direct pathway for the virus. A vendor or cook in a live-animal market may have contracted the virus through the splattering of blood when an infected bat was gutted and skinned. Through their interactions with other animals, an infected bat may have passed the virus to other caged animals before the virus leaped to humans. Or consumers may have touched contaminated surfaces in a live-animal market or inhaled infected droplets, spreading the virus through new transmission networks.

Black swan

In analyzing the events leading to the first pandemic of the twenty-first century, one origin story is that a *black swan*—an unpredictable event with severe consequences that exists beyond the scope of normal expectations—appeared unexpectedly in the form of a novel coronavirus, jumped from bats to humans in a live-animal market, moved through central China, spread throughout the region and world, and shattered the global economy.

In the field of economics, the concept of black swan is characterized by its rarity and severe impact. According to Nassim N. Taleb (2007), finance professor and former Wall Street trader who popularized the term:

> First, it is an outlier, as it lies outside of the realm of regular expectations, because nothing in the past can convincingly point to its possibility. Second, it carries an extreme impact … Third, in spite of its outlier status, human nature makes us concoct explanations for its occurrence after the fact, making it explainable and predictable.

Black swan events harm economies in unexpected ways. But the relevance of the concept that "lies outside the realm of regular expectations" depends on the characteristic of the event about which society is unsure. The unknown may be specific, such as profit for a company in the following quarter, or vague, such as a general uncertainty with respect to the future course of events. When Taleb refers to black swan events, he is referring to events that, at the time they occur, are not possibly anticipated (Faulkner et al., 2017). The implication is that, by ignoring the potential risks of a large and unforeseen event, standard methods of forecasting cannot accurately assess the risk to economic systems. However, while useful as a political tool and technically correct in explaining some economic disruptions, the black swan story is incomplete.

Black elephant

A better description of Covid-19 is *black elephant*, which crosses black swan, something whose outcome forces us to reconsider fundamental premises that society took for granted, with the concept of "elephant in the room," which everyone understands but no one wants to acknowledge (Friedman, 2020). One reason that black elephant represents a useful metaphor for Covid-19 is the disease resulted from an assault on nature, bringing humans in closer contact with animals. The term black elephant may be used for environmental applications, including pollution, climate change, and assaults on nature. But environmental problems such as these are often minimized, because solving them may disrupt economic systems. That is, addressing a black elephant event alters institutions and markets. Thus, the world minimizes the threat.

A second reason that black elephant serves as a useful metaphor is the novel coronavirus resulted from the hunting and capturing of wildlife in destroyed or vulnerable natural habitats; the abundance of generalized species such as bats, rats, and primates that host zoonotic viruses; and the selling of contaminated wildlife in live-animal markets.

A third reason is that the pandemic was not completely unexpected. In 2017, Dr. Anthony S. Fauci, director of the National Institute of Allergy and Infectious Diseases in the United States, said there was "no doubt" that a new infectious disease would soon emerge (Gallagher, 2017). In 2018, the Johns Hopkins Center for Health Security gathered U.S. government officials, public health experts, and business leaders to address the potentially devastating economic and social consequences of global threats, issuing a report, "The Characteristics of Pandemic Pathogens," that addressed bacteria, fungi, prions, protozoa, and viruses, the latter serving as the real menace (Alexopulos, 2018). In 2019, the U.S. intelligence community, in its annual "Worldwide Threat Assessment," warned of the hazards of a new outbreak (Coates, 2019). Many other warnings existed.

Once contaminated, humans passed the novel coronavirus to each other through transmission networks, first locally, then regionally, and globally. Because many governments did not initially investigate or recognize the virus and were unprepared to address its infectiousness, exposures and deaths increased to levels not seen since the 1918 Spanish flu pandemic. Like with the Spanish flu more than a century in the past, economic recovery from the novel coronavirus proved to be a long and protracted process:

> At first, the virus may have proliferated at a rate sufficient to sustain itself, but not high enough to create noticeable clusters of infection. Eventually, in pathways linked to the trade and consumption of wildlife, the virus journeyed from villages in rural China to the city of Wuhan: a modern metropolis of more than 10 million people, each a potential host with no immunity, living in dense clusters. Soon it was moving rapidly from person to person in restaurants, offices, apartment complexes, hotels, and hospitals. From there, it could have easily hopped on China's high-speed rail network, reaching Beijing and

Shanghai in under six hours. At some point in late 2019 or early 2020, the virus discovered a new way to travel: It boarded a 747.

(Jabr, 2020)

A final reason that black elephant serves as a useful metaphor is it expands the black swan framework, encouraging reflection on the global economic processes that unleashed the pandemic, such as ecological degradation and global transmission networks. The spread of microbes filled an ecological niche, especially in a world with almost eight billion people, urbanization, high population density in urban areas, and an increasing demand for exotic animals.

Previous pandemics and economic history

Pandemics are not new. "Newly emerging (and re-emerging) infectious diseases have been threatening humans since the Neolithic revolution, 12,000 years ago, when human hunter-gatherers settled into villages to domesticate animals and cultivate crops" (Morens and Fauci, 2020). These attempts at the domestication of nature led to ancient zoonotic diseases, including bubonic plague, measles, and smallpox. Because coronaviruses currently exist that are regularly found among human populations, they must have emerged prior to the determination of these viruses as human pathogens. In 2002-2003, the severe acute respiratory syndrome coronavirus (SARS-CoV) came from an animal host, most likely a civet cat, to cause a near-pandemic outbreak before the implementation of public health measures. In 2012, the Middle East respiratory syndrome coronavirus (MERS-CoV) transferred from dromedary camels to humans, but has since dissipated. Covid-19, recognized in late 2019, served as the next coronavirus disease, requiring a complex, flexible, and multifaceted response (Morens and Fauci, 2020).

Plague pandemics

Frank M. Snowden, the Andrew Downey Orrick Professor Emeritus of History and History of Medicine at Yale University, teaches a class on the history of plague pandemics and recent diseases. In Professor Snowden's (2019) book from the course, *Epidemics and Society: From the Black Death to the Present*, he explains that the concept of quarantine comes from the Italian *quaranta*, the number forty. Quarantine began long before anyone understood the characteristics of disease. A period of forty days was chosen not for reasons of health but for the biblical context of purification, which includes stories such as the Israelites wandering in the wilderness for forty years and the forty days and nights of the flood in Genesis. Countries have long applied quarantines in response to disease outbreaks.

Virulence

In Professor Snowden's (2019) narrative, plague

> represented the worst imaginable catastrophe, thereby setting the standards by which other epidemics would be judged. In later centuries, when societies experienced new and unfamiliar outbreaks of disease, they waited anxiously to see whether they would equal plague in their devastation.

Plagues cycled in waves, lasting generations or centuries. But *virulence*, the capacity of a disease to cause both pathological symptoms and infections, characterizes pandemics. The concept measures the degree to which a pathogen may overcome human defenses and inflict harm, including exposure and death. In this context, virulence strikes victims quickly, often within days of exposure. Before the advent of antibodies, virulence often killed more than half of those infected, moving through villages and towns faster than local populations could react. Unlike many diseases such as smallpox and polio, which harm the young and the old, plague would infect women and men in their primes.

By weakening local populations, pandemics would wreak havoc on economic and social institutions, leaving "in its wake vast numbers of orphans, widows, and destitute families" (Snowden, 2019). The lesson is that pandemics transform economic systems, alter demographic trends, and slow population growth. According to Morens and Fauci (2020) and Snowden (2019), three plague pandemics and additional disease outbreaks shaped history (table 1.2).

Plague of Justinian

The Plague of Justinian, named after the reigning Byzantine emperor Justinian I, began in the city of Pelusium, in northeastern Egypt, in the year AD 541, spread east and then west, and kept going. The earliest symptom, fever, was so mild that it did not make victims sick, but soon led to classic symptoms of bubonic plague, which is a type of plague caused by the bacterium *Yersinia pestis*. In victims, lumps and intense fever led to comas and violent delirium. In the year 542, the plague struck Constantinople, the capital of the Eastern Roman Empire, creating a massive death toll among both the powerful and powerless. Afterward, the emperor struggled to recruit soldiers, pay wages, and subdue revolts. The plague reached Rome in 543, Britain in 544, and again broke out in Constantinople in 558, 573, and 586. The first plague epidemic became endemic, constantly present, and did not end until 750, affecting much of the Middle East and Europe through transmission networks (Snowden, 2019).

Black Death

The Black Death began in the 1330s in central Asia and reached Europe in 1347, killing about one-third of Europeans during the next six years. Black Death led to the first formal quarantines and the end of the feudal order of serfdom. Like the first plague pandemic, the second

Table 1.2 Infectious diseases in history

Year	Disease	Deaths	Characteristics
541	Justinian Plague	30–50 million	Pandemic: killed half of the world's population
1330	Black Death	~50 million	Pandemic: killed a quarter of the world's population
1855	Modern Plague	~15 million	Pandemic: killed millions in China and India
~10,000 BC	Smallpox	~25 million	Pandemic: killed millions in the new world
1918	Spanish flu	~50 million	Pandemic: infected one-third of the world's population
~1920	AIDS	~37 million	Pandemic: first recognized in 1981 and ongoing
2002	SARS-CoV-1	700	Outbreak: quarantines ended the outbreak

Sources: Morens and Fauci (2020) and Snowden (2019)

pandemic worked in fits and starts, spreading, abating, and spreading again. Snowden (2019) argues that, in the summer of 1347, Genoese galleys carried the pandemic away from the Black Sea to ports in Sicily. Then the pandemic spread to the rest of the island and eventually to all of Italy. As the center of Mediterranean trade, Italy's early devastation reflected its geographical and economic importance. The pandemic eventually ravaged all of Europe, which was ripe for the spread of disease because of population growth, economic expansion, urbanization, and unsanitary conditions. At the time, the reduction in the number of potential workers elevated the value of labor as a scarce resource. Medieval landowners had the option of leaving grain in the fields to rot or raise wages to attract workers:

> In northern Italy, landlords tended to raise wages, which fostered the development of a middle class. In southern Italy, the nobility enacted decrees to prevent peasants from leaving to take better offers. Some historians date the separation in fortunes of the two halves of Italy—the rich north, the poor south—to these decisions.
>
> (Mann, 2020)

With waves of deadly outbreaks occurring for centuries, the Black Death eventually subsided, the last cases occurring in France in 1722 and Italy in 1743 (Snowden, 2019).

Modern Plague

In 1855, the Modern Plague erupted in China. By 1894, it ravaged Canton and Hong Kong and spread to faraway cities, including Bombay, Calcutta, and Sydney. Different from the first and second pandemics, the Modern Plague did not sicken everyone, but pursued a path of social inequality. The Modern Plague ravaged India, China, and other poor countries, but largely spared wealthier nations. During the first decade of the twentieth century, in India, the Modern Plague killed around 12 million people. But even in India, the pandemic inflicted harm on the hovels and tenements occupied by lower castes more than those with higher social status. In the United States, the total death toll from the Modern Plague was approximately 500, in minor outbreaks in Los Angeles, New Orleans, and San Francisco. According to Snowden (2019), the lasting impact was the establishment of a stable reservoir of infection among sylvatic rodents, marking the moment "when the complex etiology of the disease with its interaction between rodents, fleas, and humans was unraveled. As a result, beginning in the early twentieth century, new public health policies based on this knowledge were implemented."

By nature, plague pandemics are divisive. Neighbors that might help each other become potential sources of infection. The acts of working and socializing establish transmission networks. Governing authorities impose quarantines and become sources of oppression. Outsiders are blamed for importing the disease. Throughout history, bubonic plagues have therefore wreaked havoc, but since the middle of the twentieth century, effective antibodies have reduced the capacity of many diseases to serve as global risks.

Additional disease outbreaks

Smallpox, the Spanish flu, AIDS, and SARS, from centuries past and recent decades, also reshaped societies, providing further context for the era of Covid-19.

Smallpox

Beginning more than 2,000 years ago and continuing until it was eradicated in the mid-twentieth century, smallpox first infected humans at the time of animal domestication. By the fifteenth century, smallpox became endemic throughout Asia and Europe: during their lifetimes, most people of this era were probably exposed to it. Among young people, the fatality rate was high. Although scars lasted, those who survived smallpox acquired immunity. In subsequent generations, smallpox impacted a smaller percentage of the population and provided immunity, which, over time, gave Europeans an advantage as they explored distant lands. In 1518, when someone from Spain carried smallpox to Hispaniola, a quarter century after Columbus arrived, the process of the first New World Pandemic began, devastating communities and entire cultures, killing between 25 and 55 million people in the new world (Rosenwald, 2020).

Spanish flu

In 1918, an H1N1 virus—flu virus—with genes of avian origin, identified in military personnel, led to the deadliest strain of influenza in modern history. The Spanish flu, named because Spanish news sources were not censured during World War I and were free to report on the crisis, infected perhaps one-third of the world's population, killing about 50 million people (Rosenwald, 2020). With the Spanish flu, isolation and quarantines were used to combat the crisis. According to a study published in the *Journal of Economic History*, in the United States, large regional differences in mortality rates from the Spanish flu were related to poverty, home ownership, public health measures, quarantines, and air pollution, which may "increase susceptibility to viral infection and heighten the risk of severe complications" (Clay et al., 2018).

Acquired Immune Deficiency Syndrome

Around 1920, the virus which causes AIDS originated in the Democratic Republic of Congo when it crossed from chimpanzees to humans. In 1981, in Los Angeles, doctors first recognized AIDS in patients. Throughout the 1980s, medical researchers studied the virus to advance prevention and treatment. By the mid-1990s, although the virus mutated and acquired drug resistance, medical researchers found that an AIDS "cocktail," or combination of drugs, could curtail the viral load. Since it emerged, AIDS has killed more than 30 million people, and still kills almost a million a year (Snowden, 2019).

SARS-CoV-1

SARS, severe acute respiratory syndrome, also provides context for the era of Covid-19. In late 2002, SARS came out of the Guangdong providence in southern China, spreading to more than two dozen countries in Asia, Europe, North America, and South America, and killing people in Singapore, Toronto, and elsewhere. In 2003, a man suffering a respiratory crisis entered a Guangzhou hospital, infected dozens of healthcare workers, and became known as a "superspreader." In many of the 8,000 worldwide cases, SARS led to lethal pneumonia.

All told, more than 700 people died from SARS, but the public health strategy in southeast Asia and Canada included isolation and quarantine, so the outbreak soon ended. The virus was determined to be a coronavirus with new traits. The pathogen, named SARS-CoV, was renamed SARS-CoV-1 in 2020, so the agent of Covid-19 could be called SARS-CoV-2. SARS-CoV-1 transmitted to humans from bats, either directly or indirectly.

Disease outbreaks and scientific advance

For pandemic economics, research on plague pandemics and diseases such as smallpox, Spanish flu, AIDS, and SARS reveals three things. One, infectious diseases, if unchecked, may eventually travel in global networks. Local outbreaks may become national epidemics and then global pandemics. Two, a vaccine serves as the most valuable weapon against a disease outbreak. However, because vaccines fight specific viruses, they must be taken before infection. Moreover, viruses that mutate quickly, such as influenza, are mobile, which is why annual vaccines, by the time they are manufactured, are outdated. These limitations also exist with antibodies: countries cannot stockpile them because they apply to specific viruses. Researchers therefore work to stem disease outbreaks but are constrained by the pace of scientific advance. Three, to fight disease outbreaks, governments must prepare, maintain an appropriate capacity to comprehend the gravity of potential threats, model possible outcomes, imagine how interventions might stop the spread of disease, and allocate an appropriate level of economic resources for protective measures.

Disease outbreaks and human civilization

According to *The Economist* (2020), disease outbreaks shape human civilizations, serving as "the inevitable attendants of economic progress. Interconnected trade networks and teeming cities have made societies both richer and more vulnerable, from the empires of antiquity to the integrated global economy of the present." But past outbreaks struck human societies that were much poorer than those of today. Despite new outbreaks, advances in public health allow economies to grow and social systems to develop, leading to vaccinations, better hygiene, and urban sanitation. The point is that pandemics transform societies, including economies, healthcare systems, and networks of exchange. To prepare for the next pandemic, countries should feel the urgency, allocate resources for scientific advance, and strengthen economic and social institutions.

Rules of pandemic economics

The *rules of pandemic economics* or lessons of Covid capitalism, addressed in this book, arise from the economic analysis of pandemics and provide a "playbook" for economists (table 1.3).

To reopen the economy, control the disease

As Derek Thompson (2020) and Joshua Gans (2020) argue, saving the economy or saving lives is a false choice. To reopen an economy, a country must first stop the spread of disease. Acting quickly and forcefully serves as the most efficient option. The faster governments

Table 1.3 Rules of pandemic economics

Rule	Topic	Explanation
1	Economy	To re-open the economy, control the disease
2	Incentives	During pandemics, people respond to incentives
3	Globalization	Pandemics impede the process of globalization
4	Costs	Flattening the epidemic curve creates economic costs
5	Intervention	Government intervention is not the only cause of economic damage
6	Assistance	During economic shutdown, governments should help
7	Pathways	Economies do not follow optimal recovery paths
8	Haste	Regions that reopen with haste experience secondary outbreaks
9	Response	Pandemics require both collective responses and collaboration
10	Connection	Government and business connections influence pandemic outcomes
11	Science	Policy should rely on science
12	Shortage	In the presence of a shortage, price may not adjust
13	Vaccination	Both economics and ethics influence vaccination distribution
14	Vision	Pandemics reorient relationships and lead to calls for change

Source: author

act, the shorter intervention policies need to be. The reason is that, until the disease is under control, the economy cannot operate at full capacity. "A pandemic can be prevented in two ways: Stop an infection from ever arising, or stop an infection from becoming thousands more. The first way is likely impossible" (Yong, 2020). Two studies provide context. Analyzing the 1918 flu pandemic, economists from MIT and the Federal Reserve System investigate the costs and benefits of nonpharmaceutical interventions, finding that cities that intervene early and aggressively experience more robust economic recoveries (Clay et al., 2018). Studying the coronavirus pandemic of 2020, the Boston Consulting Group determines that, at the country level, a "crash and contain" approach is most effective, immediately limiting the spread of disease and shortening the period of time in which economies are shut down (Brimmer et al., 2020).

During pandemics, people respond to incentives

An important principle in economics, perhaps the most important, is that people respond to incentives. In the middle of health and economic crises, people without paid sick leave and health insurance have the incentive to continue to work, often in "essential" jobs, even with a greater risk of infection. They cannot afford to quit. The result is an increase in morbidity and mortality and a reduction in life expectancy. While policymakers implement aid packages for households in middle- and low-income brackets, essential workers participate in the economy during a pandemic but face the risk of repeated exposures.

Pandemics impede the process of globalization

Diseases that move through human transmission networks impede the process of globalization, because the outbreak serves as a negative global flow. The process of globalization enhances networks of production, trade, technology, information, migration, finance, and social interaction. But to prevent pandemics, countries erect barriers. The barriers impede migration, harden borders, devolve power from the international to the national, and transfer influence from the national to the local. While the process of globalization leads to multidirectional flows of goods and people, pandemics create the opposite effect: goods and people remain in place.

Flattening the epidemic curve creates economic costs

Pandemics lead to calls for flattening the *epidemic curve*, a statistical diagram used to visualize a disease outbreak. This method does not reduce the total number of infections. But it creates time for the healthcare system to increase hospital capacity. Flattening the epidemic reduces the number of visits of nonemergency patients to hospitals. This outcome safeguards public health but threatens the economic viability of hospital systems. The reason is that, for revenue generation, hospitals rely on elective procedures such as surgeries and clinic visits. But during a pandemic, hospitals cancel these procedures. As a result, revenue declines. While over-capacity in pandemic hotspots is partially offset by under-capacity elsewhere, lost patient visits lead to economic losses. At the same time, the procurement of medical equipment drives up costs. In areas where pandemic cases do not materialize and revenues fall, economic losses may extend to hospital employees.

Government intervention is not the only cause of economic damage

As policy interventions shut down segments of the economy, a deliberate recession ensues. But it is simplistic to portray the actions of public sectors as the only cause of economic damage. The reason is the disease. When comparing countries that shut down large segments of their economies at the beginning of a pandemic to those that do not, the countries in the latter category suffer from additional infection waves and inferior economic outcomes. Economic damage includes protracted economic recoveries and elevated levels of unemployment.

During economic shutdown, governments should help

During economic shutdown, public sectors should assume financial responsibility, paying workers a living wage and helping businesses shift their expenses to the future. When the disease spreads, financial assistance increases in importance, because people are both sheltering-in-place and sacrificing income. Shutdown policies enacted during pandemics reduce business revenue, but fixed costs remain. When businesses close, economic activity declines. When businesses cannot meet their financial obligations, property owners may default on mortgages. When banks falter, the financial system suffers.

Economies do not follow optimal recovery paths

Economic recoveries do not follow optimal paths. During a pandemic, countries must identify epidemiological trends and implement appropriate policy responses. But pandemics expose economic fractures. With public health, shortages persist with important medical equipment. Countries shutter their economies but may not provide adequate financial aid to workers and businesses. Structural inequality exacerbates health outcomes. During recovery, roadblocks slow progress, including political pressure from above, social pressure from below, and quarantine fatigue.

Regions that reopen with haste experience secondary outbreaks

Countries that reopen their economies with haste may experience secondary infection waves. The reason for this choice may be individualism, libertarianism, or a lack of effective leadership (Leonhardt, 2020). Depending on shutdown policies, the timeline for reopening, and human behavior, secondary infection waves may take different forms, including peaks and valleys or random patterns. When economies recover, nonpharmaceutical interventions are phased out. But then disease transmission networks may reappear. The reason is that, during the process of economic recovery, some safeguards may remain in place, such as social distancing and the requirement of masks; however, relaxed human activity may lead to noncompliance, leading to the potential return of the disease.

Government and business connections influence pandemic outcomes

During the coronavirus pandemic, businesses innovated, adapted, and accomplished important feats, notably the pharmaceutical, biotechnology, and manufacturing companies trying to fight the disease and contribute to the economy. Pharmaceutical companies developed a vaccine in record time. Grocery stores kept shelves stocked with necessities. Manufacturers redeployed factories to make personal protective equipment. But private-sector accomplishments were matched by public-sector policies. Governments channeled resources into areas of need, including healthcare and medical research, provided aid to households and businesses, and protected economies from recessionary multipliers. The most important form of collaboration between the public and private sectors occurred with vaccine development. The partnership facilitated the process of invention, innovation, and distribution.

Pandemics require collective responses and collaboration

Pandemics require collective responses and collaboration. Trust in leaders must accompany government action. While public policies boost the capacity of healthcare systems, they should also incentivize cooperation. The reason is that cooperation magnifies the impact of policy. But countries develop with spatial barricades, creating orders of separation between different socioeconomic groups (Sharkey, 2020). The problems of the "haves" are segregated from the problems of the "have-nots." As a result, the most effective response is for countries to work toward collective solutions. The disease spreads everywhere, affects the lives of everyone, and demolishes spatial barricades. While fitful cooperation may define the early pandemic interval, economic stabilization policies and the leveraging of local governments and community groups should help as many people as possible. As people develop a collective will to fight the pandemic, they learn that, in the presence of a global threat, their fates are intertwined.

Policy should rely on science

In a pandemic, the biggest problem is the unknown. When a disease spreads, scientists struggle to isolate the problem and forecast future trends. But then the science of infectiousness, mutations, and recovery improves. When the number of confirmed cases rises, a comprehensive system of testing scales up disease identification. A program of contact tracing tracks the spread of disease. The mobilization of treatments attempts to solve the problem. Meanwhile, scientific research investigates the incidence of infections among subgroups, clinical trials for vaccines, and transmission networks. In the current era, the study of pandemics involves advanced technology and data visualization. Policy implementation should rely on scientific knowledge.

In the presence of a shortage, price may not adjust

During a pandemic, essential goods, services, and medical resources in the healthcare sector, such as masks and hospital beds, may experience shortages. In response, prices may not rise to market-clearing levels. The reason rarely appears in economic models: fairness (Kahneman et al., 1986). When quantity demanded exceeds quantity supplied at a price below equilibrium, a shortage exists. Normally, market price increases to the market-clearing level. But during a pandemic, it may not be socially acceptable for businesses to raise prices. The reason is that companies value customer loyalty. In the case of medical equipment such as ventilators, gloves, and masks, hospitals sign long-term contracts with wholesalers, who want to maintain relationships.

Both economics and ethics influence vaccine distribution

The initial rollout of a vaccination does not include enough doses for everyone. As a result of the shortage, public officials must prioritize who initially receives the vaccination. Should distribution initially focus on the preservation of human life by vaccinating individuals with serious medical conditions and the elderly or reduce the rate of infection by vaccinating essential workers? The tradeoff between the two choices becomes an ethical dilemma, guided by the inequities created by the pandemic, which lead to a disproportionately high rate of infection among people with lower income levels and disparate access to testing, technology, and childcare.

Pandemics reorient relationships and lead to calls for change

Pandemics lead to the reorientation of relationships and calls for new methods of organization. During a pandemic, society's knowledge about the disease grows. After extensive research, learning occurs. But several questions remain. To prepare for the next pandemic, how should society reorient its economy? Should businesses be more flexible, especially with respect to remote work? Should employees fight for extended family leave? It may be that pandemics lead to calls for more investment in public healthcare systems, a greater reliance on local production networks, and an emphasis on preparedness. For months and potentially years, pandemics reduce economic activity. But how societies respond helps them reconsider what they value most.

Summary

The book develops the area of pandemic economics by applying economic theory to disease pandemics. In addition to drawing on the research of economists, the book incorporates research from the field of epidemiology, the area of medicine that addresses the incidence, distribution, and control of diseases. A useful description of the coronavirus pandemic is "black elephant." One, pandemics result from a combination of factors, including an attack on nature, global transmission, and a hesitation among some leaders to apply scientific principles to the outbreak. Two, the black elephant metaphor also describes the first pandemic of the twenty-first century, which originated from the hunting of wildlife in destroyed natural habitats, abundance of generalized species such as bats, rats, and some primates that host zoonotic viruses, and selling of contaminated wildlife in wet animal markets. Three, the pandemic was not completely unexpected. Finally, the concept of a black elephant expands the black swan framework, encouraging reflection on the global economic processes and institutions that unleashed the pandemic. Three plague pandemics shaped history, including the Plague of Justinian, Black Death, and the Modern Plague. Rivaling the plague pandemics in terms of lives lost, smallpox, the Spanish flu, AIDS, and SARS, from both centuries past and recent decades, reshaped societies and altered economies. These diseases serve as the inevitable attendants to globalization. Rules of pandemic economics stem from the application of economic theory to pandemic outcomes. They provide a "playbook" for economists and address many topics, including the economy, incentives, globalization, costs, interventions, assistance, pathways, haste, response, connection, science, shortage, and vision.

Chapter takeaways

LO1   Pandemic economics is the study of pandemics from an economics perspective.
LO2   To develop the field of pandemic economics, the book uses the economic approach, which combines assumptions of market equilibrium, maximizing behavior, and consumer preferences.
LO3   Humanity's polarization from the natural world triggered the novel coronavirus pandemic.
LO4   Previous pandemics and smallpox, the Spanish flu, AIDS, and SARS reshaped both economies and societies.
LO5   The rules of pandemic economics provide a playbook for economists.

Terms and concepts

Black elephant
Black swan
Economics
Efficiency
Epidemic curve
Epidemiology
Equity
Incentives
Natural reservoirs
Pandemic economics
Pathogens

Rules of pandemic economics
Scarcity
Virulence
Zoonoses

Questions

1. For the field of pandemic economics, why is it important to include empirical applications from both economics and epidemiology?
2. How might cost-benefit analysis weigh the benefit of slowing the spread of disease against the cost of economic shutdown?
3. What are the economic and public health implications of the rise of zoonoses?
4. Is "black elephant" an apt metaphor for Covid-19? Why or why not?
5. What do the first three plague pandemics reveal about the contemporary disease landscape? For reference, refer to Frank Snowden's (2019) book, *Epidemics and Society*.
6. To reopen an economy, why is it necessary to control the disease?
7. How does a pandemic impede the process of globalization?
8. In what sense is saving the economy or saving lives a false choice?
9. If it is simplistic to portray government intervention as the cause of economic damage during a pandemic, what are the causes of economic damage during a pandemic?
10. In response to a pandemic, should businesses, schools, and markets reorganize? If so, how?

References

Alexopulos, Nick. 2018. "Study by Health Security Center identifies characteristics of microorganisms most likely to cause a global pandemic," Center for Health Security, Johns Hopkins Blomberg School of Public Health, May 10.

Brimmer, Amanda, Chin, Vincent, Gjaja, Marin, Hutchinson, Rich, Kahn, Dan, Kronfellner, Bernhard, and Siegel, Phil. 2020. "It's not too late to crush and contain the coronavirus," Boston Consulting Group, July 23.

Clay, Karen, Lewis, Joshua, and Severnini, Edson. 2018. "Pollution, infectious disease, and mortality: evidence from the 1918 Spanish flu pandemic," *Journal of Economic History*, 78, 4 (December): 1179-1209.

Coates, Daniel. 2019. *Worldwide Threat Assessment of the U.S. Intelligence Community*. Office of the Director of National Intelligence, January 29. dni.gov/files/ODNI/documents/2019-ATA-SFR---SSCI.pdf.

Economist, The. 2020. "Throughout history, pandemics have had profound economic effects," March 12.

Elliott, Larry. 2020a. "Dozens of poorer nations seek IMF help amid coronavirus crisis", *The Guardian*, March 27.

Elliott, Larry. 2020b. "Blindsided: how coronavirus felled the global economy in 100 days," *The Guardian*, April 9.

Faulkner, Phil, Feduzi, Alberto, and Runde, Jochen. 2017. "Unknowns, black swans and the risk/uncertainty distinction," *Cambridge Journal of Economics*, 41: 1279-1302.

Friedman, Thomas L. 2020. "We need herd immunity from Trump and the coronavirus," *The New York Times*, April 25.

Gallagher, Gerard. 2017. "Fauci: 'No doubt' Trump will face surprise disease outbreak," *Healio*, January 11. https://www.healio.com/news/infectious-disease/20170111/fauci-no-doubt-trump-will-face-surprise-infectious-disease-outbreak.

Gans, Joshua. 2020. *Economics in the Age of Covid-19*. Cambridge, Massachusetts: MIT Press.

Georgieva, Kristalina. 2020. "Confronting the crisis: priorities for the global economy," International Monetary Fund, April 9. imf.org/en/News/Articles/2020/04/07/sp040920/-SMs2020-Curtain-Raiser.

Jabr, Ferris. 2020. "How humanity unleashed a flood of new diseases," *The New York Times*, June 17.

Kahneman, Daniel, Knetsch, Jack L., and Thaler, Richard H. 1986. "Fairness and the assumptions of economists," *The Journal of Business*, 59, 4, Part 2 (October): S285–S300.

Leonhardt, David. 2020. "The unique U.S. failure to control the virus," *The New York Times*, August 6.

Mann, Charles. 2020. "Pandemics leave us forever altered," *The Atlantic*, June.

Morens, David, and Fauci, Anthony. 2020. "Emerging pandemic diseases: how we got to Covid-19," *Cell*, 182 (September): 1077–1092.

Quammen, David. 2012. *Spillover: Animal Infections and the Next Human Pandemic*. New York: W.W. Norton & Company.

Rosenwald, Michael S. 2020. "History's deadliest pandemics, from ancient Rome to modern America," *The Washington Post*, April 7.

Sevilla, A. and Smith, S. 2020. "Baby steps: the gender division of childcare during the Covid-19 pandemic," *Oxford Review of Economic Policy*, 36 (Supplement).

Sharkey, Patrick. 2020. "In coronavirus, the U.S. faces a problem it can't fix by segregation," *Citylab*, March 24. citylabo.com/perspective/2020/03/coronavirus-solutions-collective-action-social-inequality/608644/.

Shretta, Rima. 2020. "The economic impact of Covid-19," Working Paper, University of Oxford. Research. ox.ac.uk/Article/2020-04-07-the-economic-impact-of-covid-19.

Snowden, Frank. 2019. *Epidemics and Society: From the Black Death to the Present*. New Haven: Yale University Press.

Taleb, Nassim N. 2007. *The Black Swan: The Impact of The Highly Improbable*. New York: Random House.

Thompson, Derek. 2020. "The four rules of pandemic economics," *The Atlantic*, April 2.

Tooze, Adam. 2020. "The normal economy is never coming back," *Foreign Affairs*, April 9.

World Bank. 2020a. *From Containment to Recovery: Economic Update for East Asia and the Pacific*. Washington D.C.: World Bank Group.

World Bank. 2020b. *Global Economic Prospects*. Washington D.C.: World Bank Group.

Yong, Ed. 2020. "Anatomy of an American failure," *The Atlantic* (September): 32–47.

Part I
Investigation and recognition

2 Economics of optimal disease control

Learning objectives

After reading this chapter, you will be able to:

LO1   Explain why economic analysis informs the control of infectious disease.
LO2   Contrast relativism and absolutism in the progression of economic ideas.
LO3   Discuss the scientific method from an economics perspective.
LO4   Describe the Susceptible, Infected, and Recovered (SIR) model.
LO5   Extend the SIR model to include optimal targeted lockdowns, equilibrium social distancing, and the value of human life.

Chapter outline

- Economic cost and the control of infectious disease
- Progression of ideas in economics
- Economics of science, knowledge, and information
- Optimal disease control
- The economic approach to optimal disease control
- Summary

Economic cost and the control of infectious disease

Before the coronavirus pandemic, the economic literature on the optimal control of disease was sparse. Models addressed individual behavior and the externalities that result from individual choice with respect to social distancing, treatment, and vaccination. But the topic of optimal disease control was not of great concern to economists. That perspective changed during the coronavirus pandemic. Since that period of time, extensive research in the field of economics has addressed this important topic.

One such article, written by the economist Daren Acemoglu of MIT and his co-authors (2020), argues that the risk of infectious disease varies between demographic groups. The cost of slowing the spread of disease through economic shutdowns is heterogeneous within a population. The authors use a common model from the field of epidemiology, the *Susceptible, Infected, and Recovered (SIR) model*—which demonstrates how susceptible individuals may become infected and eventually recover—to consider economic applications. They identify the benefit of optimal targeted policies that lock down alternative groups. This optimal control problem estimates the tradeoff between lives lost and economic losses, finding significant benefits for targeted lockdowns. With this research, Acemoglu et al. (2020), along with other practitioners in the field, provide a method to study the economic implications of the global spread of disease, important in a world that may experience additional pandemics.

To undertake research on the spread of disease, economists apply the SIR model to address different applications. The chapter's thesis is that the optimal method to control a disease outbreak is to implement nonpharmaceutical interventions that reduce the *reproduction number*, the expected number of cases generated by an infected person, below one. With this approach, the economic cost of saving lives increases with the length of shutdown policies. While chapter four discusses the types of nonpharmaceutical interventions available to society, this chapter develops the SIR model framework, analyzes economic applications, and considers how different assumptions for model parameters impact the results. But the chapter also provides context for this research. Economists adopting the SIR model framework from epidemiology and expanding it to include economic analysis contribute to the progression of economic ideas using the scientific method. To address these topics, this chapter discusses the progression of ideas in economics, analyzes the economics of science, knowledge, and information, and presents the economics of optimal disease control.

Progression of ideas in economics

In economics, research that leads to new ideas does not occur in isolation. On the contrary, to contribute to the discipline, researchers apply the methods and techniques of those that come before them. The study of previous pandemics, for example, provides context for the study of new pandemics. But economic applications develop in response to changes in the research environment, such as the emergence of a new disease. In this section, the progression of ideas in economics from the past contextualizes the research of the spread of disease in the present.

Competing ideas

At any time, competing ideas about the state of the world exist. In their efforts to analyze the history of economic thought, for example, the economists Werner Stark (1944), Mark Blaug (1962), and Alfred Chalk (1967) argue that two schools of interpretation, *relativism* and *absolutism*, highlight important distinctions for the progression of ideas. Stark (1944), who studied the development of knowledge, explains the difference:

> There are, in the last analysis, two ways of looking upon the history of economic thought: the one is to regard it as a steady progression from error to truth, or at least from dim and partial vision to clear and comprehensive perception (absolutism); the other is to interpret every single theory put forward in the past as a faithful expression and

reflection of contemporary conditions, and thus to understand it in its historical causa-
tion and meaning (relativism).

Although economists may admit that aspects of each view describe the progression of ideas,
many gravitate toward one view or the other.

Relativism

Relativism means that the current economic environment shapes the questions and theories
of researchers. Procedures of justification and standards of reasoning stem from assessments
of the context calling attention to them. The progression of ideas has properties relative to
a given framework of analysis. Once the framework of analysis is identified, the outcomes of
the research process are specified. Relativists argue that if an observation is relatively so,
it is dependent on the vantage point in which it is established. Stark (1944) observes that
"modern economics immediately appears as a simple product of historical development, as
a mirroring of the socioeconomic reality within which it took its origin, not unlike the various
theories which have preceded it." That is, according to Stark (1944), because the "problems
… which offer themselves to scientific economics, originate in economic life, and its solutions
must be confirmed by economic life … (p)roblems and methods … change because environments change." In this context, John Kenneth Galbraith (1958), the pre-eminent Harvard
economist and noted sage of his day, writes that "Ideas are inherently conservative. They
yield not to the attack of other ideas, but to the massive onslaught of circumstances with
which they cannot contend."

   In the relativist framework, when the events of the day warrant change, new economic
methods supplant old ideas. As a first example, one could argue that the theory of free-
market economies would always return to full employment output was more discredited by
the massive unemployment of the 1930s than the influential 1936 book by John Maynard
Keynes, the pre-eminent British economist. As a second example, the absence of certainty for
the timing of a pandemic created a research vacuum for the proper form of economic recovery. As infections diminish, should economic recovery occur quickly or methodically? Should
policy makers rely on markets to adjust or should economic policy dictate specific outcomes?
In a relativist framework, the progression of economic ideas is molded by circumstances.

   To further the idea of relativism, Wesley Mitchell (1967), an American economist known
for his work on business cycles, observes:

> One of the results of any survey of the development of economic doctrines is to show
> that in large measure the important departures in economic theory have been intel-
> lectual responses to changing current problems … The passing of ideas from one to
> another and their development by successive generations as an intellectual stunt has
> been in economics a secondary rather than a primary factor.

This idea emphasizes the connection between economic theories and their intellectual setting. Content is determined by the latter. Without the institutional setting, the principles of
economics generate empty generalities. With this connection, society evolves in endless
form, differing according to time and place. Economists fill their analytical toolboxes with
institutional content, influenced by the economic conditions of the day.

Lord Lionel Robbins (1953), British economist and faculty member at the London School of Economics, in his study of British classical political economy, adopts a relativist stance, arguing that "There can be no doubt that the stimulus to much of the abstract analysis came from interest in practical problems." Systems of economic analysis, according to Robbins (1953), proceed in their historical settings and the "stimuli of practical interest."

Absolutism

Absolutists, in contrast, argue that internal factors of the discipline, such as ongoing and unresolved questions and the discovery of new solutions, shape the progression of ideas. In this framework, absolute standards guide the judgment of theories. Analytical contributions are not traced to influences from the socioeconomic environment. A set of internal pressures and values influences researchers. Scientific advance remains on the intellectual plane of being, the level of ideas.

The reason for this argument is that disciplines, according to the absolutists, evolve in an incremental, piecemeal, and continuous process. Researchers contribute theories, information, and methods to a growing stockpile of knowledge. Once techniques of a discipline are established, fundamental views remain relatively unchanged. George Stigler (1965), the noted University of Chicago economist, argues that:

> Every major development in economic theory in the last hundred years, I believe, could have come much earlier if appropriate conditions were all that were needed ... Thus I assign a minor, and even an accidental, role to the contemporary environment in the development of economic theory since it has become a professional discipline.

Joseph Spengler (1968), an historian of economic thought at Duke University, observes that economics is "relatively immune to exogenous influences ... (taking) on the appearance of a progressive science, one in which superior theories replace inferior ones ... (and) is relatively impervious to external influence."

From this perspective, criticisms of relativism take two forms. First, relativists are myopic in thinking that economic circumstances alone furnish academic variations in the field. Second, relativists cannot explain all scientific epochs: some periods of history are more significant than others, but research continues to progress.

Synthesis of relativism and absolutism

Which of the two schools of thought is correct, relativism or absolutism? To contextualize research on the economics of optimal disease control, both perspectives offer contributions. Some theories develop in a continuing search for knowledge. Others are created in response to current conditions. But a synthesis of the two views provides a method to evaluate contemporary economic research.

Joseph Schumpeter (1961), the influential Austrian political economist, argues that, with respect to the progression of ideas, two groups exist: *innovators* and *articulators*. Innovators craft novel ideas that lead to revolutions in a discipline. In the field of economics, John Maynard Keynes (1936) fits in this category with his theory of government intervention.

Articulators are the researchers who adopt the methods of innovators and expand the ideas, thus developing the discipline. The extensive number of economists who took Keynes' theory and applied it serve as articulators.

Extraordinary and ordinary research

In this context, Thomas S. Kuhn (1962), the philosopher of science at the University of Chicago, labels the research of innovators as "extraordinary," while the research of articulators as "normal." Innovators anchor their extraordinary contributions in the conditions of the day. In the context of economics, innovators construct theories using inputs selected from the economic environment, data and information from the economy, and empirical studies of the discipline. Articulators, in contrast, accept the theories of the innovators, analyze new data and information, and advance the contours of the field. While developing empirical evidence, articulators do not craft novel theories. They use existing tools of the discipline.

To consider how research progresses, the ideas of Schumpeter (1961) and Kuhn (1962) may be synthesized. In the history of a discipline such as economics, continuity in research is followed by periods of discontinuity. In other words, revolution in the history of economic thought with innovators such as Keynes is followed by consolidation and continuity. Once an innovator creates a new theory, it grows through application and slow accretion. Extraordinary research gives way to a long period of normal science. Thus, scientific revolutions occur in discrete rushes, but are separate from each other by times of comparative quiet. Even during a pandemic, new research, important for the formulation of both economic and health policies, uses existing methods and techniques, such as the SIR model.

Paradigm and paradigm shift

A scientific revolution therefore complements the traditional research activities of normal science. In the framework of Kuhn (1962), a scientific revolution establishes a new *paradigm* in the field, "universally recognized scientific achievements that for a time provide model problems and solutions to a community of practitioners." The paradigm, according to Kuhn (1962), constitutes a "strong network of commitments—conceptual, theoretical, instrumental, and methodological" that provide the model problems and solutions. The paradigm includes a vision, conceptualized reality, model, set of theories, application of the model, set of conclusions, and policy recommendations. During the coronavirus pandemic, economists took the established model from epidemiology, the SIR model, and used it for economic applications. In this context, economists were working in a given paradigm, acting as articulators in a process of normal science.

A *paradigm shift*, which occurs infrequently, represents a fundamental change (Kuhn, 1962). The Keynesian revolution post-1936, for example, occurred when conventional theory was out of touch with the world. The conditions of the day provide new problems and solutions. Innovation leads to new visions, conceptualized realities, models, theories, applications, conclusions, and policy recommendations. Normal research becomes extraordinary and a paradigm shift occurs.

Economics of science, knowledge, and information

In the scientific method, researchers ask questions, establish hypotheses, make observations, derive predictions, and undertake experiments or investigations to test the hypotheses. In this context, knowledge is the theoretical or practical understanding of a subject, using information and data. *Contextualization* describes the domain of science, transforming data and information from a lower level of understanding to a higher level of knowledge. Reflection on the knowledge of a subject leads to wisdom in the domain of policy (figure 2.1).

The economics of science reaches decades into the past; however, it solidified when the *Journal of Economic Literature* invited Paula E. Stephan (1996), an economist at Georgia State University, to discuss the reasons why economists are interested in the production of scientific research. First, science serves as a source of economic growth. Second, both the labor market for scientists and their human capital serve as fertile grounds for economic research. Third, and most relevant to the study of pandemic economics, research on the reward structure in the scientific community helps to explain the *appropriability problem*: the ability to appropriate some gains from a contribution.

The study by economists of the scientific reward structure and associated behavior provides a foundation for contemporary research. In the current era, many factors motivate economists, including the satisfaction of solving problems, contribution to the discipline and policy discussions, compensation, and opportunity cost. Mario Coccia (2018), an economist at the National Research Council of Italy, places the economics of scientific research in several categories, including the public nature of research and financing, reward structures, careers in research, technology transfer and commercialization, knowledge spillovers, research and development, systems of innovation and knowledge, managerial and organizational behavior, research policy, and science and economic growth. While each area commands the attention of economists, systems of innovation and knowledge provide context for pandemic economics.

Researchers use factors of production—techniques, information, and other resources— to apply the scientific method. The process creates output: publications, innovations, and patents. The recipients of the output include the public, companies, government, research laboratories, and international organizations. The results of the scientific process include the spread of knowledge and information, new business methods, products, technological advance, an increase in the wealth of nations, and, in the case of a pandemic, new vaccines, antibody tests, and treatments.

Figure 2.1 Hierarchy from data and information to knowledge and wisdom.
Source: author

Optimal disease control

To study a pandemic, epidemiologists use the scientific method to forecast the spread of disease. Economists add economic costs to the framework. Approaches include simulations of both the transmission of disease and the path of recovery. From the field of epidemiology, a *compartmental model* separates individuals in a closed population into groups or compartments according to their disease status. An example is the Susceptible, Infected, and Recovered (SIR) model, which places individuals in one compartment at a time.

Susceptible, Infected, and Recovered Model

The SIR model was introduced in 1927 in the scientific community, less than a decade after the end of the 1918 influenza pandemic. In the current era, researchers value the simplicity of the model. By estimating two parameters, modelers approximate the behavior of disease. In the SIR model, a susceptible person becomes infected through contact with an infected person. When infected, the person is contagious, but then advances to a noncontagious state of recovery. At each moment in time, the SIR model (figure 2.2) predicts the number of people who are susceptible to infection, $S(t)$, infected, $I(t)$, and recovered, $R(t)$. Individuals who recover acquire immunity; therefore, the movement from $S(t)$ to $I(t)$ to $R(t)$ occurs in one direction.

Rates of infection and recovery

The entire population is susceptible. No one has immunity. But when exposed to the disease, some people become infected while others do not. Initially, newly infected people are immediately contagious and do not experience a latent period following exposure (Tolles and Luong, 2020). In the SIR model, flow between compartments depends on the *rate of infection* (movement from susceptible to infected) and the *rate of recovery* (movement from infected to recovered).

First, the rate of infection, which is the rate at which someone who is susceptible becomes infected, depends on two factors: the quantity of people in the susceptible and infected compartments and the effective contact rate (β). When infections exist among a few individuals at the beginning of an outbreak, the disease spreads slowly. But as more people become infected, the rate of infection increases. The effective contact rate measures the average number of contacts per individual and the transmissibility of the disease. Intervention measures such as school closures, social distancing, and targeted quarantines decrease β and slow the spread of disease.

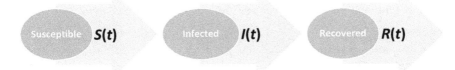

Figure 2.2 Flow in the SIR model.
Source: adapted from Toxvaerd (2020), Figure 1

Second, the rate of recovery refers to the transition from the infected compartment to the recovered compartment. But the SIR model assumes a broad meaning for "recovered." It refers to all people who are no longer contagious, not a clinical classification of disease. Because compartmental models assume closed systems without migration, people in the recovered compartment include those who either achieve immunity or die. The transition from the infected compartment to the recovered compartment depends on the length of time an individual is contagious, captured by the rate of recovery (γ).

Important parameters

The SIR model is defined by two parameters, the effective contact rate (β), which determines the movement from susceptible to infected, and the rate of recovery (γ), which determines the movement from infected to recovered (figure 2.3).

The relationship between the two important parameters determines the change in infections:

- If $\beta > \gamma$, the number of people in the infected compartment increases.
- If $\beta < \gamma$, the number of people in the infected compartment decreases.
- If $\beta = \gamma$, the number of people in the infected compartment remains constant.

The three compartments provide valuable information. During a pandemic, the number of susceptible people normally declines from the total population to a lower percentage of the population. The number of people "recovered" starts at zero and increases to a higher percentage of the population.

Epidemic curve

The number of infected individuals, graphed as an *epidemic curve* over time, serves as a marker for society's progress in fighting the disease (figure 2.4). Movements along the epidemic curve signify when infections are increasing, reaching a peak, and declining.

The epidemic curve illustrates the onset of infections after the introduction of a disease into a population. This *incubation period* is the period between exposure to an infection and the appearance of symptoms. The phrase *flattening the epidemic curve*, important as a policy goal, means a delay in peak infections and a lower number of peak cases. Epidemic curves are useful in determining the:

- character of the disease, such as an outbreak, epidemic, or pandemic
- type of disease as either *continuous source*, when exposure occurs over an extended period of time and may occur over several incubation periods, *point source*, when all

Figure 2.3 Disease status compartments.

Source: adapted from Tolles and Luong (2020), Figure 1

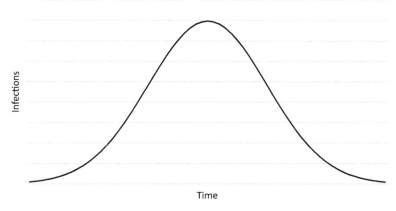

Figure 2.4 Epidemic curve.
Source: author

infections occur at the same time, or *propagated*, when the first wave of cases creates subsequent infection waves
- time of exposure of a population to a disease
- incubation period when the time of exposure is known.

Reproduction statistics

Basic reproduction number (R_0)

The parameters β to γ are relevant for the calculation of the *basic reproduction number* (R_0), "R-naught," which measures the capacity of the disease to spread: $R_0 = \beta/\gamma$. The basic reproduction number is the average number of new infections from a single infected person over the course of an illness, or "the number of secondary cases generated by the presence of one infected individual in an otherwise fully susceptible, well-mixed population" (Kwok et al., 2020). It applies to a population with no pre-existing immunity, reflecting both the infrastructure that allows the disease to spread and the intrinsic transmissibility of the disease.

An R_0 value equal to one serves as the *epidemic threshold* for public health practitioners: one person spreads the disease on average to one other person. Alternatively, if β is less than γ, no disease outbreak develops. In a pandemic, however, higher values for R_0 exist. In this case, epidemiologists and economists use values for R_0 greater than one to forecast the spread of disease, timeline, death toll, resources necessary to contain the pandemic, and proportion of a population that should be vaccinated. As a result, the estimation of R_0 is important from economic, epidemiological, and public health perspectives.

To reduce the spread of disease, R_0 must decrease below one. With respect to the parameters β and γ, three ways exist. First, a decrease in the effective contract rate β through a reduction in the number of contacts per individual and/or a reduction in the transmissibility of the disease leads to a decrease in R_0. Second, an increase in γ through higher levels of immunity leads to a decrease in R_0. Third, a decrease in β and an increase in γ lead to a decrease in R_0. The result is delaying and lowering the peak infection rate ("flattening the epidemic curve").

Measuring the value of R_o

Different methods calculate R_o. In the SIR model, R_o is estimated using three factors: a person's average susceptibility to infection, the infection rate, and the rate of removal of infection from the target population. Model solutions involve simultaneous linear differential equations, beyond the scope of this chapter. But figure 2.5, which demonstrates the SIR model in an extended framework, describes the process in which data are entered into the model and R_o is calculated. Note the model now includes the possibility of an *asymptomatic incubation period*, the time in which an infected individual does not exhibit characteristics of the disease.

Variance in potential outcomes

The calculation of R_o is important because small differences in R_o lead to a large variance in potential outcomes. A value greater than one leads to exponential growth. For example, when R_o = 0.5, 1,000 people infect 500 others, which turns into 250, and then 125, and so forth, depicted with the lowest line in figure 2.6. But when R_o = 2, 1,000 people infect 2,000, which turns into 4,000, and then 8,000, and so on, depicted with the highest line in figure 2.6. Higher levels of R_o explain why infections quickly spread.

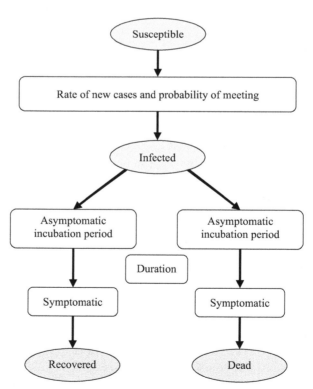

Figure 2.5 Extension of the SIR model used to calculate R_o.
Source: adapted from Aronson et al. (2020), Figure 3

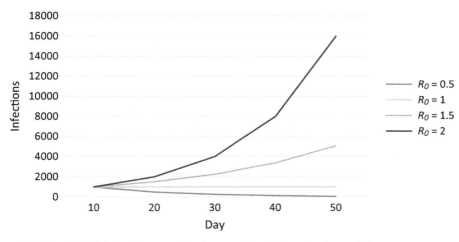

Figure 2.6 How 1,000 infections would change with different values of R_0.

Source: author

Characteristics of the basic reproduction number

In a pandemic, R_0 is not fixed but changes according to the infectiousness of the disease, population density, interventions, lockdown policies, and transmission networks. For example, early in a pandemic, areas with higher population density experience larger values of R_0 as people unknowingly infect others. But when shelter-in-place interventions occur, R_0 declines. As research progresses, the challenge is to determine each factor's significance. What is the relative significance of social distancing, wearing masks, and sheltering-in-place? How effective is a targeted process of recovery? The answers to these questions are important because a slight uptick in the value of R_0 may cause secondary infection waves, complicating the process of recovery.

Shapes of additional infection waves

Depending on the value of R_0, the effectiveness of lockdown policies, and the recovery timeline, additional infection waves assume different forms. These forms both highlight characteristics of the disease and forecast future pandemic intervals. In a report from the Center for Infectious Disease Research and Policy at the University of Minnesota, Moore et al. (2020) model the shape of subsequent waves, including (a) peaks and valleys, (b) a fall peak, and (c) a slow burn. In the peaks and valleys scenario, over a one- to two-year period, the first wave is followed by several smaller waves that gradually diminish over time. In the fall peak scenario, the first wave is followed by another significant wave, such as the trajectories of the 1918 flu and 2020 coronavirus pandemics in many countries. This scenario requires strong intervention measures such as social distancing, sheltering-in-place, and mask wearing soon after the original lockdown policies. In the slow burn scenario, after the original wave, subsequent infection waves appear without clear patterns. The latter scenario may not require additional lockdown measures, but the continuous monitoring of infections and R_0.

Social distancing

In a research study in *Science*, Kissler et al. (2020) analyze the relationship between policies of intermittent social distancing and infections. When the number of infections reaches a certain threshold, for example, 20 cases per 1,000 people, regions should activate geographically appropriate policies of social distancing. When cases fall to a medically safe level, for example, 5 cases per 1,000 people, the policy of social distancing should end. Another scenario characterizes the strategy. When hospitals increase their intensive care capacity, governments may establish social distancing at higher rates of infection, for example, 75 cases per 1,000 people, because one-time social distancing measures may not sufficiently slow infections. With these and other scenarios, stress on the healthcare system follows the rise in infections. But before the stress overwhelms hospitals, this strategy prepares the healthcare system.

Effective reproduction number (R_e)

In practice, the entire population will rarely be susceptible to infection. As a result, the average number of secondary cases will be less than the basic reproduction number. To account for this reality, scientists use R_e, the *effective reproduction number*, "a more practical real-life version … which uses real-life data (from diagnostic testing and/or clinical surveillance) to estimate the reproductive number for an ongoing epidemic" (Kwok et al., 2020). In effect, R_e is the average number of secondary cases per infected person in a population of both susceptible and nonsusceptible hosts. The value of R_e may be estimated by multiplying the basic reproduction number (R_0) by the fraction of the host population that is susceptible (δ): $R_e = \delta R_0$. For example, if $R_0 = 3$ for the novel coronavirus but 10 percent of the population is immune, $R_e = (0.90)(3) = 2.7$, meaning the average infected person infects 2.7 others. The value of R_e is important because it impacts the trajectory of the disease:

- When $R_e > 1$, cases increase.
- When $R_e = 1$, the disease is *endemic*, constantly maintained at a baseline level for a specific population.
- When $R_e < 1$, cases decline.

As the level of immunity among survivors and the death toll increase, people alter their behavior. As a result, R_e changes. The struggle to end the pandemic becomes a challenge of reducing R_e below one. However, R_e is a function of several variables. Lockdown measures reduce R_e, but quarantine fatigue does not. To consider an example, at the beginning of the coronavirus pandemic, in March 2020, in the UK, R_e was estimated to be between two and three, lower than the measles but higher than the seasonal flu. By the end of April 2020, in the UK, R_e declined to between 0.5 and 0.7, depending on the region (Devlin, 2020). For comparison, in March 2020, R_e was 5.17 in Spain (Kwok et al., 2020). Spain, with 5,232 cases in the middle of March 2020, would have experienced, in the absence of strict lockdown measures, total cases equal to almost 4 million in 40 days. For a population, a low and stable value of R_e accelerates the process of recovery. When the spread of disease slows, recovery policies reignite economic activity, encourage social gatherings, and maintain sufficient resources for the medical system. When R_e is low and stable, a population may begin to move on from a pandemic.

Herd immunity

For a population, the point of vaccination is to create *herd immunity*, the protection from infectious disease that occurs when a sufficient percentage of the population becomes immune. This process stimulates antibodies that confer immunity without giving the disease. Vaccination creates a pathway directly from the susceptible compartment to the recovered compartment (figure 2.7).

If a population is to achieve herd immunity, R_0, the basic reproduction number, determines the percentage of required immunizations. To halt the spread of infection, the minimum critical level of population immunity (P_{crit}), acquired in an induced manner, may be expressed as: $P_{crit} = 1 - (1/R_0)$. The higher is the value of R_0, the greater is the percentage of people in the population that needs to be immune through vaccination (table 2.1).

The value of P_{crit} depends on the value of R_0. If $R_0 = 2$, a person with the disease will infect two others on average. In this case, herd immunity requires immunization in 50 percent of the population. If $R_0 = 4$, a person with the disease will infect four others on average if they are susceptible. In this situation, herd immunity requires immunization in 75 percent of the population. The relationship between R_0 and P_{crit} demonstrates a nonlinear pattern (figure 2.8).

Consider another example. If $R_0 = 8$, herd immunity requires immunization in 88 percent of the population. In this case, an infected person will infect eight others if they are susceptible. But when other people start becoming immune, the infected person who encounters eight others will not infect them all. The number infected will depend on the level of R_e, the effective reproduction rate. The size of the appropriate reproduction statistic is therefore important for public policy and allocation of resources for vaccinations. During a pandemic,

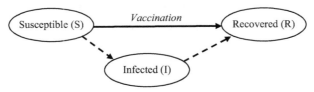

Figure 2.7 Herd immunity through vaccination.

Source: author

Table 2.1 Percentage for herd immunity

R_0	$P_{crit} = 1 - (1/R_0)$	Percentage for herd immunity
2	0.50	50%
3	0.67	67%
4	0.75	75%
5	0.80	80%
6	0.83	83%
7	0.86	86%
8	0.88	88%

Source: author using the equation from Kwok et al. (2020)

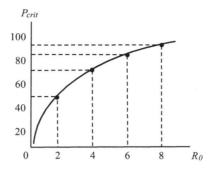

Figure 2.8 Relationship between R_0 and P_{crit}.
Source: author

the effective reproduction statistic proceeds through stages, starting at a high level, main-taining this level in the absence of interventions, declining rapidly during lockdown, decreasing further with quarantines, treatment, and medical resources, and decreasing toward zero with comprehensive testing, *contact tracing*, and treatment (Inglesby, 2020).

Limitations of the SIR model

The structure of the SIR model makes it easy to apply; however, it oversimplifies the complexity of infectious diseases. The model may not accurately characterize the latent period when asymptomatic cases become prevalent. This is the important period in which an individual is exposed to a disease but not yet contagious. Extensions of the model that include asymptomatic cases, such as the SEIR model, where "E" denotes exposed but not yet contagious, increase the model's predictive capacity. The SIR model also assumes a homogenous mixing of the population, meaning that each person has an equal probability of coming into contact with every other person. This, of course, does not reflect actual human interaction. Most people move within a limited space. The SIR model also assumes a closed structure without immigration, births, or deaths from causes other than the pandemic. Finally, the SIR model does not allow for the quantification of uncertainty with respect to parameter values. The numerical values for the rate of infection and the rate of recovery represent the modeler's best estimates. But the rates change. As a result, the best applications of the SIR model simulate different trajectories with alternative parameter values. The most complex applications apply distributions for the parameters instead of point estimates, characterizing the probability of potential outcomes and offering more realistic forecasts for the spread of disease (Tolles and Luong, 2020).

The economic approach to optimal disease control

During the coronavirus pandemic, economists used the SIR model to study the economics of optimal disease control. Economists extended the SIR framework to include different aspects of economic analysis, including optimal targeted lockdowns, equilibrium social distancing, and the value of human life. Two benefits existed with this hybrid approach: it led to forecasts of the long-run impact of a pandemic and estimates of economic costs of policy intervention. The following sections discuss three areas of economic analysis that use the SIR model.

Optimal targeted lockdowns

The economist Daren Acemoglu of MIT and his co-authors' (2020) study targeted lockdown policies in an extended SIR model where fatalities, hospitalizations, and infections differ between groups, focusing on the coronavirus pandemic. The groups include "old," "middle-aged," and "young." The economists argue that both the risk of infection and the serious consequences from the spread of disease vary between groups. In addition, the costs of a slowdown in the economy demonstrate heterogeneous effects on different members of the population.

In this framework, Acemoglu et al. (2020) analyze policy choices, finding that policies that differentiate between age and risk groups outperform uniform policies that are the same for all. From society's perspective, most welfare gains come from lockdown policies targeting the oldest and riskiest group. To stop the spread of disease, longer and focused lockdowns for the riskiest and most vulnerable groups complement shorter and flexible lockdowns for lower-risk groups.

From a modeling perspective, Acemoglu et al. (2020) assume people are partitioned into groups (*j*), where *j* = 1...*J*. Each group has a certain number of members, represented by N_j. In modeling terminology, the total population is "normalized" to unity, $\Sigma_j N_j = 1$, so the total number of people in all groups cannot exceed 100 percent. As an extension of the SIR model, at any moment in time (*t*), people in each group may be categorized as susceptible (*S*), infected (*I*), recovered (*R*), or deceased (*D*):

$$N_j = S_j(t) + I_j(t) + R_j(t) + D_j(t) \tag{2.1}$$

Individuals move from susceptible to infected and then recover or die. But if policy interventions target each group and restrict contacts between groups, society may limit the spread of disease.

Assume two groups, S_1 and S_2, where the risk of infection for S_1 is less than the risk of infection for S_2. If infected individuals come into contact with those who are susceptible, the latter may become infected. But some who become infected require time in an intensive care unit (ICU) with ventilators and other forms of medical care, while others do not require time in an ICU. Those who do not need time in ICUs recover, but individuals who spend time in ICUs either recover or die. In figure 2.9, solid arrows demonstrate flows between groups, but dotted arrows represent potential contact between groups.

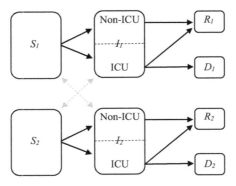

Figure 2.9 Multiple group SIR model.
Source: adapted from Acemoglu et al. (2020), Figure 2.1

In this framework, policy options include uniform lockdown policies that affect all people equally or targeted lockdown policies that focus on specific groups and limit the cross interaction between groups with different risk factors. This model acknowledges a tradeoff between extended lockdowns and economic activity. With a safety-first approach, the economy experiences a substantial economic loss through shutdown measures in order to minimize the fatality rate. With an economy-first approach, a higher mortality rate is the cost of minimizing losses in economic activity. Acemoglu at el. (2020) have an important conclusion:

> Better social outcomes are possible with targeted policies. Differential lockdowns on groups with differential risks can significantly improve policy tradeoffs, enabling large reductions in economic damages or excess deaths or both … a majority of these gains can be achieved with a simple targeted policy that applies an aggressive lockdown on the oldest group and treats the rest of the population uniformly.

Equilibrium social distancing

The economist Flavio Toxvaerd of the University of Cambridge (2020) addresses the case in which susceptible individuals engage in *social distancing*, a nonpharmaceutical intervention that decreases the contact rate between susceptible and infected individuals. Social distancing is used as a tool to flatten the epidemic curve and reduce the spread of infections. In the model, an individual's optimal strategy is a function of the probability of infection, which depends on the prevalence of disease, $I(t)$. At each moment in time, individuals noncooperatively choose whether to adopt a position of social distancing. The optimal strategy of individuals takes the form of a *threshold infection probability*, which means the act of social distancing is a function of the risk of interaction. At the beginning and end of a pandemic, the prevalence of disease is low. During these periods, the risk of infection is also low; individuals may not maximize their opportunities to socially distance. But during the period of high disease prevalence, during the middle of a pandemic, the risk of exposure outweighs the benefit of interaction, so individuals take advantage of the opportunities to socially distance.

In the absence of strict policy interventions, Toxvaerd (2020) determines the equilibrium level of social distancing. This focus on behavior is relevant for understanding the extent to which governments should limit human interaction. While the SIR model serves as a starting point, the addition of human decision-making and behavior develops the framework. The decision to socially distance acts as a flow regulator between susceptible, infected, and recovered individuals, reflecting the biological characteristics of disease. In Toxvaerd's (2020) model, even though the equilibrium level of social distancing may not be socially optimal, aggregate equilibrium infections are lower than the prediction from a standard SIR model. In the absence of the assumption of rational behavior, a purely epidemiological SIR model may overstate the severity of the pandemic.

Value of human life

After a period of economic shutdown to fight the spread of disease, governments debate how to reopen economies without causing a resurgence. During shutdown, businesses close. People lose their jobs. The unemployment rate rises. Governments provide financial aid. At the same time, the costs of loneliness and isolation from sheltering-in-place rise. Professors Robert Rowthorn and Jan Maciejowski (2020) of the University of Cambridge recognize this balance between economic and human health, extend the SIR model, and present a cost-benefit analysis of the optimal path of government intervention for economic and epidemiological conditions.

When government shuts down the economy to minimize disease transmission, economic and social costs must be weighed against the public health benefits of intervention. In this case, an optimal control problem includes the scale, timeline, costs, and benefits of public policy. While the SIR model focuses on the health status of individuals—susceptible, infected, or recovered—Rowthorn and Maciejowski (2020) address the costs of locking down society. If government treats infected individuals after the fact, almost 100 percent of the population becomes infected and the death toll is high. Rather, from a public health perspective, the optimal government response is to impose an extensive lockdown at the beginning of the pandemic.

The contribution of Rowthorn and Maciejowski (2020) is to include the value of human life in their cost-benefit analysis. With disease control, policymakers may refuse to publicly acknowledge the concept, but actual policy implies a tacit valuation of life. With this addition, a model simulation finds that an increase in the value of human life requires a longer economic shutdown (figure 2.10). But as an extended shutdown minimizes the number of deaths, the economic cost of unemployment increases.

Summary

After the onset of the coronavirus pandemic, economists studied the optimal control of disease by adding economic costs to the standard SIR model from epidemiology. In this chapter, a discussion of the history of economic thought contextualizes this research. Two schools of thought view the progression of economic ideas: relativism, when the current economic environment shapes the questions and theories of inquisitors and absolutism, when internal factors of a discipline such as ongoing and unresolved questions and the discovery of new solutions shape the progression of ideas. A synthesis of the two schools of thought, Kuhn's (1962) idea of paradigm, explains the application of the scientific method in this case. The SIR model exists as a paradigm to address the spread of disease. Economic extensions of the

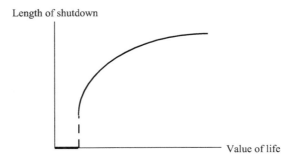

Figure 2.10 Optimal shutdown.
Source: adapted from Rowthorn and Maciejowski (2020), Figure 8

model use the scientific method to analyze optimal targeted lockdowns, equilibrium social distancing, and the value of human life.

Chapter takeaways

LO1   The optimal disease control problem estimates the tradeoff between lives saved and economic losses, demonstrating the benefits of targeted lockdowns.

LO2   The theory of absolutism regards the progression of economic ideas as a steady movement from error to truth, while the theory of relativism means that the current economic environment shapes the questions and theories of researchers.

LO3   For several reasons, economists are interested in the production of scientific research, including science as a source of economic growth, labor markets for scientists as fertile grounds for economic research, and the reward structure in the scientific community.

LO4   The SIR model computes the number of people infected with a contagious illness in a closed population.

LO5   Economists extend the SIR framework to include different aspects of economic analysis, including optimal targeted lockdowns, equilibrium social distancing, and the value of human life.

Terms and concepts

Absolutism
Appropriability problem
Articulators
Asymptomatic incubation period
Basic reproduction number
Compartmental model
Contact tracing
Contextualization
Continuous source
Effective reproduction number
Endemic
Epidemic curve
Epidemic threshold
Flattening the epidemic curve
Herd immunity
Incubation period
Innovators
Paradigm
Paradigm shift
Point source
Propagated
Rate of infection
Rate of recovery
Relativism

Reproduction number
Social distancing
Susceptible, Infected, and Recovered (SIR) model
Threshold infection probability

Questions

1. What are the methods economists use to incorporate the economic perspective in the SIR model? From a policy perspective, why are these methods important?
2. In the study of the coronavirus pandemic, why did economists adopt the SIR model from epidemiology?
3. This chapter argues that, in the history of economic thought, relativists and absolutists claim that economic ideas progress in different ways. Contrast the position of the relativists and the absolutists. In what circumstances, if any, is each position correct?
4. Does the concept of paradigm provide a method to synthesize the position of absolutism and relativism? In your answer, define paradigm and paradigm shift, referring to the famous book by Thomas Kuhn (1962), *The Structure of Scientific Revolutions*.
5. Are the economists who adopt the SIR model from epidemiology innovators or articulators? Explain.
6. Explain the standard SIR model. Why is its "simplicity" useful to address a disease pandemic? What are the model assumptions? What are the model limitations?
7. With the SIR model, do economists use an existing paradigm? With economic applications of the SIR model, do they undertake normal or extraordinary research? Explain.
8. Discuss the optimal targeted lockdown extension of the SIR model. What are the contributions of this economic analysis?
9. Discuss the equilibrium social distancing extension of the SIR model. What are the contributions of this economic analysis?
10. Discuss the value of human life extension of the SIR model. What are the contributions of this economic analysis?

References

Acemoglu, Daron, Chernozhukov, Victor, Werning, Iván, and Whinston, Michael D. 2020. "Optimal targeted lockdowns in a multi-group SIR model," NBER Working Paper 27102.

Aronson, Jeffrey, Brassey, Jon, and Mahtani, Kamal. 2020. "An introduction to viral reproduction numbers, R_0 and R_e," Oxford Covid-19 Evidence Service, Centre for Evidence-Based Medicine, University of Oxford.

Blaug, Mark. 1962. *Economic Theory in Retrospect*. Homewood, Illinois: Richard Irwin.

Chalk, Alfred F. 1967. "Relativist and absolutist approaches to the history of economic theory," *The Southwestern Social Science Quarterly*, 48, 1 (June): 5-12.

Coccia, Mario. 2018. "Evolution of the economics of science in the twentieth century," *Journal of Economics Library*, 5, 1 (March): 65-84.

Devlin, Hannah. 2020. "What does the 'R' number of coronavirus actually signify," *The Guardian*, April 30.

Galbraith, John K. 1958. *The Affluent Society*. Boston: Houghton Mifflin.

Inglesby, Thomas. 2020. "Public health measures and the reproduction Number of SARS-CoV-2," *JAMA Insights*, 323, 21 (May). doi:10.1001/jama.2020.7878.

Keynes, John M. 1936. *The General Theory of Employment, Interest, and Money*. London: Macmillan.

Kissler, Stephen, Tedijanto, Christine, Goldstein, Edward, Grad, Yonatan, and Lipsitch, Marc. 2020. "Projecting the transmission dynamics of SARS-CoV-2 through the postpandemic period," *Science*, 368, 6493: 860-868.

Kuhn, Thomas S. 1962. *The Structure of Scientific Revolutions*. Chicago: The University of Chicago Press.

Kwok, Kin O., Lai, Florence, Wai, Wan I., Wong, Samuel, and Tang, Julian. 2020. "Herd immunity–estimating the level required to halt the Covid-19 epidemics in affected countries," *The Journal of Infection*, 80, 6 (June): e32–e33.

Mitchell, Wesley. 1967. *Types of Economic Theory: From Mercantilism to Institutionalism*. New York: A.M. Kelley.

Moore, Kristine A., Lipsitch, Marc, Barry, John M., and Osterholm, Michael T. 2020. *Covid-19: The CIDRAP Viewpoint*. Center for Infectious Disease Research and Policy, University of Minnesota. https://www.cidrap.umn.edu/sites/default/files/public/downloads/cidrap-covid19-viewpoint-part1_0.pdf.

Robbins, Lionel. 1953. *An Essay on the Nature and Significance of Economic Science*. London: Macmillan and Co.

Rowthorn, Robert, and Maciejowski, Jan. 2020. "A cost-benefit analysis of the Covid-19 disease," *Oxford Review of Economic Policy*, 36 (Supplement).

Schumpeter, Joseph A. 1961. *The Theory of Economic Development*. Translated by Redvers Opie. New York: Galaxy Books of Oxford University Press [1911].

Spengler, Joseph. 1968. "Economics: its histories, themes, approaches," *Journal of Economic Issues*, 2, 1: 5-30.

Stark, Werner. 1944. *The History of Economics in its Relation to Social Development*. Oxford: Oxford University Press.

Stephan, Paula E. 1996. "The economics of science," *Journal of Economic Literature*, 34, 3 (September): 1199-1235.

Stigler, George J. 1965. *Essays in the History of Economics*. Chicago: University of Chicago Press.

Tolles, Juliana, and Luong, ThaiBinh. 2020. "Modeling epidemics with compartmental models," *JAMA*, 323, 24 (June): 2515-2516.

Toxvaerd, Flavio. 2020. "Equilibrium social distancing," Working Paper, Cambridge Working Paper Series in Economics, 2020/08.

3 Globalization, networks, and contagion

Learning objectives

After reading this chapter, you will be able to:

LO1 Explain why systems of interconnection cause diseases to spread.
LO2 Analyze the process of globalization, the widening and deepening interconnec-
     tions among the world's peoples through all forms of exchange.
LO3 Describe the characteristics of networks.
LO4 Discuss network applications, including disease, energy, supply chains, and
     innovation.
LO5 Explain how contagion, the spread of crisis from one area to another, may occur.

Chapter outline

- Systems of interconnection
- Globalization
- Networks
- Network applications
- Contagion
- Summary

Systems of interconnection

Through networks–systems of interconnection–disease outbreaks spread. Because of airline travel, transmission networks span the globe. But the speed in which a disease spreads
depends on infectiousness, the degree of interconnection of transmission networks, and the
effectiveness of policy interventions. Interconnected countries assume higher risks of infection. But after the identification of an initial outbreak, countries that close their borders and
shut down internal transmission networks have a better chance of containing an outbreak.
The carriers of disease in one region will not infect people in others.

The policy prescription seems straightforward: "Stop travel, stop the virus from spreading around the world" (Wu et al., 2020). But it is not that easy. After the disclosure of the novel coronavirus, in January 2020, more than 430,000 people flew from China to the United States, before a travel ban was enacted (Eder et al., 2020). As the virus spread, international travel from China continued to South Korea and Japan, the Middle East, Europe, and North America. Of the infected travelers, most were asymptomatic, but some were not. By the end of January 2020, cases appeared in Bangkok, Sydney, Tokyo, Singapore, New York, Seattle, London, and Paris.

As this chapter explains, the study of networks, common in the field of economics, provides a framework of analysis. The chapter first explains the process of globalization. It then addresses network theory, network characteristics, and applications. The chapter finishes with a discussion of contagion, the possibility that a crisis may spread from one part of the world to another.

Globalization

Globalization—the widening and deepening interconnections among the world's peoples through all forms of exchange (Khanna, 2008)—does not imply an inevitable movement toward integration. When resources, goods, and people flow from one area to another, specific networks of globalization, such as supply chains, may strengthen. When countries erect barriers and close their borders, integration declines. The point is that, over time, interconnections ebb and flow.

Globalization is nothing new. Trade routes have existed for millennia. The Silk Road, for example, a network between China, the Middle East, and Europe, emerged thousands of years ago, lasting until at least the sixteenth century. Over time, as empires grew and diminished, the routes expanded, contracted, and changed course, crossing deserts and mountains, and eventually the ocean. On the Silk Road, trade generally covered food items, raw materials, and luxury goods, from surplus to shortage areas. In early centuries, caravans left the historical Chinese city of Chang'an with spices, tea, and silk, traveling on the 4,000-mile (6,400-kilometer) route to Constantinople or Rome. In return, goods such as fruit, glassware, and textiles flowed east. But merchants on the Silk Road transported more than tangible goods. They created a network that developed technologies, ideas, and philosophies. An example of international capitalism, the Silk Road also advanced the human need to connect.

The Silk Road, however, helped spread some of the world's worst diseases, including the Justinian Plague of the sixth century, Black Death of the 1340s, and tuberculosis epidemic of the 1500s. In the late thirteenth century, Italy's ties to the Silk Road extended to China during the days of Marco Polo. In 1271, Polo, his father, and other Venetian traders left Italy and arrived on the Silk Road via Central Asia, but returned by sea, spending time in Sri Lanka along the way. As Salvatore Babones (2020) of the University of Sydney, who studies the macro-level structure of the global economy, explains in *Foreign Policy*:

> Barely 50 years after the Polos' return from China, an outbreak of bubonic plague traveled those very same routes to the West, where the disease became known as the Black Death. It is believed to have been spread by both land and sea, originating in China and following the trade routes to Europe and the Middle East. Both routes ultimately

converged on Italy, where the plague killed up to 75 percent of the population in some areas. Northern Italy's thoroughly internationalized merchant traders probably played a key role in transmitting the disease onward to the rest of Europe.

Like the Black Death in the fourteenth century, Covid-19 in the twenty-first century killed more people outside of China. During both pandemics, Europe struggled to contain outbreaks. More than 700 years ago, Marco Polo chronicled the wet markets in China that existed during his day, marveling at their "ample supply of every meat and game" (Babones, 2020). In the twenty-first century, one of these markets contributed to the rise of Covid-19.

Epochs of globalization

Jan Pieterse (2012), a Dutch-born scholar whose work focuses on global political economy, argues that, in history, globalization enhanced connectivity, but developed according to different economic influences. In the Oriental Phase I, circa 500 AD to 1100 AD, caravan trade in the Middle East enhanced connections between regions. In the Oriental Phase II, circa 1100 to 1500, urbanization and the Silk Road increased trade, technology, and productivity. In the Multicentric Phase, circa 1500 to 1800, Europeans expanded trade across the Atlantic Ocean. In the Euro-Atlantic Phase, circa 1800 to 1950, industrialization, specialization, and division of labor developed the European and North American economies. In the post-World War II Phase, circa 1950 to 1991, global value chains and multinational corporations in Europe, Japan, and North America experienced the beginning and end of the Cold War.

The Current Phase of Globalization, circa 1991 to the present, is characterized in several ways, including Thomas L. Friedman's (2005) vision of a "flattening" world in which technological advances level the economic playing field for countries, companies, and workers: "When the world is flat, you can innovate without having to emigrate." As urbanization expands and more than fifty percent of the world's people now live in cities, Richard Florida's (2005) vision of the current era is that globalization is spiky: "although one might not have to emigrate to innovate, it certainly appears that innovation, economic growth, and prosperity occur in those places that attract a critical mass of top creative talent."

While both of these visions characterize the global economy, during pandemics, the world may also restore borders, slow migration, devolve power from the international to the national, and shift influence from the national to the local. That is, as a disease moves through transmission networks, a local outbreak may become a national epidemic and then an international pandemic, stifling the process of globalization. The reason is that, to slow the spread of the disease, countries implement policies of intervention, including border closings. Even though globalization leads to multidirectional flows of people and output, pandemics slow this process.

The current epoch

In a closed economy, people, output, and information are tied to place. A country's resource inputs are used to create output. Social relationships are restricted. Because people do not travel far, information is not widely disseminated. In this world of limited mobility, exports do not exist. Closed economies, such as Japan (1639–1853), erect barriers to trade. During the Cold War (1946–1991), impediments to commerce were propagated by the influence of the Soviet Union. The Berlin Wall, erected in 1961 and dismantled in 1989, kept East Berliners in and ideas of the Western world out. Prior to the Berlin Wall, a fluid relationship existed between all members of the city, but the wall froze relationships in place. Until 1989, relatively little movement of people, goods, and information occurred between East and West.

At the end of 1991, the breakup of the Soviet Union and the end of the Cold War precipitated the current era of globalization. Germany reunited. International trade accelerated. Between 1991 and 2020, the global economy grew, with the Great Recession of 2008-2009 serving as the only setback. In the three decades between 1991 and 2020, global trade networks expanded far beyond the geography of the Silk Road.

Global flows

The current epoch of globalization is characterized by *global flows*—the movement of people, resources, goods, capital, and information. The ubiquitous iPhone, manufactured in China, is sold in global markets. French wine, a favorite of many countries for centuries, is sold in markets on five continents. Some of the largest exports from the U.K., such as machinery, computers, and vehicles, flow to countries in Asia, Africa, and Latin America. New Zealand's largest trade partner is Australia, but New Zealand also trades with the U.K., Germany, Canada, and many other countries. Every year, hundreds of thousands of students from China study in the United States and Europe. Designs by companies for electric cars, solar panels, social media, entertainment videos, smart watches, and other forms of output occur on a collaborative basis across geographical space and time zones. With expanding global flows, many forms of output considered transformational in one period, such as modems, camera phones, and flash drives, become commonplace in the next.

Types of global flows

In their book on globalization, Ritzer and Dean (2015) discuss four types of global flows. *Interconnected flows* coalesce at different points in time. During picking season, food networks rely on migrant labor, which increases market supply. *Multidirectional flows* transport many types of things, including entertainment. Not a one-way process, movies, videos, and music flow from East to West and vice versa. *Negative flows* create friction, such as disease outbreaks or polluting emissions. When sufficiently serious, negative flows stifle economic activity. *Reverse flows* proceed in one direction but then turn back on their source. Lines of code may flow from a source to a collaborator, who revises it and sends it back.

Liquid modernity

Zygmunt Bauman (2006), a Polish-British social theorist, characterizes the world as *liquid modernity*. In effect, the conditions that encourage action change faster than the establishment of routines and habits. As a result, a liquid society is one that experiences uncertainty. In Bauman's framework, neither modern nor post-modern, the current epoch of globalization exhibits characteristics that are modifying, interweaving, and disintegrating. It is difficult to distinguish between local and global, public and private, and work and leisure.

In contemporary and liquid economic life, widespread fear exists with respect to both potential dangers and society's ability to address them: "fear is the name we give to our uncertainty; to our ignorance of the threat of what is to be done," whereas the unpredictability of the liquid and modern world gives rise to "negative globalization" (Bauman, 2006). While the existence of negative global flows provides context for pandemic economics, Bauman (2006) argues for an extreme position: the current epoch of globalization is "wholly negative ... unchecked, unsupplemented and uncompensated for by a positive counterpart."

While global networks create negative flows, the current epoch of globalization also creates conditions for integration, technological advance, and the flow of information. The point is that the process of globalization is nuanced. Through *offshoring*, some workers gain jobs, while others lose them. With new technology, students gain access to knowledge and information, but must experience more online education. Globalization may extend markets but increase income inequality. Finally, globalization involves institutions; however, institutions such as the World Health Organization and the Centers for Disease Control and Prevention do not have the resources necessary to prevent a pandemic.

Choke points

Global systems, including connections, patterns, and flows, determine how global production is impacted by disruptions or shocks (Gertz, 2020). In this framework, disruptions occur at *choke points*—crucial points of connection. As an example, with the flow of energy resources, the South China Sea and the adjacent Straits of Malacca serve as choke points, acting as geographical thoroughfares to and from Asia. In these choke points, economic, political, and military conflict may disrupt the flow of oil. As Henry Farrell and Abraham L. Newman (2020) argue, in the *Harvard Business Review*, the current epoch of globalization has not created a decentralized and flat global economy (more Richard Florida than Thomas Friedman). It is characterized by imbalanced networks, hierarchical structures, and economic hubs. Technology companies in the United States, for example, host most of the world's information storage for cloud computing. But with global flows, economic hubs may serve as choke points:

> These choke points allow seemingly neutral infrastructure to be manipulated by governments to further their national strategic goals. China's push into 5G equipment has raised concerns in the West precisely because it might give the Chinese access to key parts of emerging communications networks. Japan recently restricted the export to South Korea of three chemicals crucial to the production of semiconductors, because of a political spat with Seoul. And the United States has aggressively exploited its control of a variety of seemingly technical structures that make global trade possible; it now appears increasingly willing to turn those structures into a machinery of domination.
>
> (Farrell and Newman, 2020)

But the identification of choke points, a priori, is not always possible. Global shocks may impact the flow of goods through hubs, independent of national policies. As a result of this complexity, a pandemic may sever connections between countries.

Global arrangements

While the world is characterized by the flows of people, goods, resources, information, technology, and capital, global arrangements may either expedite or establish barriers to those flows. Trade agreements, country borders, regulatory agencies, standards, and customs may enhance, hinder, or block global flows. Trade agreements, for example, include economic unions (such as the European Union), which encourage the flow of goods, resources, and workers between members, and free trade agreements (such as the former North American Free Trade Agreement), which eliminates trade barriers.

The point is that the current epoch of globalization includes an interplay between arrangements and flows, a simultaneous movement toward openness and oversight, and the existence of agents—private-sector companies and public-sector entities—who "carve the channels through which things flow" (Ritzer and Dean, 2015). Those in superordinate positions such as multi-national corporations enhance the flows that benefit their positions, such as encouraging the global "brain-drain" from the global South to the North or the flow of construction workers from low-income to high-income countries. A focus on this nuanced framework of structures, flows, openness, and oversight envisions a critical but realistic orientation to globalization in terms of who creates global structure, manages global flows, and benefits from the existing order.

The framework includes *friction*, the unstable interconnection across difference. In a system, a movement toward greater flow and integration means the reduction of friction. But friction, while restrictive, may lead to both costs and benefits. Highways restrict how travelers may flow from one point to another but accelerate the process. Unions encourage higher salaries and better working conditions for members but oppose nonunion businesses. During a pandemic, comprehensive interventions restrict human connections but slow the spread of the disease. Depending on one's position within the socio-economic hierarchy, these outcomes create different costs and benefits.

Relevant to pandemic economics, socio-economic structures may subordinate individuals according to race, class, ethnicity, and gender. The intersection of poverty and discrimination amplifies the problems of those in need. During a disease outbreak, pre-existing health conditions and inadequate access to healthcare—common with lower socio-economic classes—exacerbate health outcomes. During a pandemic, those in lower income brackets suffer the most.

But a framework that includes flows, structures, friction, and interconnection is useful for pandemic economics when it values these characteristics. But several questions remain. For global networks, how extensive are interconnections and flows, especially with respect to disease outbreaks? What is the velocity of transmission? During a pandemic, is it possible to introduce friction in a system or sever the link between connections? To answer these questions, the study of networks provides a useful framework.

Networks

A *network* or web is a system of interconnected elements that includes a set of agents or *nodes* and a set of *connections* that link them. A node is a physical point in which connections intersect. The structure of nodes and connections differs according to the system under consideration. For example, a communication network in a business environment facilitates economic activity, so nodes include all members of the organization while links include the pathways of communication. This network does not experience value relative to other networks but establishes a method to enhance business performance. To identify network structure, common queries include the degree of *small-worldness* (when most nodes are not neighbors but may reach each other with a small number of links) and *scale-free* (when the characteristics of the network are independent of the size of the network, so if the network grows its structure remains the same). Within a network structure, different shocks, methods of transmission, and connections facilitate flows.

Economics of networks

For economists, networks have become an important area of research. First, the expansion of game theory—the study of mutual interdependence, strategies, and payoffs—provides a network perspective. Second, important economic applications include communication networks, cellphones, and social media. Third, the rise of data and computing power has encouraged research on networks. Fourth, the growth of network research in economics patterns the growth of network research in related fields, including computer science and finance (Bramoullé et al., 2016).

Alan Kirman (2016), Professor Emeritus of Economics at the Aix-Marseille University and a researcher on complex heterogeneous networks, argues that a focus on the structure of interactions should underlie economic modeling. This focus facilitates an understanding of a wide range of economic phenomena, such as wholesale markets and financial crises. The application of economic theory to markets requires assumptions concerning both individual behavior and methods of interaction among agents. That is, to understand aggregate economic outcomes, economic models should include assumptions about the behavior of agents and connections between them. Because agents are embedded in networks, the connections between them impact their choices and actions.

Network structure

A network or web (W) includes two sets, nodes $N = \{n_1, n_2, ..., n_n\}$ and connections (C): $W = (N, C)$. Examples of nodes include computers, bridges, companies, researchers, suppliers, and infected individuals. For an ordered pair of nodes n_1 and n_2, a connection is defined as a link or pathway between them: $c(n_1, n_2)$. As an example, figure 3.1 demonstrates a network with a set of six nodes in physical space: $N = \{n_1, n_2, n_3, n_4, n_5, n_6\}$. Normalizing the distance between any two adjacent nodes to unity, the model identifies $c(n_1, n_2) = 1$ as the shortest path between them, represented with solid lines in figure 3.1.

At the same time, agents who are geographically distanced may interact in social networks. In social networks, ongoing value-generating flows $F = \{f_1, f_2, ..., f_n\}$ are overseen by network agents. For example, in an organizational network, the flow of information (f_1) between two nodes may accompany the flow of technology (f_2) between two other nodes, identified in figure 3.1 with dotted lines. The distance in a social network between nodes $\varphi(n, n_n)$ entails the shortest pathway, which may be greater than, equal to, or less than their

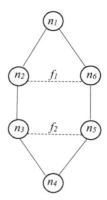

Figure 3.1 Network structure.

Source: author

geographic distance $c(n, n_n)$. The physical distance between n_2 and n_6, $c(n_2, n_6) = 2$ (solid lines) is greater than the distance of the social connection $\varphi(n_2, n_6) = 1$ (dotted line).

This reality means that the social network–which includes both business and personal connections–is the main channel through which agents discover new opportunities. In geographic space, economic exchange occurs at different levels. As scale increases, the resources necessary to undertake exchange rise. But social networks offer shorter connections. When social networks expand, economic growth occurs (Duernecker and Vega-Redondo, 2018).

As previously mentioned, different flows exist in network space. In a supply chain network, an interconnected flow of resources exists between raw material extraction, suppliers, and manufacturers. Multidirectional flows of output occur between developed and developing countries. Negative flows of polluting emissions accompany production. Reverse flows of information exist between the first set of nodes (raw materials) through intermediate nodes (supplier, manufacturer, retail, and distribution) to the last set of nodes (consumers), and back again. Modeling these flows requires an understanding of network structure.

Network characteristics

For the study of networks, areas of analysis include node identification, the relative importance of nodes, distance between connections, types of friction, interventions that stop network flows, and network topologies. Connections may be simple with direct and unweighted links or more complex with multidirectional and weighted links. Connections exist at different lengths and widths. Some connections may be relatively short, such as when a programmer shares code with a colleague in the same physical space; long, when the code is shared around the world; or of medium length. Some connections may be wide, relative to other connections, as when one power plant provides electricity to a city; narrow, such as a wind turbine providing power to a few homes; or in between. Networks may contain *walks* between nodes n_1 and o, paths that persist without node repetition: $(n_1, n_2), (n_3, n_4)...(n_n, o)$ or $n_1- n_2- n_3- n_4-...- n_n-o$. Networks may also contain *node-disjoints*, two or more paths that do not possess common intermediate nodes.

Network size

Network size refers to the number of nodes in a network. In terms of distribution, networks may be local (fresh food), regional (energy), national (production), or global (supply chain). With diseases, depending on network characteristics and interventions, an outbreak may become a regional problem, national epidemic, or global pandemic. The *boundary specification problem* is related to the difference between groups and networks. For groups, the existence of boundaries serves as a point of distinction. Group members may be full-time or part-time, but the group distinguishes between insiders and outsiders. For networks, natural boundaries may not exist. While a researcher may choose to study a set of well-defined organizational nodes, networks may expand and contract according to conditions and rules, without well-defined boundaries (Borgatti and Halgin, 2011).

When nodes cannot reach other nodes through pathways, networks include disconnections or *network fragments*. The advantage of identifying fragments is the ability to study how networks evolve. For example, at a university, a network of incoming freshmen may include hundreds of student nodes but few connections between them. That is, many network fragments exist. For two students, no connecting pathways may be apparent. But over time, students establish friendships and meet colleagues. As a result, network fragments decline. Eventually, each person or node may connect to every other person or node through links of various length and width. Eventually, transfers join, and the network expands. In this framework, the nodes, pathways, and degree of fragmentation change (Borgatti and Halgin, 2011).

Network topologies

Networks demonstrate two types of node distributions: *Poisson distributions* and *power-law functions*. The former describes random network structure, when nodes have about the same number of connections, close to the average. This characterization, typical of point-to-point networks such as supply chains, occurs when many connections may be profitably operated. The latter characterizes networks with a small number of nodes that cluster at the end of a distribution but have many connections and direct a large percentage of the flow.

Networks may contain hubs, which are clusters of nodes (H), where $H < N$. When businesses cluster in geographic space, neighborhoods serve as economic hubs. When airlines cluster in airports, cities serve as transportation hubs. When financial service organizations cluster in regions, states serve as financial hubs. In a network, the ratio of nodes in hubs to total nodes determines the degree to which the network is "spiky," using Richard Florida's (2005) term.

Superspreaders

Networks demonstrate the potential existence of a set of *superspreaders* $S = \{s_1, s_2, ..., s_n\}$, nodes or hubs that facilitate a high degree of network flow. In social networks, superspreaders have a relatively large number of connections and spread the most information. In technology networks, superspreaders are the individuals or companies, well connected,

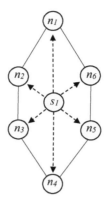

Figure 3.2 Network superspreader.

Source: author

that innovate and spread new technology in the network. When a disease appears in a transmission network, a superspreader (s_i) spreads the disease to others, creating an outbreak (figure 3.2).

In a disease outbreak, early epidemiological studies assumed that susceptible nodes had equal chance of infection. But subsequent studies documented heterogeneity in transmission: some people have a greater propensity of infecting others (Issues in Pandemic Economics 3.1). What emerged as the 20/80 rule, a concept found in empirical studies in epidemiology, 20 percent of a given population is thought to hold 80 percent of the "transmission potential" (Stein, 2011). For networks, the extent of this rule determines both the capacity for superspreader events and the heterogeneity of nodes. As an example, with the SARS epidemic of 2003, which began in southern China, most cases were barely infectious (73 percent), but a small number were highly infectious (6 percent) (Chan, 2016). As a result, an infectious disease with a small individual variation of infectiousness shows frequent but weak transmission after the initial infection. But an infectious disease with a large individual variation of infectiousness shows infrequent but explosive transmission after the initial infection.

Issues in pandemic economics 3.1: Superspreaders

Because of social habits, infectiousness, and timing, superspreaders in disease networks infect a disproportionate number of people. The disease carriers in the middle of superspreader events drive outbreaks, making it important to identify the potential events, establish interventions, and prevent the gatherings where superspreading may occur. However, distinguishing between superspreaders and those at the other end of the distribution who are infected but unlikely to spread the disease makes a large difference with respect to resource allocation and the speed in which a disease spreads (Kolata, 2020). For superspreaders, contact tracing is important. For those who do not spread the disease, contact tracing is a waste of resources. Early in a disease outbreak, identification of the two groups is paramount. For a disease to spread, connections must exist;

however, connections are necessary but not sufficient for the disease to spread. Other factors are at play, including pre-existing conditions, access to healthcare resources, and age. For these reasons, identifying potential superspreader events *a priori* is a difficult task. Nevertheless, network spreading studies range from technology diffusion to online social media to epidemic disease identification. In different networks, superspreader identification strategies are identified and accelerated to increase product exposure, identify profitable marketing strategies, and in the case of disease execute early interventions. With the latter, one study estimated that, with Covid-19, most transmissions were caused by a small fraction of those who were infected (Endo et al., 2020). The implication is that, although the initial size of the network is important in estimating potential dispersion, it is not directly applicable early in an outbreak, because the final size is not observed. In a disease network and a heterogeneous distribution, it is important for policy makers to focus on the prevention of superspreading events as well as the underlying factors that cause higher levels of infectiousness.

Network applications

Systematic differences between networks exist across income levels, regions, and political predilections but they facilitate global flows. It is now easier than ever to communicate, distribute, and innovate but also spread disease. Although not mutually exclusive, the networks relevant to pandemic economics in the following chapters include, but are not limited to, disease, energy, supply chain, and innovation. The result of these networks is an ever-expanding web of linkages.

Disease networks

Disease networks spread negative flows. Suppose targeted interventions (X) are successful in severing connections between a superspreader (s_1) and individuals n_1, n_2, n_3 (figure 3.3). But the interventions do not spare others. An example is an infectious person who travels through an airport (superspreader event one), flies on a plane (superspreader event two), and

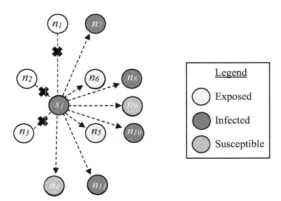

Figure 3.3 Superspreader event, interventions (X), and multiple outcomes.
Source: author

upon arrival attends a large gathering with family and friends (superspreader event three). Depending on characteristics of the event, connected agents may be exposed, infected, or susceptible.

Superspreader events are "normal features of disease spread" (Chan, 2016). Even though the basic reproductive number (R_o)—the average number of people to whom an infected person passes on a new disease in the absence of interventions—was thought to be between two and three during the majority of the coronavirus pandemic, meaning an infected person passed the disease on average to between two and three other people, a superspreader possessed a basic reproductive number beyond this range.

A basic reproductive number possesses a normal distribution. As a result, R_o does not convey the fact that, in a disease outbreak, some people infect very few others, but superspreaders infect many. For this reason, another important variable informs disease networks: k, the *dispersion factor*, which captures the range of possible infections and the potential for superspreader events. That is, k captures how much a disease clusters. All else equal, "the lower k is, the more transmission comes from a small number of people" (Kupferschmidt, 2020). The viruses SARS-CoV-1 in 2003 and SARS-CoV-2 in 2020 commonly infected groups but a majority of cases stemmed from a small percentage of infectors (Adam et al., 2020). This result is important. Superspreading events serve as sources of disease outbreaks. As a result, eliminating the potential for superspreader events through targeted interventions both severs network connections and slows disease transmission. Targeting superspreader events may therefore serve as a cost-effective intervention during a pandemic.

Energy networks

Energy networks—interrelated markets of energy sources, transmission, and distribution—include links between consumer nodes and energy resources. Within an energy network, several sectors exist, including power, electricity, fuel, buildings, industry, and transportation. Power sources for electricity generation are traditional (coal, natural gas, oil, and nuclear) and alternative (biomass, geothermal, hydropower, solar, and wind). Both electricity and fuel networks energize transportation, industrial, and building sectors. Electricity networks burn fossil fuels in power plants, emit greenhouse gas emissions, and contribute negative global flows (chapter 9). Greenhouse gas emissions—gases in the atmosphere that absorb radiation in the thermal infrared range—stem from the burning of fossil fuels, accumulate in the atmosphere, and increase average global temperatures. In electricity networks, the nodes are power plants and end-use consumers, while transmission lines serve as connections. With electricity, network structure elucidates the energy conversion chain, how sources of primary energy are transformed into end-use form.

The energy conversion chain includes energy sources, refining, carriers, storage, end-use conversion, and demand. The three categories of primary energy sources (fossil fuels, nuclear, and renewables) power the global economy. But in many cases, refining must occur, such as when oil refineries turn petroleum into gasoline or ethanol is refined out of plant matter. The result of refining or processing is the creation of a secondary form of energy, an energy carrier. Four energy carriers may be converted into mechanical work or heat: electricity, refined natural gas, refined petroleum products, and refined biomass. But in the conversion process from primary energy to energy carrier, energy is often stored, especially with respect to transportation. With gasoline, energy is stored in tanks at refineries, tanker trucks, filling stations, and in vehicles. End-use-conversion refers to the process in which energy is transformed from one form to another, such as when heat energy from fuels is converted into mechanical energy to power vehicles. Finally, the energy conversion chain satisfies the demand for energy for transportation, buildings, and industry.

During different steps of the chain, however, polluting emissions flow into the environment. With energy processing and the conversion of crude oil into gasoline, for example, carbon emissions, nitrogen oxides, carbon monoxide, and unburned hydrocarbon–all greenhouse gases–are released into the atmosphere. In addition, during the end-use stage, driving with combustion engines leads to the release of these gases. In the generation of electricity, the burning of coal, oil, and natural gas also leads to greenhouse gas emissions. The point of these examples is that the transportation and power sectors generate greenhouse gas emissions, a negative flow.

Supply chain networks

Supply chains–value-adding activities that start with raw materials and end with consumption–both characterize the current epoch of globalization and demonstrate how a pandemic may impact the global economy. In *global supply chains*, different nodes exist, including companies that spread their production processes across suppliers and countries, and consumers that demand output. The average automobile, for example, contains about 30,000 parts; for production, automobile manufacturers rely on hundreds of firms, often clustered in hubs. While these global connections enhance efficiency, they also introduce vulnerabilities. When a link on the chain weakens through regulatory friction or breaks because of lockdown, consumers, upstream suppliers, and downstream manufactures struggle.

In the current epoch of globalization, global supply chains are so elaborate and circuitous that they are designed as *complex networks*–networks that do not have the characteristic of simplicity–exhibiting chain reactions and nontrivial topological features. Patterns of connection may be neither random nor regular but nonlinear with feedback loops. They exhibit high levels of clustering, reciprocity, and community structure. Complex networks often experience both thin profit margins and outsourcing. Although pervasive on a global scale, they create system vulnerabilities. As a result, disruptions such as trade wars, choke points, tariffs, and disease outbreaks alter network flows and impact supplier, producer, and consumer nodes.

In the case of disease outbreaks that lead to global pandemics, shutdown interventions both restrict the movement of resources and close factories. As a result, the shock spreads, virus-like, through a global supply chain. Inventories either in transit or already among wholesalers and retailers provide a short-term cushion. But as inventories are depleted, the shock deconstructs supply chain mechanisms. As more companies chase fewer resource inputs, production slows. As consumers peruse fewer items on the shelves, shortages emerge.

The reason for shortages is that, when workers are in lockdown and factories idle, output collects at ports, container ships sail without cargo, and initial shopping sprees empty shelves of essentials. While factories shutter, some producers find themselves without resource inputs. When key global industries such as industrial machinery and electronics shut down, laptop exports and cellphone imports plummet, while the demand for remote work and distance learning soars. As a pandemic proceeds, countries prohibit exports, consumers hoard necessities–medicine, toilet paper, diapers, nonperishable food, etc.–and supply chain disruptions accelerate.

During a pandemic, shortages and chain reactions impact specific markets, altering both aggregate demand and supply. While pillars of economic activity such as airlines, apparel, arenas, fitness, lodging, and restaurants close, online retailers report higher earnings. With an increase in cooking, the demand for groceries rises. In the presence of sheltering-in-place interventions, home projects increase. The demand for certain forms of entertainment increases, including e-books, movies, news media, music, video streaming, and gaming. Attempting to meet changes in demand, some supply chain networks are more robust than others.

Innovation networks

Innovation networks include agents who create and develop new products, services, and production methods (chapter 11). In these networks, variations across performance and regions depend on two sets of factors. One set includes resources, data, and information. The other set includes organizational and institutional structures, human capital, capabilities, and knowledge. While the first set includes flows that travel between nodes, the second set of characteristics is often tied to place and not mobile. As a result, innovation networks exhibit a high *clustering coefficient*–the degree to which nodes in a network cluster together–so resources, data, and information are shared between colleagues and connected researchers.

Following the Nobel-prize winning economist Paul Krugman's (1991) seminal article on increasing returns and economic geography, economists study the geographic dimension of innovating activities, particularly the companies in high-tech and technology-based industries. According to Breschi and Malerba (2005), this research analyzes innovation, geographic clustering, and the implications for economic activity. For example, *localized knowledge spillovers* serve as explanatory factors in the clustering of innovating firms. Localized knowledge spillovers imply that, in a world of global information networks, new knowledge occurs more efficiently in research clusters. The properties of innovating firms, such as their tacit nature and complexity, mean that spatial proximity decreases the cost of the transmission of knowledge. As a result, knowledge flows through the interfirm mobility of researchers and interpersonal contacts, characteristic of close geographical proximity. But the knowledge developed in clusters flows through network connections locally but takes time to flow regionally. Innovating clusters differ from industries, depending on tacit knowledge and the state of the industry life cycle (Breschi and Malerba, 2005).

Another area of research for innovation networks involves evolutionary theory, in which knowledge and learning are elements of change in an economic system. Innovation is a process in which researchers engage in trial and error, select among the best methods, and learn about economic conditions. However, their decisions and actions are both enabled and constrained by the knowledge base of other members of the network. Therefore, in addition to individual contributions, collective contributions from hubs are important (Breschi and Malerba, 2005).

Contagion

In networks, *contagion*—the spread of crisis from one area to another—may occur in two ways. One, contagion may occur when something spreads in a network, such as the flow of disease (f_d) infecting members of a community. In this context, contagion is contained to the network under consideration. Two, if networks are interdependent, they are vulnerable to shocks that begin in one network and spread to others (figure 3.4).

Contagion and negative flows

When contagion spreads between networks, it may entail the same or different negative flows. An example of the former is the flow of a disease. An example of the latter, the Asian financial crisis of 1997, occurred when a series of currency devaluations began in Thailand, spread to other east-Asian countries, and raised fears about a regional or global economic meltdown. Because financial networks link to economic networks, the Asian financial crisis led to the collapse of banks, decrease in investment, and decrease in the production of output. The contagion demonstrated how problems in the banking sector could scare foreign investors, devalue currencies, and lead to recession. In response, the global community mobilized bank loans and implemented policies of currency stabilization.

Financial contagion depends on "phase transition," the magnitude of negative shocks impacting financial institutions (Acemoglu et al., 2015). For example, when the negative shocks that impact financial institutions are sufficiently small, a densely connected network enhances financial stability. But, beyond a certain level, a densely connected network serves to propagate higher-order shocks, spreading contagion through a financial system. In this context, the network characteristics that promote stability may also serve as sources of systematic risk.

Contagion as a process

In a disease pandemic, contagion unfolds as a process. First, disease spreads in global transmission networks, creating a healthcare crisis. This leads to a decrease in the production of output, recession, and rising unemployment, as countries lock down their economies. As

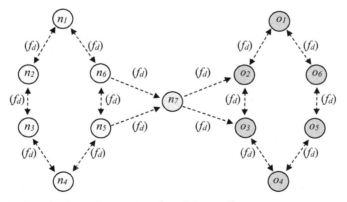

Figure 3.4 Contagion (f_d) flows from one network to another.
Source: author

business investment declines, bankruptcies and layoffs rise. Following the economic crisis is the danger of a financial crisis with countries and companies defaulting on loans. Countries with the highest levels of debt per GDP are at the greatest risk as they borrow money to combat economic downturns. For many companies, revenue generation is too low to make interest payments on debt, so they issue new debt. The debt problems cause investors to become pessimistic. As these epidemiological, economic, and financial problems unfold, contagion spreads to developing countries. As a result, infections rise and economic activity declines. Finally, global markets such as transportation and manufacturing experience a demand-side shock and lower levels of economic activity. While contagion may be global, national responses complicate efforts to combat the problem (Zakaria, 2020).

Measuring the likelihood of outcomes

In the presence of contagion, how is it possible to measure the likelihood of outcomes across countries? The researchers Eswar Prasad of Brookings and Ethan Wu of Cornell (2020) answer this question with their TIGER model: Tracking Indexes for the Global Economic Recovery. Using economic, financial, and confidence variables, the model forecasts country-level outcomes. At the beginning of the coronavirus pandemic, the model forecasted that "the combined public health and economic crises (made) a rapid recovery less likely … Europe and Japan … (were) likely to suffer substantial declines in output … France, Germany, and the U.K. face(d) historic recessions" (Prasad and Wu, 2020).

What are the lessons of contagion? First, the more that networks are integrated, the more likely negative flows will spread across regions. Second, as governments borrow beyond their means, they are likely to experience budget crises when economic and financial activity decline. Third, the longer the initial outbreak continues to spread, the greater the risk of contagion. Finally, an inability of countries to stop economic, epidemiological, and financial crises leads to a greater likelihood that contagion will infect multiple networks.

Summary

The process of globalization leads to a higher level of interconnection between countries, companies, and individuals but does not imply an inevitable movement toward integration. The epochs of globalization demonstrate the expansion of trade, information, and transmission networks. While connections may expand, globalization also propagates negative flows, which may lead the world to restore borders, slow migration, devolve power from the international to the national, and shift influence from the national to the local. In a disease outbreak, countries implement policy interventions such as border closings. Multidirectional flows of output and people characterize global networks, but disease pandemics stop these flows. The process of globalization may be viewed as an example of liquid modernity: the conditions that cause people to act change faster than the ability of people to establish routines. As a result, liquid societies exhibit characteristics of conflict and uncertainty.

A network is a system of interconnected elements, including a set of nodes and a set of connections. For economists, networks are an important area of research because many applications have arisen, including game theory, supply chaining, social media, and systems of innovation. The pattern of nodes, connections, flows, and friction creates structure. In networks, agents who are geographically distanced may interact in social networks. As a result, the social network serves as the main channel through which agents discover new opportunities. Connections assume different lengths and widths, but when nodes cannot reach others through pathways, network fragments exist. Networks may contain hubs and superspreaders that facilitate a high degree of network flow.

Applications demonstrate network characteristics. Disease networks spread negative flows. Energy networks include links between consumer nodes and energy resource nodes. Supply chain networks characterize the current epoch of globalization and demonstrate how a pandemic may impact the global economy. Innovation networks include agents who create and develop new policies, products, services, procedures, and solutions.

Contagion—the spread of crisis from one area to another—may occur in one network or between networks. If networks are interdependent, they are vulnerable to shocks that begin in one network and cascading failures that spread. Financial contagion depends on phase transition, the magnitude of negative shocks impacting financial institutions. In a disease pandemic, contagion occurs as a process, including collapses in the economy, financial system, and public health. The lesson of contagion is that the more that networks are integrated, the more likely negative flows will spread across regions.

Chapter takeaways

LO1   In systems of interconnection, the speed in which a disease spreads depends on infectiousness, the degree of interconnection of transmission networks, and the effectiveness of interventions.

LO2   The process of globalization does not imply an inevitable movement toward integration.

LO3   A network is a system of interconnected elements that includes a set of nodes and a set of connections.

LO4   Networks relevant to pandemic economics include, but are not limited to, disease, energy, supply chain, and innovation networks.

LO5   Contagion occurs when a negative flow spreads through a network or interconnected networks.

Terms and concepts

Boundary specification problem
Choke points
Clustering coefficient
Complex networks
Connections
Contagion
Dispersion factor
Friction
Global flows
Global supply chains
Globalization
Interconnected flows
Liquid modernity

Localized knowledge spillovers
Multidirectional flows
Negative flows
Network
Network fragments
Node-disjoints
Nodes
Offshoring
Poisson distributions
Power-law functions
Reverse flows
Scale-free
Small-worldness
Superspreaders
Supply chains
Walks

Questions

1. Characterize the current epoch of globalization. Does 1991 serve as the beginning? In the current epoch, what economic factors are important?
2. Does the concept of globalization refer to the opening of international borders to flows of trade and investment? Or should the concept of globalization include additional flows such as information, migration, and technology?
3. What are examples of positive and negative global flows? Over the epochs of globalization, what are the trends for each?
4. With respect to countries, companies, and businesses, do you think Thomas Friedman's (2005) vision that the world is flat or Richard Florida's (2005) vision that the world is spiky best characterizes the process of globalization? Why?
5. Diagram a supply chain network. Identify nodes, connections, and types of flows. What is the degree of small-worldness? Is the network scale-free? How may disruptions occur? What interventions would effectively address the disruptions?
6. Diagram a disease network. Identify nodes, connections, and types of flows. What is the degree of small-worldness? Is the network scale-free? How may disruptions occur? What interventions would effectively address the disruptions?
7. Diagram an energy network. Identify nodes, connections, and types of flows. What is the degree of small-worldness? Is the network scale-free? How may disruptions occur? What interventions would effectively address the disruptions?
8. Diagram an innovation network. Identify nodes, connections, and types of flows. What is the degree of small-worldness? Is the network scale-free? How may disruptions occur? What interventions would effectively address the disruptions?
9. Study contagion in the articles by Zakaria (2020) and Acemoglu et al. (2015). How does contagion proceed? What interventions slow contagion? Does a positive counterexample to contagion exist? If so, explain.

10. Is the present system of globalization more vulnerable to contagion than previous systems?

References

Acemoglu, Daron, Ozdaglar, Asuman, and Tahbaz-Salehi, Alireza. 2015. "Systematic risk and stability in financial networks," *American Economic Review*, 105, 2 (February): 564-608.

Adam, Dillon, Wu, Peng, Wong, Jessica, Lau, Eric, Tsang, Tim, Chauchemez, Simon, Leung, Gabriel, and Cowling, Benjamin. 2020. "Clustering and superspreading potential of severe acute respiratory syndrome coronavirus 2 (SARS-CoV-2) infections in Hong Kong," *Nature Medicine*, 26: 1714-1719.

Babones, Salvatore. 2020. "The 'Chinese Virus' spread along the New Silk Road." *Foreign Policy*, April 6.

Bauman, Zygmunt. 2006. *Liquid Fear*. Cambridge: Polity Press.

Borgatti, Stephen P., and Halgin, Daniel S. 2011. "On network theory," *Organization Science*, 22, 5 (September-October): 1168-1181.

Bramoullê, Yann, Galeotti, Andrea, and Rogers, Brian W. 2016. "Introduction to the handbook," in Bramoullê, Yann, Galeotti, Andrea, and Rogers, Brian W. (Eds.), *The Oxford Handbook of the Economics of Networks*. New York: Oxford University Press.

Breschi, Stefano, and Malerba, Franco. 2005. "Clusters, networks, and innovation: research results and new direction," in Breschi, Stefano and Malerba, Franco (Eds.), *Clusters, Networks, and Innovation*. Oxford: Oxford University Press.

Chan, Byung C. 2016. "Understanding and modeling the super-spreader events of the Middle East respiratory syndrome outbreak in Korea," *Infection & Chemotherapy*, 48, 2 (June): 147-149.

Duernecker, Georg, and Vega-Redondo, Fernando. 2018. "Social networks and the process of globalization," *The Review of Economic Studies*, 85, 3 (July): 1716-1751.

Eder, Steve, Fountain, Henry, Keller, Michael H., Xiao, Muyi, and Stevenson, Alexandra. 2020. "430,000 people have traveled from China to U.S. since coronavirus surfaced," *The New York Times*, April 15.

Endo, Akira, Abott, Sam, Kucharski, Adam, and Funk, Sebastian. 2020. "Estimating the overdispersion in Covid-19 transmission using outbreak sizes outside China," *Wellcome Open Resource*, 10, 5 (July): 67.

Farrell, Henry, and Newman, Abraham L. 2020. "Choke points," *Harvard Business Review*, January-February.

Florida, Richard. 2005. "The world is spiky," *The Atlantic Monthly*, October: 48-51.

Friedman, Thomas L. 2005. *The World is Flat: A Brief History of the Twenty-first Century*. New York: Farrar, Straus, and Giroux.

Gertz, Geoffrey. 2020. "The coronavirus will reveal hidden vulnerabilities in complex global supply chains," *Brookings*, March 5.

Khanna, Parag. 2008. *The Second World: Empires and Influence in the New Global Order*. New York: Random House.

Kirman, Alan. 2016. "Networks: a paradigm shift for economics?" in Bramoullê, Yann, Galeotti, Andrea, and Rogers, Brian W. (Eds.), *The Oxford Handbook of the Economics of Networks*. New York: Oxford University Press.

Kolata, Gina. 2020. "Why are some people so much more infectious than others?" *The New York Times*, April 12.

Krugman, Paul. 1991. "Increasing returns and economic geography," *Journal of Political Economy*, 99, 3 (June): 483-499.

Kupferschmidt, Kai. 2020. "Why do some Covid-19 patients infect many others, whereas most don't spread the virus at all?" *Science*, May 19. doi:10.1126/science.abc8931.

Pieterse, Jan. 2012. "Periodizing globalization: histories of globalization," *New Global Studies*, 6, 2 (July): 1-27.

Prasad, Eswar, and Wu, Ethan. 2020. "April 2020 update to TIGER: the coronavirus collapse is upon us," *Brookings*, April 12.

Ritzer, George, and Dean, Paul. 2015. *Globalization: A Basic Text*, 2nd edition. Oxford, England: John Wiley & Sons.

Stein, Richard A. 2011. "Super-spreaders in infectious diseases," *International Journal of Infectious Diseases*, 15, 8 (August): e510-e513.

Wu, Jin, Cai, Weiyi, Watkins, Derek, and Glanz, James. 2020. "How the virus got out," *The New York Times*, March 22.

Zakaria, Fareed. 2020. "This is just the first in a series of cascading crises," *The Washington Post*, April 2.

Part II

The pandemic phase: shutdown, recession, and recovery

4 Theories of economic shutdown

Learning objectives

After reading this chapter, you will be able to:

LO1 Discuss the first economic interval of the pandemic phase: shutdown.
LO2 Explain why flattening the epidemic curve serves as an epidemiological goal.
LO3 Analyze nonpharmaceutical interventions.
LO4 Address the tradeoff between economic health and public health.
LO5 Contrast theories of economic shutdown.
LO6 Explain why countries should prioritize health before wealth.
LO7 Determine the loss in income when laborers shelter-in-place.
LO8 Analyze models of economic assistance.

Chapter outline

- Shutdown interval
- Flattening the epidemic curve
- Nonpharmaceutical interventions
- Tradeoff between health and the economy
- Theories of economic shutdown
- Health before wealth
- Labor market and lost income
- Economic systems and income assistance
- Summary

Shutdown interval

This chapter analyzes the first economic interval of the pandemic phase: *shutdown* (figure 4.1).

To reduce infections, slow the spread of the disease, and decrease the number of deaths, shutdown interventions limit human contact. For most countries, shutdown interventions follow a script: nonessential members of the labor force stop reporting to their places of

Figure 4.1 Three economic intervals of the pandemic phase.
Source: author

employment, while essential workers remain. But when nonessential workers leave, they may or may not remain employed with their companies. This chapter addresses the implication of this reality, arguing that, to maintain economic viability, public economic assistance for workers must accompany shutdown interventions. In particular, when infections are rising, the public sector should support workers while they stay home.

This chapter uses an economic systems framework to demonstrate that countries that approach social policy in a statist framework, such as the implementation of universal health-care, are more likely to keep workers tied to their jobs. During economic shutdown, the public sector subsidizes their wages. But countries that implement social policy in a more market-oriented approach, such as a combination of public and private healthcare, are less likely to keep workers tied to their jobs. In this situation, during economic shutdown, the public sector provides unemployment benefits. If successful, shutdown interventions stabilize public health, measured with a reduction in confirmed cases. But at the same time, economic activity declines. The extent to which a country maximizes public health and minimizes economic losses depends on the efficacy of targeted policy. Before addressing policy interventions, the next section discusses why shutdown interventions occur at the beginning of a pandemic phase: to flatten the epidemic curve.

Flattening the epidemic curve

Flattening the epidemic curve, a public health strategy of protective measures, attempts to slow the spread of disease. After an outbreak, infections rise, peak, and decline. Flattening the epidemic curve leads to both a delay in peak infections and a lower number of peak cases. When the epidemic curve flattens, it takes longer for infections to spread through a population. The argument for flattening the epidemic curve is twofold. First, slowing the spread of disease provides time for a network of scientists to create a vaccine and other treatments. With a susceptible population, infections rise exponentially at the beginning of a pandemic (Harris, 2020). Second, slowing the spread of disease addresses the potential of shortages in capacity in hospitals. When cases rise, hospitals may not have the capacity to treat all of the patients or enough resources necessary to fight the disease, including doctors, nurses, and protective equipment.

Nonpharmaceutical interventions

Nonpharmaceutical interventions flatten the epidemic curve. They sever transmission networks before the creation and distribution of a vaccine. In this context, physical distancing serves as the primary mechanism to slow the spread of disease. But the interventions differ with respect to structure, function, and income effects. In the absence of a national lockdown mandate, for example, individuals in higher income neighborhoods are more likely to experience a greater number of days at home, whereas individuals in lower income neighborhoods are more likely to experience more work outside the home (Jay et al., 2020). The reason is that individuals in lower income neighborhoods face specific barriers, including financial constraints and insufficient savings. As a result, government support for workers in all income levels must accompany nonpharmaceutical interventions.

Swiss cheese model of pandemic defense

During the ongoing debate of government intervention during the coronavirus pandemic, experts referred to the "Swiss cheese model" of pandemic defense (Roberts, 2020). This framework provides multiple layers of protection and blocks the spread of disease; however, no one layer is perfect. Each contains holes (weaknesses). When the holes align, the risk of disease transmission increases. But when the holes are not aligned, the layers provide a method to reduce the spread of disease. Therefore, a country's success depends on multiple layers of response, not a single policy. Organized according to personal and collective responsibility, the model includes hand washing, mask wearing, ventilation, air filtration, sheltering-in-place, social distancing, quarantines, testing and tracing, and government messaging. When a vaccination arrives, it provides an additional layer of protection. The following sections discuss sheltering-in-place, social distancing, and quarantines. Chapter 6 addresses testing, tracing, and government messaging. Chapter 11 discusses vaccination.

Sheltering-in-place

With a *sheltering-in-place* directive, people remain home for all but essential activities, including work, care for others, and trips to grocery stores and pharmacies. As an alternative to quarantine, sheltering-in-place separates individuals to stop the spread of disease. The difference, however, is that sheltering-in-place provides more flexibility. As a result, the extent to which members of a population participate is a function of both the perceived threat from the disease and extent of the directive. The more a disease spreads through a community, the more time people spend sheltering-in-place. With this intervention, people living in areas with higher population density experience more time sheltering-in-place. In rural areas, people spend more time away from home, in large part because places of work, healthcare facilities, and stores are farther away.

The socioeconomic implications of sheltering-in-place include changes in demand for necessities and luxuries such as streaming video services, but also anxiety, depression, apathy, the need for social connection, and loneliness, the latter serving as "the leprosy of the 21st century," according to *The Economist* (Fergusson, 2018). Sheltering-in-place directives follow heterogeneity across regions: high population density areas and early adopters benefit more from the intervention (Dave et al., 2020). But one other issue, the composition of trips outside the home, provides additional insight. During a pandemic, when people are not sheltering-in-place or working, where do they go? The answer is trips to grocery stores, pharmacies, and parks, "essential" aspects of economic and psychological well-being (Schaul et al., 2020).

Social distancing

The process of physical or *social distancing* means maintaining an acceptable amount of space, believed to be six feet (1.83 meters), between individuals. With social distancing, individuals may work, shop for groceries and pharmaceuticals, and exercise, while avoiding infection. Especially important for people in high-risk categories, such as pre-existing medical conditions or less access to healthcare services, the motivation for social distancing is that asymptomatic cases may spread disease to others without knowledge. The *incubation period* between exposure to a disease and the appearance of the first symptoms was on average five days for Covid-19 but could last two weeks. The average *infectious period*—when an infected individual may spread the disease to others—was 10 days for Covid-19, starting with the last two or three days of incubation.

The process of social distancing raises important questions of accommodation, especially in urban areas. On many city sidewalks, six feet of social distancing is impossible. Temporarily closing traffic lanes, or restricting transportation to biking, accommodates pedestrians. Converting traffic signals to four-way stops reduces human bunching on sidewalks. Markings on the floors of stores and grounds of outdoor spaces remind people of social distancing requirements.

Public policy may dictate that returning to places of employment after working from home should occur incrementally for employees who work in close proximity to others. To the extent that employees vary systematically across these characteristics, social distancing creates uneven outcomes. Understanding these differences is therefore important in evaluating the effectiveness of social distancing policies.

Two important labor market outcomes exist. First, social distancing impacts employees who cannot work from home or are economically vulnerable because of lower levels of education, health insurance, and income. Second, a greater level of economic diversity exists among employees who work in higher levels of physical proximity to others, such as sales assistants and salon workers. As a result, the economic costs of social distancing are correlated with economic status, while the economic costs for those who work in environments with low levels of physical proximity may be more broadly distributed (Mongey et al., 2020).

Quarantines

A state, period, or place of *quarantine* is characterized as the "deliberate separation of individuals exposed to a contagious agent, irrespective of their infectivity or symptomatic status, from a population of susceptible individuals" (Mubayi et al., 2010). During a pandemic, a percentage of the exposed individuals are sent to quarantine. Monitoring demonstrates who shows symptoms or tests positive. But the acceleration of infections leads to the isolation of at-risk individuals. For those in quarantine, preventive and protective measures apply. But in the presence of testing, the isolation of positive infections serves as an appropriate epidemiological response, followed by treatment (Mubayi et al., 2010). In practice, quarantine applies to different members of a population. One option is to quarantine everyone at a large social cost. Another option is to quarantine targeted individuals, based on the results of testing. In Beijing, China, for example, during the coronavirus pandemic, an infection wave hit the city six months after the initial round of infections. In response, Beijing imposed quarantine measures on targeted neighborhoods.

Public health benefits of nonpharmaceutical interventions

The public health benefits of nonpharmaceutical interventions stem from physical distancing. First, Seth Flaxman of Imperial College London and his co-authors (2020), writing in *Nature*, argue that the objective of shutdown interventions is to reduce the effective reproduction number (R_e) below one, a quantity representing the average number of infections generated by an infected person at a point in time. During the coronavirus pandemic, European countries such as Austria, Denmark, France, Germany, Italy, and the U.K. implemented nonpharmaceutical interventions and reduced disease transmission in varying degrees, leading to "large reductions in the reproduction number" and the avoidance of millions of deaths (Flaxman et al., 2020).

Second, the economist Soloman Hsiang of the University of California, Berkeley and his co-authors (2020), also writing in *Nature*, argue that shutdown interventions "significantly and substantially slowed" the growth of the virus during the pandemic, preventing or delaying tens of millions of confirmed cases, and hundreds of millions of total infections.

Third, the economist Sangmin Aum of the South Korean Development Institute and his co-authors (2020) apply a quantitative economic-epidemiological model to study the effects of shutdown policies, including heterogeneity in people, sectors, and occupations with the ability of employees to work at home. They find that, early in a pandemic, "there may not be a clear tradeoff between GDP and public health," as shutdown measures encourage people to work from home (Aum et al., 2020).

Tradeoff between health and the economy

If a country prioritizes public health, shuts down segments of the economy, and fights the spread of disease, the country must eventually ease restrictions on economic activity. At this point, further improvements in the economy may come at the expense of public health (figure 4.2).

Assimilation of workers

The tradeoff between health and the economy stems from the fact that countries must eventually ease restrictions and open the segments of the economy that were closed. The idea is to assimilate workers back into the economy. But higher levels of economic activity lead to more human interaction and the potential for additional infection waves. At this point, the benefit of economic activity must be weighed against the cost of a subsequent decline in public health. The tradeoff between public health and the economy includes a dynamic element, the extent to which businesses adapt to new economic circumstances. To adjust, businesses invest in technology, maintaining economic activity while employees work from home. But few businesses are equipped to handle a sustained loss of revenue. Even if they furlough workers, cut spending, and receive public assistance, many businesses do not survive

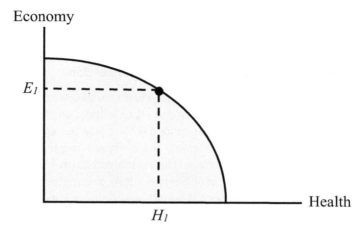

Figure 4.2 Tradeoff between public health and the economy.
Source: author

a government-mandated economic shutdown. As a result, the longer shutdown measures prioritize public health, the more businesses will fail.

Suboptimal position

When workers re-emerge from their homes after sheltering-in-place, they experience an economy operating in a suboptimal position with less production and consumer spending. One reason is that, on the supply side of the market, pandemics sever global supply chains. Businesses that remain open and offer essential services may have suppliers further up the supply chain that cannot continue to offer raw materials or packaging. Another reason is that, on the demand side of the market, households reduce spending on services, such as restaurant meals and haircuts. A reduction in consumption expenditure alters production patterns, such as dairies that must dump milk when retailers experience lower sales.

The tradeoff between public health and the economy depends on the relationship between shutdown interventions and economic activity. For businesses that rely on face-to-face interaction, such as hair salons and dentists, shutdown policies reduce economic activity. Empirically, the benefit to society of shutdown interventions is the present value of lives saved, measured as the difference in mortality between shutdown and no shutdown policies. The cost to society is the present value of a decline in GDP. In plausible scenarios, the economic value of lives saved far outweighs the economic losses from economic activity (Thunstrom et al., 2020).

Theories of economic shutdown

Early in a pandemic, countries may choose to shutter all, some, or no parts of the economy. In practice, policies of economic shutdown relate to the epidemic curve. A full economic shutdown flattens the curve in the most substantial manner. But the prioritization of public health may take different forms. What economic shutdown measures occur? As this section

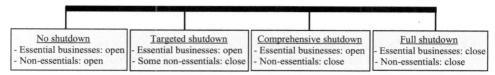

No shutdown	Targeted shutdown	Comprehensive shutdown	Full shutdown
- Essential businesses: open	- Essential businesses: open	- Essential businesses: open	- Essential businesses: close
- Non-essentials: open	- Some non-essentials: close	- Non-essentials: close	- Non-essentials: close

Figure 4.3 Theories of economic shutdown.

Source: author

explains, different theories of economic shutdown demonstrate the extent to which inter-ventions shutter the business environment, lead to tradeoffs between public health and the economy, and exist along a spectrum of choices (figure 4.3).

At one end of the spectrum, a lack of economic shutdown interventions keeps all businesses open, does not flatten the epidemic curve, and accelerates the movement toward herd immu-nity. Depending on spatial and market variables, a targeted shutdown keeps some nonessen-tial businesses open, closes others, and slowly flattens the epidemic curve. A comprehensive economic shutdown uses a full range of protective measures, shutters all nonessential forms of economic activity, keeps essential businesses open, and aggressively flattens the epidemic curve. At the other end of the spectrum, a full economic shutdown closes all businesses (essen-tial and nonessential), prioritizes public health, and aggressively flattens the epidemic curve.

No economic shutdown

The theory of not shutting down any businesses is to build herd immunity as quickly as pos-sible when a critical mass of infections thwarts transmission. With this option, a country does not attempt to flatten the epidemic curve. As chapter 2 explains, herd immunity exists after an infection threshold is achieved, occurring between 60 percent and 80 percent of a population, when the disease no longer spreads. The short-term economic benefit of this approach is the continuity of economic activity. No businesses are shuttered. The short-term epidemiological cost is the rise in confirmed cases.

But compared to targeted, comprehensive, and full shutdowns, other costs exist. First, during the acceleration interval of the epidemic curve, more exposures and deaths occur. Second, many of the infected establish short-term immunity. Third, a strategy for achieving herd immunity is not universal in process across countries, depending on the level of public health and average age of the population. Fourth, the strategy does not protect at-risk mem-bers of the population from obtaining the disease.

This approach therefore leads to several challenges. Herd immunity differs by region, depending on social interaction and population density. With rapid transmission, the thresh-old for herd immunity may be higher than the consensus of public health officials. With new diseases, immunity lasts different periods of time. It may not prevent multiple infection waves.

Targeted economic shutdown

A *targeted economic shutdown*, which includes spatial and market dimensions, protects public health with less economic cost than a comprehensive shutdown. The approach first visualizes individual cities as a group of neighborhoods. It then identifies the neighborhoods experiencing a higher risk of infection. With this information, a targeted and dynamic process of business closures occurs. Compared to a comprehensive shutdown, cost savings result from a strategic choice of targeted neighborhoods for business shutdowns, calibrating the impact on jobs with the risk of obtaining the infection. The idea is that cities should keep businesses open if the chance of spreading the disease among these businesses is low and the economic cost of closing the businesses is high.

This approach considers geography, market structure, epidemiological conditions, and an appropriate timeframe. Compared to a comprehensive or full shutdown, the keys to the process include the use of a data-driven method, fewer restrictions, identification of neighborhood hotspots, and businesses that conduct high-value economic activity. The resulting framework is a spatial epidemic spread model with neighborhoods that accounts for the "spillovers" of infections from other areas (Birge et al., 2020).

When a disease spreads through transmission networks, some neighborhoods are exposed more than others. As a result, each neighborhood is evaluated based on five disease components: susceptible, exposed, infected clinical, infected subclinical, recovered. Using these components, a planner determines which business entities in an exposed neighborhood should be shut down at lowest economic cost. In theory, the neighborhoods with higher infection rates may not experience the most business closures: the decision depends on the "structure of the spatial spread patterns between these neighborhoods and the others" (Birge et al., 2020). But a balance exists between the losses to society from rising infection rates—based on current epidemiological characteristics and transmission spillovers from other neighborhoods—and losses to society from high-value economic activities shutting down. For neighborhoods characterized with lower risks of infection, the planner minimizes the reduction in economic activity subject to the constraint that the remaining economic activity does not increase infections.

Comprehensive economic shutdown

A *comprehensive economic shutdown* distinguishes between essential and nonessential workers. *Essential workers*—those engaged with the safety of human life—continue to operate in their physical workspace. *Nonessential workers*—who do not have to be physically present in the workspace for a city to function—are sent home to engage in remote work. In general, essential work includes childcare, social workers, health care providers, emergency personnel, energy sector employees, mass transit workers, pharmacy employees, food production and agricultural workers, and many public sector employees. During a pandemic, society asks essential workers to carry a heavy workload and remain present in the workspace, while public health risks remain.

For essential workers, both safety and socioeconomic challenges exist. First, they must take precautions. But even if employers attempt to ensure their safety, essential workers experience a higher risk of exposure. During a pandemic, the nature of their work changes. Public guidelines for the safety of workers, such as social distancing, sanitizing, and wearing masks, should accompany essential work. Second, research has documented that essential workers tend to have lower incomes (Nunn et al., 2020). Because they face a greater risk during a pandemic, they should receive more compensation. Third, essential work is gendered. For example, in the United States, during the coronavirus pandemic, one in three jobs held by women were designated as essential, the majority of total essential workers were women, and more women than men remained in the labor force (Robertson and Gebeloff, 2020). Fourth, women's "essential" work is traditionally underpaid, especially in public health. In the United States, most healthcare workers infected with Covid-19 were women (Robertson and Gebeloff, 2020).

Full economic shutdown

A *full economic shutdown*, the most extensive intervention, prioritizes public health, shutters all business activity, and creates the highest economic costs. New infections result from the average number of contacts per person and infectivity of the disease. But aggressive forms of intervention decrease the average number of contacts per person. The idea of a full economic shutdown is that, if 100 percent of the population shelters-in-place, the disease will not spread. A full economic shutdown therefore flattens the epidemic curve in the fastest manner.

A spectrum of choices

While these four theories provide a useful method of categorization, a country's actual choice exists along the spectrum. A country's policy measures entail a multifaceted approach, including containment policies, economic measures, and health interventions. In general, some countries pursue aggressive measures to slow the spread of disease while others adopt a *laissez-faire* approach. Within countries, policy interventions may differ, with some states adopting a more aggressive approach than others. This variation creates an inevitable debate over the structure and speed of an appropriate response.

During the coronavirus pandemic, many national and state governments imposed severe restrictions. State governments in the United States, Russia, and Brazil, for example, implemented some of the strongest interventions, such as shuttering a wide range of businesses. Overall, these countries imposed stricter policies than South Korea, Taiwan, and Japan, even though the latter set of countries experienced shorter infection waves. The difference between the two sets was that the national governments of the United States, Russia, and Brazil did not implement a central response, leaving local governments to address the problem on their own.

Stringency index

To compare shutdown policies between countries, Oxford University developed the Oxford Covid-19 Government Response Tracker, a *stringency index*, which provides a cross-national and cross-temporal method to measure the evolution of government responses (Hale et al., 2020). The tracker tabulates government policies across 19 indicators (table 4.1). The stringency index uses the indicators—each assigned a number between 0 and 100 to represent the government's response—to calculate an overall score.

Table 4.1 Oxford Covid-19 Government Response Tracker: indicators

Containment and closure		E3	Fiscal measures
C1	School closing	E4	Giving international support
C2	Workplace closing	Health systems	
C3	Cancel public events	H1	Public information campaign
C4	Restrictions on gathering size	H2	Testing policy
C5	Close public transport	H3	Contract tracing
C6	Stay at home requirements	H4	Emergency investment in healthcare
C7	Restrictions on internal movement	H5	Investment in Covid-19 vaccines
C8	Restrictions on international travel	H6	Facial coverings
Economic response		Miscellaneous	
E1	Income support	M1	Other responses
E2	Debt/contract relief for households		

Source: Hale et al. (2020)

The stringency indices, however, are not used as a measure of the effectiveness of government policy. Researchers use them to assess whether the indicators, confirmed cases, and deaths are correlated across countries or states:

> They do not provide information on how well policies are enforced, nor do they capture demographic or cultural characteristics that may affect the spread of Covid-19. Furthermore, they are not comprehensive measures of policy. They only reflect the indicators measured by (the Oxford Tracker) and thus will miss important aspects of a government response … The value and purpose of the indices is instead to allow for efficient and simple cross-national comparisons of government interventions.
>
> (Hale et al., 2020)

The change in stringency scores

During the coronavirus pandemic, stringency index scores varied between countries such as the United Kingdom and United States (figure 4.4). In addition, the composite score changed over time according to a country's need to combat the disease through policy interventions. For many countries, including the U.S. and U.K., the change in the stringency index score highlighted how the countries implemented strong shutdown policies at the beginning of the coronavirus pandemic, in the spring of 2020, and then eased restrictions during the summer. In the case of the U.S., when confirmed cases and deaths rose again during the fall of 2020, the stringency index increased.

Stringency scores and epidemiological outcomes

Countries that limit the spread of disease impose strong shutdown measures early in the pandemic (with higher stringency scores) and then transition to a testing- and information-based focus to encourage defensive behavior among individuals. Less successful countries do not implement early shutdown interventions. Statistically, the earlier a country implements a comprehensive set of policy interventions, the larger is the decrease in the cumulative infection growth rate (World Bank, 2020). Even more, the increase in confirmed cases is larger when policy measures do not maintain strong disease containment efforts over time or fail

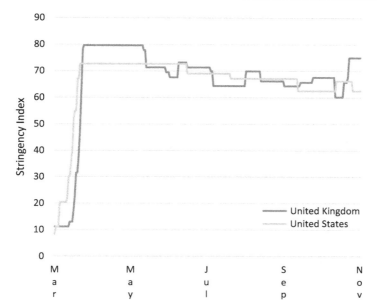

Figure 4.4 Stringency index for the United States and United Kingdom during 2020.

Source: author using data from the Oxford Covid-19 Government Response Tracker, accessed on Our World in Data, https://ourworldindata.org/grapher/covid-stringency-index

to induce social distancing and mask wearing. In the United States, after the initial infection wave during the coronavirus pandemic, outbreaks during the fall of 2020 were smaller in states that experienced larger stringency index scores. In fact, states that maintained control policies experienced a smaller number of confirmed cases in the fall and winter. By the end of 2020, the worst outbreaks in the United States were in states where "policymakers did the least to prevent transmission," according to the Oxford Stringency Index (Leatherby and Harris, 2020).

The health-economy tradeoff

The stringency index reveals a country's preference for the health-economy tradeoff. The shutdown approaches, as measured by the stringency index, demonstrate a preference along the health-economy production frontier, where the highest possible score represents a complete focus on health and the lowest possible score represents a complete focus on the economy (figure 4.5). In practice, countries choose to operate somewhere on the frontier, represented by their stringency score, choosing a bundle that balances health and the economy.

Health before wealth

Economists think "at the margin," meaning they consider the implication of a decision or policy moving the economy in one direction or another. This type of thinking narrows the process of analysis. For example, with economic shutdown policies, thinking at the margin

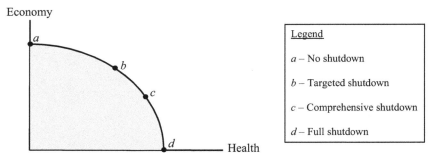

Figure 4.5 Shutdown approaches.

Source: author

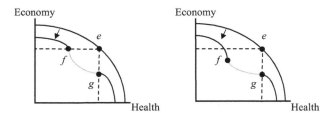

Figure 4.6 Hollowing out and drifting away.

Source: adapted from Gans (2020)

implies a tradeoff between the economy and public health: reducing infections by closing businesses leads to a decrease in economic activity. However, Professor Joshua Gans (2020), the Jeffrey Skoll Chair in Technical Innovation and Entrepreneurship at the Rotman School of Management, University of Toronto, in his book on *Economics in the Age of Covid-19*, emphasizes that, in a pandemic, thinking at the margin has caveats. Early in a pandemic, he argues, countries should not trade lives for economic livelihood. Instead, to fight the disease, countries should prioritize public health. Countries that intervene earlier and more aggressively experience faster economic recoveries. In other words, countries should use all of their policy tools—including containment and closure, economic policies, and health measures—to generate a high stringency index score.

Model framework

According to Professor Gans (2020), two reasons exist for prioritizing health before wealth. First, a pandemic hollows out the ability of a country to balance public health and the economy. Second, the options for prioritizing public health may drift away from their original position (figure 4.6).

The original and outer production possibility frontier demonstrates a tradeoff between health and the economy at the beginning of the pandemic. Point e represents the starting position. What happens when the pandemic hits? The pandemic means that the possibilities for both the production of health and economic output contract. The original bundles of health and the economy on the outer PPF are no longer feasible. Society must decide whether to absorb the impact of the pandemic more through a decline in economic activity, human health, or a combination of the two. On the left-hand side diagram, point *g* demonstrates the choice of maintaining health while experiencing the cost of the pandemic through a reduction in economic activity. Point *f* demonstrates the choice of maintaining economic activity while experiencing the cost of the pandemic through a reduction in human health.

Hollowing out

The new and inward production possibility frontier possesses a shallow curve between points *f* and *g*, which arises from the pandemic and represents the concept of *hollowing out*. In the left-hand side graph, consider two scenarios.

In the first scenario, if society begins at point *f* and desires more health during the pandemic and a movement to point *g*, it must sacrifice more economic activity to achieve it. In this context, hollowing out means the pandemic increases the opportunity cost of marginal improvements in public health. To obtain the same marginal increase in public health, economies must sacrifice more resources. That is, to marginally increase public health, society must disengage from even more economic activity. This argument points to the need for extensive nonpharmaceutical interventions, such as social distancing, mask wearing, and sheltering-in-place. A small level of nonpharmaceutical interventions among the population will not have much effect on the spread of disease.

In the second scenario, if society begins at point *g* and desires more economic activity and a movement to point *f*, it must sacrifice a larger amount of health to achieve it. Even if society maintains its level of health, society must employ a large amount of nonpharmaceutical interventions to achieve an increase in economic activity.

Magnitude of hollowing out

What determines the magnitude of the shallow curve between points *f* and *g*? The more virulent the disease, the larger is the inflection of the shallow curve. The implication is that, during a pandemic, the option of sacrificing a little economic activity for more public health is no longer an option. Society cannot maintain the same tradeoff. On the new PPF, additional improvements in public health create higher costs. To enhance healthcare outcomes, it would not be possible for a country to dial up a few economic resources. In other words, if a country chooses a middle ground with nonenforceable policy interventions and slightly less economic activity, suboptimal outcomes will occur. With this weak approach, the country will experience a large decline in both health and the economy. On the contrary, at the beginning of the pandemic, society should prioritize public health with a strong set of intervention policies. Otherwise, future economic costs are too high (Gans, 2020).

Shutdown interventions and health outcomes

Prioritizing public health requires collective sacrifice, but early in a pandemic, this is the optimal choice. Unless the public sector contains the disease, it may spiral out of control. In the presence of visible health risks, individuals abide by nonpharmaceutical interventions at higher levels. Stopping the spread of disease with strong and early interventions lowers the

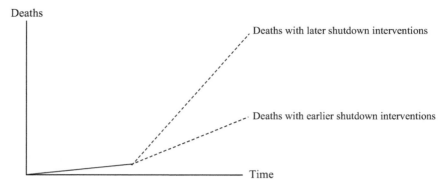

Figure 4.7 The earliest shutdown interventions save the most lives.

Source: author

trajectory of future deaths (figure 4.7). Therefore, the pursuit of a high level of public health in the short term is consistent with better economic performance.

Drifting away

Suppose society prioritizes economic activity. As the pandemic worsens, health costs rise, and the economy declines even further, demonstrated by point *f* in the right-hand side graph (figure 4.6). According to Professor Gans (2020), this is the concept of *drifting away*. Drifting away means the longer it takes society to address the health crisis, the fewer the number of available options. Taking a long time to recognize the problem and to investigate appropriate solutions decreases the number of pathways forward. If society wants to maintain public health, it must act quickly and comprehensively. After the pandemic worsens, the option of protecting the same level of public health will no longer be available. As Professor Gans (2020) explains, in the presence of inactivity, an option to "buy" more public health through a reduction in economic activity no longer exists.

Labor market and lost income

Shutdown interventions create economic costs. First, both business profits and labor income decrease. Second, business investment declines. Third, consumer spending falls by a multiple of the decrease in output. Finally, the economy's productive potential decreases (Barrero et al., 2020). Using a labor market model, this section demonstrates the impact of an economic shutdown on income. Labor supply represents *marginal resource cost (MRC)*, the additional cost to the firm of employing one more unit of labor. In a competitive resource market, the firm does not impact the price of the labor input (wage), regardless of how many laborers are employed. Labor demand represents *marginal revenue product (MRP)*, the additional revenue to the firm from the employment of one more laborer. If output sells in a competitive market, marginal revenue = price. Therefore, *MRP* equals the change in output from employing one more unit of input (marginal product or *MP*) multiplied by the price (*P*) of output: $MRP = (MP)(P)$. The intersection of MRC and MRP occurs at equilibrium, leading to equilibrium wage (W_e) and employment (L_e). If *MRP* > *MRC*, the firm should hire more workers, to the point where *MRP* = *MRC* (figure 4.8).

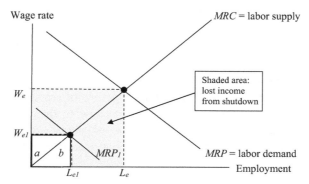

Figure 4.8 The labor market and lost income.

Source: author

In the shutdown interval, businesses close. As a result, labor demand decreases, shifting left to MRP_1. Employment declines from L_e to L_{e1}. Wages decline from W_e to W_{e1}. The determination of the value of lost income requires the identification of the difference between total income before and after shutdown. Before shutdown, total income equals the rectangle with base (L_e) and height (W_e): $(L_e)(W_e)$. After the decrease in labor demand, income equals area a + b. Lost income from the economic shutdown therefore equals the shaded area.

Economic systems and income assistance

When countries shut down segments of their economies, they must provide financial assistance to workers, equal to the value of lost income. Financial assistance is critical to align public health with economic expectations. This section discusses two models: the "European model of income assistance" and the "U.S. model of income assistance." These models include government intervention in the form of income support but differ with respect to the employment status of workers. In the European model, workers remain tied to their places of employment. In the U.S. model, workers are not tied to their places of employment.

Economic systems

The models highlight the role of *economic systems*. Policies of financial assistance do not exist in isolation. They exist as part of a country's economic system, which includes the set of arrangements through which society make choices about the allocation of scarce resources and apportionment of output. In a modern framework that moves beyond the traditional capitalist-socialist tradeoff with respect to the ownership of the means of production, countries debate how to balance economic growth, working conditions, living standards, and the role of government. Countries may be categorized by their willingness to integrate into the global economy, provide social assistance, and implement public policy. For many countries, high levels of integration into the global economy, a change in the traditional nature of households, and evolving labor market conditions create the need for new social policies. Attitudes toward political economy shape how countries decide to address these challenges. Pre-existing risks, including inequality of healthcare outcomes; care for children, the elderly, and infirm; equality of labor market opportunities; and assistance to households during economic downturns become more pronounced during a pandemic. The composition of an economic system determines how a society reacts to shutdown conditions, the labor market, and income support.

The point is that a society's view of the role of government informs the models of income assistance. On the one hand, a statist view of big government promotes the belief that the public sector has an important role in directing the economy, corresponding to the European model of income assistance. On the other hand, a free market view of government intervention reflects a *laissez-faire* attitude toward public support, corresponding to the U.S. model of income assistance.

European model of income assistance

In the European model, workers remain tied to their places of employment. The objective of the model is to maintain the economy's level of employment. During economic shutdown, businesses continue to pay workers, aided by government reimbursement. The public sector reimburses businesses between 60 to 90 percent of labor income (Hirsh and Johnson, 2020). The approach is intended to soften the economic blow. Workers continue to pay their bills with certainty. Businesses do not have to hire and train a new set of employees. This approach signals to workers that their economic livelihoods will remain and to businesses that they will retain their workers.

The strength of the model is demonstrated on both the supply and demand sides of the labor market. During shutdown, employees continue to earn a high percentage of their incomes from government with businesses covering the rest. They do not lose their jobs. When the shutdown interval ends, companies move forward with the same employees. The risk is that, in the presence of a longer shutdown interval, governments are saddled with escalating responsibilities for financial support. In addition, when the pandemic ends, production diverges, so locking the workforce in place both reduces the level of flexibility necessary to adapt and slows the pace of adjustment. For example, during a pandemic, industries such as travel and related services face extended reductions in demand and do not expediently return to pre-pandemic levels of economic activity. For these industries, a government subsidy program is not cost effective, but it does spare the economy from a sudden shock of unemployment. Moreover, households adapt to pandemic conditions and alter their consumption patterns, such as online purchasing and food delivery. The problems of the European model include keeping some companies afloat that have few economic prospects, while under-allocating resources to companies that thrive.

U.S. model of income assistance

The U.S. model is comparable to its European counterpart in terms of providing financial assistance; however, it differs in two ways. First, it offers an alternative relief program. Second, it does not avoid layoffs. This approach creates a support system of unemployment benefits, including one-time payments to the unemployed based on income status, a small business loan initiative—which forgives loans if they are dedicated to payroll, utilities, rent, or mortgage interest—and a program of weekly compensation to the unemployed.

The strength of the model is the ability to adjust to exogenous shocks. The pandemic alters economic activity, sending a wave of disease through human transmission networks. After the pandemic ends, the economy operates on a different trajectory. In sectors such as telemedicine, video streaming, and grocery delivery, economic expansion occurs with rising consumer spending. Other sectors such as airlines, hotels, and movie theaters experience economic contraction. In this context, the pandemic is a "reallocation" shock (Barrero et al., 2020). A certain number of new hires exist for every layoff. In the labor market, from a demand-side perspective, layoffs create future flexibility. In the post-pandemic phase, firms decide how to best move forward, with either their pre-pandemic employees or new employees.

The benefit of the U.S. model is keeping companies afloat that may grow. But a problem exists. On the supply side of the labor market, unemployed workers experience income insecurity, depending on their status as temporary or permanent unemployed. For the temporarily unemployed, income assistance minimizes uncertainty. For the permanently unemployed, it provides short-term benefits but does not address future prospects. Permanent layoffs exist for three reasons. Jobs are lost due to shifts in consumer spending. Jobs at the margin before the pandemic are eliminated and do not return. Jobs are lost due to the intra-industry reallocation of resources (Barrero et al., 2020). On the demand side of the labor market, the ratio of average benefits to average pre-pandemic earnings demonstrates heterogeneity in outcomes. Some unemployed workers receive benefits that exceed pre-pandemic earnings, but the benefits flowing to others fall short. Thus, the U.S. model does not provide a systematic approach to all workers. Some benefit more than others. The results vary across income status, economic sector, and geography (Ganong et al., 2020).

Summary

To slow the spread of disease, reduce infections, and decrease the number of deaths, shutdown interventions limit human contact and flatten the epidemic curve. Nonpharmaceutical interventions sever transmission networks before the creation and distribution of a vaccine. In this context, physical distancing serves as the primary mechanism to slow the number of confirmed cases. If a country prioritizes public health, shuts down segments of the economy, and fights the spread of disease, the country must eventually ease restrictions on economic activity. At this point, further improvements in the economy may come at the expense of public health. Early in a pandemic, countries may choose to shutter all, some, or no parts of the economy. In practice, policies of economic shutdown relate to the epidemic curve. A full economic shutdown flattens the curve in the most substantial manner. But the prioritization of public health may take different forms, including targeted and comprehensive shutdowns. Countries should not trade lives for economic livelihood. Instead, to fight the disease, countries should prioritize public health. Countries that intervene earlier and more aggressively experience faster economic recoveries. From an economics perspective, when people are asked to leave the workplace, they may or may not remain tied to their places of employment. When confirmed cases rise, the public sector should support workers during the shutdown interval. Policies of financial assistance do not exist in isolation. They exist as part of a country's economic system, which includes the set of arrangements through which society make choices about the allocation of scarce resources and apportionment of output.

Chapter takeaways

LO1   The shutdown interval leads to a decrease in economic activity.
LO2   Flattening the epidemic curve reduces infections and maintains hospital capacity.
LO3   Nonpharmaceutical interventions limit human contact.
LO4   With respect to resource allocation, a tradeoff exists between health and the economy.
LO5   Theories of economic shutdown demonstrate different levels of intervention.
LO6   Early in a pandemic, countries should prioritize health before wealth.
LO7   When workers shelter-in-place, they lose income.
LO8   Models of economic assistance demonstrate different methods of financial support.

Terms and concepts

Comprehensive economic shutdown
Drifting away
Economic systems
Essential workers
Flattening the epidemic curve
Full economic shutdown
Hollowing out
Incubation period
Infection period
Laissez-faire
Marginal resource cost
Marginal revenue product
No economic shutdown
Nonessential workers
Nonpharmaceutical interventions
Quarantine
Sheltering-in-place
Shutdown
Social distancing
Stringency index
Targeted economic shutdown

Questions

1. Describe the shutdown interval. For different countries, how does the shutdown interval differ?
2. What are the costs and benefits of flattening the epidemic curve?
3. What do economic shutdown interventions accomplish? What are the costs and benefits? What is the optimal mix of shutdown interventions?
4. At the beginning of a pandemic, should countries prioritize health before wealth?
5. Using the graphical depiction of the economy-health tradeoff, what factors impact the concepts of hollowing out and drifting away?

6. Explain the stringency index. What does it measure? How do stringency scores correlate with the change in confirmed cases?
7. Contrast the theories of economic shutdown. Which is the most effective in balancing the need to maximize public health and minimize economic losses?
8. During the coronavirus pandemic, which countries experienced high stringency index scores? Were these countries successful in minimizing the spread of disease?
9. How does a country's view about the free market relate to its program of income assistance?
10. Contrast the European and U.S. models of income assistance. What are the costs and benefits of each model?

References

Aum, Sangmin, Lee, Sang, and Shin, Yongseok. 2020. "Inequality of fear and self-quarantine: is there a trade-off between GDP and public health?" NBER Working Paper 27100 (May): National Bureau of Economic Research.

Barrero, Jose, Bloom, Nick, and Davis, Steven J. 2020. "Covid-19 is also a reallocation shock," Becker Friedman Institute Working Paper 2020-59 (May), University of Chicago.

Birge, John R., Candogan, Ozan, and Feng, Yiding. 2020. "Controlling epidemic spread: reducing economic losses with targeted closures," Becker Friedman Institute Working Paper 2020-57 (May), University of Chicago.

Dave, Dhavel M., Friedson, Andrew I., Matsuzawa, Kyutaro, and Sabia, Joseph J. 2020. "When do shelter-in-place orders fight Covid-19 best? Policy heterogeneity across states and adoption time," *Economic Inquiry*. doi:10/1111/ecin.12944.

Fergusson, Maggie. 2018. "How does it really feel to be lonely?" *1843* Magazine, February/March. 1843magazine.com/features/how-does-it-really-feel-to-be-lonely.

Flaxman, Seth, Mishra, Swapnil, Gandy, Axel, Unwin, H., Mellan, Thomas, Coupland, Helen, … Bhatt, Samir. 2020. "Estimating the effects of non-pharmaceutical interventions on Covid-19 in Europe," *Nature*, June 8. https://doi.org/10.1038/s41586-020-2405-7.

Ganong, Peter, Noel, Pascal, and Vavra, Joseph. 2020. "US unemployment insurance replacement rates during the pandemic," *Journal of Public Economics*, 191 (November): 104273.

Gans, Joshua. 2020. *Economics in the Age of Covid-19*. Cambridge, Massachusetts: MIT Press.

Hale, Thomas, Angrist, Noam, Cameron-Blake, Emily, Hallas, Laura, Kira, Beatriz, Majumdar, Saptarshi, … Webster, Samuel. 2020. "Variation in government responses to Covid-19," BSG Working Paper 2020/32, Version 9.0, Blavatnik School of Government, University of Oxford.

Harris, Jeffrey E. 2020. "The coronavirus epidemic curve is already flattening in New York City," NBER Working Paper 26917 (April), National Bureau of Economic Research.

Hirsh, Michael, and Johnson, Keith. 2020. "A tale of two rescue plans," *Foreign Policy*, April 24.

Hsiang, Soloman, Allen, Daniel, Annan-Phan, Sebastien, Bell, Kendon, Bolliger, Ian, Chong, Trinetta, … and Wu, Tiffany. 2020. "The effect of large-scale anti-contagion policies on the Covid-19 pandemic," *Nature*, June 8. https://doi.org/10.1038/s41586-020-2404-8.

Jay, Jonathan, Bor, Jacob, Nsoesie, Elaine, Lipson, Sarah, Jones, David, Galea, Sandro, and Raifman, Julia. 2020. "Neighbourhood income and physical distancing during the Covid-19 panic in the U.S.," *Nature Human Behaviour*. https://doi.org/10.1038/s41562-020-00998-2.

Leatherby, Lauren, and Harris, Rich. 2020. "States that imposed few restrictions now have the worst outbreaks," *The New York Times*, November 18.

Mongey, Simon, Pilossoph, Laura, and Weinberg, Alex. 2020. "Which workers bear the burden of social distancing policies?" NBER Working Paper 27085 (May), National Bureau of Economic Research.

Mubayi, Anuj, Zaleta, Christopher, Martcheva, Maia, and Castillo-Chavez, Carlos. 2010. "A cost-based comparison of quarantine strategies for new emerging diseases," *Mathematical Biosciences and Engineering*, 7, 3 (July): 687-717.

Nunn, Ryan, O'Donnell, Jimmy, and Shambaugh, Jay. 2020. "Examining options to boost essential worker wages during the pandemic," *Brookings*, June 4.

Roberts, Siobhan. 2020. "The Swiss cheese model of pandemic defense," *The New York Times*, December 5.

Robertson, Campbell, and Gebeloff, Robert. 2020. "How millions of women became the most essential workers in America," *The New York Times*, April 18.

Schaul, Kevin, Mayes, Brittany, and Berkowitz, Bonnie. 2020. "Where Americans are still staying at home the most," *The Washington Post*, May 6.

Thunstrom, Linda, Newbold, Steven C., Finnoff, David, Ashworth, Madison, and Shogren, Jason F. 2020. "The benefits and costs of using social distancing to flatten the curve for Covid-19," *Journal of Benefit-Cost Analysis*: 1–17. doi:10.1017/bca.2020.12.

World Bank. 2020. *From Containment to Recovery: Economic Update for East Asia and the Pacific*. Washington D.C.: World Bank Group.

5 Recession, forecasting, and economic policy

Learning objectives

After reading this chapter, you will be able to:

LO1 Describe the recession interval of the pandemic phase.
LO2 Use the circular-flow model to explain the relationship between output and income.
LO3 Discuss business cycles, focusing on the contractionary stage.
LO4 Establish an aggregate supply-aggregate demand model to explain the recession.
LO5 Incorporate a Keynesian framework for the analysis of market outcomes.
LO6 Explain that a pandemic recession is unique because of the precipitating event.
LO7 Analyze both fiscal and monetary policies as methods to stimulate aggregate demand.
LO8 Discuss the challenge of macroeconomic forecasting during a pandemic.

Chapter outline

- Recession interval
- Circular flow of economic activity
- Business cycles
- The *AS-AD* model and economic fluctuations
- A Keynesian perspective
- Characteristics of recession
- Economic stimulus policy
- The challenge of macroeconomic forecasting during a pandemic
- Summary

Recession interval

This chapter analyzes the second economic interval of the pandemic phase: *recession* (figure 5.1).

Figure 5.1 Three economic intervals of the pandemic phase.

Source: author

When a disease spreads through a population, economic shutdown interventions–the first interval–close businesses. As chapter 4 explains, the goal is to flatten the epidemic curve. But after shutdown occurs, a deliberate recession begins with declining output and employment. During a recession, household income declines. The consumption of services decreases. The circular flow of economic activity slows. Depending on the spread of disease, economic stimulus policies, and economic resilience, the recession continues.

To discuss the recessionary interval, this chapter uses the tools of *macroeconomics*, the study of economy-wide phenomena, including production and employment. First, the *circular-flow model* shows that households and firms interact in both the product and resource markets, demonstrating the flows of output and income. Second, the business cycle model, which shows fluctuations in economic activity, demonstrates that recessionary intervals vary according to macroeconomic conditions. Third, the *aggregate supply-aggregate demand (AS-AD) model* shows that, during a pandemic, *AS* and *AD* both decrease, leading to lower levels of output and employment. In this framework, fiscal and monetary policies stimulate economic activity. Finally, with respect to macroeconomic forecasting, the interaction of epidemiological and economic conditions complicates the process of identifying potential future outcomes. The chapter's thesis is that, while economic shutdown interventions inevitably lead to recession, the severity of the recession depends on the extent to which society first stabilizes public health and then addresses the economic shortfalls of production and employment through fiscal and monetary policies.

Circular flow of economic activity

The economy consists of individuals engaged in economic activities, including working, manufacturing, producing, buying, and selling. The economy provides a mechanism in which consumption spending leads to business revenue and eventually household income. By including two types of decision makers–households and businesses–and two types of markets–product and resource–the circular-flow model demonstrates economic activity (figure 5.2).

The circular-flow model demonstrates connection between the demand and supply sides of the market. But it also shows how a pandemic severs the connections between economic agents and markets. On the supply side, businesses produce output (goods and services) using resource inputs (factors of production), including land, labor, and capital (buildings, machinery, and equipment). On the demand side, households serve as the owners of the factors of production and consume the output of businesses. With respect to economic transactions, businesses and households interact in product and resource markets. In *product markets*, businesses sell and households buy goods and services. In *resource markets*, households supply factors of production and businesses employ them. In these latter markets, households provide the resource inputs that businesses use to produce output.

In the circular-flow model, two loops, distinct but related, demonstrate the interconnection between output and income. With the outer loop, which represents the flow of output,

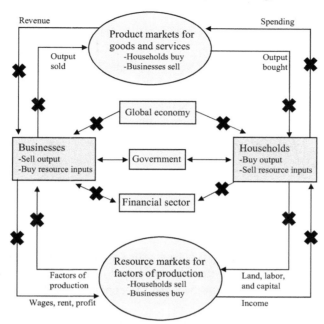

Figure 5.2 Circular flow of economic activity.

Source: author

households—as the owners of the factors of production—sell the use of their land, labor, and capital to businesses. Businesses, in turn, use these resource inputs to make output in the form of goods and services. To complete the flow, households then purchase the output. With the inner loop, which represents the flow of dollars, households spend their income to purchase goods and services. The businesses use some of the revenue they earn through sales to pay for labor inputs, in the form of wages, while the rest of the revenue is allocated as rent or profit.

The loops in the circular-flow model provide a framework to address the sequence of events that begin with economic shutdown and continue with recession. The shutdown interval first sends workers home to shelter-in-place, which reduces the factors of production flowing from households to businesses. This intervention decreases the production of output by businesses. At the same time, when the production of output declines and sales decrease, the level of revenue flowing to businesses decreases. This effect leads to a decrease in both household income and spending. At the same time, connections between the global economy, financial sector, businesses, and households are severed. The overall result is a decline in economic activity.

Business cycles

Macroeconomic trends demonstrate changes in economic activity. Short-run fluctuations in these variables play an important role in *business cycles*—the unpredictable and irregular fluctuations in economic activity (figure 5.3).

Economists characterize business cycles in four stages of varying length: *expansion* (increasing real GDP), peak, recession (decreasing real GDP), and trough. In the

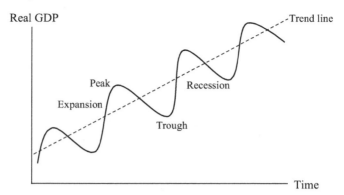

Figure 5.3 Business cycle.

Source: author

expansionary phase, the production of output rises until it reaches the peak. In the reces-sionary phase, the production of output declines until it reaches the trough. An upward-sloping trend line demonstrates that, because of economic growth, each peak is higher than the previous peak.

The business cycle shows the production of output as measured by real GDP increases over time, but contracts in some periods. During contractionary periods, businesses can-not sell all the goods and services that they have to offer, so they lay off employees and unemployment rises. As the circular-flow model makes clear, when the production of output declines, household income decreases. A relatively mild downturn is a recession, but a more severe downturn is a depression.

As Professor N. Gregory Mankiw (2018) of Harvard University explains, business cycles have three important properties. First, fluctuations in economic activity are irregular and almost impossible to forecast. Second, many macroeconomic variables, including income, spending, and production, fluctuate in tandem. Third, output and unemployment move in opposite directions. That is, a decrease in a nation's production of goods and services is cor-related with its use of the labor force. When real GDP declines, fewer people are employed. But when a recession ends and expansion begins, the unemployment rate decreases.

With respect to pandemic economics, the business cycle demonstrates that economic shutdown policies (chapter 4) lead to the end of the expansionary stage, leading the econ-omy into recession (chapter 5). Among macroeconomists, some debate exists concerning how to best analyze economic downturns, but most macroeconomists use an aggregate sup-ply-aggregate demand model, the subject of the next section.

The *AS-AD* model and economic fluctuations

The *AS-AD* model includes the behavior of two variables. The first variable, the economy's output, is characterized by *real GDP*, an inflation-adjusted measure of the value of goods and services produced in an economy annually, often called "constant-price GDP." The second variable, the average price level, is measured by a consumer price index or GDP deflator, a nominal variable.

Aggregate demand

The *aggregate demand curve* demonstrates the quantity of output demanded in the economy at any given price level. In both the short run and long run, the *AD* curve slopes downward: as the price level increases, quantity demanded for goods and services decreases. An economy's GDP, noted with the variable *Y*, is the sum of consumption (*C*), investment (*I*), government spending (*G*), and net exports (*NX*), which equals exports minus imports:

$$Y = C + I + G + NX \tag{5.1}$$

Each component contributes to *AD*. If government spending is fixed, *C*, *I*, and *NX* depend on economic conditions and the price level. A decrease in the price level increases the quantity of output demanded, because consumers are wealthier and spend more, investment increases because of falling interest rates, and an increase in net exports is stimulated by currency depreciation. Aggregate demand is therefore a function of *C*, *I*, *G*, and *NX*. When one or more of these components increase, *AD* increases and shifts right. When one or more of these components decrease, *AD* decreases and shifts left. When *G* increases through stimulus policy, *AD* shifts right.

Long-run aggregate supply and the natural level of output

Unlike the *AD* curve, which always slopes downward, the *AS* curve depends on the time horizon. In the long run, long-run aggregate supply (*LRAS*) is vertical. The intersection of *LRAS* and *AD* (point *a* in figure 5.4) leads to the equilibrium price level (P_e) and output (Q_e).

The *LRAS* curve is vertical because the price level does not impact the long-run determinants of real GDP. An economy's production of output depends on the supply of labor, capital, natural resources, and availability of technology. But the price level does not impact an economy's ability to produce output. If two economies are identical with respect to factors of production and output, but economy one has twice as much money in circulation, economy one would also have a price level that is twice as high. Otherwise, the economies are the same. In other words, in the long run, the factors of production and technology determine

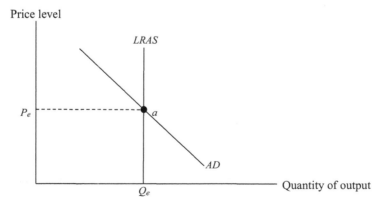

Figure 5.4 *LRAS, AD,* and equilibrium.
Source: author

the quantity of aggregate supply. In this context, the vertical *LRAS* exemplifies the theory of monetary neutrality. Most economists argue this principle applies to the economy over a timeframe of many years, but not month-by-month changes in economic activity (Mankiw, 2018).

Shifts in LRAS

An economy's long-run equilibrium level of output equals its potential or *natural level of output* (Q_e) in figure 5.4. In the long run, the economy gravitates to the natural level. Because output in this classical model is a function of labor, capital, natural resources, and technology, changes in these variables cause *LRAS* to shift, adjusting the natural level of output. That is, in the long run, the natural level of output may increase or decrease. A permanent increase in labor force participation shifts *LRAS* to the right, increasing the natural level of output. A permanent increase in an economy's capital stock raises both labor productivity and the quantity of output supplied, shifting *LRAS* to the right, increasing the natural level of output. With natural resources, a decrease in the availability of fossil fuels or an exacerbation of the climate crisis that reduces the supply of agricultural crops shifts *LRAS* to the left, decreasing the natural level of output. Finally, technological advances in areas such as cloud computing lead to a greater production of goods and services, shifting *LRAS* to the right and increasing the natural level of output.

Short-run aggregate supply

In the model, the difference between the short run and the long run is the shape of aggregate supply. The *short-run aggregate supply curve* (*SRAS*) demonstrates the quantity of output that businesses produce and sell at each price level. In the long run, the price level does not impact the production of output, but in the short run it does. As a result, in the short run, the *SRAS* curve slopes upward: as the price level increases, quantity supplied increases (figure 5.5).

The short-run *AS-AD* model departs from the classical assumption that real and nominal variables are separate, acknowledging that, with short-run economic fluctuations, real and

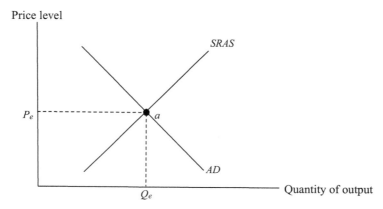

Figure 5.5 Short-run *AS-AD* model.

Source: author

nominal variables interact. When compared to the long run, market imperfections in the short run cause the supply side to behave differently: when the actual price level deviates from the expected price level, the quantity supplied of output differs from its natural level (Mankiw, 2018).

Shifts in SRAS

The SRAS curve demonstrates the quantity of output supplied for any given price level. Like LRAS, the SRAS curve is a function of labor, capital, natural resources, and technology. Changes in these variables shift SRAS. For example, when economic shutdown occurs during a pandemic, SRAS shifts to the left. But, in the short run, the expected price level also impacts the position of SRAS. The reason is that the quantity of output supplied in the short run is also a function of sticky prices, sticky wages, and economic perceptions. It is these latter variables that depend on the expected price level. So, when expectations of the price level change, SRAS shifts. That is, if the expected price level differs from the actual level, expectations adjust, and SRAS increases or decreases. As an example, a decrease in the expected price level leads to the establishment of new business contracts with lower wages and operating costs, which shifts SRAS right.

Causes of economic downturn: the case of a pandemic

Suppose the economy is operating in a position of long-run equilibrium (point a in figure 5.6). When the pandemic strikes, two effects occur. First, on the supply side, after the spread of infections, economic shutdown policies decrease the production of output by forcing workers to shelter-in-place. By reducing labor force participation, the pandemic decreases the economy's productive capacity, shifting aggregate supply left from SRAS to $SRAS_1$.

Second, on the demand side, when businesses send workers home, household income decreases, leading to a reduction in consumption and a decrease in aggregate demand from AD to AD_1. But the extent to which consumption declines and AD shifts to the left depends on the *marginal propensity to consume (MPC)*, the change in consumption divided by the change in disposable income. For example, if disposable income declines by $100 billion and

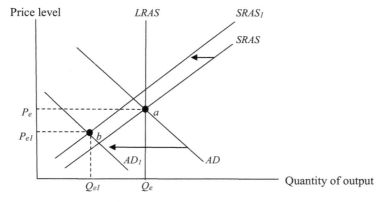

Figure 5.6 A reduction of SRAS and AD reduces output.

Source: author

the *MPC* = 0.9, consumer spending will decrease by $90 billion, and *AD* will shift to the left by this amount.

In sum, the two-step process means an initial supply shock leads to a demand-side disruption. In the pandemic, the combined shifts in *SRAS* and *AD* cause a decline in equilibrium output from Q_e to Q_{e1} and a decrease in the price level from P_e to P_{e1}.

A Keynesian perspective

During the 1920s, after World War I, companies experienced a prosperous decade. But in many countries, the rate of population growth was decreasing. Before the growth of global trade networks, it was difficult to envision a process of globalization establishing markets in far-off countries. Toward the end of the decade, as income and saving increased, aggregate supply outpaced aggregate demand; however, no new inventions such as the steam engine, automobile, electricity, or railroad came into the marketplace to stimulate capital investments.

The analysis of John Maynard Keynes (1936), the influential British economist, spread throughout the field of economics during a time of growing concern about secular stagnation and economic contraction. During the Great Depression, Keynes' ideas ushered in a new paradigm in the field of economics, "Keynesianism," replacing the classical belief that free-market economies, if left to themselves, would naturally gravitate to a full employment level of output.

The Keynesian framework addressed the pressing problem of the day: economic contraction during the 1930s. Although policy solutions for economic contraction were presented both inside and outside the economics profession before Keynes published his 1936 magnum opus, *The General Theory of Employment, Interest, and Money*, Keynes' recommendations for government intervention during a time of contraction came to be known as "Keynesian policies," because Keynes developed the analytical framework.

Along the way, Keynes, as an innovator, touched off the Keynesian revolution in the field of economics, leading to generations of articulators applying his framework, which includes five major tenets. First, a macroeconomic focus includes total or aggregate levels of production, consumption, income, savings, and employment. Second, the framework emphasizes aggregate expenditures as the determinant of national output, employment, and income. Third, economic instability leads to recurring booms and busts, now called business cycles. Fourth, market rigidity creates downward inflexibility with respect to wages and prices, especially during times of crisis, leading to layoffs and lower levels of production. Finally, during a period of contraction, the public sector should adopt an active approach of intervention to promote full employment and economic growth. During the Great Depression, businesses lacked incentive to expand production, so they reduced investment. The resulting *demand shock* led to a downward economic spiral. The implication is that, to combat an economic downturn, government should intervene, to increase business investment and employment.

Keynesian supply shock

When shutdown policies shutter businesses, a *supply shock* ripples through the economy, eventually triggering changes in aggregate demand that may exceed the size of the supply shock itself. That is, in figure 5.6, the magnitude of the leftward shift in *AD* exceeds the magnitude of the leftward shift in *SRAS*. Two explanations exist. The first explanation comes from the University of Chicago economist Veronica Guerriero and her co-authors (2020), who describe this outcome as a *Keynesian supply shock*: the economic impact of the pandemic is an inversion of the demand-driven crisis of the Great Depression of the 1930s as described by Keynes (1936).

Economies with multiple sectors provide an environment for a substantial decrease in *AD*. Supply shocks that occur during a pandemic, including shutdowns, layoffs, and business closings, impact demand-side variables. That is, aggregate demand is *endogenous*–experiencing an internal cause in the economy–and shifts to the left after employment declines. The intuition of the Keynesian supply shock is that it reduces employment, income, and aggregate demand. But when supply shocks exist in multiple sectors, the potential exists for a contraction in total spending.

The presence of multiple sectors creates two effects. The first effect refers to sectors in which the pandemic leads to business closings and layoffs. With this effect, an economic shutdown increases the *shadow price*–monetary value of currently unknowable or difficult-to-calculate costs–of goods and services in these sectors, discouraging consumption. The second effect refers to sectors in which the pandemic does not lead to business closings and layoffs. With the second effect, shortages in these sectors lead to a partial substitution, in which consumers shift spending into those sectors impacted directly by the supply shock (Guerriero et al., 2020).

Whether or not full employment remains in the sectors that are not subject to business closings and layoffs depends on the relative magnitude of the first and second effects. A contraction in employment may eventually occur in sectors not initially impacted by the pandemic shutdown when (a) consumers in affected sectors decrease their consumption significantly, are credit constrained, and have high MPCs, and (b) workers in the unaffected sectors do not increase their consumption of the remaining goods and services sufficiently. If the goods and services produced in the sectors are not close substitutes, *AD* contracts more than *SRAS* and employment in the sectors initially unaffected by the pandemic declines (Guerriero et al., 2020).

Fear and economic shutdown

The second explanation of why the magnitude of the decrease in *AD* might exceed the magnitude of the decrease in *SRAS* comes from the University of Chicago economists Austin Goolsbee and Chad Syverson (2020), who estimate the relative impact on aggregate output from people voluntarily staying home to avoid infection (demand-side effect) and government-imposed restrictions on economic activity (supply-side effect). By analyzing cellular phone data on customer visits to businesses, consumer behavior reveals how much a decrease in economic activity stems from government stay-at-home mandates or personal choice. In a pandemic, customers reduce their purchasing behavior for several reasons, including the avoidance of disease while it spreads through the community, avoidance of potential human contact in businesses with relatively more customer traffic, and government mandates.

Countries that repeal their shutdown interventions earlier do not experience a large increase in economic activity; however, the repeals shift spending from nonessential to essential businesses. At the same time, individuals engage in social distancing of their own accord, with or without shutdown interventions. Fear rather than economic directives dictate a portion of the economic decision-making process. Furthermore, within industries, a decline in economic activity is disproportionately larger in businesses with more foot traffic. The impact of the pandemic on economic activity may result more from individuals exhibiting the desire to avoid others than the implementation of policy interventions (Goolsbee and Syverson, 2020).

Characteristics of recession

A pandemic recession differs from other recessions because of the precipitating event. When the pandemic hits, the public sector intentionally shuts down segments of the economy, reducing production. The result is characterized as a "deliberate recession."

Types of recessions

- *Real recession*—Over-production in the private sector leads to layoffs, rising unemployment, lower levels of household income, and economic contraction.
- *Financial recession*—Financial imbalances build slowly but then unwind, disrupting financial markets and the real economy.
- *Policy recession*—Central banks leave interest rates high, tightening credit intermediation and financial conditions, and choking off economic activity.
- *Deliberate recession*—A deliberate economic shutdown decreases aggregate supply, sending workers home, thus reducing production and employment.

Severity of recessions

How severe is a recession? The answer depends on two factors: the extent to which output declines below the natural level and how long this position lasts. Using figure 5.6, four steps characterize the severity of a deliberate recession. First, the pandemic reduces SRAS. Second, the decline in SRAS leads to a decrease in AD. Third, the new equilibrium (Q_{e1}) is less than the natural level of output (Q_e). Fourth, while a new short-term equilibrium exists (Q_{e1}), whether LRAS shifts depends on the potential for permanent outcomes.

Recall that LRAS, like SRAS, is a function of the levels of labor, capital, natural resources, and technology. Because fewer workers participate in the economy during a pandemic, SRAS shifts left. But whether LRAS also shifts left depends on the extent to which the decrease in the number of workers leads to a permanent decline in the labor force. Two possibilities exist. First, the pandemic may impact the economy for a few months and not fundamentally alter its structure, leading workers to fully reintegrate into previous employment or new jobs after the pandemic ends. The first possibility leaves both the size of the labor force and the position of LRAS unchanged in the post-pandemic phase. (This is the scenario depicted in figure 5.6.) Second, the pandemic may last a longer period of time and fundamentally alter the structure of the economy, leaving some people unable to integrate back into the workforce in the post-pandemic phase. The second possibility decreases the size of the labor force and shifts *LRAS* to the left. Whether an economy experiences the first or second possibility is an empirical question and subject to investigation.

Impact on employment

Because employment is a function of production, a decrease in production reduces the level of employment during a pandemic. When output falls, unemployment rises. But recall from chapter 4 that two models of income assistance, the European and U.S. models, create different employment outcomes. During the coronavirus pandemic, when shutdown interventions closed businesses and sent workers home, the United States expanded its program of unemployment insurance, providing short-term income assistance to tens of millions of people who lost their jobs. The assumption was that the unemployed workers would be re-hired once the pandemic ended. In contrast, many European countries, including Austria, the United Kingdom, Denmark, France, Ireland, and Spain, prevented joblessness by nationalizing payrolls and subsidizing wages. While the U.S. model provided short-term assistance for labor, economies that adopted the European model were better poised to recover from the economic contraction. The difference between these approaches mattered with respect to changes in employment. Unemployment data during the year 2020 revealed that the U.S. unemployment rate soared by 10 percent during the pandemic, while the European Union experienced a much smaller increase in the unemployment rate (Issues in Pandemic Economics 5.1).

Issues in pandemic economics 5.1: Covid-19 unemployment in the U.S. and E.U.

During the coronavirus pandemic, recessions decreased economic activity in the United States and European Union (figure 5.7). The official unemployment rate is the total number of unemployed as a percentage of the civilian labor force. In the United States, starting in April 2020, the pandemic led to a large increase in unemployment and began a severe recession. In the European Union, the pandemic increased unemployment marginally. One reason is the E.U. contained the disease more effectively. A second reason is the European model of income assistance kept workers tied to their jobs. For the two regions, a comparative analysis of recessionary outcomes demonstrates the differences between shutdown and employment approaches. In the United States, shutdown interventions began at the end of March 2020, closing nonessential business activity. In April 2020, the unemployment rate rose. In the European Union, unemployment remained steady until June 2020.

Adjustment to the natural level of output

Macroeconomic theory posits that the short-run level of output will eventually adjust back to the natural level. But if the process lingers, the economy experiences a longer recession. As an example, because the magnitude of the decrease in *AD* may exceed the magnitude of the decrease in *SRAS*, a new equilibrium is established. Figure 5.8 begins at this pandemic

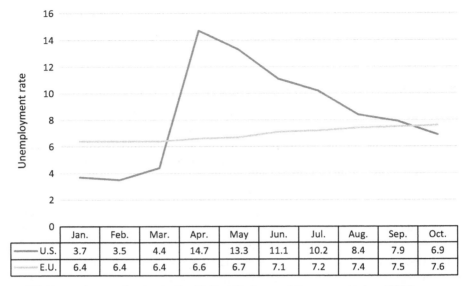

	Jan.	Feb.	Mar.	Apr.	May	Jun.	Jul.	Aug.	Sep.	Oct.
U.S.	3.7	3.5	4.4	14.7	13.3	11.1	10.2	8.4	7.9	6.9
E.U.	6.4	6.4	6.4	6.6	6.7	7.1	7.2	7.4	7.5	7.6

Figure 5.7 Unemployment rates in the United States and European Union, 2020.
Source: author using data from the Bureau of Labor Statistics (U.S.) and Eurostat (E.U.)

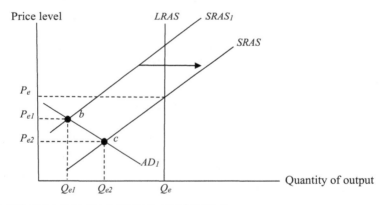

Figure 5.8 Adjustment to the natural level of output.
Source: author

equilibrium, with a price level P_{e1} and quantity Q_{e1} (point b). The price level (P_{e1}) exists at a position below the level that businesses were expecting in the pre-pandemic phase (P_e).

The change from the pre-pandemic price level of P_e to the pandemic price level of P_{e1} may surprise economic agents in the short run, but the agents eventually adjust their expectations, leading to a forecast of P_{e1}. Compared to P_e, the price level P_{e1} encourages businesses to alter wages, salaries, and perceptions, which in turn impacts the position of $SRAS_1$. According to *sticky-wage theory*, when businesses expect lower future prices, they reduce labor costs by lowering nominal wages. But over time, this lower cost structure initiates an expansion of output at the given price level, shifting $SRAS_1$ to the right to its original position $SRAS$, leading to equilibrium point c and output level Q_{e2}.

Increase in aggregate demand

At the end of the recession, consumers purchase more output, boosting aggregate demand. But the extent to which AD_1 shifts right and increases output toward its original position at Q_e depends on the integration of workers into the labor force, the extent to which their incomes compare to pre-pandemic levels, and consumption. The problem is that, for many workers, lower price expectations lead to a decrease in income as businesses hire at wages and salaries below their pre-pandemic levels. In the post-pandemic phase, it is challenging for many workers to resume their previous levels of employment, receive the same flow of income, and undertake consumption. In this situation, AD_1 will not shift all the way back to its original position. Figure 5.9 begins at point c with AD_1 shifting right to AD_2, leading to price level P_{e3}, output level Q_{e3}, and equilibrium point d. To fully restore aggregate demand to its original position at the natural level of output (Q_e), an economic stimulus policy is required.

Economic stimulus policy

To analyze policies of economic stimulus, a Keynesian framework emphasizes that society gains from a movement to the natural level of output. At the natural level, a tight labor market exists. Businesses benefit from an increase in production. Consumers benefit from higher levels of disposable income. From the perspective of the public sector, the cost of economic stimulus equals the increase in government borrowing.

The economic justification for government intervention during economic contraction may be traced to Keynes (1936). The Great Depression of the 1930s gave impetus to his ideas, but Keynes began forming his important theory about government intervention before that time, when the National Bureau of Economic Research started analyzing aggregate economics. Keynes adopted this macroeconomic approach. During the 1920s, the growth of large-scale manufacturing and international trade led to the gathering of aggregate data, encouraging a macroeconomic perspective. By the 1930s, as policy makers addressed rising levels of unemployment, this empirical approach grew.

Keynes (1936) described the Great Depression as a period in which the rate of utilization of productive capital and the number of employed workers declined. Because aggregate

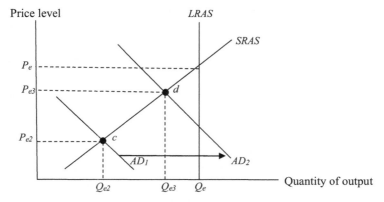

Figure 5.9 Increase in aggregate demand.

Source: author

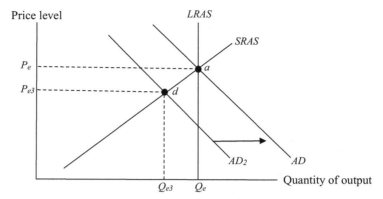

Figure 5.10 Stimulus policy and adjustment to the natural level of output.

Source: author

demand decreased, inventories rose, and businesses reduced their levels of production. The results were decreases in aggregate supply, employment, and income. Because household consumption was a function of income, lower income levels led to lower levels of consumption. Keynes argued that, when inadequate levels of aggregate demand led to prolonged periods of recession, government intervention may stabilize the economy.

An economic stimulus takes the form of *monetary policy* or *fiscal policy*. Monetary policy refers to the management of the money supply and interest rates. Fiscal policy involves altering government spending and taxation. During a recession, policymakers stimulate aggregate demand. Figure 5.10 demonstrates this objective, beginning at point *d*. An increase in government spending (fiscal policy) and/or the money supply (monetary policy) increases aggregate demand, shifting AD_2 rightward to its original position (*AD*) at point *a*. With appropriate policy, an increase in *AD* will return the economy to Q_e. If successful, stimulus policies lead to the end of the pandemic recession, returning output and employment to their pre-pandemic levels.

Monetary policy

To stimulate *AD* with expansionary monetary policy, central banks buy securities in the open market, injecting money into the banking system. When this process occurs, the banking system deposits the money, increases bank reserves, and enhances the system's lending capacity. To disperse reserves, banks lower interest rates, which increases the quantity of goods and services demanded, because the cost of borrowing declines. During the coronavirus pandemic, many central banks implemented swift responses to the disease outbreak, including expansionary monetary policy, commitments to low interest rates, and the easing of financial constraints.

Fiscal policy

Expansionary fiscal policy increases *AD*. When the government increases its own purchases or decreases taxes, aggregate demand increases. During a pandemic, government spending is usually the choice. When government provides stimulus checks, for example, household income rises, and consumption expenditure increases. The result is an increase in demand for goods and services and a rightward shift in *AD*. The rightward shift in *AD* is influenced by two macroeconomic effects. First, the *multiplier effect* creates an additional impact on *AD*, larger than the size of the fiscal policy. Stimulus money sent to households leads to more consumption expenditure across different economic sectors. Higher business revenue stimulates production, leading to more employment, additional income, and subsequent rounds of spending. The size of the multiplier effect increases with a positive change in the marginal propensity to consume. Second, the *crowding-out effect*, the smaller of the two, partially offsets the multiplier effect. When stimulus policy increases spending, households hold more of their assets in liquid form, increasing the demand for money. This outcome puts upward pressure on interest rates, increasing the cost of borrowing, and potentially reducing quantity demanded. Under "normal" conditions, this effect chokes off some household consumption or business investment, but during a pandemic, strong levels of monetary policy keep interest rates relatively low, so the crowding-out effect does not manifest itself during the pandemic phase. The overall impact, therefore, of the multiplier effect and the crowding-out effect is to increase output.

Automatic stabilizers

With monetary and fiscal policies, policymakers react to previous events. But when the economy changes, *automatic stabilizers*, such as unemployment insurance in the United States, activate. For example, a rise in unemployment triggers an increase in federal outlays. As a policy characteristic, the production of output or the unemployment rate may serve as automatic stabilizing triggers, ensuring economic resilience during times of crisis. In a pandemic, a program of automatic stabilizers calibrates funding from the public sector with economic and epidemiological trends. When the disease spreads and the economy contracts, aid flows to businesses and households.

As an application, the flattening of the epidemic curve slows the spread of disease through a population. Similarly, the flattening of the *recession curve*–which characterizes an economic downturn–slows the loss of jobs. But the epidemic curve and the recession curve are related (figure 5.11). In the short term, flattening the former steepens the latter.

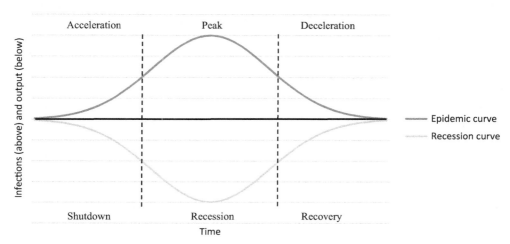

Figure 5.11 Relationship between the epidemic curve (above) and recession curve (below).

Source: author

Shutdown interventions lead to the closing of nonessential businesses. Overall economic activity declines.

These epidemiological and economic trends could trigger automatic stabilizers. The idea is to flatten the recession curve, even as medical containment measures reduce the spread of infections. That is, automatic stabilizers would sever the link between the epidemic and recession curves, providing income to workers and assistance to businesses during stay-at-home orders. In effect, workers would pay their bills, businesses would continue to operate, and the economic downturn would not turn into a financial crisis with foreclosures and bankruptcies. In practice, as production and employment decrease, the stabilizers would increase. As production and employment increase, the stabilizers would decrease. Overall, during a pandemic, countries must stabilize public health and economic activity. The right combination of policies would limit the spread of the disease and the economic fallout from recession.

The challenge of macroeconomic forecasting during a pandemic

For effective policy decisions, *macroeconomic forecasting*, the use of statistical techniques to estimate future trends in macroeconomic variables, is essential. Before policymakers implement a directive such as stimulus policy, they forecast outcomes on important variables such as production and employment. But forecasting differs from prediction. The latter occurs in a world in which events are preordained. In this scenario of future certainty, current events do not alter future outcomes. But forecasting examines how present trends signal potential changes in the future direction of economies. That is, forecasting identifies potential outcomes, not a limited set of certainties. The role of the forecaster is to model uncertainty: the actions of the present impact future outcomes. Uncertainty serves as an opportunity for understanding (Saffo, 2007).

Rules of forecasting

Several rules apply. First, the forecaster should embrace uncertainty by delineating the possible outcomes of a current event. Second, the forecaster should acknowledge that change rarely happens linearly. Change may unfold slowly, proceed methodically, but then accelerate, before tapering off, and returning to normal. Third, the forecaster should embrace indicators of change that are already apparent, especially subtle differences. Fourth, the forecaster should not rely on pre-existing conceptions of reality that may be wrong. Fifth, the forecaster should use as much data as possible, to understand current indicators and map future trajectories. Sixth, the forecaster should acknowledge that sometimes forecasting is straightforward but other times impossible. Finally, the forecaster should publish results with humility, as the future may usher in unexpected outcomes, especially during periods of uncertainty (Saffo, 2007).

Challenges of forecasting

Forecasting presents several challenges, including modeling assumptions, a changing economy, and statistical techniques; however, during a pandemic, macroeconomic forecasting presents additional challenges. How long will the pandemic last? How many people will become infected? How will the labor force participation rate change? How many workers will become permanently unemployed? How will remote work impact productivity? How will businesses react to policy interventions, such as wage subsidies and unemployment insurance? What is the interplay between school reopenings, childcare, and the return to work? During a pandemic, the answers to these questions impact individual forecasts.

The act of forecasting

To make a forecast, economists use forecasting tools to project the likely path of economic variables. For example, they need to know what the economy looks like under current policy and how the economy will change under new policy. Three categories of forecasting models exist, each with strengths and weaknesses: structural, nonstructural, and large-scale models. Structural models use economic theory to learn about economic processes, at the expense of matching with incoming data. Nonstructural models represent correlations of historical data and provide flexible forecasts, at the expense of economic structure. Large-scale models, a middle ground between structural and nonstructural techniques, are built from equations that derive from economic data and use economic theory. The strength of the latter technique is the ability to provide a thorough description of economic events, but the challenge is the level of complexity, which may limit their application.

Forecasting during the coronavirus pandemic

During the coronavirus pandemic, uncertainty was manifest in economic forecasts. Early in the crisis, economists commonly made inaccurate projections, forecasting large spreads that included large and sustained increases in unemployment for the most pessimistic scenarios. One reason that large and sustained increases in unemployment turned out to be inaccurate was that economic policies stimulated economies more than expected. Another reason was that the pandemic was an unprecedented event. Over time, economists consolidated the forecasting spread, but continued to struggle to make accurate projections. Why did forecasting problems persist? The short answer was that no one had experience forecasting during a pandemic. But three deeper reasons existed.

First, stimulus policies quickly improved economic activity. Normally, a predictable time lag exists between policy implementation and subsequent effects. But shutdown interventions quickly shuttered economic activity. Production immediately slowed. Recovery policies then reopened parts of the economy, putting employees back to work. During this process, miscalculating the dates for nationwide lockdowns or economic recoveries substantially altered the spread of potential outcomes. In addition, fiscal and monetary policy responses during the pandemic dwarfed actions in previous downturns and were therefore difficult to model (Pohlman and Reynolds, 2020).

Second, the pandemic undermined the reliability of economic data, the foundation of forecasting. Economic shutdown directives reduced business and household response rates for survey data—a common sampling technique—and sampling error increased. During the shutdown interval, the institutions and individuals that provided survey data were not representative, pronouncements of spending underestimated online purchases, and many businesses were not open to answer questions about sales (Pohlman and Reynolds, 2020).

Third, economists were challenged by unfamiliar epidemiological trends. During the pandemic, the spread of disease was intertwined with economic activity, but economists struggled to incorporate epidemiological data. This problem was also apparent for public health officials. The existence of mutations, infectiousness, and reproductive variance complicated the process of forecasting. For the first nine months of the pandemic, no generally accepted timeline existed for vaccinations (Pohlman and Reynolds, 2020).

Eventually, economists compared previous forecasts to actual trends. They learned about the pandemic and the strengths and weakness of existing techniques. As more information became available and the impact of policy interventions became apparent, greater clarity emerged. Economic recovery facilitated the collection of survey data. Knowledge improved with respect to the spread of disease, effective interventions, and the optimal path of economic recovery. Economists applied knowledge, information, and data from previous downturns, including the Great Recession of 2008-2009, and implemented adaptive techniques.

Summary

Economic shutdown interventions, the first economic interval of the pandemic phase, lead to recession, the second interval; however, the severity of recession depends on the extent to which society first stabilizes public health and then addresses the economic downturn with fiscal and monetary policies. By including two types of decision makers—households and businesses—and two types of markets—product and resource—the circular-flow model demonstrates the process in which a decline in the production of output from businesses leads to a decrease in household income, which slows economic transactions. Four stages characterize business cycles—expansion, peak, recession, and trough. The business cycle model demonstrates that the recessionary stage follows economic expansion, but a recession may last for varying lengths of time, depending on economic conditions and government stimulus policy.

The *AS-AD* model demonstrates that, during a recession, the magnitude of the decrease in aggregate demand exceeds the magnitude of the decrease in aggregate supply. Because long-run aggregate supply is vertical and exists at the natural level of output, recession decreases output below the natural level. But the extent that output falls below the natural level determines the length and depth of the recession.

The Keynesian framework addresses the problem of economic contraction. In the Great Depression, a demand shock, a lack of business investment, initiated the downward spiral that reduced employment and income. But, during a period of economic contraction, Keynes argued that the public sector should adopt an active approach of intervention to promote full employment and economic growth. In a pandemic, a Keynesian supply shock leads to the shuttering of business activity, a decrease in employment, and a lower level of household income. That is, a decrease in *SRAS* leads to a decrease in *AD*. At the same time, individuals choose defensive measures to avoid infections, with or without government mandates for social distancing and sheltering-in-place. Taken together, the decreases in income and defensive measures lead to a large impact on the aggregate demand side of the market. Eventually, market forces create a movement back to the natural level of employment. From the perspective of businesses, lower price expectations increase aggregated supply. Higher levels of employment, and income increase aggregate demand. A stimulus in the form of monetary or fiscal policy enhances household consumption.

During a pandemic, macroeconomic forecasting aids the process of policymaking. Forecasting examines how present trends signal potential changes in the future direction of economies. That is, forecasting identifies potential outcomes, not a limited set of certainties. Forecasting presents challenges to economists, including modeling assumptions, the economic environment, and statistical techniques; however, during a pandemic, macroeconomic forecasting presents several additional problems, including the uncertainty with respect to the spread of disease and other epidemiological trends. The existence of mutations, infectiousness, and reproductive variance complicated the process of forecasting.

Chapter takeaways

LO1   The recession interval entails a decline in output and an increase in unemployment.

LO2   The circular-flow model of economic activity demonstrates that a pandemic disrupts the flows of output and income.

LO3   Business cycles demonstrate alternating increases and decreases in real GDP.

LO4   The *AS-AD* model demonstrates how the production and spending sides of the economy lead to equilibrium price and quantity.

LO5   A Keynesian supply shock and fear of the future could cause *AD* to shift more than *SRAS*.

LO6   A pandemic causes governments to induce a deliberate recession to fight the spread of disease.

LO7   Expansionary fiscal and monetary policy may be used to fight a recession.

LO8   A pandemic complicates the process of macroeconomic forecasting.

Terms and concepts

Aggregate demand curve
Aggregate supply-aggregate demand model
Automatic stabilizers
Business cycles
Circular-flow model
Crowding-out effect
Deliberate recession
Demand shock
Endogenous
Expansion
Financial recession
Fiscal policy
Keynesian supply shock
Macroeconomic forecasting
Macroeconomics

Marginal propensity to consume
Monetary policy
Multiplier effect
Natural level of output
Policy recession
Product markets
Real GDP
Real recession
Recession
Recession curve
Resource markets
Shadow price
Short-run aggregate supply curve
Sticky-wage theory
Supply shock

Questions

1. Using the circular-flow model, explain what happens to household income in the recessionary interval when the production of output declines.
2. For the most recent business cycle in an economy, identify the last expansion, peak, recession, and trough. How long was the recession? Compared to previous recessions, how severe was it?
3. During a pandemic, what factors might shift the aggregate-supply curve to the left? What factors might shift the aggregate demand curve to the left?
4. Using the *AS-AD* framework, trace the short-run and long-run effects of a pandemic on output and the price level.
5. In an *AS-AD* framework, under what short-run conditions will a pandemic create a greater impact on the demand side than on the supply side? For specific countries, was the decrease in *AD* greater than the decrease in *SRAS*? If so, why?
6. Does a pandemic shift *LRAS*? If so, what factors create this outcome?
7. A link exists between the epidemic curve and the recession curve. In the absence of policy intervention, flattening the epidemic curve steepens the recession curve. In a two-graph model, draw this scenario. For a relationship between the two curves, what assumptions are necessary? Should a country use automatic stabilizers to address the recessionary problem?
8. Suppose an economic recovery after a pandemic leaves aggregate demand short of its pre-pandemic level. What types of fiscal and monetary policies would boost aggregate demand? After the pandemic ends, how long should the policies continue? Will crowding out occur? Will a tradeoff between output and inflation occur?
9. For the year 2020, gather unemployment data. For individual countries, graph the month-by-month unemployment rates. Which countries had the highest unemployment rates? Which countries experienced higher unemployment rates for the longest periods of time? What factors account for these trends?
10. How does a pandemic alter the process of forecasting?

References

Goolsbee, Austin, and Syverson, Chad. 2020. "Fear, lockdown, and diversion: comparing drivers of pandemic economic decline 2020," Becker Friedman Institute Working Paper 2020-80 (June), University of Chicago.

Guerriero, Veronica, Lorenzoni, Guido, Straub, Ludwig, and Werning, Iván. 2020. "Macroeconomic implications of Covid-19: can negative supply shocks cause demand shortages?" Becker Friedman Institute Working Paper 2020-35 (April), University of Chicago.

Keynes, John M. 1936. *The General Theory of Employment, Interest, and Money*. London: Macmillan.

Mankiw, N. Gregory. 2018. *Brief Principles of Macroeconomics*, 8th Edition. Boston, MA: Cengage Learning.

Pohlman, Arne, and Reynolds, Oliver. 2020. "Why economic forecasting is so difficult in the pandemic," *Harvard Business Review*, May 18.

Saffo, Paul. 2007. "Six rules for effective forecasting," *Harvard Business Review*, July–August.

6 Economics of recovery

Learning objectives

After reading this chapter, you will be able to:

LO1 Describe the recovery interval of the pandemic phase.
LO2 Establish historical perspective for economic recoveries.
LO3 Explain the components of economic recovery.
LO4 Address the importance of strong pre-existing conditions.
LO5 Discuss roadblocks to economic recovery.
LO6 Contrast different strategies to fight the disease.
LO7 Consider potential shapes of economic recovery.

Chapter outline

- Recovery interval
- Economic recovery in historical perspective
- Components of economic recovery
- The importance of strong pre-existing conditions
- Roadblocks to economic recovery
- Strategies to fight the disease
- The shape of economic recovery
- Summary

Recovery interval

This chapter analyzes the third economic interval of the pandemic phase: *recovery* (figure 6.1).

During the pandemic phase–after economic shutdown and during recession–planning begins for economic recovery. When the disease is under control, businesses reopen. People re-emerge from their homes. Public sectors reduce restrictions on economic activity. But challenges remain. People may be anxious to return to work, concerned about lingering health effects. Some individuals become permanently unemployed. Governments may have

Figure 6.1 Three economic intervals of the pandemic phase.
Source: author

an accelerating debt load. A further complication is that countries do not move directly from recession to complete recovery. Instead, they experience lingering effects.

The reason that the process of economic recovery is challenging for policymakers is that the consequences of a new disease are unforeseen and multisectoral, impacting individuals in all areas of society. With sound guidelines, policymakers may reduce uncertainty. But pandemics are not one-time events that unfold over a limited time, such as hurricanes or earthquakes. They unfold over a protracted period in several waves, until the distribution of a vaccination. Because each infection wave possesses unique characteristics, flexible policy must accompany changing economic circumstances (Fakhruddin et al., 2020).

During economic recovery, households, businesses, and governments attempt to re-energize the circular flow of economic activity, transitioning the economy in a fluid and dynamic process from recession to expansion. When disaster strikes, a pandemic response—aided by data management—will lead to an initial transition and process of recovery, but then a secondary infection wave might lead to another response, transition, and process of recovery. A third wave could then follow. In this unpredictable process, both consumer spending and business activity may rise and fall and rise again. But as this chapter explains, countries with pre-existing strengths, including efficient forms of governance, lower debt loads, and adaptive methods of industrial organization, provide the best opportunities to move forward.

The point is that unpredictable epidemiological conditions lead to challenging policy realities. The process of economic recovery, for example, includes school re-openings; however, schools may implement programs of online education. If parents return to their jobs, but children work online from home, who provides childcare? In addition, when businesses reopen, society may experience additional infection waves. During this time, political support for additional government borrowing to finance assistance programs may dwindle. If the disease re-emerges but businesses begin to reopen, the public sector may struggle to find additional resources for both income assistance and economic stimulus. In this economic environment, should the process of economic recovery proceed or halt? These questions reveal important challenges for economic recovery. The chapter's thesis is that, while a blueprint for an optimal recovery includes testing, contact tracing, targeted isolation, a reasonable timeline, appropriate jurisdiction, and economic mobilization, the process requires flexible decision making. Business investment may be sluggish. Consumer confidence may be low. Individuals may be slow to return to restaurants, movies, and public transportation. As the World Bank (2020) explains, economic recovery depends on suppression of the disease, the strength of government containment policies, government capacity to provide economic stimulus, and global economic conditions (figure 6.2).

To analyze the process of economic recovery, the chapter first discusses the topic in historical perspective. It then establishes a recovery roadmap, addresses both economic and epidemiological components, and considers the importance of strong pre-existing conditions. Because actual economic recovery differs from an optimal process, the chapter then

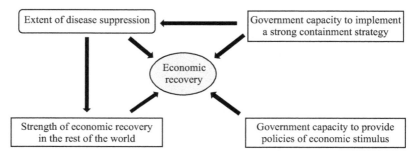

Figure 6.2 Economic recovery.

Source: adapted from World Bank (2020), Figure 14

introduces potential roadblocks, arguing that economic, epidemiological, political, and social factors, unknown at the beginning of the pandemic, may inhibit a timely recovery. The final sections address strategies to fight the disease and the shape of economic recovery.

Economic recovery in historical perspective

With respect to lethality and global reach, the 1918 influenza pandemic establishes historical perspective for the 2020 coronavirus pandemic. For both mortality and economic outcomes, the influenza pandemic provides a reasonable upper bound. Many countries reacted to the influenza pandemic, which began and peaked in 1918 but lasted until 1920, with lockdowns and other nonpharmaceutical interventions, including social distancing, school closings, and targeted quarantines, the same measures taken during the coronavirus pandemic.

The influenza pandemic proceeded in three waves, the first in the spring of 1918, the second during the fall of 1918 and continuing until early 1919, and the third during the remainder of 1919. (In 1920, some countries experienced a fourth wave.) The influenza pandemic killed around 50 million people, approximately 2.1 percent of the global population, representing a likely peak in mortality from a natural disaster in modern times (Barro et al., 2020).

But important differences exist between 1918 and 2020. First, the 1918 influenza pandemic occurred during the aftermath of World War I. In contrast, the 2020 coronavirus pandemic followed a decade-long period of economic expansion. In 1918, the economic recovery was intertwined with the end of war; as a result, debtor and creditor nations emerged. Depending on demobilization, the relative strength of economic institutions, and repatriation of veterans, labor shortages either diminished or persisted in different countries (Asquith and Austin, 2020).

Second, the 1918 pandemic sickened and killed prime-age workers, but the 2020 pandemic disproportionately sickened and killed the elderly. As a result, areas hit by the 1918 influenza pandemic experienced declines in economic activity that lasted for years. With the 2020 coronavirus pandemic, many workers re-entering the workforce after sheltering-in-place required re-training, but labor shortages did not exist. In 2020, economic recovery did not lead to upward pressure on wages as workers integrated into the economy (Asquith and Austin, 2020).

Third, compared to the 1920s, capital markets in the 2020s are more sophisticated. During the recessionary interval of the 2020 pandemic, central banks maintained a position of easy monetary policy, lowering interest rates to increase the supply of money. The effect was to provide liquidity to economies and finance government borrowing to prop up businesses and households. This expansionary monetary policy aided the process of economic recovery.

Fourth, compared to the 1920s, more employees in the 2020s in advanced economies worked in the service sector as opposed to manufacturing. This distribution led to mixed results. For employees in finance, policy, research, and other areas, working remotely during economic recovery did not reduce productivity; however, frontline employees in the service sector who rely on person-to-person interaction confronted health risks.

Fifth, like the 1918 pandemic, cities during the 2020 pandemic remained susceptible to the spread of disease, even after the first infection wave. But after the 1918 pandemic, policymakers took a laissez-faire approach because the roaring twenties created a period of economic expansion. With the 2020 pandemic, many governments maintained activist forms of policy intervention.

Finally, like the 1918 pandemic, the 2020 pandemic may leave the world with a pool of workers either in poor health or disabled. Survivors of the 1918 pandemic appeared to have higher rates of heart disease, neurological disorders, and shorter life spans (Asquith and Austin, 2020). But survivors of the 2020 pandemic complained of persistent fatigue, lung congestion, sore throats, poor appetites, headaches, and other ailments (Cha and Bernstein, 2020).

Components of economic recovery

After shutdown and recession, data-driven epidemiological and economic instructions guide economic recovery. The recovery begins after the disease is contained. The process includes a roadmap to pandemic resilience.

Roadmap to pandemic resilience

Economic recovery entails a process of economic mobilization in sync with the stabilization of public health. Investment in pandemic resilience includes the testing tools necessary to fight the disease, supporting institutions such as hospitals and treatment centers, and flexible industries that transition from shutdown to recession to recovery. The benefits of this approach are fivefold: preventing a recurrence of the disease, avoiding an economic depression, protecting frontline workers, managing the recovery process before the development of a vaccine, and addressing the fraying social fabric of isolation (Allen et al., 2020). A Harvard University study, *Roadmap to Pandemic Resilience*, establishes the strategy, arguing that, before economic recovery, public sectors must establish three components: a system of testing, tracing, and supported isolation (TTSI)–ambitious enough to replace national quarantines–appropriate policy jurisdiction, and a plan for economic mobilization (Allen et al., 2020).

Testing, tracing, and supported isolation

The system for TTSI recommends the establishment of testing oversight for the disease at the national level, guidance at the state level, and innovation in testing methods at the local level.

Ideally, individuals should be tested as often as resources allow. While test availability varies between regions, four reasons exist for a program of comprehensive testing. First, when individuals feel sick, they should get a test. Second, testing should occur soon after potential exposure. Third, individuals should have the ability to get tested as a safeguard. Fourth, widespread testing in a community or neighborhood at hospitals, pharmacies, and health clinics helps to measure the spread of disease (Parker-Pope and Wu, 2020). With contact tracing, health officials identify individuals who may have come in contact with infected people. The process informs people of contacts with infected individuals, collects data, and provides oversight for symptomatic and asymptomatic cases. When a country maintains control over the spread of disease, contact tracing serves as an effective mechanism. If the disease increases exponentially, contact tracing becomes cost prohibitive. For individuals with infections that have to isolate, support provides a method of reducing anxiety and vulnerability.

Policy jurisdiction

The national government should provide surge capacity for the healthcare system, establish a pandemic testing board, provide scientific guidelines to states or provinces, monitor the spread of the disease, and maintain fiscal viability for the whole network. National responsibilities include the clarification of social distancing rules, technology for establishing a database of contact tracing, and procurement of medical supplies and personal protection equipment. States should activate surge capacity in the healthcare system, establish municipal safety guidelines, and supply testing resources. Local governments should design and administer testing programs, support people emerging from isolation, and report epidemiological data, including new cases, recoveries, and deaths. A feedback loop, in which epidemiological trends at the local level are reported to state and national levels, strengthens the system by providing data on the spread of the disease, successful treatments, and public health outcomes.

Economic mobilization

After implementing a strong disease containment strategy, policymakers should establish a staggered process of economic mobilization, which includes the consideration of disease networks, transmission hubs, new forms of business activity, phases, and a targeted business approach.

Because the clustering of disease propagates the crisis, a network framework guides policymakers. This reality is why economic recovery begins with the premise that sheltering-in-place interventions sever disease networks. When people return to work, production increases, but disease networks may return.

Limiting the spread of the disease while reopening the economy includes the minimization of transmission hubs, locations where people interact, such as central business districts, schools, and places of worship. As the disease is contained, hubs may begin to operate at low levels of occupation, and then expand.

Policies to reopen the economy must acknowledge that, during shutdown and recession, new forms of business activity emerge. More employees work from home. Telework establishes new methods of communication. Essential work is prioritized over nonessential work. Businesses establish safety protocols, ease workers into the office environment, and develop methods of preparedness for efficient work experiences. An effective process of economic recovery encompasses these private-sector initiatives.

The *Roadmap to Pandemic Resilience* argues for a staggered and intentional approach to economic recovery with four phases of economic mobilization (Allen et al., 2020). In the presence of targeted sheltering-at-home requirements, phase one focuses on essential workers. While the disease spreads, essential workers in healthcare, food production, pharmacy, delivery, and other areas keep the economy running. The healthcare system provides disease identification, treatment, and support. This step provides information to epidemiologists about the spread of the disease within the essential workforce.

Phase two of economic recovery, expansion of essential employees and relaxation of sheltering-at-home requirements, builds on phase one. This phase addresses shortages in the essential workforce through training programs, expanding the definition of essential workers to include medium-term essential and long-term essential workers–construction, maintenance, research and development, and others–and modifying social distancing practices by maintaining more stringent restrictions on larger gatherings.

Phase three, which ends the sheltering-in-place requirement, maintains strong testing, contact tracing, and treatment protocols, but relaxes social distancing for those with proper testing certification. This phase integrates the nonessential employees into the economy who could not work from home. These employees, in nonessential services, manufacturing, and vulnerable sectors of the economy, require the modification of regulations that prohibit business activity.

Phase four occurs with rigorous testing, disease certification, safe business practices and full economic mobilization. The final phase re-integrates all remaining workers into the economy and increases aggregate supply and aggregate demand. Throughout the four phases, an aggressive program of research and development in both vaccines and therapeutics complements the process.

Market considerations

With a phased-in approach, some businesses reopen before others. Three reasons exist. First, not all business activity is essential. Second, business activity differs with respect to crowding. Third, the existence of latent periods for the disease leads to exploitation of the disease's weak spot.

Crowding approach

The crowding approach to reopening businesses sorts them by the average visit length and average number of weekly visits per square foot (figure 6.3). Fast food establishments are small and busy with several weekly visits per square foot, located in the lower right-hand portion of the diagram. Gyms are larger in size but have fewer visits per square foot, existing in the upper left-hand portion of the diagram. Bars and sit-down restaurants, represented by shaded circles in the top middle portion of the diagram, have longer average stays and larger crowds. Using the lens of contagion, this latter category is more likely to facilitate

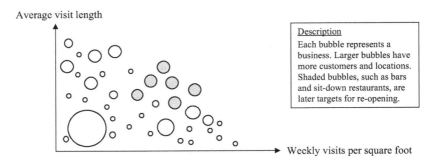

Figure 6.3 Business crowding.

Source: adapted from Baicker et al. (2020)

superspreader events, because the average visit length and weekly visits per square foot are both relatively high. As a result, bars, sit-down restaurants, and businesses with similar characteristics should reopen last (Baicker et al., 2020).

The problem with this approach is that data on weekly visits and average visit lengths do not reveal how customers interact with each other or divide their time between indoor and outdoor activities. Some businesses, such as nail and beauty salons, have high levels of indoor activity and contact. In a process of economic recovery, these businesses and others with similar characteristics should open last (Baicker et al., 2020).

Latent-period approach

Another approach to reopening businesses involves the exploitation of the disease's weak spot. Research during the coronavirus pandemic revealed that the disease's *latent period*– the period between infection and the time a person may infect others–averaged five days. The idea of a latent-period approach is that people work in two-week cycles: on the job for four days and then 10 days of quarantine, to safeguard against the spread of the disease. Workers could serve in two groups, alternating the weeks spent on the job, keeping businesses open, and stabilizing the supply side of the market.

This approach entails several benefits. First, the approach reduces the reproductive number–the average number of people infected by each person with the disease–while invigorating the economy. If employees are infected but asymptomatic, they would interact with others less, reducing work density and slowing the spread of the disease. Second, the approach reduces the psychological cost of opening and then closing sectors of the economy. Providing the hope of economic mobilization and then taking it away increases the level of social anxiety. Third, the approach provides at least some employment for those sent home because of the pandemic. For subsistence workers, four days of earnings could provide income. Finally, a cyclical method is fair, easy to oversee, and applies at any scale. While businesses reopen, infections coming from outside of a region would not perpetuate the crisis (Alon et al., 2020).

The importance of strong pre-existing conditions

An effective economic recovery requires a strategic response, but it benefits from strong pre-existing economic conditions, such as efficient government, low deficits, innovation, the capacity to create new business models, technological advance, and a flexible labor market. With stimulus policy, countries with lower annual deficits or budget surpluses may offer sustained income assistance. These countries may also be able to aid their neighbors, energizing trade networks. In terms of technological advance, countries that devote a relatively large amount of national income to research and development provide an environment for new business models that include telework and cloud computing. Effective responses that lead to economic recovery while minimizing health risks include transparent communication, collaborative structures, information technology, and communication systems (Fakhruddin et al., 2020). Ineffective responses entail a lack of data management, bureaucratic structures, weak communication strategies, and inefficient public health measures (table 6.1).

Roadblocks to economic recovery

During economic recovery, *roadblocks* emerge, because no single intervention is completely effective in stopping the spread of disease. Each has holes or weaknesses. To fight a pandemic, both personal responsibilities and shared responsibilities are necessary. While governments implement, monitor, and enforce shared responsibilities such as quarantines and sheltering-in-place requirements, they recommend personal responsibilities such as social distancing and mask wearing. As a result, some members of society may choose not to participate. In addition, other factors inhibit the process that result from economic, political, and social forces. Taken together, the roadblocks complicate the process of economic recovery (table 6.2).

Table 6.1 Government responses

Effective responses	Ineffective responses
Transparent governance, collaborative structures	Top-down governance, bureaucratic structures
Efficient and effective information dissemination	Lack of information dissemination
Modern information technology	Poor technology
Information dissemination to specific populations	Misinformation
Strong community vigilance	Weak community vigilance
Collaboration	Lack of collaboration
Evidence-based decision-making	Lack of data consideration

Source: Fakhruddin et al. (2020).

Table 6.2 Roadblocks to economic recovery

Roadblock	Explanation
Economic haste	Entails the prioritization of the economy over health
Hesitation	Results from doubts about the safety of the marketplace
Lack of childcare	Inhibits the ability of parents to return to work
Political pressure from above	Prevents a coordinated process of recovery
Protracted medical advances	Slows the development of a vaccine
Quarantine fatigue	Complicates the process of recovery
Social pressure from below	Pressures leaders to deviate from recovery guidelines
Uncoordinated strategy	Complicates the process of an effective and coordinated response

Source: author

Economic haste

Economic haste causes governments to prioritize economic mobilization at the expense of public health. During the coronavirus pandemic, an example was the jurisdiction of state-level governments in the United States, meant to provide a decentralized method of control. In April 2020, two months after the beginning of the pandemic, governors in the states of Georgia and Tennessee reopened their economies against the wishes of their own medical advisors and even before hospitals could estimate if their equipment could withstand another surge in the disease. In May 2020, governors in Texas and Florida did the same. The governors were advised how an early reopening of nonessential parts of the economy—including bowling alleys, tattoo parlors, and hair salons—could intensify the spread of disease, but they acted to reopen their economies anyway. In these states, by July 2020, this economic haste served as a roadblock to economic recovery, as infections surged during a secondary wave. To slow the spread of the disease, businesses had to close again.

Hesitation

When the economy reopens, some people hesitate to return to work or the marketplace. One reason is that, even if the disease is under control, they lack confidence in public health. For these people, the elimination of restrictions on economic activity do not matter. They fear that they may become infected. The problem with this hesitation is that, before an economy recovers, people must be confident in public health. But residual fears of the disease may prevent some people from returning to theaters, sports stadiums, airplanes, shopping malls, and social events. Another reason for hesitation is that, after the end of shutdown interventions, individuals may decide that they are more efficient and happier when they work from home. They may worry that they will lose the economic benefits of telework, including the elimination of commuting, productivity gains, money saved, higher job satisfaction, less sickness, and more time for fitness (Cramer and Zaveri, 2020).

Lack of childcare

Economic recovery requires many employees to return to the office but what about their children? The answer is normally schools and childcare centers. However, an uneven process of economic recovery may exist. Once businesses reopen, they may have to shutter again if infections return. As a result, parents may have to enter and then exit the office environment in an unstable cycle. At the same time, in the public sector, a lack of coordination may exist between institutions that should be in sync, particularly businesses and schools. If the disease is under control and businesses reopen, schools should also reopen. But decentralized school systems that control educational resources may offer online courses, independent of business activity.

   The problem of childcare is therefore deeper than an inability of parents to return to work because they must take care of children. The problem is the potential for economic policy to differ from educational policy. The mobilization of businesses may not correspond to the mobilization of schools. With a lack of coordination, the necessity of childcare prohibits some members of the labor force from re-entering the economy, hindering economic recovery.

The effects of this discordance differ by industry and income class. While some companies provide employees with flexible telework options, essential and "blue-collar" industries, such as fast food, grocery stores, and sanitation, do not. During a pandemic, working-class or low-income employees and small businesses may feel the greatest burden from this roadblock. As a result, childcare should feature prominently in the process of economic recovery (Dingel et al., 2020).

Political pressure from above

If national governments establish recovery guidelines but empower state authorities to implement the plans, political pressure from above may serve as a roadblock to economic recovery. Early in the process, this pressure may exist if national leaders value the economy over public health. The national leaders may conclude that the political costs of a gradual recovery are too high. As a result, they may apply pressure to accelerate the process of economic recovery, even if the disease re-emerges. Political pressure from above may exist in countries with records of individual liberty, free speech, and national leaders that face re-election.

Protracted medical advances

Protracted medical advances serve as a roadblock to economic recovery. While the spread of disease in a pandemic may galvanize the scientific community to establish medical solutions, the slow process of scientific advance may conflict with the desire to reopen the economy. Before the coronavirus pandemic in 2020, the record for development of a vaccine was four years, which occurred with the mumps (McNeil, 2020). But as a result of an expediated process during the coronavirus pandemic, the development and initial dissemination of a vaccine took less than one year (Mueller, 2020).

Vaccine development

Accelerating the process of vaccine development depends on modern biotechnology techniques, using RNA or DNA platforms. Scientists do not rush antibodies into the human body. Vaccine candidates may trigger "antibody-dependent enhancement," making recipients more susceptible to infection, not less (McNeil, 2020). During a pandemic, scientists use *challenge trials* when a disease is curable. In the process, scientists vaccinate a few volunteers, observe the patients until they develop antibodies, initiate a process of deliberate infection, and evaluate whether the vaccine protects them. In developing a vaccine, the scientific community must decide whether the risk of challenge trials is more ethical than leaving millions of people exposed to the virus. Whatever method is used to create a vaccine, developing hundreds of millions of doses presents a substantial challenge.

Treatment development

Compared to vaccines, the development of a treatment occurs faster. Reopening the economy requires the tabulation of confirmed cases. If a country cannot identify infected individuals, it cannot ascertain the degree of infectiousness of the disease. Over time, testing for anti-bodies determines the existence of *asymptomatic carriers*–those who are contagious but do not show symptoms–helping to determine who may safely return to work. The production of antibody tests then serves as an important element to ease stay-at-home restrictions. In general, higher levels of antibodies lead to stronger physiological responses. When the body encounters a disease, time is necessary for both disease identification and the establishment of a defense.

Antibody determination

The identification of antibodies, or immune molecules, is crucial to the process. Scientists must determine what levels are needed to create immunity. With one option, *convalescent serum*, medical professionals first draw blood from those who have previously been infected. To remove everything but antibodies, they filter the blood. The antibody-rich immunoglobulin, injected into healthy patients, requires several survivors from the virus. With another option, *monoclonal antibodies*, which was associated with the Ebola problem in eastern Congo, the most effective antibodies are spliced into a benign virus, grown in cellular mixtures, and given to healthy patients. But with these and other possible treatments, antibodies may last for weeks before breaking down. They may not demonstrate an ability to kill disease cells. An ongoing challenge with economic recovery is that it occurs when many members of the population are uninfected. Barring the development of a vaccine, the disease may re-appear in higher-order rounds of infection.

Quarantine fatigue

When a quarantine policy requires people to stay in their homes, *quarantine fatigue* emerges, which is a profound burden from physical distancing. Quarantine fatigue may reduce psycho-logical well-being, especially for those who already suffer from depression. For some people, extended isolation worsens mental health conditions. The problem is that a premature reo-pening of the economy may compromise public health. An influx of people into public spaces could increase daily infections. But quarantine fatigue threatens to prematurely push some people out of isolation, strengthen disease networks, and extend the timeline for economic recovery.

Even in the presence of a crisis, some people will take risks. A strategic response acknowl-edges quarantine fatigue: people act in a broader context of public health. A strategy of risk reduction involves the identification of high-risk and low-risk activities, such as gathering in large crowds and speaking loudly versus physical distancing and wearing masks. In this framework, contextual factors demonstrate why some people may shun sheltering require-ments: they seek human connection in response to feelings of anxiety or loneliness. As a result, the health benefit of human connection must be weighed against the risk of disease transmission, when the connection entails a conversation in a park, exercise with a friend, or some other activity.

In this debate, ethics may guide the decision-making process. One reason is that, from the perspective of society, the loss in value from higher orders of mental anguish may outweigh economic losses from under-employment. Another reason is that, for structural reasons, some people cannot abide by distancing interventions. Discrimination, racism, and income inequality may create an environment in which physical distancing is a privilege. In this sense, marginalized members of society may bear a greater burden during the pandemic (Marcus, 2020).

Social pressure from below

Social pressure from below may serve as a roadblock to economic recovery. First, protesters of "excessive quarantine" may argue for a premature reopening of the economy. By prioritizing personal liberties over sheltering-in-place and violating shutdown interventions, the protesters may impede economic recovery. Second, local jurisdictions may flout phased-in recovery mandates. With a lack of sanctions, this choice may stem from a belief that the consequences of a methodical and phased-in approach are anxiety, isolation, and lost income. Both forms of social pressure from below demonstrate acts of defiance, the resistance of public health requirements. In the first case the defiance exists between individuals and policymakers. In the second case it exists between local elected officials and national leaders.

Uncoordinated strategy

An effective process of economic recovery requires coordination between different levels of government. Uncoordinated strategy serves as a roadblock. An uneven patchwork of national, state, and local decisions leaves a country susceptible to recurrent waves of infection. An effective response, in contrast, requires vision, planning, and a calibrated response. A combination of smart strategy and public cooperation reduces infections and provides a framework for recovery.

Strategies to fight the disease

The Boston Consulting Group identifies three strategies to fight the disease: *crush and contain*, *flatten and fight*, and *sustain and support* (Gjaja et al., 2020). Each strategy differs with respect to objectives and outcomes. In addition, each strategy includes different methods of combining the economic and epidemiological components of recovery (table 6.3).

Crush and contain

During the coronavirus pandemic, the most successful strategy was crush and contain, decisively crushing the disease when it appeared and aggressively containing it during additional outbreaks (Brimmer et al., 2020). This strategy prioritizes health before wealth, because containing the disease leads to a shorter period of economic shutdown. During the coronavirus pandemic, some countries successfully adopted this approach. For example, New Zealand (population 5 million) and South Korea (population 52 million), and World Bank population densities (number of people per square kilometer of land area) equal to 18 and 529 respectively (world average = 60), minimized the growth of new cases below 20 per day per million people, allowing their economies to reopen soon after the onset of the disease

Table 6.3 Public sector strategies to fight the disease

	Crush and contain	*Flatten and fight*	*Sustain and support*
Objectives	Full containment to reduce the number of new cases close to zero with stringent lockdowns and aggressive testing, tracking, contract tracing, quarantining, and isolating	Attempted containment with interventions to decrease the number of cases and avoid overwhelming the healthcare system's capacity	Open containment with moderate interventions and primary reliance on voluntary restraint to limit the number of cases until herd immunity, vaccine, or cure
Implications for restarting the economy	Opening the economy in a walled society, focusing on strict border controls, and restoring economic vitality	Progressively lifting the restrictions and reopening the economy without surpassing the healthcare system's limits	Prolonged quarantining of the vulnerable population, while the less vulnerable pursue economic activities
Prerequisites	• Early, stringent interventions • Acceptance of prolonged lockdowns • Strict border controls	• Resources to expand the healthcare system's capacity • Ability to increase testing and contact tracing • Adherence to safety protocols during reopening	• Ability to isolate and support the vulnerable • High trust in government translating into high compliance levels • Favorable demographics
Country examples	China, New Zealand, South Korea, and Taiwan	Austria, Australia, Denmark, Germany, Italy, Norway, and U.K.	Sweden

Source: Boston Consulting Group (Gjaja et al., 2020)

and remain open (figure 6.4). When the pandemic began in early 2020, both countries shut their borders, locked down their populations, implemented strong economic shutdown measures, and contained disease outbreaks, although South Korea experienced a rising number of confirmed cases toward the end of the year.

Flatten and fight

During the coronavirus pandemic, many countries struggled to stop the spread of the disease. The inability to prevent disease hotspots led to a lack of containment during the first infection wave. Because the spread of disease risks extending the healthcare system beyond capacity, localized lockdowns must reduce the number of confirmed cases. Two countries, Germany (population 83 million) and Norway (population 5 million), and World Bank population densities equal to 237 and 15 respectively (world average = 60), struggled with early cases, flattened the epidemic curve during the summer months, and experienced new cases at the end of the year (figure 6.5).

Sustain and support

Another approach avoids disease containment but includes moderate economic shutdown interventions. This approach involves selective and largely voluntary restrictions, protecting vulnerable members of the population while keeping much of the economy open. The goal

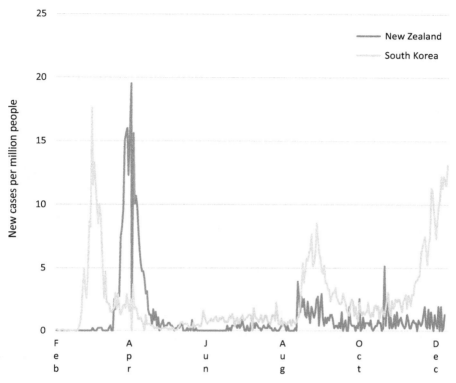

Figure 6.4 New Zealand and South Korea epidemic curves in 2020: crush and contain.

Source: author using data from Our World in Data, github.com/owid/covid-19-data/tree/master/public/data

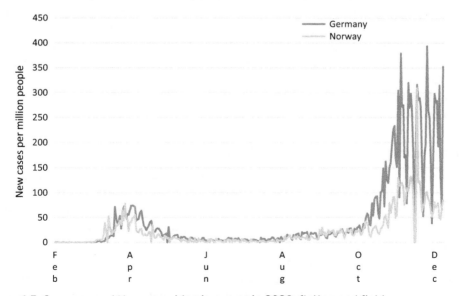

Figure 6.5 Germany and Norway epidemic curves in 2020: flatten and fight.

Source: author using data from Our World in Data, github.com/owid/covid-19-data/tree/master/public/data

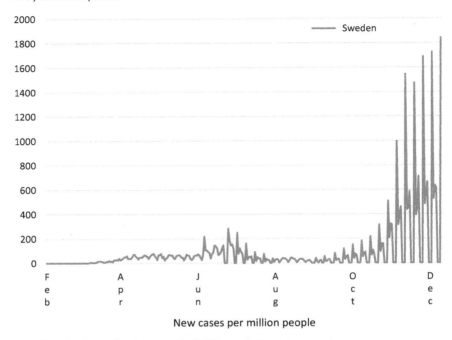

Figure 6.6 Sweden's epidemic curve in 2020: sustain and support.

Source: author using data from Our World in Data, github.com/owid/covid-19-data/tree/master/public/
data

is not to flatten the epidemic curve but to achieve herd immunity among the healthy and young. During the coronavirus pandemic, Sweden implemented this approach; however, it struggled with more infections than its Nordic peers, especially with older members of the population. But the number of cases did not overwhelm the Swedish healthcare system, and the economy remained open throughout the pandemic (Gjaja et al., 2020). With a population of 10 million people and a World Bank population density equal to 25 (world average = 60), Sweden kept new cases below 300 per day per million people until October, when new cases escalated (figure 6.6).

Countries may struggle to contain the disease

Even with the implementation of shutdown interventions, some countries experience uncontrolled transmissions, characterized by the continued growth of confirmed cases. Two examples during the coronavirus pandemic, Brazil and the United States, demonstrated countries that struggled to balance public health and economic activity. Brazil, with a population of 210 million and the United States, with a population of 330 million, and World Bank population densities equal to 25 and 36 respectively, attempted early economic recoveries, but the disease returned in regional outbreaks, leading to an increasing number of cases after the onset of the pandemic (figure 6.7). These results suggest that countries that prioritize public health and contain the disease early, in contrast to the experiences of Brazil and the United States, experience better results.

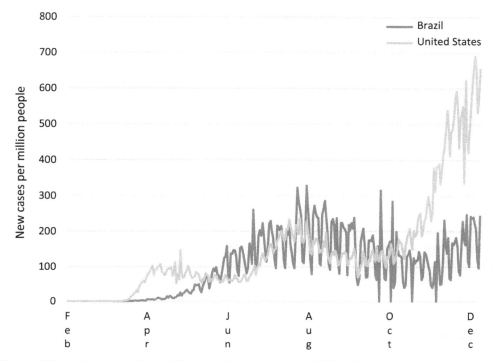

Figure 6.7 Brazil and the United States epidemic curves in 2020: rising cases.

Source: author using data from Our World in Data, github.com/owid/covid-19-data/tree/master/public/data

As the epidemic curves demonstrate, the countries that moved rapidly with shutdown interventions experienced early benefits. They eliminated or minimized secondary infection waves. For countries that experienced second waves, some implemented slower and weaker interventions. In many cases the interventions were not strictly enforced, limiting their effectiveness, even in places suffering disruption and economic losses. Roadblocks to recovery made it harder to achieve widespread support and compliance for additional lockdowns. The result was that, for many countries, the peak deaths per 100,000 people were much higher in the second wave than the first (table 6.4).

The shape of economic recovery

Economic and epidemiological factors determine the shape of economic recovery, including infection waves, changes in economic activity, and the appearance of a vaccine. During the process, one country may control the disease and experience a rapid economic recovery. Another country may experience secondary infection waves with rising unemployment, public sector debt, loan defaults, and bankruptcies. In a third country, economic recovery may occur slowly as economic mobilization unfolds. Whatever the case, the shape of economic recovery is only clear in hindsight, and may assume different shapes, including V, U, W, reverse radicals, and L.

Table 6.4 Deaths in the second wave compared to the first during 2020

Country	First wave deaths per 100,000 people	Second wave deaths per 100,000 people	Second wave as % of first wave
Czech Republic	0.10	1.97	2,011%
Greece	0.05	0.93	1,950%
Hungary	0.14	1.42	1,031%
Austria	0.24	1.21	495%
Iceland	0.16	0.44	275%
Portugal	0.31	0.75	241%
Germany	0.33	0.41	123%

Source: Holder et al. (2020)

V-shaped recovery: best-case scenario

With a V-shaped recovery, the best-case scenario, output increases soon after a pandemic shock. When sheltering-in-place requirements end, employees return to work, consumers spend their disposable income, and businesses return to their pre-pandemic levels of production. With this trajectory, the recession is short and the economy returns to the natural level of output.

U-shaped recovery: persistent shock

Additional infection waves may create a U-shaped or slow recovery. In this scenario, the shock persists, the recession lingers, and a sustained loss in output occurs. (For perspective, the Great Recession lasted a year and a half in many countries, between the end of 2007 and the middle of 2009.) With a U-shaped recovery, a lack of consumer confidence and business investment temper expansionary forces. Businesses struggle to assimilate workers back into their production processes. Even if the economic growth rate returns to pre-pandemic levels, it takes several periods for the economy to return to the natural level of output.

W-shaped recovery: return of recession

With a W-shaped recovery, another recession occurs. The reasons include expediated but ill-advised processes of reopening, additional disease outbreaks, a large negative wealth effect as markets fall and household wealth contracts, or a crisis in the banking sector as households and businesses default on their loans. The potential for a W-shaped recovery hinges on tertiary rounds of infections and additional lockdown measures.

Reverse-radical recovery: bumpy process

A reverse-radical pattern (a mirrored version of the square root symbol) entails a sharp decline in output, a partial rebound, and a slow recovery. In this case, a steep decline in economic activity is followed by a rapid partial recovery and a long period of mixed growth. But the process is not smooth. Secondary infection waves, hospitalizations, bankruptcies, and a lack of income assistance create the reverse-radical recovery.

L-shaped recovery: structural damage

An L-shaped recovery, the worst-case scenario, means structural damage. Recessions are normally cyclical and not structural. But if a severe economic shock causes production to plummet, the recession may linger. The slump is characterized by labor market inefficiencies, inadequate capital formation, and a decline in productivity. In the business cycle, when output reaches the trough, it remains for an extended period. (For further perspective, the Great Depression, which was characterized by a sustained period of contraction, lasted from 1929 to 1939.) With the L-shape, previous business patterns do not hold. Businesses operate below capacity. An example is Japan during the "lost decade" of the 1990s, when production did not return to previous levels until after the end of the decade.

A new shape of recovery

Pandemics create their own legacies. The shape of previous recoveries may not hold. Microeconomic outcomes may include new business models and forms of investment. Macroeconomic outcomes may include lower price levels and natural levels of output. Political outcomes may involve the actions taken by leaders to shelter their populations. Educational outcomes may entail more online education. Policy outcomes may include the allocation of resources to prepare for future pandemics. As a result, for a pandemic economy, the shape of recovery may exhibit a new pattern.

Tracking economic recovery

Ultimately, the fate of the economy depends on the ability to contain the disease. As infections rise and economic activity declines, businesses are at risk of failing. In practical terms, several indicators help to identify economic inflection points. These indicators serve as inputs into an economy's *recovery index*, which reveals the reasons for the shape of recovery, including infection trends, the extent of lockdown, employment statistics, labor force participation, energy consumption, public transit ridership, travel, vehicle sales, home sales, stock prices, income assistance, and unemployment claims (Issues in pandemic economics 6.1). During recession, if home sales, employment, labor force participation, and energy consumption increase, while infections and jobless claims decrease, the recession may soon end, and expansion may begin. Identifying these trends helps to explain the shape of recovery. One example is Bloomberg's "Recovery Tracker," which includes these variables. Using time-series data, the Tracker follows economic trends, determines when inflection points occur, and identifies the end of recessions (Pickert et al., 2020).

Issues in pandemic economics 6.1: The shape of economic recovery

During the coronavirus pandemic, the shape of economic recovery differed by country. In the United States, during the year 2020, the recovery exhibited a reverse-radical shape (figure 6.8).

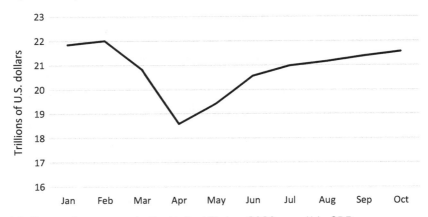

Figure 6.8 Economic recovery in the United States, 2020: monthly GDP.

Source: author using data from YCharts, https://ycharts.com/indicators/us_monthly_gdp

Summary

After shutdown and recession, recovery serves as the third economic interval of the pandemic phase. Meeting the challenge of a global, complex, and multi-dimensional pandemic requires a comprehensive data ecosystem that links the economy with public health. The recovery interval begins when the spread of disease is under control and it is safe to reopen businesses and send employees back to work. Several components of the recovery process exist, including testing, tracing, supported isolation, an appropriate timeline, policy jurisdiction, and economic mobilization. Economic and epidemiological trends determine the shape of economic recovery. Additional infection waves, consumer confidence, and the appearance of a vaccine impact the process. Potential shapes of economic recovery include V, U, W, L, and reverse-radical patterns, but a pandemic may create a new shape of recovery.

During economic recovery, roadblocks emerge. These economic, social, and political barricades, while different in form, complicate the process of economic recovery. An effective economic recovery requires a strategic response to the pandemic and an ability to overcome roadblocks. Recovery also benefits from strong pre-existing economic conditions, such as an efficient government, low annual deficits, propensity for innovation, a growing capacity to create new business models, technological advance, and a flexible labor market. Effective responses that lead to economic recovery while minimizing health risks also include transparent communication, collaborative structures, information technology, and communication systems.

Chapter takeaways

LO1 Recovery serves as the third economic interval of the pandemic phase.

LO2 Compared to the 1918 influenza pandemic, the 2020 coronavirus pandemic differed with respect to the average age of affected individuals, capital markets, the size of the service sector, and policy interventions.

LO3 A strategy for economic recovery includes testing, tracing, supported isolation, an appropriate timeline, policy jurisdiction, and economic mobilization.

LO4 Strong pre-existing conditions complement the process of economic recovery.
LO5 Roadblocks complicate the process of economic recovery.
LO6 A crush and contain strategy stops the disease most effectively during a pandemic.
LO7 Economic recovery assumes different shapes.

Terms and concepts

Asymptomatic carriers
Challenge trials
Convalescent serum
Crush and contain
Flatten and fight
Latent period
Monoclonal antibodies
Quarantine fatigue
Recovery
Recovery index
Roadblocks to economic recovery
Sustain and support

Questions

1. During the pandemic phase, what are the characteristics of economic recovery? What economic data may be used to document a country's economic recovery?
2. What components impact the shape of a country's economic recovery? Which are most important?
3. With respect to economic recovery, does the 1918 influenza pandemic offer an historical precedent for the 2020 coronavirus pandemic? Explain.
4. Review Harvard University's *Roadmap to Pandemic Resilience*, available online (Allen et al., 2020). List and explain the public health and economic components.
5. For an effective economic recovery, is it crucial to first minimize daily infections? Or is it possible to reopen an economy while infections persist?
6. How should a country structure the process of economic mobilization? Should all shuttered businesses open at once? Should a staggered process occur? What are the costs and benefits of each approach?
7. For a country, find time-series data on GDP, including several periods before the coronavirus pandemic, during the pandemic, and after. Graph the data, with GDP on the vertical axis and time on the horizontal axis. What is the shape of recession and economic recovery? Does the pattern fit a V, U, W, L, or reverse-radical shape?
8. Which roadblocks are most important in impacting the process of economic recovery? Why? What components of economic recovery may restrict or eliminate the roadblocks? Besides the roadblocks listed in this chapter, what other roadblocks exist?
9. Are quarantine fatigue and economic haste related? Explain your answer. How do they complicate the process of economic recovery?

10. What pre-existing economic conditions strengthen a country's process of economic recovery?

References

Allen, Danielle, Block, Sharon, Cohen, Joshua, Eckersley, Peter, Eifler, M., Gostin, Lawrence, … Weyl, E. 2020. *Roadmap to Pandemic Resilience*. Cambridge, Massachusetts: Edmond J. Safra Center for Ethics, Harvard University.

Alon, Uri, Milo, Ron, and Yashiv, Eron. 2020. "How to reopen the economy by exploiting the coronavirus's weak spot," *The New York Times*, May 11.

Asquith, Brian, and Austin, John. 2020. "What can the past teach us about a coronavirus economic recovery?" *Barron's*, May 21.

Baicker, Katherine, Dube, Oeindrila, Mullainathan, Sendhil, Pope, Devin, and Wekerek, Gus. 2020. "Is it safer to visit a coffee shop or a gym?" *The New York Times*, May 6.

Barro, Robert, Ursua, Jose, and Weng, Joanna. 2020. "The coronavirus and the great influenza pandemic: lessons from the 'Spanish Flu' for the coronavirus potential effects on mortality and economic activity," NBER Working Paper 26866 (March), National Bureau of Economic Research.

Brimmer, Amanda, Chin, Vincent, Gjaja, Marin, Hutchinson, Rich, Kahn, Dan, Kronfellner, Bernhard, and Siegel, Phil. 2020. "It's not too late to crush and contain the coronavirus," Boston Consulting Group, July 23.

Cha, Ariana, and Bernstein, Lenny. 2020. "These people have been sick with coronavirus for more than 60 days," *The Washington Post*, June 11.

Cramer, Maria, and Zaveri, Mihir. 2020. "What if you don't want to go back to the office?" *The New York Times*, May 5.

Dingel, Jonathan I., Patterson, Christina, and Vavra, Joseph. 2020. "Childcare obligations will constrain many workers when reopening the US economy," Becker Friedman Institute Working Paper 2020-46 (April), University of Chicago.

Fakhruddin, Bapon, Blanchard, Kevin, and Ragupathy, Durga. 2020. "Are we there yet? The transition from response to recovery for the Covid-19 pandemic," *Progress in Disaster Science*, 7: 100102.

Gjaja, Marin, Hutchinson, Rich, Farber, Adam, and Brimmer, Amanda. 2020. "Three paths to the future," Boston Consulting Group, May 27.

Holder, Josh, Stevis-Gridneff, Matina, and McCann, Allison. 2020. "Europe's deadly second wave: how did it happen again?" *The New York Times*, December 4.

Marcus, Julia. 2020. "Quarantine fatigue is real," *The Atlantic*, May 11.

McNeil Jr., Donald G. 2020. "What the next year (or two) may look like," *The New York Times*, April 19.

Mueller, Benjamin. 2020. "U.K. approves Pfizer coronavirus vaccine, a first in the West," *The New York Times*, December 2.

Parker-Pope, Tara, and Wu, Katherine. 2020. "What you need to know about getting tested for coronavirus." *The New York Times*, December 9.

Pickert, Reade, Qiu, Yue, and McIntyre, Alexander. 2020. "Economic activity point to U.S. recovery stalling," *Bloomberg*, July 20.

World Bank. 2020. *From Containment to Recovery: Economic Update for East Asia and the Pacific*. Washington D.C.: World Bank Group.

Part III
Economic analysis of pandemic outcomes

7 Healthcare economics

Learning objectives

After reading this chapter, you will be able to:

LO1 Explain the challenges of providing healthcare during a pandemic.
LO2 Discuss the unique characteristics of healthcare markets.
LO3 Analyze the production of health, including population health and health inputs.
LO4 Examine the shape and components of health production functions, the marginal production of health, and rotations.
LO5 Address the impacts of a pandemic on healthcare systems, including shortages of medical equipment and the economic viability of hospitals.
LO6 Consider the importance of universal healthcare coverage during a pandemic.

Chapter outline

- Introduction to healthcare economics
- Characteristics of healthcare markets
- Production of health
- Health production function
- The impacts of a pandemic on healthcare systems
- Universal coverage
- Summary

Introduction to healthcare economics

A pandemic alters the processes and institutions that constitute healthcare systems. For example, a pandemic complicates the delivery of healthcare services. It leads to shortages for personal protective equipment. It muddles the exchange of information on infectiousness and patient care. It motivates research programs for the development of a vaccine. It challenges the set of protocols for quality control from the approval of treatments to guidelines for clinical care. In each area, a pandemic exposes weaknesses, fractures, and points of fragility.

Healthcare systems that are self-sustaining are susceptible to turbulence with an external shock as large as a pandemic.

This chapter addresses the impact of a pandemic on *healthcare*, the management, prevention, and treatment of illnesses and the promotion of mental and physical well-being. Early in the coronavirus pandemic, for example, health departments were hampered by a *shortage* of testing capacity. This problem left them without the information necessary to track and contain the disease. While some countries strengthened testing capacity, many struggled with detection and the procurement of testing equipment. Even in the presence of rising hospitalizations, many countries were reluctant to invest in new testing capacity without assurances of sustained levels of demand. In many cases, the result was an inability to conduct the widespread surveillance that would slow the spread of the disease.

During a pandemic, several healthcare challenges exist: infectiousness of the disease, asymptomatic cases, disease mutations, patient surges, infection waves, shortages of medical equipment—including hospital beds, ventilators, and masks—and the development of a vaccine. This chapter uses the tools of economics to address the impact of a pandemic on *public health* and *population health*.

Public health includes disease prevention, the extension of life, and the promotion of health through informed choices. The objective of public health is to identify and establish the conditions for healthy lives. Healthcare policies and programs, both public and private, improve accessibility, disease control, education, equity, preparation, and response. With respect to economics, public health systems promote quality and monitor costs. In this context, public health professionals administer health services such as medical and preventive care, diagnose and treat the sick, educate the public, control infectious diseases, provide access to family planning, prevent chronic diseases, and undertake medical research.

Population health refers to a country's health status. It is a function of health inputs or determinants, including public health, climate factors, education, environmental quality, income, the distribution of outcomes, and health policies. Healthcare economists analyze the components of population health with respect to geographic space (countries, provinces, cities) and social disparities (race, gender, poverty), the relationship between health inputs and output (mortality, life expectancy, morbidity), health policies, and cost-effective programs. The study of population health underscores the idea that communities bridge individual health and population health. That is, population health does not exist in isolation. As communities or groups suffer during a pandemic, population health declines. In this context, population health provides an organizing framework that aligns public health, the healthcare system, and health policy.

The chapter's thesis is that pandemics pose unique threats to both public and population health. Asymptomatic cases may not be diagnosed. A disease may spread rapidly. The pandemic may pressure hospitals beyond surge capacity. Medical equipment may be in short supply. Because doctors, nurses, and medical professionals work on the frontline as essential workers, they may become infected. Members of marginalized communities may suffer more than other groups. Isolation and targeted quarantines may lead to mental health problems. The accumulation of these pandemic outcomes leads to a decrease in population health; however, as this chapter explains, counter forces exist, such as targeted policies and programs. To address these points, the chapter analyzes characteristics of healthcare markets, production of health, the health production function, equipment shortages, and the economic viability of hospitals.

Characteristics of healthcare markets

Healthcare markets seek cost-effective methods of providing care to patients. From an economics perspective, one way to provide cost-effective care is to constrain the growth of costs. Another method is to improve quality. Both approaches address the provision of healthcare, focusing on different aspects of the process.

The provision of healthcare includes four levels: individuals, groups, organizations, and systems (Ferlie and Shortell, 2001). Taken together, they provide a framework to analyze both the characteristics of healthcare markets and the impact of a pandemic. People demand healthcare services but may increase their knowledge with education and individual choices. Professional groups, including doctors, nurses, and healthcare assistants, deliver services to individuals, focusing on quality care, positive outcomes, and cost constraints. Organizations such as hospitals and clinics employ healthcare professionals to provide services, focusing on management, organizational culture, and quality. Healthcare systems, which include markets, public sectors, and legal environments, establish the methods, policies, and regulations that govern healthcare networks (universal care, public options, healthcare markets).

Healthcare markets

The standard theory of markets is the supply and demand model:

* Buyers and sellers are the main agents.
* Buyers judge the value of what they purchase from sellers.
* Buyers pay sellers directly for goods and services.
* Market prices serve as the mechanism for exchange.
* The invisible hand of the market, if left to itself, guides resources to their optimal use.

Healthcare markets, in contrast, are more complex:

* Patients may not know their affliction or the kind of service they need.
* Governments, insurers, and pharmaceutical companies have an interest in healthcare.
* The public sector or insurance companies may pay providers for healthcare services.
* The public sector or insurance companies may establish the rules for resource allocation.
* The invisible hand of the market does not serve as the organizing mechanism.

These characteristics stem from the uniqueness of medical care and the existence of market failure.

Uniqueness of medical care

Important differences exist between the supply of medical care and other commodities. According to the influential economist Kenneth Arrow (1963), "the *laissez-faire* solution for medicine is intolerable" because of the distinguishing characteristics of medical care:

* Asymmetric information: patients may collect information about medical services, but the task may prove challenging because of the complexity of medical knowledge. With medical care, the typical patient is not well informed.

- Barriers to entry: educational standards, licensing requirements, accreditation, and codes of conduct ensure quality among the providers of medical care but serve as barriers to entry into the profession.
- Payment practices: in markets, payments are made through third-party insurance, severing ties to the full price of care. With universal healthcare, government covers costs.
- Trust: Because of asymmetric information, patients trust their physicians for assessments, diagnoses, and prescriptions. As a result, medical care relies on ethical decision making.
- Unpredictability: with the exception of preventive care, the demand for medical care exhibits irregular patterns, rising and falling with illnesses and accidents.

Market failure

Market imperfections complicate the provision of efficient services. That is, market imperfections do not deliver the *optimal level of output*, when the marginal benefit of every unit is greater than or equal to the marginal cost of production. In healthcare markets, *market failure* exists: market imperfection prevents the forces of supply and demand from providing an optimal outcome. This reality forms the basis for government intervention. Depending on the type of healthcare, four sources of market failure may exist: public goods, externalities, market power, and inequity.

Public goods

Economists identify two attributes of economic goods: *excludability* and *rivalry*. Excludability is a function of both the legal system and technology. If a producer prevents some people from using a good, such as computer code, it is excludable. Through encryption or legal restrictions, coders may exclude others from using their output. When the consumption of goods such as food items precludes consumption by others, it is rivalrous. Using the attributes of excludability and rivalry, an identification matrix distinguishes between different types of goods (table 7.1).

Private goods, rivalrous and excludable, are traded in markets. When the consumption of private goods increases, that quantity is not available for others. In this case, prices efficiently allocate resources. In the absence of external effects, government intervention is unnecessary for the provision of private goods.

Public goods, nonrivalrous and nonexcludable, are shared by many people and not withheld from those who cannot pay. Nonrival in consumption, one consumer may enjoy the benefits of public goods without decreasing the quantity enjoyed by other consumers. With

Table 7.1 Types of economic goods

	Excludable	Non-excludable
Rivalrous	Private goods	Congestible goods
Non-rivalrous	Impure public goods	Public goods

Source: author

nonexclusion, it is too costly for society to develop a mechanism to exclude those who do not pay from enjoying the benefits of public goods. Normally with public goods government determines how much to supply. As an example, universal healthcare serves as a public good. The adoption of social insurance or publicly financed healthcare systems, in which all members of a population may consume healthcare services regardless of their ability to pay, ensures that the provision of healthcare is nonrivalrous and nonexcludable.

Public health represents a shared benefit from a shared good. Even though individuals benefit from better health, society also gains. Public health therefore represents a collective benefit, especially with infectious disease reduction and herd immunity. In this context, healthcare is a good that depends on the conditions that create the system, including the economic, political, and social forces that produce healthcare, rather than free markets. These structural features are not owned or consumed by individuals. They are linked to government actions. Therefore, the conditions that promote healthy outcomes have many of the properties that exist with other public goods.

Two other possibilities exist. From a practical standpoint, nonrival goods may be exclusive. For example, private hospitals that maximize profit are considered impure public goods, nonrivalrous in consumption but exclusive in terms of restricting those who cannot pay. Impure public goods may be produced by government or business and distributed in markets. A direct unit charge may exist, subsidized by the public sector. As a result, revenue from the sale of the service plus taxes that raise revenue for the subsidy finance impure public goods.

In contrast, after consumption increases beyond a certain level, congestible goods remain nonexclusive but may become rivalrous. Collectively consumed benefits are subject to crowding. These goods flow from shared facilities, distributed by government or businesses. When businesses supply congestible goods, such as theaters or sporting events, they use prices to allocate resources. When government supplies congestible goods, such as parks or public schools, a partial charge may exist, and the potential for crowding remains. In these latter cases, political institutions determine quality and quantity, while the tax system finances the costs.

During a pandemic, the availability of public health, nonrivalrous in consumption, should not exclude anyone. In this context, public health serves as a *pure public good*, nonrival and nonexclusive in consumption for an entire population. However, during a pandemic, when infections accelerate and crowding emerges in healthcare systems, hospitals may receive patients at levels beyond surge capacity. When crowding leads to a shortage of hospital beds, congestion emerges. Public health remains nonexclusive, but the shortage of hospital beds creates rivalry: consumption of healthcare by one precludes consumption by others.

The ethical dilemma of congestible goods

The movement of hospital beds from a pure public good to a congestible good raises an ethical question: for whom should doctors provide care? As a framework for analysis, the ethics of healthcare include four principles: provision of compassionate care, respect for employees, public spirit, and efficient resource allocation (Winkler and Gruen, 2005). With hospital congestion, the latter principle applies. As an example, suppose the arrival at a hospital of two infected patients. One hospital bed remains. (During the multiple infection waves of the coronavirus pandemic, hospital bed shortages were common.) Which person should the doctors treat? Several factors influence the decision. One, screening may determine the relative necessity of critical care and whether the patients are high risk. Two, testing may determine appropriate action. Three, transfer protocols may elucidate additional options. Four, the problem may reveal additional choices, including treatment options and help from other doctors. A systematic and collective choice should determine resource allocation. Doctors should not operate in isolation, choosing between patients.

Externalities

The act of personal consumption may impact the welfare of others. An *externality*, either positive or negative, exists when the benefit or cost of one person's actions affects others. An example is a *positive externality*, when the actions of one person confer spillover benefits. At every level of output, *marginal private benefit* (MPB), the additional benefit to individuals from consuming another unit, is less than *marginal social benefit* (MSB), the benefit to society from additional consumption (figure 7.1).

During a pandemic, vaccination creates positive spillover effects. By reducing the probability of infection and the number of hosts with the disease, the vaccination benefits those who receive it and other members of the population. As a result, vaccinations reduce the probability of outbreaks, including for those who do not receive the treatment. The external benefit equals the reduction in the probability of infection for those who do not receive the vaccination. However, because markets do not capture spillover benefits, they do not account for positive externalities. In the absence of government intervention, the result is a nonoptimal level of output.

The difference between *MSB* and *MPB*, *marginal external benefit* (MEB), represents the spillover effect:

$$MSB - MPB = MEB \tag{7.1}$$

The optimal level of output (Q_o) exceeds the market level (Q_m), while the optimal price (P_o) exceeds the market price (P_m). On the supply side, the supply curve equals *marginal social cost* (MSC), the additional cost to society of supplying one more unit. At point *a* in figure 7.1, the market equilibrium, inefficiency exists: $MSB > MSC$. At Q_m, the market fails to deliver the

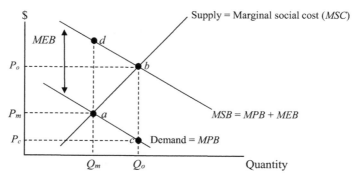

Figure 7.1 Positive externality.
Source: author

optimal level of output. At point *b*, the efficient level of inoculations occurs: the *MSB* of inocu-lations equals the *MSC* of producing them. Point *b* satisfies the marginal efficiency condition:

$$MPB + MEB = MSB = MSC \tag{7.2}$$

To reach Q_o, consumer price must decline to P_c. At point *c*, the quantity demanded by con-sumers equals Q_o, but a lower price does not provide the incentive for producers to bring more inoculations to the marketplace. Therefore, in the presence of the positive externality, government must intervene. If government intervenes, the increase in net benefits of the movement from *a* to *b* is represented by area *abd*.

With a positive externality, government may intervene with a *corrective subsidy*, a pay-ment by government to either sellers or buyers that reduces the price to buyers. By subsidiz-ing the process of creating a vaccination, government accounts for *MEB*. A corrective subsidy is a per-unit payment equal to the *MEB* of a vaccination. With a subsidy, the demand curve shifts rightward from *D* = *MPB* to *MPB* + subsidy = *MSB*, stopping at point *b*. At that point, market price increases from P_m to P_o, covering the marginal cost of production. The correc-tive subsidy decreases the net price to consumers from P_m to P_c, provides incentive for more inoculations, and increases quantity demanded from Q_m to Q_o.

A *negative externality* arises when the actions of individual agents impose a spillover cost on others. The provision of healthcare, for example, leads to the disposal of personal protec-tive equipment, polluting emissions, and alteration of natural ecological systems of bacteria. During a pandemic, infectious diseases and asymptomatic cases escalate. In the marketplace, people may unknowingly spread the disease to others.

In the presence of a negative externality, market price does not reflect the marginal social cost of production. Instead, producers focus their decisions on *marginal private cost (MPC)*, the additional cost to the producer of supplying one more unit of output. As an example, suppose reopening an economy leads to a secondary infection wave. The consumption of restaurant meals, movies, and other services increases the spread of disease from asympto-matic carriers. Because buyers and sellers believe they are meeting safety standards, neither considers the growing level of risk. In this case, *marginal external cost (MEC)* represents the additional risk of infection accruing to people not involved in the economic activities. The vari-able *MEC* is part of the marginal social cost of bringing the goods and services to the market:

$$MPC + MEC = MSC \tag{7.3}$$

In figure 7.2, the market equilibrium (point *e*) occurs at the intersection of *MSB* (demand) and *MPC* (supply). The *MSB* curve represents the additional benefit to society from the consump-tion of one more unit of output. The *MPC* curve represents marginal cost that each supplier faces to produce an additional unit of output. But the *MPC* curve does not reflect *MEC*. As a result, *MPC* falls short of the *MSC* of production.

With a negative externality, a market produces too much output, relative to the efficient level. To move to the efficient level, price must rise from P_m to the optimal price (P_o). At point *f*, the efficient equilibrium occurs:

$$MSC = MPC + MEC = MSB \tag{7.4}$$

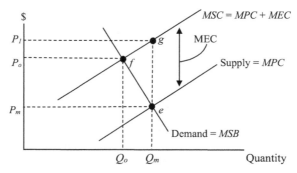

Figure 7.2 Negative externality.

Source: author

Moving to the optimal price reduces the marginal social cost per unit of output, resulting in net gains of area *efg*. Internalization of the negative externality occurs when the market accounts for marginal external cost, price increases from P_m to P_o, and output decreases from Q_m to Q_o.

But economic theory posits that the internalization of spillover cost requires identification of the monetary value of *MEC*. During a pandemic, it is difficult to acquire the information necessary to identify the spread of disease from asymptomatic carriers. As a result, during a pandemic, the standard prescription to address a negative externality, a corrective tax, which equals the monetary value of *MEC* at Q_m, is not appropriate to address the problem. The policy would increase the marginal private cost of restaurant meals or concert tickets and reduce output to Q_o. Producers would compare the extra cost of the corrective tax with other alternatives of reducing output. But during a pandemic, actions that spread infections require other forms of public intervention, rather than a corrective tax. The problem is not the consumption of restaurant meals or concerts *per se*, but the spreading of disease. As a result, the public sector chooses economic shutdown interventions, rather than a corrective tax, reducing quantity directly from Q_m to Q_o.

Market power

With public goods and externalities, the market fails to achieve an optimal level of output because of a flaw in the price signal. Market price does not reflect marginal external cost or benefit. But even in the presence of accurate price signals, markets may fail. Rather than a failure of the price signal, the response to price signals may be flawed. This outcome may occur in the presence of *market power*, the ability of an economic agent to manipulate price.

Market power occurs in different industries. The most extreme form of market power, a monopoly, exists when one firm produces the entire market supply of output. A monopolist may increase price without losing customers. A higher price reflects the importance of the good or service. Optimally, a higher price would signal to producers to increase quantity supplied. But the monopolist may not choose this option, opting instead to enjoy higher profits without increasing the supply of the service. The consequence is that the supplier gains influence over the response of consumers to price signals. It may use the influence for personal gain.

With respect to healthcare, does market power exist? In a market system without competition, market power may exist. When hospitals, specialists, and other providers operate in isolation, they may restrict the provision of healthcare services and raise prices. In particular, rising healthcare costs in market systems are linked to the presence of market power, not an increase in the quality of care. More expensive hospitals and medical providers often exist in rural areas with greater leverage, including a lack of competition, large market share, and monopoly status. The lack of provision of an optimal level of output requires government intervention.

Inequity

Public goods, externalities, and market power create a misallocation of resources. The market fails to deliver an optimal mix of output in a cost-effective way. But an important question relates to the demand side of the market: for whom is output produced? The market answers this question by delivering a larger share of output to those who have larger incomes. While this result may lead to efficient outcomes, it is not equitable.

A global pandemic reveals an inequality of healthcare outcomes. A pandemic disturbs the global economy, upsets industries, and removes employees from the work environment. But the economic upheaval exposes inequities, thrusting the world's most vulnerable people into inferior situations because of unequal access to healthcare services and pre-existing medical conditions. Problems such as unemployment are most acute for vulnerable members of a society. They may lack a social safety net. They may not have the human capital to hold stable jobs. During a deliberate recession, poverty rises and low-income households suffer. The fallout from an economic downturn includes food insecurity, less access to medical care, and higher risks from pre-existing health conditions. Health inequities reflect the difference in distribution of health resources between those who have access to the system and those that do not.

Production of health

The goal of a healthcare system is to achieve a positive health status for the population. But this goal includes cognitive health (concentration, judgment, intuition, learning, memory, language, planning, reason), cultural health (attitudes, behaviors, beliefs, values), physical health (accessibility to medical care and resources, diet, environment, exercise, socioeconomic status), and social health (hope, interaction, purpose).

Population health

Successful efforts in achieving population health require the development and validation of appropriate measures of public health, associated costs, and intended benefits. This process guides the allocation of scare resources among competing wants. To the extent that a country strengthens its healthcare system, establishes methods to provide surge capacity, and creates protocols for the procurement of additional healthcare resources determines how well it operates during a pandemic. To assess the health status of a population, economists examine two variables: *mortality* and *morbidity*. A third variable, *life expectancy*, results from changes in the first two.

Mortality

Mortality is measured by the death rate, which equals the number of deaths per unit of the population over a period of time. For centuries, this variable has been used to estimate the burden of disease. Depending on age groups, ethnicity, and socioeconomic status, several factors serve as the leading causes of mortality, including cardiovascular disease, cancer, and diabetes. Using age-specific, ethnic, or socioeconomic mortality rates, policymakers may allocate resources to aid specific groups. For example, the coronavirus pandemic infected older people at relatively higher rates than younger people, leading to a focus on the prevention of infections in nursing homes for the elderly. Also, it disproportionately impacted people with pre-existing conditions and lower socioeconomic status, leading to the allocation of resources to marginalized communities.

During the coronavirus pandemic, several trends emerged. First, deaths lagged behind infections. It took time for symptoms and complications from the disease to create life-threatening situations. Second, at the beginning of the pandemic, limited resources for testing restricted the evaluation of infectiousness. As a result, resources were allocated to the high-risk and severely ill members of the population. Over time, as testing became more prevalent, resources were allocated to the prevention of the spread of the disease for all members of the population. Third, during the pandemic, medical options improved, resources increased, and doctors were able to treat patients with more information and experience. Finally, in some countries, additional infection waves resulted from economic haste in reopening economies. Taken together, these outcomes impacted mortality rates across countries and regions, as measured by *excess deaths*, deaths resulting from a pandemic above the deaths that are expected. Excess deaths increase early in a pandemic and decrease when the disease is under control.

Morbidity

Morbidity, the disability from disease, a multidimensional variable, measures the consequences, duration, and qualitative severity of disease. In a medical context, disability from disease may entail functional, mental, physical, or social outcomes. These outcomes are identified with hospital inpatient statistics, discharge records, and survey data on biomarkers such as blood pressure, incidence rate of chronic conditions, sick days, and self-assessments of health status. But the onset of disease, physiological dysregulation, and functioning loss vary over time. Because disability is a commonly used measure of morbidity, it is influenced by the environment in which it occurs. A pandemic may alter morbidity through the prevalence and incidence of disease, functioning ability, and psychological status.

Life expectancy

Life expectancy, which results from changes in mortality, morbidity, and other variables, refers to the average number of years that people are expected to live. Per unit of healthcare expenditure, some countries experience higher life expectancies than others. Several reasons exist. First, life expectancy is correlated with income. In a population, a gap in longevity exists between the richest and poorest members. Second, inequality of life expectancy may increase. In the absence of an equitable distribution of healthcare resources, an increase in life expectancy for the richest members of a population may exceed the increase in life expectancy for the poorest members. Third, life expectancy varies with geographic space according to economic development, political stability, and conflict. Fourth, differences in life expectancy for members of the lowest income quintile correlate with government expenditure, environmental quality, and the number of immigrants in a region. In this framework, a difference in life expectancy between pre- and post-pandemic statistics—resulting from mortality and morbidity—reveals the potential for lasting effects. For example, with the coronavirus pandemic, an increase in mortality, stress on healthcare systems, and a rise in morbidity caused a decrease in life expectancy for people with lower socioeconomic status.

Health inputs

The inputs or determinants of population health include public health, climate factors, education, environmental quality, income, the distribution of outcomes in society, and health policies. As people adopt healthier lifestyles, mortality and morbidity decrease and population health increases. Climate factors may improve environmental conditions, increasing population health. Access to healthcare may reduce inequities and increase population health. A public sector may raise public health expenditure as a percentage of GDP, increasing population health.

Health production function

Economists depict production as a functional relationship between resource inputs and output. A *health production function* depicts the relationship between health inputs and population health (figure 7.3).

The health production function shows the relationship between population health (*PH*)—the dependent variable—and health inputs (*HI*)—the independent variables—which include public health, climate, education, environmental quality, income, equity, and healthcare policy:

$$PH = f(HI) \tag{7.5}$$

As *HI* alter mortality, life expectancy, and morbidity, population health changes.

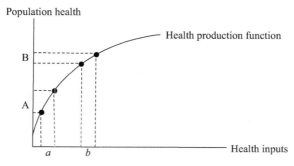

Figure 7.3 Health production function.
Source: author

Marginal product of health

A change in public health causes a movement along the health production function. Disease prevention, life extension, and the promotion of health lead to an upward movement along the function. The marginal product (*MP*) is the change in population health resulting from an additional unit of health inputs, where Δ equals "change in":

$$MP = \Delta PH / \Delta HI \qquad\qquad (7.6)$$

Additional spending on medical care increases population health by decreasing morbidity and mortality and increasing life expectancy. But as health inputs increase, *MP* diminishes, reflecting the *law of diminishing marginal returns*: in productive processes, adding one more factor input, holding all other inputs constant, will eventually yield lower returns.

This concept is demonstrated in figure 7.3. The increase in health inputs in range *a* equals the increase in health inputs in range *b*; however, the resulting change in population health *A* is greater than the change in *B*. The implication is that continued increases in health inputs will lead to smaller outcomes, an important result for policymakers. In this model, *MP* may differ according to demographic or age groups, such as the young or poor. As a result, a given level of expenditure in healthcare may help the young more than the old, or the poor more than the wealthy.

Rotation of the health production function

Besides public health, other independent variables impact population health, including climate, education, environmental quality, equitable outcomes, income, and health policies. When these inputs change, the health production function rotates. In this framework, a pandemic serves as a complicating factor, altering the inputs in different ways (table 7.2).

As an example, the shutdown interval of the pandemic phase reduces economic activity, which decreases pollution from P_0 to P_1 and increases environmental quality, all else equal (figure 7.4). This outcome reduces mortality and morbidity, raises life expectancy, and improves population health. The health production function rotates upward. But pollution

Table 7.2 Rotation of the health production function

Independent variable	Pandemic effect	Explanation	Health production function
Climate	Fewer emissions	The pandemic reduces business activity and the burning of fossil fuels	Rotates up
Education	Less education	The pandemic reduces the amount of time students spend in school	Rotates down
Environment	Less pollution	The pandemic reduces business activity and polluting emissions	Rotates up
Equity	Less equitable	The pandemic leads to inequitable health outcomes	Rotates down
Income	Less income	The pandemic reduces business activity and disposable income	Rotates down
Policies	More health	The pandemic leads to policies to strengthen healthcare systems	Rotates up

Source: author

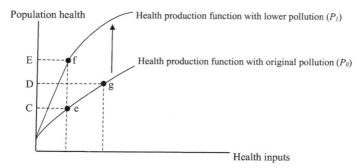

Figure 7.4 Upward rotation of the health production function.
Source: author

reduction increases population health (*e* to *f*) more than a marginal increase in health inputs (*e* to *g*).

This environmental impact, occurring in isolation, flows from the model framework; however, the overall impact of the pandemic on the health production function depends on the relative interaction of changes in public health, climate, education, environmental quality, equity, income, and policy. Because of the negative impacts from the spread of disease, less school time, lower income levels, and inequitable outcomes, the most likely result of a pandemic is a downward rotation of the health production function.

The impacts of a pandemic on healthcare systems

In addition to the impact of a pandemic on population health, other important outcomes occur. The following examples demonstrate why a pandemic may lead to shortages and alter the economic viability of hospitals.

Shortages of medical equipment

Pandemics create shortages of medical equipment and supplies, including ventilators, dialysis units, drugs, and masks. During a pandemic, what happens to the laws of supply and demand? In the presence of shortage conditions, when will market price adjust and when will it remain sticky? In the presence of a shortage, quantity demanded exceeds quantity supplied at a price below equilibrium (figure 7.5). But in "normal" market circumstances, market forces will provide the conditions for price to rise to the market-clearing position (P_e), eliminating the shortage.

In a typical market, the *supply curve* demonstrates the quantity of a good or service that sellers are willing and able to sell at different prices, all else equal. Because price and quantity are directly related, the supply curve slopes upward. Movements along the supply curve are a response to a change in price. As price rises, sellers have the incentive to bring more units of output to the market. But the supply curve may also shift. The determinants of supply, which serve as shift variables, include technology, factor costs, taxes and subsidies, expectations, number of sellers, and prices of related goods and services.

The *demand curve* demonstrates the quantity of a good or service that consumers are willing and able to buy at different prices, all else equal. Because price and quantity are

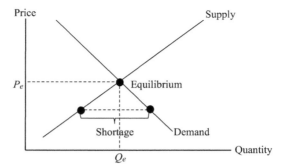

Figure 7.5 The case of a shortage.

Source: author

inversely related, the demand curve slopes downward. Movements along the demand curve are a response to a change in price. As price rises, buyers have incentive to purchase fewer units of output, resulting in a decrease in quantity demanded. But the demand curve may also shift. The determinants of demand, which serve as shift variables, include tastes, income, expectations, number of buyers, and prices of other goods and services. Equilibrium price (P_e) and quantity (Q_e) exist at the point where quantity supplied equals quantity demanded. This market-clearing position is compatible with the intentions of both sellers and buyers.

Sticky prices

In a pandemic, suppliers may hesitate to raise price. To consider this scenario, assume a market for medical equipment. Different from the aggregate supply-aggregate demand model in chapter 5, this market includes the supply of and demand for medical equipment. Assume no external effects. In a pandemic, a position of disequilibrium may persist for important medical equipment. A shortage exists at a price below equilibrium. At the shortage price, suppliers sell a level of output equal to quantity supplied, but this position falls short of quantity demanded. In the absence of price controls, disequilibrium normally signals that price should self-adjust. For example, if a shortage exists, consumers are willing and able to pay a higher price. With a higher price, sellers supply more output. The invisible hand of the market guides price until it reaches equilibrium. But a pandemic complicates the process. Richard Thaler (2020), Professor of Economics and Behavioral Science at the University of Chicago, explains why: in times of crisis, people may value the concept of fairness. That is, they may feel that it is not socially acceptable to profit from a pandemic.

In research conducted on the economic implications of crisis, Richard Thaler and his co-authors, notably the Nobel-Prize winning psychologist Daniel Kahneman, and Jack Knetsch (1986) argue that businesses understand that abiding by standards of fairness should be a part of their operational procedures. Applying this concept to a pandemic, businesses may feel that they should not raise price, even in the presence of a shortage. Instead, they limit the amount each consumer may buy.

Kahneman, Knetsch, and Thaler (1986) consider the example of a hurricane. After the storm, demand increases for plywood and bottled water. Big retailers anticipate shortages and send extra supplies of plywood and bottled water to regions close to the danger zone. When the coast is clear, retailers continue to sell the plywood at low prices and give the water away for free. But at the same time, "entrepreneurs" seize the opportunity, load up on plywood and water, go to the storm site, and sell the items at higher prices. From the perspective of equity, the business preference for fairness should persist, but the profit-seeking behavior of the enterprising individuals should be discouraged.

This result explains the shortages of medical equipment such as ventilators, dialysis units, drugs, and masks during the coronavirus pandemic (Thaler, 2020). Hospitals in disease hotspots struggle to maintain adequate supplies. They normally sign contracts with buying associations for the provision of medical supplies from wholesalers. The wholesalers maintain relationships with hospitals, feeling that a pandemic is not a good time to raise prices. But when demand increases, other institutions along the supply chain divert medical equipment to agents willing and able to pay higher prices, creating the opportunity for profit. When hospitals search for additional medical equipment to meet the surge in patients, the regular stock of supplies is short.

Adjusting prices

During the coronavirus pandemic, shortages existed in other markets. In the food industry, for example, several disease outbreaks in meatpacking plants led to market disruptions. When some pork processing plants closed, millions of pigs that were living on farms grew too big to be processed in meatpacking plants. With the disruption in the market, many of the pigs were euthanized. But despite cases such as these, the food supply chain remained relatively stable. Shortages in grocery stores for individual items appeared on an intermittent basis throughout initial and subsequent infection waves, but for the most part the market worked. Shortage conditions for some items, notably pork chops and whole chickens, led to price increases, which eliminated the shortages. The higher prices encouraged consumers to seek alternatives, such as beef and fish. The higher prices also encouraged producers and supply chain managers to ensure that shortages did not last. The result was that, although grocery stores did experience empty shelves for some items for short periods of time, no widespread food shortages existed (Irwin, 2020).

Views on shortages

There are two ways to view the problem of shortages. The market perspective argues that maintaining the social norm of fairness during a pandemic is not efficient: it does not allow markets to clear, such as in the food industry, preventing a solution to the shortage problem. Higher prices discourage panic buying and increase the flow of essential goods and services to the markets and institutions that need them. In contrast, the ethical perspective argues for a principle of fairness. During a pandemic, hospitals require additional medical equipment. But relying on market forces means the medical equipment flows to the highest bidders, not the institutions that may need them the most.

Economic viability of hospitals

During a pandemic, hospitals postpone elective surgeries, scans, and other well-reimbursed services to meet the needs of patients and maintain surge capacity. The result is less revenue for private hospitals and less compensation for healthcare workers. Therefore, a pandemic raises a question about the economic viability of the hospital system. Four models of health-care exist: *Beveridge model, Bismarck model, national health insurance model,* and *out-of-pocket model* (Chung, 2017). The economic impact of a pandemic on hospitals depends on the type of healthcare system. Countries may implement a combination of the approaches, which is why one country may have examples of several of the models.

Beveridge model

The Beveridge model, a single-payer national health system, such as in New Zealand, Spain, and the United Kingdom, offers healthcare services in a centralized framework. Government acts as a single payer, eliminates competition, and maintains low prices. Because the tax sys-tem provides funding, healthcare is free for patients at the point of delivery. No out-of-pocket expenses or *premiums*–monthly healthcare payments–exist. A central motivation of the sys-tem, healthcare as a human right, guarantees universal coverage. The criticism is that, while government attempts to control costs, over-utilization creates waiting lists and escalates costs. An additional concern is that, during a pandemic, tax revenue declines, exacerbating the ability of the healthcare system to allocate resources to care for a large influx of patients. Addressing these concerns requires the allocation of resources to contingencies before the onset of crisis (Chung, 2017).

Bismarck model

The Bismarck model, a social but more decentralized health insurance system, in Belgium, Germany, Japan, and the United States (employer-based healthcare plans), is funded by employers and employees through payroll deductions. Employees have access to "sickness funds" through their insurance plans, regardless of pre-existing conditions. Even though the social health insurance fund is public, private institutions serve as health providers. The model offers a single insurer, multiple and competing insurers, or multiple and noncompeting insurers. But in all cases the government regulates prices and insurers do not earn profits, leading to cost controls. The benefit is the system provides quality healthcare to the insured. Problems result from a lack of cost-effective coverage for those who cannot work, the elderly, and marginalized members of society (Chung, 2017).

National health insurance model

The national health insurance model, a single-payer system, such as in Canada, South Korea, and the United States (similar to Medicare), uses aspects of the Beveridge and Bismarck models. Like the Beveridge system, government serves as a single payer. Like the Bismarck system, providers are private. Universal coverage does not deny claims or profit from the provision of services. In some countries, the mixed framework provides private insurance for those who demand it. Hospitals maintain independence, decrease complications with insurance policies, and balance private practice with public insurance. On the demand side, patients choose their healthcare providers. On the supply side, low financial barriers lead to the management of costs, government processes claims, and the system minimizes the duplication of services. But the problem is that the system may lead to long waiting lists for services such as nonemergency procedures and elective surgeries. Also, in nonurgent cases, the over-utilization of healthcare resources threatens the long-term viability of the system (Chung, 2017).

Out-of-pocket model

The out-of-pocket model, a market-driven system, such as in China, India, and the United States (for the uninsured or underinsured), requires patients to pay for their services. In countries lacking in resources for national plans or choosing not to cover everyone, a market system provides unequal access to treatment and disparities in healthcare outcomes, depending on socioeconomic status. With a market system, people with low-income status, pre-existing conditions, and less access to healthcare suffer the most during a pandemic (Chung, 2017).

Universal coverage

A pandemic creates shortages in medical equipment, overloads hospitals with patients, and weakens private insurance models. Centralized systems of universal coverage, while providing incentive for excessive treatments and requiring an ongoing investment of public resources, provide healthcare for all citizens. This model of universal access is crucial during a pandemic. A centralized system, when run by capable administrators, allocates healthcare resources in an equitable manner. A market system, in contrast, provides exclusive and rivalrous services, an inefficient outcome during a pandemic.

Summary

Healthcare systems include the management, prevention, and treatment of illness and the preservation of mental and physical well-being through healthcare services. During a pandemic, several healthcare challenges exist, including infectiousness, asymptomatic cases, disease mutations, patient surges beyond capacity, repeated infection waves, shortages of medical equipment and testing capacity, and development of a vaccine.

Healthcare markets differ from other markets because of the unique nature of medical care and market failure. The unique factors of medical care include asymmetric information, barriers to entry for healthcare professionals, payment practices, trust, and unpredictability. The forms of market failure include public goods, externalities, market power, and inequity. The existence of market failure provides an economic justification for government intervention.

A model of the production of health demonstrates how health inputs determine population health. Population health refers to the health outcomes of society, including the distribution of outcomes. Population health is a function of health inputs or determinants, including public health, climate factors, education, environmental quality, income, the distribution of outcomes in society, and health policies. A change in the health inputs leads to a change in population health.

A pandemic creates shortages of medical equipment and threatens the economic via-bility of hospitals. When a shortage exists, quantity demanded exceeds quantity supplied. In typical market circumstances, price then rises to a market-clearing level, eliminating the shortage. In a pandemic, suppliers may hesitate to raise prices of important equipment and supplies because of an issue of fairness. Also, hospitals postpone elective surgeries, scans, and other well-reimbursed services to meet the needs of patients, satisfy social distancing requirements, and maintain surge capacity. The result is less revenue for private hospitals and compensation for healthcare workers. Therefore, a pandemic raises a question about the economic viability of the hospital system. Centralized systems of universal coverage, while providing incentive for excessive treatments and requiring an ongoing investment of public resources, provide healthcare for all citizens. This model of universal access is crucial during a pandemic.

Chapter takeaways

LO1   Public health includes disease prevention, the extension of life, and the promotion of health, while population health refers to the health outcomes of society, including the distribution of outcomes within the group.

LO2   The uniqueness of medical care differentiates it from output in typical markets. Market failure in healthcare exists in the form of public goods, externalities, market power, and inequity.

LO3   Successful efforts in achieving population health require the development and valida-tion of appropriate measures of public health, associated costs, and intended benefits.

LO4   A health production function demonstrates the relationship between health inputs and population health, but diminishing marginal returns holds.

LO5   Because of the potential for sticky prices, a pandemic may lead to shortages of medical equipment, while threatening the economic viability of hospitals.

LO6   During a pandemic, a system of universal healthcare provides a way to treat all mem-bers of a population.

Terms and concepts

Beveridge model
Bismarck model
Corrective subsidy
Demand curve
Excess deaths
Excludability
Externality
Healthcare
Health production function
Law of diminishing marginal returns
Life expectancy
Marginal external benefit

Marginal external cost
Marginal private benefit
Marginal private cost
Marginal social benefit
Marginal social cost
Market failure
Market power
Morbidity
Mortality
National health insurance model
Negative externality
Optimal level of output
Out-of-pocket model
Population health
Positive externality
Premiums
Private goods
Public goods
Public health
Pure public good
Rivalry
Shortage
Supply curve

Questions

1. During a pandemic, what factors pressure healthcare systems? What are the economic implications of these factors?
2. What are the costs and benefits of public health? How does a pandemic impact these costs and benefits?
3. List and explain the variables that determine population health: mortality, morbidity, and life expectancy. For a country, graph the change in these variables over time. Why do the trends exist? How did the coronavirus pandemic impact the variables?
4. What types of market failure exist with healthcare? During pandemic, which types are most pronounced?
5. How are excess deaths from a pandemic calculated? For a country, find data on excess deaths during the coronavirus pandemic. How would you characterize excess deaths?
6. Graph a health production function. With respect to the dependent variable, what data requirements are involved? How do the independent variables, including public health, climate, education, environmental quality, equitable outcomes, income, and policy impact population health?
7. For each of the following scenarios, demonstrate the impact on the health production function, noting the difference between a movement along the function and rotations of the function.

a. The level of public health expenditure increases as a percentage of GDP.
b. A pandemic reduces economic activity, which leads to fewer carbon dioxide emissions flowing into the atmosphere.
c. A pandemic reduces the amount of time students spend in school.
d. A pandemic reduces economic activity, lowering pollution levels and improving environmental quality.
e. A pandemic increases the inequity of healthcare outcomes.
f. A pandemic reduces economic activity, leading to lower income levels.

8. A problem during a pandemic is a shortage of medical equipment such as ventilators, face masks, and gowns. On a supply and demand graph, draw the scenario. With respect to the problem, explain the market and ethical perspectives. During a pandemic, which perspective should prevail?

9. How does a pandemic threaten the economic viability of hospitals? What measures may hospitals take to plan for a future pandemic?

10. What is the ethical argument for universal healthcare during a pandemic?

References

Arrow, Kenneth J. 1963. "Uncertainty and the welfare economics of medical care," *American Economic Review*, 53(5), December: 941–973.
Chung, Mimi. 2017. "Health care reform: learning from other major health care systems," *Princeton Public Health Review*, December 2.
Ferlie, Ewan B., and Shortell, Stephen M. 2001. "Improving the quality of healthcare in the United Kingdom and the United States: a framework for change," *The Milbank Quarterly*, 79, 2: 281–315.
Irwin, Neil. 2020. "Capitalism is amazing! (It's also inadequate)." *The New York Times*, November 15.
Kahneman, Daniel, Knetsch, Jack L., and Thaler, Richard H. 1986. "Fairness and the assumptions of economists," *The Journal of Business*, 59, 4, Part 2 (October): S285–S300.
Thaler, Richard. 2020. "When the law of supply and demand isn't fair," *The New York Times*, May 24.
Winkler, Eva C., and Gruen, Russell L. 2005. "First principles: substantive ethics for healthcare organizations," *Journal of Healthcare Management*, 50, 2 (March/April): 109–119.

8 Inequality of outcomes

Learning objectives

After reading this chapter, you will be able to:

LO1 Explain why inequality of wealth becomes inequality of health.
LO2 Discuss the components of the demand for healthcare.
LO3 Analyze why physician factors impact the demand for healthcare.
LO4 Describe how demographic characteristics impact the demand for healthcare.
LO5 Assess the relationship between health status and the demand for healthcare.
LO6 Address how socioeconomic standing impacts the demand for healthcare.
LO7 Identify the relationship between structural inequality and the demand for healthcare

Chapter outline

- Inequality of wealth becomes inequality of health
- Demand for healthcare
- Physician factors
- Demographic characteristics
- Health status
- Socioeconomic standing
- Structural inequality
- Summary

Inequality of wealth becomes inequality of health

A pandemic exposes disparities of health outcomes between socioeconomic groups. With less access to healthcare, individuals in lower income classes or marginalized communities experience negative health outcomes at higher rates than other members of the population. Although no one has natural immunity to a new disease, socioeconomic and structural disparities demonstrate what happens when a pandemic is layered upon entrenched inequalities.

Because of pre-existing medical conditions and less access to healthcare, those who are disadvantaged may experience infections at a higher rate than their percentage in the general population. Free market economies make members of the working poor especially vulnerable. Even during times of economic growth, they may lack the economic wherewithal to maintain their health status and the status of family members. During a pandemic, the working poor risk daily harmful health effects while those with higher socioeconomic status work from home or benefit from income assistance. As this chapter explains, an inequality of health outcomes depends on precipitating events, the vulnerability of healthcare systems, and factors that determine the demand for healthcare. During a pandemic, "The inequalities of wealth … become inequalities of health" (Editorial, 2020).

This chapter addresses the inequality of pandemic outcomes. Economists debate whether or not economic inequality hurts a country's prospect for economic growth; however, economic inequality creates inferior health outcomes for those with lower socioeconomic and/or marginalized status. The individuals in these categories may suffer from pre-existing health conditions, a lack of nutritious food, and adequate resources for healthcare. According to one study, "income inequality creates a propensity to disease pathways over the course of human development" (Vega and Shribney, 2017). Many reasons exist. Poor people spend a higher percentage of their income on healthcare. Life expectancy declines for people with lower socioeconomic status. Individuals with relatively less income early in life are statistically more likely to report poorer health in their later years. Greater exposure to pollution stunts the developmental process of children. These realities demonstrate that health risk is a societally imbedded issue. A reduction in health inequality requires the reduction of economic inequality.

To analyze these issues in the context of a pandemic, the chapter first discusses the demand for healthcare. The chapter then applies this framework to consider the determinants of demand, including physician factors, demographic characteristics, health status, socioeconomic standing, and structural inequality. The chapter's thesis is that these determinants place individuals with relatively more access to resources in a better position, while those with fewer resources are more likely to suffer harmful consequences.

Demand for healthcare

Economists treat health like other investments that enhance future productivity. Michael Grossman's (1972) model of health demand views investment in health as the consumption of medical care. In this framework, individuals have a level of health that depreciates with age. They invest in the process because better health status leads to more time for both market and nonmarket activities. At any age, a person determines an optimal stock of health by equating the user price of investment in health with marginal efficiency. In this model, improvements in health increase *human capital*, the knowledge and skills embodied in work effort that lead to the creation of economic value. But the allocation of resources to enhance health reduces the money available to purchase other goods and services, resulting in lower levels of current consumption. The implication is that better health will increase future productivity, income, and consumption. Several factors determine the willingness to invest in health: the timing of the future payoff, level of the future payoff, and cost of healthcare.

People willing to invest more in health tend to have higher levels of education and income. As a result, correlation exists between better health, educational attainment, and income (Henderson, 2018).

Model of derived demand

The model of *derived demand* provides a framework. The demand for healthcare is derived from an individual's demand for health. It is inversely related to price. The demand for healthcare is defined in terms of what an individual is willing to sacrifice to obtain better health outcomes. Following the analysis of Henderson (2018), figure 8.1 depicts the demand for healthcare (D_I), where Q_m equals the minimum level of healthcare necessary to maintain a person's health status. An assumption is that society will not allow anyone's health to fall below (Q_m). In the model, the healthcare community guarantees a *clinical quantity of care* for each patient (D_{cl}) without consideration of cost. Policymakers and administrators use D_{cl} to determine resource needs, including personnel, equipment, and facilities. Because the clinical quantity of care does not consider cost, D_{cl} is perfectly inelastic: individuals demand a level of care (Q_{cl}) regardless of price.

Demand curves highlight willingness and ability to pay. As chapter 7 explains, four general healthcare models assume different methods of payment: the Beveridge model, Bismarck model, national health insurance model, and out-of-pocket model. In figure 8.1, quantity demanded changes with price along D_I. If the price of healthcare equals zero, quantity demanded equals Q_{cl}. But as patients pay more (P_0) for healthcare out-of-pocket, quantity demanded decreases to Q_I. The minimum level of healthcare varies according to health status. People with stellar health records and healthy lifestyles require less formal healthcare.

Determinants of demand

The demand for healthcare is a function of both physician and patient factors (Henderson, 2018). Physicians impact the demand for healthcare through their positions in the system. They are both agents of their patients and providers of healthcare. By recommending additional care, physicians create demand for their own services. Patient factors include

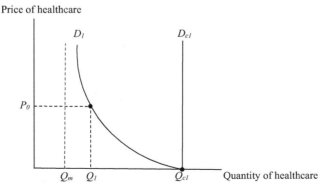

Figure 8.1 The demand for healthcare.

Source: adapted from Henderson (2018), Figure 5.2

demographic characteristics, health status, socioeconomic standing, and structural inequities. For person j over time t, the demand for healthcare (HC_{jt}) is written as a function of its determinants:

$$HC_{jt} = f\left(P_t, D_{jt}, H_{jt}, S_{jt}, I_{jt}\right) \tag{8.1}$$

where P_t denotes physician factors, D_{jt} includes demographic characteristics, H_{jt} connotes health status, S_{jt} refers to socioeconomic standing, and I_{jt} refers to structural inequality. Changes among variables on the right-hand side of the equation shift the demand for healthcare.

Physician factors

Physicians impact the demand for healthcare in their roles as service providers and patient advisors. They admit patients to hospitals, diagnose illnesses, order tests, care for patients, administer treatments, and prescribe drugs.

Principal-agent relationship

The physician-patient relationship is characterized as a *principal-agent relationship*, when an agent, the physician, is granted authority to make decisions for an individual, the principal. The relationship functions when they agree on treatment. If the interests of the principal and agent align, efficiencies exist. But patients may lack knowledge on diagnoses, treatments, and prescriptions. They trust physicians to make decisions on their behalf. In the role of medical supplier, the physician's interests may diverge from the patient's interests. The reason is the type of care. Preventive care includes the measures taken for the prevention of disease or illness, including counseling. Providing these services at low cost helps patients remain healthy and decreases future healthcare expenditure. Medical services, however, include the procedures that address illness and disease after they are present. In this case, providing testing and treatment provides the economic livelihood for physicians and hospitals. Physicians have the economic incentive to prescribe additional tests and procedures. That is, from an economics perspective, physician agents have the incentive to act in an opportunistic manner.

Adverse selection and moral hazard

This behavior is linked to *adverse selection* and *moral hazard*. Adverse selection exists when one member of a transaction benefits from asymmetric information, distorting the market with a lack of shared information. Due to asymmetric information, physicians may prescribe additional procedures at higher prices. Moral hazard exists if an individual assumes more risk when not bearing the entire cost of exposure to risk. With healthcare, a person may demand additional procedures in the presence of insurance coverage, even if the procedures are unnecessary. The difference between the relatively lower benefit of additional care to patients and the relatively higher cost to providers represents an inefficiency.

The principal-agent relationship creates an environment for these factors. In a modeling framework, the opportunistic agent, the physician, occurs in the presence of adverse selection. But the opportunistic principal, the patient, stems from the existence of moral hazard. Taken together, opportunism of the agent occurs with power asymmetries, while opportunism of the principal rests with insurance coverage. The economic rationale for this game of opportunism is short-term maximizing behavior, not behavior-oriented or outcome-oriented solutions (Wagner, 2019).

Induced demand

Physicians may induce demand. Two possibilities exist. One, physicians may be "perfect" agents, serving the interests of patients. Two, physicians may be "imperfect" agents, serving their own interests. In either case, physicians may influence the demand for healthcare. In theory, the cost and potential effectiveness of medical services guide the decisions. In practice, a physician may choose more cost-effective treatments to benefit the patient or more expensive procedures for personal gain (Henderson, 2018).

In a market, economic theory posits independence for supply and demand. An increase in supply means a rightward-shift, a decline in equilibrium price, and an increase in equilibrium quantity. But when supply and demand are dependent, *supplier-induced demand* may exist. An increase in the supply of healthcare may raise healthcare expenditure per capita. Doctors, acting as agents for their patients, use their discretionary power to undertake demand-shifting activities.

To demonstrate supplier-induced demand, assume equilibrium point *a* in figure 8.2. An increase in supply from S_1 to S_2 induces demand to increase from D_1 to D_2. Physicians advise their patients to consume more healthcare services. To hedge against uncertainty or a decline in revenue, physicians recommend additional treatments, surgeries, and consultations. The result is equilibrium point *b*. The change in price depends on the magnitude of the shifts.

Demand-shifting activities

Demand-shifting activities take the form of medical services and/or additional treatments. The practice includes two types of assistance: *referrals* (written orders by doctors to see specialists) and *consultations* (the act of seeking assistance from another healthcare provider

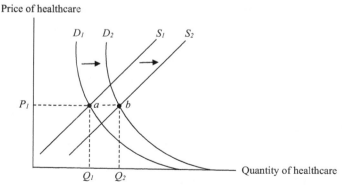

Figure 8.2 Induced demand.

Source: author

for therapeutic interventions, diagnostic studies, or other forms of care). One motive for demand-shifting activities is self-interest: doctors seek to boost their incomes. But supply-induced demand may also result when physicians consider the well-being of patients. If a physician acts in the absence of full information on a new disease or underestimates the ability of a patient to pay for the costs of additional treatments, recommended care may exceed nominated care. In either the case of self-interest or altruism, the result is an increase in demand for healthcare.

Interaction between physicians and patients

This conceptual framework for supply-induced demand provides a method of characterizing the interactions between physicians and patients (Mohammadshahi et al., 2019). The supply side includes nine components:

- Current income
- Target income
- Physician/population ratio
- Service price
- Payment method
- Consultation time
- Type of employment of physicians
- Observable physician characteristics
- Size and type of hospital.

The demand side includes three components:

- Observable characteristics of patients
- Nonclinical characteristics of patients
- Insurance coverage.

The potential for supplier-induced demand is a function of circumstance. If the patient has clear and observable characteristics and full information about treatment plans, while the physician's current income equals target income and acts in the best interest of the patient, no induced demand occurs. If the patient has several unobservable characteristics and is uninformed, while the physician's current income is less than target income and acts in self-interest, induced demand exists. Several other scenarios may occur. But the issue of importance is not whether physicians have the ability to induce demand, but whether the practice actually exists.

Several behavioral, institutional, and market factors provide incentive for supply-induced demand. Doctors make decisions to improve the health of patients, but their behavior is also influenced by payment arrangements and clinical uncertainty. The design of insurance or universal healthcare systems may not provide incentive to restrain demand. Information gaps and asymmetries encourage the expertise and medical advice of physicians.

The result is that supply-induced demand may not lead to net benefits in the healthcare market. From the perspective of the patient, providing additional services may exceed the level of treatment the patient would choose, leading to a better health outcome, but increasing cost. From the perspective of the physician, additional treatments may hedge against the uncertainty of disease or illness but increase compensation.

Economic research on supplier-induced demand has two implications. First, while physicians have the ability to induce demand, it is not clear empirically the extent to which the practice occurs. Incentive for the activity stems from the structure of the healthcare system, the physician's personal circumstance, the health of the patient, and the opportunity for personal gain. Second, even in the presence of asymmetric information, physicians may not have the ability to induce the demand for healthcare services. As policy, oversight, and the flow of information standardize medical practices, physician-induced demand may decrease (Henderson, 2018).

The impact of a pandemic

A pandemic creates a unique challenge. In theory, flattening the epidemic curve allows hospitals to obtain additional equipment, boost capacity, and prepare for the onset of cases. The supply of healthcare increases. Demand inducement means a subsequent increase in demand: healthcare providers advise patients to consume more medical care. There are two ways to view this case. On one hand, asymmetric information is present. With a new disease, patients have little information with respect to symptoms, treatments, and potential outcomes. On the other hand, while physicians benefit from experience, during a pandemic they have an evolving set of beliefs and circumstances. They may require additional procedures but are constrained by hospital capacity and personal knowledge. In a crisis, they may not be in position to advise patients on an optimal path of medical care.

Demographic characteristics

Demography is the study of the changing structure of human populations, including family structure, labor force participation, fertility, migration, and population. Demographic characteristics shift the demand for healthcare. In many countries, family structure evolves. Single parent households, blended families, cohabitation, divorce, and remarriage are on the rise. No one family form prevails. Throughout the course of a child's life, family structure may change. Several demographic characteristics are important. A change in labor force participation reflects the movement of more women into the workforce. The higher the level of a mother's education, the more likely she will participate in the labor force. Accompanying this trend is a decrease in the share of stay-at-home mothers. Among the entire population, the declining percentage of children living in "traditional" families, supplanted by children living with single or cohabiting parents, and more women in the labor force means a decrease in demand for family care and an increase in demand for medical providers.

Fertility

Fertility is a function of education, contraception, income, and labor force participation for women. As these factors increase, fertility falls. While fertility is linked to ethnicity and race, when women seek more education and training, enter the labor force at earlier ages, and delay family and children, fertility declines. In higher-income countries, the share of women reaching the end of childbearing years with two or fewer children is rising. In addition, while parents are more likely to be unmarried than in the past, they are more likely to have higher levels of education.

Migration

Migration patterns link to changes in the demand for healthcare. Immigrant women are less likely to be part of the labor force, relative to their domestically born counterparts. Foreign-born mothers do not hold jobs at comparable levels. Immigrants are also less likely to partici-pate in the formal healthcare system. As a result, as immigration increases, all else equal, the demand for healthcare decreases. In a pandemic, the lower level of assimilation of immigrant communities into formal institutional systems makes them vulnerable to the spread of dis-ease. If they have pre-existing conditions and less access to medical care, they may struggle to slow the spread of disease in their networks of families, friends, and colleagues.

Population

A change in population links directly to the demand for healthcare. At the aggregate level, rising population increases the demand for healthcare services. But the trend in many high-income countries is population decline as lower fertility rates lead to fewer children per couple. In this situation, two competing factors exist. In the aggregate, a lower population decreases the demand for healthcare. But as societies grow older, the stock of health capital declines. To offset hearing loss, osteoporosis, and poor eyesight, older people increase their demand for medical care. As costs increase, these procedures contribute to a rise in per capita spending on healthcare.

Health status

A change in health status shifts the demand for healthcare. A patient seeking treatment nor-mally initiates the process. In response to an accident, disease, illness, or injury, the demand for medical care (emergency visits, hospitalizations, outpatient visits) increases. Also, lifestyle choices impact demand. Exercise, better diets, and regular blood pressure tests increase the demand for preventive care (health examinations). With preventive care, healthcare services ensure that healthy people maintain their positive health status. With medical care, health-care services address current problems, relieve discomfort, or slow the spread of disease.

Change in demand

During a pandemic, as the disease spreads throughout a population, the demand for health-care increases from D_1 to D_2 (figure 8.3). At a price of P_0, quantity demanded increases from Q_1 to Q_2. When demand shifts to D_2, the clinical quantity of care increases from Q_{c1} to Q_{c2}, the level of care guaranteed to each patient.

Recall that the clinical quantity of care exists without consideration of price. As a result, D_{c2} is perfectly inelastic. Policymakers and healthcare administrators use D_{c2} to determine

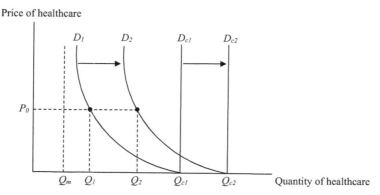

Figure 8.3 Increase in the demand for healthcare.

Source: author

additional resource needs, including personnel, equipment, and facilities. During a pandemic, shortages of these resources may exist, depending on whether a hospital exists near a disease hotspot, the level of preparation, and ability to acquire resources. For example, a hospital that exists in a disease hotspot with little preparation or ability to acquire resources may not be able to provide the clinical quantity of care for all patients. In this situation, the hospital may transfer patients to other facilities, if possible, and attempt to acquire proper equipment. In contrast, a hospital that exists in a disease hotspot but has protocols and resources in place has a better chance of providing the clinical quantity of care.

Acute care and chronic health problems

Acute care or short-term treatment consists of a patient developing a condition, seeking a physician, receiving treatment, and either recovering or dying. But with some patients the condition does not end. They live with *chronic health problems*, not recovering or dying, when a cure does not exist. Chronic health problems such as asthma, diabetes, heart disease, hypertension, and mood disorders contribute to the total cost of healthcare.

Socioeconomic standing

A change in socioeconomic status shifts the demand for healthcare through education and income. Even though these variables are correlated, each may lead to a change in demand for healthcare. Educational policies and programs serve as important public health interventions. From a social perspective, education engages the receptive capacity of individuals by imbuing them with awareness, knowledge, reason, and social skills. But education occurs at schools, home, and the community. When linking education with health outcomes, the process includes more than formal education (Hahn and Truman, 2015).

Education

Education is an attribute. The quality and quantity of schooling impacts lifetime opportunity, employability, and earnings. Even though a person possesses a level of educational attainment at a moment in time, learning is a dynamic process, including an evolving capacity for skills, knowledge, and capabilities. While education occurs in both formal and informal settings, much of the research linking education with health focuses on formal schooling (Hahn and Truman, 2015).

The information economy provides rising incomes for those with higher levels of education and training—engineers, doctors, lawyers, corporate managers, etc.—who invest in the education of their children. Compared to students of poorer families, by high school the children of higher-income families are several grade levels ahead. As an example, at the 150 most competitive colleges in the United States, more than 70 percent of the students come from families in the top income quintile; less than 5 percent come from the lowest income quintile (Markovits, 2020).

Several principal relationships exist between education and health. First, in order to learn, individuals require positive health status. Second, education includes courses on health. Third, physical education emphasizes the importance of physical activity. Fourth, education as a personal attribute serves as a component of health. Fifth, additional education provides more information on healthy choices. Taken together, these relationships demonstrate that educational attainment is both a component and contributing cause of health (Hahn and Truman, 2015).

With respect to specific pathways, higher levels of education are correlated with lower rates of diabetes, heart disease, and missed workdays and higher rates of self-reported health. The reason is that people with higher levels of education demand more preventive care, including vaccines, cancer screenings, flu shots, blood pressure tests, and health counseling.

During a pandemic, educational challenges relate to the alteration of the formal classroom model. Normally, educational attainment encourages people to be more effective consumers of healthcare services. Education improves the ability of individuals to understand diseases, treatments, and risk. But in a pandemic, as children are sent home and learn in an online environment, the formal classroom setting no longer provides the same educational service. To the extent to which this switch to online learning benefits some students at the expense of others, inferior health outcomes may result. In addition, during a pandemic, people of all ages must learn about health risks and disease outcomes from healthcare professionals and political leaders, who vary with respect to their abilities to convey information to the public. For individuals, a lack of knowledge and information during a pandemic may serve as a barrier to effective behavior.

Income

Income is linked to both educational attainment and healthcare outcomes. An increase in income precedes and predicts educational achievement. In addition, higher levels of income lead to an increase in demand for health-related resources, including healthcare, healthy food, and exercise, and decrease the demand for medical care. This outcome means that people with lower levels of income may experience higher levels of demand for medical care.

The challenge is especially acute for children. For children, a growing scholarly consensus exists on the outcomes of low income. First, living in poverty, even briefly, may create an environment for inferior health outcomes. Second, raising the incomes of poor families increases children's health, education, and earnings later in life (National Academies of Science, Engineering, and Medicine, 2019).

When disease spreads during a pandemic, children below the poverty line face several challenges. Classrooms close, hunger rises, and parental stress increases. These outcomes could leave low-income children with permanent scars (DeParle, 2020). Many countries have social systems that address these challenges, including child allowances for low-income families, which help children because they lead to an increase in housing, food, and education. But money and resources also reduce the stress on parents. This outcome is important for children because excessive stress may lead to "permanent changes in brain structure and function," creating inferior health outcomes later in life (National Academies of Science, Engineering, and Medicine, 2019). A pandemic exacerbates pre-existing problems with school closings, rising unemployment, fears of contagion, and additional stress.

Socioeconomic gradients in health

In a pandemic, young people may struggle to join the labor force. A rise in the unemployment rate reduces the compensation received by young workers because they work less and have lower wages. For individuals with lower levels of education, it may take years for potential income to recover. They may switch jobs more and experience higher levels of stress. But the impacts extend beyond wages. Workers that begin their careers during recession have higher rates of divorce, mortality, and disease later in life. The timing of entry into the labor market during a crisis may shorten their lifespans (Schwandt and von Wachter, 2019).

These health outcomes refer to *socioeconomic gradients in health*: those with higher incomes and levels of education experience better health outcomes. Gradients in income and education exist for racial and ethnic groups, measured by life expectancy, mortality, and other health indicators. Causal pathways lead to specific health outcomes, although the results vary across indicators, depending on age, historical period, gender, geographic location, life stage, nativity, and race (Braveman et al., 2010).

The need for targeted policies

The existence of socioeconomic gradients suggests the need for targeted policies that reduce health disparities. Gradient patterns reveal disparities across the socioeconomic spectrum, not just those with the least privilege. While tension exists with the allocation of resources between population-wide versus targeted approaches, a better understanding of socioeconomic gradients leads to policies that halt the perpetuation of social disparities. In this framework, the health available to the most advantaged members of society indicates what is possible for everyone. From an economics standpoint, the question is the allocation of healthcare resources. From an ethical standpoint, it may be unacceptable for some members of a society to experience inferior health outcomes (Braveman et al., 2010).

Insurance coverage

In addition to education and income, the rise of third-party insurance coverage impacts the demand for healthcare. An increase in the supply of insurance leads to a decrease in out-of-pocket payments by consumers. When out-of-pocket payments decline, the demand for medical care rises. This result means that, when the patient is not paying the full cost of medical care, an incentive exists for additional treatment, and output exceeds the social optimum.

Because insurance increases the demand for medical care, insurance companies dampen the effect with *coinsurance, copayments*, and *deductibles*. Coinsurance requires patients with insurance to pay a certain percentage of the medical bill. Copayments require fixed payments for each hospital visit, checkup, or prescription drug. Deductibles refer to the payments that must occur before insurance pays for medical expenses.

Countries vary with respect to the use of these requirements. With publicly funded health-care systems, copayments are normally low. An increase in the size of copayments raises the cost of an illness relative to the benefit of being insured. Taken together, the ability of an individual to afford better third-party insurance and pay for coinsurance, copayments, and deductibles rises with income.

Insurance coverage alters the demand for healthcare (figure 8.4). If a person does not have insurance, total out-of-pocket payment equals 100 percent of the cost, demand is D_{100}, and the policyholder consumes Q_1 at price P_1. A coinsurance rate of 25 percent means the insurance company pays 75 percent of expenses, demand is D_{25}, and the policyholder consumes Q_2 at price P_1. A reduction in the coinsurance rate rotates the demand curve, leading to a higher level of quantity demanded at a given price. With full insurance coverage and a coinsurance rate of zero, the demand curve rotates to D_0 with quantity demanded equal to Q_3 at a price of zero. If the healthcare system reduces costs and is able to decrease the price of care, P_1 falls to P_0 and patients without insurance consume Q_2 (Henderson, 2018).

In a pandemic, infected individuals may need emergency care. Systems of universal coverage that provide healthcare with little or no coinsurance, copayments, or deductibles are able to alleviate cost barriers that impede management of the pandemic. In systems without universal coverage, some members of the population lack insurance while the insurance for others is tied to employment.

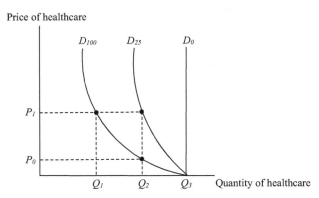

Figure 8.4 The impact of insurance on the demand for healthcare.
Source: adapted from Henderson (2018), Figure 5.3

Structural inequality

Structural inequality refers to the condition in which some members of a population receive unequal status relative to others. A society may perpetuate this arrangement through its decisions, opportunities, rights, and roles. Structural inequalities are observed in institutions such as the economy, education, law, and healthcare. They result from an economic and political imbalance of power. While certain members of a population establish the existing economic and political order, access to opportunity and wealth by marginalized groups may be limited. Historical patterns establish structural inequalities through discrimination, racism, and segregation; the targets of these beliefs and practices do not have the same access to resources. Structural inequalities alter people's sense of justice. They also lead to inferior health outcomes. While health is patterned according to socioeconomic conditions, it is also a function of structural inequality. A link exists between health and hierarchies of social advantage (Braveman et al., 2010).

Sources of inequality

Although socioeconomic factors such as education and income are associated with public policies toward poverty and education, a consideration of the sources of inequality reveals the degree to which structural inequality exists. When public policies address structural inequality, they focus on the link between inequality and opportunity. In mixed economies, inequality of outcomes occurs because capabilities, circumstances, knowledge, motivation, and skills are unequally distributed. These factors impact lifetime opportunities, employment, and earnings. The market places a higher value on human capital, so inequality of outcomes rises in societies that do not provide these characteristics for everyone. As an example, maldistribution in the quality and quantity of schooling leads to earnings gaps. The career choices of young people are influenced by their communities, creating an inequality of opportunities resulting from wealth, crime, and environmental degradation.

The role of institutions

Fiscal, educational, political, and business institutions play significant roles in inequality dynamics, especially with respect to the modern welfare state, labor markets, collective bargaining, minimum wages, privatization, corporate governance, and deregulation. The development of these institutions and processes, according to Piketty (2014), leads to capital accumulation in the hands of the few: "Capital is not an immutable concept: it reflects the state of development and prevailing social relations of each society ... The boundary between what private individuals can and cannot own has evolved considerably over time." The more that particular members of a population have access to capital, the more they benefit from the existing order.

The role of income

With structural inequality, income plays an important role. Families in lower income quintiles do not have the same access to healthcare services. The existence of a job does not guarantee access to a healthcare network. Lower levels of real income and living standards decrease health status because markets do not work for everyone and political systems may not correct market failures such as inequity (Stiglitz, 2012). The rise of the top income shares results from the rising inequality of labor earnings. This outcome, in turn, is a function of two factors: the rising inequality in access to education and an increase in compensation to members of the managerial class. Households with diversified categories of wealth—such as homes, business equity, financial investments, retirement, and insurance assets—have higher positions in the income distribution, compared to households with either no wealth or wealth dominated by a main residence. But this positive wealth effect is less significant for households with lower socioeconomic status.

The role of discrimination

An important source of inequality is racial and sexual *discrimination*, the behaviors, policies, and practices that perpetuate inequalities between groups. Due to discriminatory practices, women and those with minority status face additional challenges. For women, labor market discrimination may lead to different wages and employment opportunities. Marginalized members of a population may experience overcrowded housing, environmental hazards, and lower levels of air quality. During a pandemic, marginalized groups are more likely to have types of employment that limit their ability to quarantine.

Intersectionality

Intersectionality—the interconnected nature of social categorizations such as ethnicity, gender, race, and sex—provides a framework to assess the experience of people with multiple areas of marginalized status. By addressing how inequality and power manifest themselves through racism and sexism and the ways in which they are linked, intersectionality highlights the experiences of all people, not just those who benefit most from the existing order. Intersectionality reveals how inequality and power and their interlocking dynamics are structured for different members of a population, especially oppressed groups. By identifying how a group may suffer from marginalized and/or low-income status, intersectionality questions the notion of the same economic opportunity for all (Bowleg, 2020).

Inferior health status may result from discrimination, less access to economic resources, or the denial of healthcare. While racism may lead to deleterious health effects, evidence of discrimination exists with multiple social identities. But a focus on one form of discrimination may mask the experiences of groups facing multiple forms of discrimination. In this context, health inequalities may not increase linearly with the addition of a nondominant form of identity. "Intersectionality has become a central framework for understanding multiple, interacting, and context-dependent forms of social and health (dis)advantage based on social identity and position" (Schiem and Bauer, 2019).

Health risks from structural inequality

A pandemic reveals disproportionate health risk from structural inequality at the intersection of class, ethnicity, race, and occupation. Many frontline jobs deemed "essential" offer lower pay and higher risk and are staffed by members of the population "at the most marginalized intersections" (Bowleg, 2020). A pandemic also exposes inequality with respect to healthcare outcomes. For individuals, the elements of risk assemble in an interconnected framework. The foundation consists of age, biological sex, and genes. Cellular factors that attend these features alter the vulnerability to microbes. The next level includes chronic conditions and diseases, acquired over time, which impact the ability of viruses to enter the body. The outer layer consists of the socioeconomic circumstance and conditions that permeate life: access to healthcare, employment conditions, housing arrangements, nutritional status, exposure to environmental toxins, systematic discrimination, and racism (Wallis, 2020).

Health effects of Covid-19

This framework provides a method to analyze the health effects of Covid-19, the disease from the coronavirus pandemic. First, older people were more likely to get infected and die. But age is related to the quality of the immune system: as people get older, it is more difficult for the body to fight infections. Second, sex played a role during the coronavirus pandemic in that men were more likely to die from Covid-19 than women. This result stems from stronger immune systems among women and behaviors such as a greater propensity to smoke among men. Third, patients with chronic conditions were more vulnerable. Diabetes, heart disease, hypertension, and obesity provided the virus with more entry points into the body, including blood clots, heart attacks, heart failure, kidney injuries, and strokes. Fourth, structural inequality and racism served as external stressors. The risk of becoming infected occurred at work and home. Low-income and marginalized populations were less likely to shelter-in-place and avoid infections. They live in higher-density neighborhoods. They have higher levels of exposure to toxic environments. They have less access to medical care and face discrimination in the system. Once an infection occurs, they are more likely to experience a severe course and die. Overall, stressors from ethnic and racial discrimination worsen health status (Wallis, 2020).

An *infection gap* between majority and minority populations serves as a topic of investigation and part of the research on pandemics. Unless a country makes the effort to allocate healthcare resources equitably, a pandemic exacerbates pre-existing health inequalities for people who already have lower life expectancies than average.

Health justice

This analysis of structural inequality exists in a framework of *health justice*: the correlation between health outcomes on one hand and income, race/ethnicity, and sex on the other. Health justice provides a method to use laws, policies, and regulations to eliminate health disparities. In a pandemic, a framework of health justice offers a policy toolkit. The objective is to provide access to healthcare resource for all people, even those with multiple nondominant forms of identity.

In a pandemic, policy interventions slow the spread of disease, including isolation, quarantines, sheltering-in-place, social distancing, and shutting down nonessential businesses. But as public policies restrict personal liberties, the potential for discriminatory practices escalates, especially for people with intersectional identity. This reality holds true for people who are impacted by negative social determinants of health, including those who cannot stay home, lack flexible work schedules, have disabilities, experience food or housing insecurity, or do not have the housing space to separate the sick from the healthy. These members of society have less control over their living environments, have higher probabilities of living in substandard housing, and may suffer from segregation.

A focus on health justice means affordable and universal access to quality healthcare, policies to address the determinants of health outcomes, and financial, legal, and social protections to accompany interventions such as sheltering-in-place and social distancing. But efforts to improve the health of marginalized communities are impeded by inequitable legal systems, regulatory systems, social structures, and stereotypes that are not set up to address widespread health disparities (Benfer, 2015).

Freedom, justice, and liberty do not exist for all members of a population when they are reserved for those in middle- and upper-socioeconomic classes. To establish an equal opportunity for positive health status, interventions are necessary to address social health determinants. This process begins with the recognition that poor health status, poverty, and social injustice are interconnected.

> Health justice requires a regulatory and jurisprudential approach that consistently and reliably considers the health ramifications of judicial and legislative decision making. The preponderance of the evidence clearly indicates the urgent need for robust measures that address the deleterious effects of economic, societal, cultural, environmental, and social conditions, as well as the policies and legal systems that have devastating effects on health.
>
> (Benfer, 2015)

Laws, policies, and social structures must be designed to anticipate and address the social outcomes of poor health and the effects of inequality. In many societies, precedent exists with universal healthcare, early childhood interventions, access to education, social support services, workplace safety, consumer protection, and accommodations for the disabled (Benfer, 2015). Health justice protects the liberty of all members of a population while improving the health of marginalized communities.

Summary

A pandemic exposes disparities of health outcomes between different socioeconomic and marginalized groups. With less access to healthcare resources, people in lower socioeconomic classes or marginalized status may suffer infections at higher rates than other members of the population. Although no one has natural immunity to a new disease, socioeconomic and structural disparities demonstrate what happens when a pandemic is layered upon entrenched inequalities. Because of less access to healthcare resources and pre-existing medical conditions, those with marginalized status have a higher potential of inferior health outcomes.

With respect to healthcare, economists treat health like other investments that enhance future productivity. The model of health demand views investment in health as the consumption of medical care and other areas of healthcare. Individuals have a level of health that depreciates with age. Individuals invest in their health because greater health leads to more time for both market and nonmarket activities. At any age, a person determines an optimal stock of health by equating the user price of investment in health with the marginal efficiency. In this framework, improvements in health increase human capital, the knowledge and skills embodied in work effort that leads to the creation of economic value.

The demand for healthcare is a function of both physician and patient factors. Physicians impact the demand for healthcare through their positions in the system. They are agents of their patients and providers of healthcare. By recommending additional care, physicians create demand for their own services. Patient factors include demographic characteristics, health status, socioeconomic status, and structural inequities.

During a pandemic, policy interventions slow the spread of disease, including isolation, quarantines, sheltering-in-place, social distancing, and shutting down nonessential businesses. But as public policies restrict personal liberties, the potential for discriminatory practices escalates, especially for people with intersectional identity. This reality holds true for people who are impacted by negative social determinants of health, including those who cannot stay home, lack flexible work schedules, have disabilities, experience food or housing insecurity, or do not have the housing space to separate the sick from the healthy.

Chapter takeaways

LO1   Individuals with relatively more access to resources are in a better position to address the healthcare crisis during a pandemic, while those with fewer resources are more likely to suffer harmful consequences.

LO2   The demand for healthcare is a function of physician factors and patient factors, including demographic characteristics, health status, and socioeconomic status.

LO3   Physicians shift the demand for healthcare by serving as agents for patients.

LO4   Demographic characteristics shift the demand for healthcare by altering population size, family structure, labor force participation, average number of children per family, opportunities for family care, and reliance on medical providers.

LO5   Health status shifts the demand for healthcare through a desire for treatment, which is a function of lifestyle choices, accidents, illnesses, injuries, and diseases.

LO6   Socioeconomic status shifts the demand for healthcare through several factors, including education, income, healthcare spending, poverty, and inequality.

LO7   Structural inequality shifts the demand for healthcare through discrimination and racism.

Terms and concepts

Acute care
Adverse selection
Chronic health problems
Clinical quantity of care
Coinsurance

Consultations

Copayments

Deductibles

Demography

Derived demand

Discrimination

Health justice

Human capital

Infection gap

Intersectionality

Moral hazard

Principal-agent relationship

Referrals

Socioeconomic gradients in health

Structural inequality

Supplier-induced demand

Questions

1. During a pandemic, explain how inequality of wealth may became inequality of health. What are the characteristics of groups of people that are in the most precarious position with respect to health outcomes? Why?

2. Explain why economists treat health like other investments that enhance future productivity. What is the implication of this approach?

3. Explain the model of derived demand in figure 8.1. In what sense is demand derived? How does a healthcare system determine Q_m, the minimum health requirement? How does a healthcare system determine Q_{cf}, the clinical quantity of care? To answer these questions, think about the provision of healthcare in terms of costs and benefits.

4. For person j over time t, the demand for healthcare (HC_{jt}) is written as a functional relationship between healthcare and its determinants: $HC_{jt} = f(P_t, D_{jt}, H_{jt}, S_{jt}, I_{jt})$. During a pandemic, how do the independent (right-hand-side) variables interact to impact HC_{jt}?

5. Explain how physicians serve as a determinant of the demand for healthcare. In your answer, discuss the principal-agent relationship. In the process of delivering healthcare, what motivates physicians? How does a pandemic alter the framework?

6. With respect to the model of induced demand (figure 8.2), explain why an increase in supply leads to an increase in demand. Under what circumstance would price increase? During a pandemic, how is this model relevant?

7. How do demographic characteristics of a population, including family structure, labor force participation, fertility, migration, and population, impact the demand for healthcare? During a pandemic, how important are these factors?

8. In a pandemic, an increase in demand for medical services (figure 8.3) leads to an increase in the clinical quantity of care. What is the implication of this change in the clinical quantity of care with respect to costs, benefits, the surge in patients, and hospital capacity?

9. Explain the link between education/income and healthcare outcomes. How do higher levels of education and income lead to better health? During a pandemic, how important are education and income in determining healthcare outcomes?

10. What types of structural inequalities impact human health and the demand for healthcare? What are the roles of pre-existing conditions and a lack of resources for healthcare services? During a pandemic, how does structural inequality complicate the provision of healthcare?

References

Benfer, Emily. 2015. "Health justice: a framework (and call to action) for the elimination of health inequality and social justice," *American University Law Review*, 65, 2: 275–351.

Bowleg, Lisa. 2020. "We're not all in this together: on Covid-19, intersectionality, structural inequality," *American Journal of Public Health*, 110, 7 (July): 917.

Braveman, Paula A., Cubbin, Catherine, Egerter, Susan, Williams, David R., and Pamuk, Elsie. 2010. "Socioeconomic disparities in health in the United States: what the patterns tell us," *American Journal of Public Health*, 100, S1 (April): S186–S196.

DeParle, Jason. 2020. "The coronavirus generation," *The New York Times*, August 23.

Editorial. 2020. "The America we need," *The New York Times*, April 9.

Grossman, Michael. 1972. "On the concept of health capital and the demand for health," *Journal of Political Economy*, 80, 2, (March–April): 223–255.

Hahn, Robert A., and Truman, Benedict I. 2015. "Education improves public health and improves health equity," *International Journal of Health Services*, 45, 4 (May): 657–678.

Henderson, James W. 2018. *Health Economics and Policy*. Boston, Massachusetts: Cengage Learning Inc.

Markovits, Daniel. 2020. *The Meritocracy Trap: How America's Foundational Myth Feeds Inequality, Dismantles the Middle Class, and Devours the Elite*. New York: Penguin Random House.

Mohammadshahi, Marita, Yazdani, Shahrooz, Olyaeemanesh, Alireza, Sari, Ali, Yaseri, Mehdi, and Sefiddashti, Sara. 2019. "A scoping review of components of physician-induced demand for designing a conceptual framework," *Journal of Preventive Medicine and Public Health*, 52, 2 (March): 72–81.

National Academies of Science, Engineering, and Medicine. 2019. *A Roadmap to Reducing Child Poverty*. Washington D.C.: The National Academies Press.

Piketty, Thomas. 2014. *Capital in the Twenty-First Century*. Cambridge, Massachusetts: Belknap Press: An Imprint of Harvard University Press.

Schiem, Ayden I., and Bauer, Greta R. 2019. "The intersectional discrimination index: development and validation of measures of self-reported enacted and anticipated discrimination for intercategorical analysis," *Social Science & Medicine*, 226: 225–235.

Schwandt, Hannes, and von Wachter, Till. 2019. "Unlucky cohorts: estimating the long-term effects of entering the labor market in a recession in large cross-sectional data sets," *Journal of Labor Economics*, 37, S1 (January): S161–S198.

Stiglitz, Joseph. 2012. *The Price of Inequality*. New York: W.W. Norton & Company.

Vega, William A., and Shribney, William M. 2017. "Growing income inequality sustains health disparities," *American Journal of Public Health*, 107, 10 (October): 1606–1607.

Wagner, Dirk N. 2019. "The opportunistic principal," *Kyklos*, 72, 4 (November): 637–657.

Wallis, Claudia. 2020. "Why some people get terribly sick from Covid-19," *Scientific American*, August 20. https:///www.scientificamerican.com/article/why-some-people-get-terribly-sick-from-covid19/.

9 Energy, the environment, and climate change

Learning objectives

After reading this chapter, you will be able to:

LO1 Explain how a pandemic impacts the global environment.

LO2 Present a model framework that shows how a pandemic impacts energy, the environment, and climate.

LO3 Analyze why a pandemic disrupts energy markets.

LO4 Discuss the mechanism in which a pandemic alters the flow of pollution from the economy into the environment.

LO5 Explain how a reduction in economic activity impacts the release of greenhouse gas emissions and whether this leads to lasting climate effects.

LO6 Discuss strategies for a sustainable future.

Chapter outline

- Global environment
- Environmental framework
- Energy effects
- Environmental effects
- Climate effects
- Strategies for environmental sustainability
- Summary

Global environment

During the coronavirus pandemic, an unprecedented event occurred. In April 2020, because of a substantial decrease in the global demand for oil, the price per barrel plunged. In fact, for a few days, the price of a contract to supply West Texas Intermediate crude fell below zero. The price of oil is determined in the futures market, in which futures contracts establish agreements to buy and sell oil at a future date. Normally, the futures contract is bought and sold many times before the date of delivery. During April 2020, traders were caught in a market to sell their contracts before they received the oil. The economic shutdown that decreased economic activity led to a reduction in global consumption by over 20 million barrels per day (figure 9.1). With a surplus of oil on land and in tankers at sea and no buyers in the market, storage capacity filled. Oil prices fell below zero, meaning suppliers had to pay customers to take the oil off of their hands.

A pandemic forces countries to implement interventions that both reduce human contact and shutter nonessential forms of economic activity. During the process of economic shutdown, recessionary forces emerge. The provision of services declines. Global supply chains sever. Travel decreases. Unemployment rises. But several indirect effects occur, which serve as this chapter's topics, including a reduction in energy consumption, a change in environmental quality, and an impact on the climate. These outcomes reinforce the need to strengthen energy transitions, maintain environmental quality, and contribute to programs that lead to climate solutions.

First, a reduction in economic activity from shutdown interventions leads to a decrease in energy demand. The impact on energy sectors, especially buildings, industry, transportation, and electricity generation, is widespread. Factories and manufacturing plants consume less natural gas. The severing of global supply chains decreases the consumption of oil. Individuals drive less and cycle more. As more people work from home, the demand for electricity declines for office buildings. Taken together, these effects alter the trajectory of energy consumption.

Second, a reduction in the production of output leads to less pollution and an improvement in environmental quality. In this context, the environment provides raw materials, energy, and water to the economy. After the economy uses these resources for the production of output and provision of ecosystem services, they return to the environment in the form of pollution

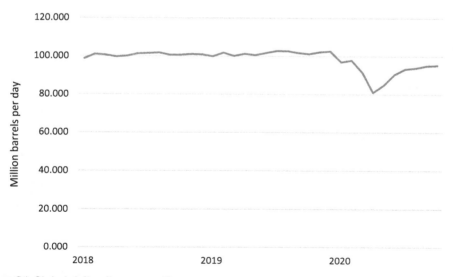

Figure 9.1 Global daily oil consumption.

Source: author using data from the U.S. Energy Information Administration, https://www.eia.gov/outlooks/steo/data.php

and waste. But when economic activity declines, less pollution flows into the air, water, and ground. Urban areas experience cleaner skies.

Third, a decline in energy demand reduces fossil fuel consumption, the process of burning coal, oil, and natural gas as fuels and sources of power. This outcome leads to a decrease in *greenhouse gases* (GHG), a byproduct of combustion. Because a change in the atmospheric concentration of GHG alters climate effects, an evaluation of the overall process demonstrates potential convergence between the pandemic and climate crises. But whether a short-run change in GHG impacts the long-term process of climate change depends on lasting effects. This chapter addresses these impacts on energy, the environment, and climate, arguing that both positive and negative environmental outcomes occur.

Environmental framework

Because of a reduction in economic activity, including transportation, industry, and tourism, both fossil fuel consumption and GHG decline while air quality improves. But the disposal of personal protective equipment (PPE), including face masks and hand gloves, and the generation of hospital waste lead to negative environmental outcomes. Taken together, a pandemic creates both positive and negative effects (figure 9.2).

Energy effects

To analyze the impact of a pandemic on energy, it is important to distinguish between an *energy system* and an *energy sector*. An energy system is a network that links energy sources, storage, and transmission to the agents of energy demand. An energy sector serves a purpose within the energy system, including power sources, fuels, electricity generation,

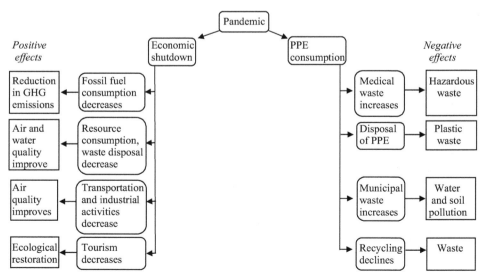

Figure 9.2 Energy, environmental, and climate effects of a pandemic.
Source: adapted from Rume and Didar Ul-Islam (2020)

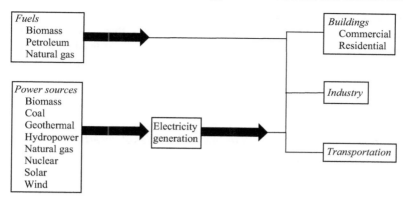

Figure 9.3 Model of an energy system.
Source: adapted from Sadler (2020), Figure 2.1

buildings, industry, and transportation. The primary sources of energy, including renewables, nuclear power, and fossil fuels, flow into the buildings, industrial, transportation, and electricity sectors (figure 9.3).

Every time individuals consume energy to cool their homes, fuel their vehicles, or undertake other energy-intensive activities, they convert energy from one form to another. As an example, in vehicles, the engine converts the chemical energy in petroleum into mechanical work. The mechanical work powers the wheels. This example of the *energy conversion chain* demonstrates how primary energy is converted into final form. The chain is used to analyze how the supply of energy in the form of fuel and power sources satisfies the demand for energy from buildings, industry, transportation, and electricity generation.

Global energy trends

According to the International Energy Agency (2019), energy markets demonstrate disparities. Parts of developing countries do not have access to electricity. Both carbon emission targets and climate targets are difficult to reach. Differing levels of air quality depend on the patterns of globalization, urbanization, and industrialization. A gap exists between the expectation of renewable energy satisfying energy demand on a global scale and the incremental infusion of solar, wind, and geothermal technologies. In this environment, the IEA (2019) forecasts global energy demand to increase one percent annually until 2040. Low-carbon sources such as solar photovoltaics will supply half the growth, with natural gas supplying one-third. The global demand for coal will flatten in the 2020s while the global demand for oil will flatten in the 2030s. The infusion of clean energy technology will not offset the consumption of fossil fuels.

Energy security–the ability to satisfy energy demand in the absence of high energy prices, environmental degradation, and conflict–remains an important global priority. Natural disasters, volatile prices, and geopolitical conflict threaten global energy supply. Growing interconnection increases the integration of global energy systems but enhances their vulnerability. In this framework, the provision of electricity complements energy security. In developing countries, advances in digital technology and cost reductions create opportunities. But new challenges stem from data privacy, the integration of electric vehicles, and energy storage (IEA, 2019). Finally, to power Asia's growing economies, a three-way race exists between renewables, natural gas, and coal. While the existing stock of coal-fired power plants and factories that burn coal provide "staying power," investment in new coal technology is declining (IEA, 2019).

Energy transition

Energy transition is the "complex socio-technical processes of *decarbonization* within energy systems, and involves both bringing in low, or zero, carbon energy and phasing out old, high carbon energy" (Kuzemko et al., 2020). It signifies the period between the introduction of a new resource or technology and growth into a significant share of the market. Transition includes growth in renewable technology, energy efficiency, and synergies between the two. Reasons for the transition include cost-effectiveness, scalable technology, and climate targets. To meet a rising global energy demand, renewable energy technology could satisfy up to two-thirds of the total while contributing to a reduction in greenhouse gas emissions (Gielen et al., 2019).

Accelerating the transition to clean energy requires innovation in the buildings, industry, transportation, and electricity sectors. But forecasting the timeframe for energy transition is challenging. Projections of the growth of renewables and natural gas have been unreliable. The ages of hydrogen and nuclear have not come to pass. Energy transition requires decades for new technologies to assume a significant market share.

> Although a successful transformation is found to be technically possible, it will require the rapid introduction of policies and fundamental political changes toward concerted and coordinated efforts to integrate global concerns, such as climate change, into local and national policy priorities.
>
> (Gielen et al., 2019)

Presence of uncertainty

In the presence of uncertainty, it is important to recognize the limitations of reaching definitive conclusions; however, the following sections, which incorporate the analysis of Kuzemko et al. (2020), highlight the continuities and discontinuities with pre-pandemic and post-pandemic energy trends in four areas: temporalities of energy system change, finance and investment, governance, and social practices. In a pandemic, shutdown and recession define the short term, economic recovery defines the medium term, and the following years define the long term. In this process, some countries experience protracted downturns and recoveries, leading to consequential long-term effects. In other countries, shorter downturns and recoveries lead to the status quo.

Temporalities of energy system change

Public policies and market conditions determine the temporalities for the nature and pace of energy system change, especially with respect to a decline in fossil fuel technology and growth in low-carbon energy. The short-term impact of a pandemic includes a decrease in energy demand, especially electricity, oil, and liquified natural gas. At the same time, a pandemic slows the installation of new energy platforms for power facilities, offshore wind technology, and power infrastructure. Global supply chain interruptions push governments and markets to accelerate processes of de-globalization with respect to energy components, materials, and assembled goods. In the medium term, the fate of fossil fuel networks depends on the evolving conditions of decarbonization programs. If investment in fossil fuel technology continues to decline, the supply of coal, natural gas, and oil will exhibit decreasing trends. But long-term effects are empirical in nature and subject to several factors, including the shape of economic recovery and the extent to which government stimulus plans both accelerate clean energy production and support existing fossil fuel infrastructure (Kuzemko et al., 2020).

Investment in clean technology and divestment from fossil fuels

Important aspects of energy transition entail the financial power of energy actors and support for fossil fuels industries. Multinational fossil fuel companies propagate investments in coal in developing countries, expanding the supply of coal-fired electricity. But growing awareness of the financial risks of fossil fuel investments coupled with concerns about stranded fossil fuel reserves has led to investments in energy efficiency, grid management, renewables, and energy storage. The pandemic may accelerate these trends. The growing cost-effectiveness and rising returns from solar, wind, and geothermal technologies underpins investment in clean technology and potential divestment from fossil fuels. But a majority of energy investment comes from government spending. In the medium term, a pandemic forces public sectors to finance extensive economic recovery packages. Therefore, in the long term, investments in clean energy depend on the level of economic and job multipliers that stem from infrastructure projects, building retrofits, renewable technology, and whether policymakers and business leaders choose the path of clean energy transition (Kuzemko et al., 2020).

Energy governance

A pandemic interrupts the movement toward global interconnection. As countries look inward, a pandemic highlights the lack of coordinated global energy governance. Reacting to a pandemic, policymakers prioritize energy security rather than decarbonization or clean energy technology. Rising levels of government intervention create discontinuities with respect to market trends. Global climate conferences that discuss clean energy technology are postponed. But innovation in global governance, such as the Paris Agreement (2016), the United Nations Sustainable Development Goals (2015), and the International Renewable Energy Agency (2009) provide mechanisms to diversify the global energy supply. But the "frailty of the current system of global cooperation might reinforce the decentralization of energy governance from the multilateral to national and transnational to local scales" (Kuzemko et al., 2020).

Social practices

How energy transition impacts social groups differs between and within countries. Seaside communities facing rising ocean levels may value a movement toward renewables more than members of the fossil fuel industry. But a rising consensus about the ill effects of the climate crisis creates momentum for appropriate solutions, including clean energy technology. While a pandemic mobilizes societies to address problems of public health, security, and employment, both high carbon and clean energy industries seek support in government recovery programs. But pre-pandemic environmental concerns, attitudes toward cleaner air, and the demand for alternative modes of transportation influence policymakers. A link exists between economic activity, the consumption of fossil fuels, environmental quality, and human health. A pandemic highlights this interconnection (Kuzemko et al., 2020).

Energy innovation

A pandemic creates unique challenges for the process of *energy innovation*, the set of programs and procedures that lead to new or improved energy technologies. Economies that innovate in energy markets adopt different approaches, but public sectors play an important role by initiating and incentivizing the process (IEA, 2020a). A basic role for government is funding the research, development, and diffusion (RD&D) of new technology. But a gap exists between RD&D budgets and clean energy goals. The budgets are insufficient to maintain the resilience of energy systems while delivering reductions in greenhouse gas emissions (IEA, 2020a). Through measures such as countercyclical spending on technology demonstration and RD&D, public sectors accelerate innovation in clean energy technology. But during a pandemic, companies reduce spending on clean technology. In addition, governments finance recovery programs, straining their budgets. A pandemic impacts the areas of energy system innovation—decentralization, digitization, flexibility, and electrification—by altering the processes of systems operation, infrastructure development, and regulation (Gielen et al., 2019). Policy and market uncertainties reduce the flow of resources for RD&D. The "world's capacity to bring new technologies to market will be weaker as a result of the disruptions caused by the pandemic" (IEA, 2020a).

One study on the impact of the coronavirus pandemic on the electricity sector in the province of Ontario, Canada concluded that electrical demand declined in the months following economic shutdown, compared to the previous year (Abu-Rayash and Dincer, 2020). Specific changes were the decrease in daily demand and demand during peak hours. The highest daily reductions in demand were observed on weekends. In addition, the previous year exhibited a weekly pattern in which electricity demand would increase throughout the week and peak on the weekend. During the pandemic, electricity demand would reach a peak during the middle of the week and then decline throughout the weekend. This pattern resulted from a change in economic activity. During the first few days of the week, people working from home were experiencing greater workloads, compared to the rest of the week. During shutdown, individuals could not seek social and recreational activities. The result of the electricity demand footprint demonstrates that, due to the pandemic, business and lifestyle changes occurred (Abu-Rayash and Dincer, 2020).

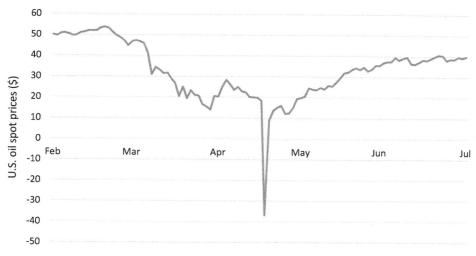

Figure 9.4 U.S. oil spot prices become negative during April 2020.

Source: author using data from the U.S Energy Information Association, https://www.eia.gov/opendata/qb.php?sdid+PET.RWTC.D.

Issues in pandemic economics 9.1: Disruption in the oil market

In 2020, the coronavirus pandemic impacted the global oil market more than geo-political events such as OPEC embargos or conflict between oil-producing countries. The pandemic weakened the ability of oil suppliers to control the market, driving down oil spot prices to levels not previously experienced in the marketplace (figure 9.4). A large decline in price resulted from a decrease in global demand, especially transportation:

> In the run-up to the collapse of crude oil prices in early 2020 it was primarily a division between Russia and Saudi Arabia within OPEC which appeared to be the main force at work, but then the Covid-19 pandemic took over, followed by US oil price turning negative in April 2020, as May contracts expired and traders had to offload stocks with ongoing storage becoming extremely limited.
>
> (Jefferson, 2020)

Environmental effects

In the field of economics, the environment is considered an asset that provides services for the economy. It is an important asset, of course, as it provides the life-sustaining services that support human existence. Similar to other assets, however, economies should maintain or enhance environmental quality, or at least prevent accelerated depreciation. As an asset, the environment provides raw materials such as metals, water, and wood. In production processes accompanied by energy resources, which also flow from the environment to the economy, raw materials are transformed into output. But the environment also provides eco-system services, including air, biodiversity, carbon sequestration, and water quality. But after production and human consumption, energy and raw materials eventually return to the environment in the form of air and water pollution, solid waste, and waste heat (Tietenberg and Lewis, 2018).

Pollution taxonomy

The damage from pollution depends on the environment's *absorptive capacity*, the ability of the environment to assimilate waste and pollution. Two categories of pollutants exist. The environment has little or no absorptive capacity for *stock pollutants* such as lead, persistent synthetic chemicals, and nonbiodegradable bottles. As a result, the optimal level of these pollutants is zero. Stock pollutants accumulate in the environment, increase their persistence as pollution continues to flow, and create an interdependent effect between the present and the future. As stock pollutants increase in the present, their future environmental damage effects rise.

The environment has higher absorptive capacity for *fund pollutants*, the pollutants that become diluted, disperse, or transform into substances that are harmless to ecological systems and human health. If the environmental rate of absorption exceeds the rate of polluting emissions, environmental assimilation occurs. An important fund pollutant is carbon dioxide, a biproduct of the burning of fossil fuels, absorbed by plants, trees, and oceans (Tietenberg and Lewis, 2018).

The efficient allocation of fund pollutants depends on damage cost and abatement cost (figure 9.5). As emissions rise, marginal damage cost from pollution increases. The environment assimilates smaller levels of pollution but is less tolerant of larger levels. Marginal abatement cost increases as more pollution is controlled. Together, these costs establish an efficient allocation (P^*). If the polluter emits P_0, the benefit to society from reducing pollution (reflected by marginal damage cost) exceeds marginal abatement cost. Pollution reduction should occur until marginal damage cost equals marginal abatement cost (P^*). At P^*, total

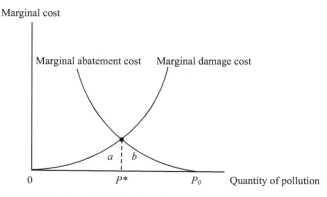

Figure 9.5 Fund pollutants–the efficient allocation.

Source: adapted from Tietenberg and Lewis (2018), Figure 14.2

damage cost equals area *a* while total control cost equals area *b*. From an economics per-spective, reducing pollution below $P*$ would not be cost-effective.

Another way to classify pollution is through a nonmutually exclusive *zone of influence*: the impact of pollution on the natural environment in terms of geographic space. The zone of influ-ence includes horizontal and vertical elements. A *local pollutant* has low horizontal impact. A *regional pollutant* has greater potential to inflict environmental damage and larger horizontal impact. A *global pollutant* has the greatest horizontal impact. Because zones of influence are not mutually exclusive, pollutants such as nitrogen oxide, produced in combustion processes, may be both local and regional. With vertical elements, pollutants possess *spatial variability*, attributable to their chemistry and dispersion. Polluting effects may concentrate close to the Earth's surface, such as with lead, alter atmospheric concentrations, such as with carbon dioxide, or possess intermediate effects. With environmental management, each category of pollution requires its own policy response (Tietenberg and Lewis, 2018).

Pollution during a pandemic

In this economy/environment framework, the major sources of ambient (outdoor) air pol-lution are industry, power generation, residential energy consumption, and transportation. When economic activity declines during a deliberate recession, pollution flows decrease. But a pandemic alters these flows. Some factories close. Global supply chains suspend product distribution. Retail establishments switch to online markets. Meatpacking and power generation remain. Transportation between and within countries declines, including business and leisure activities. As countries close their borders, airlines cancel flights. But as hospitals discharge personal protective equipment, waste increases. The spatial vari-ability of pollution between countries changes because shutdown measures have differ-ent effects on emissions and waste. In some countries, a decrease in polluting emissions results from changes in the transportation sector more than power generation or buildings (Venter et al., 2020).

As an example, nitrogen oxide (NO_2), a highly reactive pollutant, with local and regional effects, creates pathways to human health, increasing mortality rates through respiratory problems and cellular inflammation. Pollution from the flow of traffic serves as the major source of NO_2 emissions. At the local and regional levels, millions of people die annually from air pollution and poor air quality from the release of pollutants such as NO_2 (Muhammad et al., 2020). During the coronavirus pandemic, ground level NO_2 concentrations declined in multiple countries when they implemented economic shutdown measures (Venter et al., 2020).

A pandemic impacts industrial and transportation sectors as factories and drivers respond to a decline in business activity and lockdown policies. The overall effect is a decrease in the global demand for coal, natural gas, and oil. When the consumption of fossil fuels declines, carbon dioxide emissions decrease, a pollutant with an extensive vertical element. Overall, a pandemic leads to reductions in local, regional, and global air pollutants but an increase in waste from the healthcare sector. Therefore, a pandemic impacts the natural environment in both positive and negative ways (Berman and Ebisu, 2020; Muhammad et al., 2020; Venter et al., 2020).

Future pollution flows

Similar to previous economic downturns, the environmental concern is that after a pandemic the global economy will quickly return to previous pollution patterns. When economic activity returns to pre-pandemic levels, economic growth resumes. The flow of pollution increases. But the environmental changes resulting from a pandemic demonstrate the potential for reducing the risk to public health. Less pollution leads to a reduction in pollution-related mortality. A cleaner environment reduces pollution-related deaths. The extent to which countries maintain lower pollution levels depends on environmental and energy policy, collective behavior, and economic restructuring (Venter et al., 2020).

Pollution, disease, and mortality

An important empirical question relates to these interrelated outcomes. On a global scale, does the decrease in deaths from lower pollution levels outweigh the increase in deaths from disease? A working hypothesis is that, over the long term, the outcome of lower levels of global mortality that result from less pollution is stronger than the outcomes of higher levels of global mortality from a disease pandemic. To study the hypothesis, research compares the pathway between pollution and mortality on one hand to the pathway between the pandemic disease and mortality on the other. (Complicating the research is the fact that the two effects are not mutually exclusive. Lower levels of air pollution make individuals less susceptible to disease.) As research occurs, "empirical data will emerge to fill in the knowledge gaps and uncertainties associated with the air pollution health burden attribution" (Venter et al., 2020).

Climate effects

The Earth is smoldering. Heat waves in Australia and the Middle East, hurricanes on the Atlantic and Gulf coasts, droughts in Argentina and Mexico, and wildfires in California, Oregon, and Washington ravage human populations. Over time, these climate effects become more pronounced. *Climate change*, the alteration of climate patterns resulting from higher global average surface temperatures, serves as the world's most important environmental challenge. When the world battles a pandemic, it has "a much bigger and stronger opponent ... called the climate emergency" (Dans, 2020). In the post-pandemic phase, production rises, employment increases, and economies recover; however, without drastic changes to economic activity and energy choices, especially with respect to decarbonization, renewable energy, and climate policy, the climate crisis will continue.

Integrated assessment model of climate change

Integrated assessment models (IAMs) use both economic and climate research to simulate economic, energy, and climate activity, address how economic choices lead to climate outcomes, and determine how changes in average global surface temperature alter climate effects. The IAMs include the incentives and choices that underlie economic decision making and the physical laws of environmental systems. The IAMs require several simplifying assumptions, including the relationship between changes in atmospheric concentrations and climate

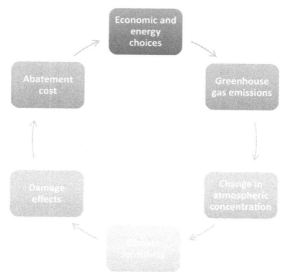

Figure 9.6 Integrated assessment model of climate change.
Source: author

outcomes and the value of environmental damage; however, IAMs establish a framework to understand how climate policy slows greenhouse gas emissions. One of the most important IAMs is the Dynamic Integrated Economy/Climate (DICE) model of Professor William Nordhaus (2019) of Yale University, the 2018 co-recipient of the Nobel Prize in Economics for his work on the economics of climate change. A computer model, DICE integrates economics and climate science, assesses the costs of economic and energy activity, and the benefits of emission abatement. The model (figure 9.6) demonstrates that, if the global economy continues on its current trajectory, global average surface temperature will rise, leading to volatile climate outcomes and extensive economic damages.

Economic and energy choices

Globalization, modernization, and urbanization characterize the global economy. Globalization leads to global networks of finance, information, migration, production, social connection, technology, and trade. By bringing agents closer together, the networks facilitate the process of exchange. The result is an ever-expanding web of global linkages. Modernization transforms society, from rural and agrarian to urban and industrial. Although countries develop at their own pace, modernity entails an emphasis on technological change, the flow of information, and economic evolution. The global migration of people from rural to urban areas demonstrates the process of urbanization. The United Nations estimates that, in the year 2007, the world's urban residents equaled the number of rural inhabitants for the first time. According to a forecast by the United Nations Population Division, by the year 2050, 70 percent of the world's population will live in cities. During the next several decades, almost all of the world's population growth will occur in urban areas. According to International Energy Agency (2020b), the result of these trends will be an increase in the demand for energy, especially natural gas and oil.

Greenhouse gas emissions

Economic and energy choices lead to fossil fuel combustion and GHG, including carbon dioxide, methane, and nitrous oxide, which absorb and emit radiant energy within the infrared range. The GHG, similar to economic problems like pollution, involve a *negative externality*, impacting people on a global scale at no cost to the responsible agents. With regulatory jurisdiction, full information, and perfect competition, economic theory argues for either direct regulation, a tax equal to the marginal external costs of additional emissions, or the allocation of property rights. But the world has multiple jurisdictions, long time horizons, multiple market structures, and weak representation of future generations. As a result, a deep and complex set of problems exists, including intertemporal collective action and interconnection with other forms of market failure (Stern, 2006).

Since the Industrial Revolution, the world has burned oil, natural gas, and coal in furnaces, power plants, and vehicles. These processes increase the flow of carbon dioxide (CO_2), a byproduct of the combustion process, into the atmosphere. On a global scale, CO_2 emissions, the most prominent greenhouse gas, come from fossil fuel combustion in industry, forestry practices, industrial processes, and other uses of land. Economic growth leads to an increase in both industrial and nonindustrial CO_2 emissions, although economic growth impacts industrial emissions to a greater extent (Sanchez and Stern, 2016). This century has experienced a rising level of CO_2 from fossil fuel combustion and industrial processes. But the coronavirus pandemic led to an abrupt decrease in global CO_2 emissions of almost 10 percent in the first half of 2020 compared to the same six-month period in 2019 (Liu et al., 2020).

Change in atmospheric concentration

The accumulation of greenhouse gases in the atmosphere absorbs heat from the sun, causing the *greenhouse effect*, the natural process that warms the Earth's surface. The concentration of CO_2 in the atmosphere is measured in parts per million (ppm), the number of molecules of gases per million molecules of air. At the beginning of industrialization, in 1750, the concentration of CO_2 in the atmosphere equaled 277 ppm. At the end of 2020, CO_2 concentration was 413 ppm, a level the Earth has not experienced in more than a million years (figure 9.7).

Climate sensitivity

The planet's energy balance results from the flow of the Sun's solar energy and the flow from Earth back into space. Average global surface temperature is a function of changes in radiated and absorbed energy within the energy balance. In equilibrium, stable temperature patterns occur. But average global surface temperature may rise. *Climate sensitivity*—the link between greenhouse gas concentrations in the atmosphere and average global surface temperatures—is determined by the factors that alter the energy balance of the Earth, including a change in GHG, intensity of the Sun's energy, and cloud reflectivity. Changes in these natural and anthropogenic factors may increase GHG atmospheric concentration. The result is higher average global surface temperatures. In a simulation, Stern (2008) finds that a CO_2 concentration of 450 ppm has a 78 percent likelihood of increasing average global surface temperature

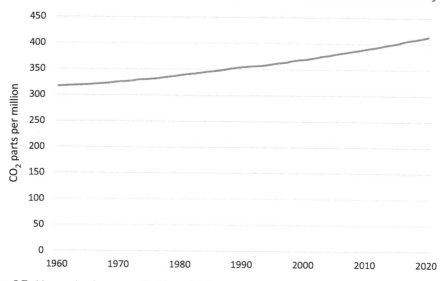

Figure 9.7 Atmospheric concentration of CO_2.

Source: author using data from Our World in Data, Ourworldindata.org/co2-and-other-greenhouse-gas -emissions.

by 2°C by the end of the century relative to pre-industrial levels. Another research study concludes that with current trends for rising atmospheric concentration of CO_2 that global average surface temperature is likely to rise 1.5°C by 2040 and 4°C by 2100 (IPCC, 2018).

To meet the objective of the 2016 Paris Agreement of limiting the increase in average global surface temperature below 2°C during this century, the world must implement renew-able technology in a concerted and coordinated process of energy transition (Gielen et al., 2019). As discussed earlier in this chapter, energy transition must reduce GHG from the com-bustion of fossil fuels, increase energy efficiency, decarbonize the economy, increase renew-ables as a share of total energy supply, and ensure that enough energy is available to meet future global economic growth.

Damage effects

Climate sensitivity demonstrates the link between higher average surface temperatures and a change in climate effects. Higher average global temperatures lead to more intense and severe heat waves, hurricanes, habitat degradation, droughts, water stress, wildfires, and extreme weather events (Wallace-Wells, 2019). Overall, negative climate effects lead to a loss in global GDP. But damages are not equivalent. A difference exists between damages that accompany catastrophic events and those that do not (Irwin, 2019).

If extreme weather events continue, regions with specific weather patterns such as heavy rainfall and flooding will experience the same events but with greater frequency and inten-sity. Higher temperatures melt ice sheets on land in areas such as Greenland. When the water flows into the ocean, the global ocean level rises, putting cities on the coast at risk. Even more, when ice sheets melt, the resulting lakes absorb additional heat from the sun, accelerating the melting process. More volatile weather conditions such as droughts and wildfires compromise the functionality of terrestrial ecosystems. In agricultural regions, climate change alters growing patterns, irrigation requirements, and the ability of small-scale farmers to maintain their yields. Climate volatility impacts infrastructure, including bridges, energy systems, roads, and telecommunication networks.

Taken together, these damage effects increase the potential for climate conflict. If global average surface temperature increases 2°C above pre-industrial levels, 300 million people will suffer from reduced crop yields, 680 million people from habitat destruction, 3.66 billion people from water stress, and 5.99 billion people from severe heat waves (Wallace-Wells, 2019). As a result, the concept of security for individual countries must expand beyond traditional military and political threats to include the effects of climate change. As humans flee rising ocean levels, desertification, resource scarcity, and declining crop yields, dislocation will rise, increasing stress on areas of the world that are already experiencing problems of migration and assimilation.

Economists quantify the monetary value of emission damage, the *social cost of carbon* (SCC), which is the harm that additional carbon emissions will cause in future decades. For policy, the SCC provides an economic valuation of damages. The SCC translates damage from climate change into economic terms, helping policymakers allocate resources to address the climate crisis. Nordhaus (2019) determines the value of the SCC as equal to $31.20 per ton of CO_2. Accordingly, a reduction of 1,000,000,000 emission tons would yield a benefit equal to $31,200,000,000, the value of damages avoided.

Abatement cost

In upcoming years, the climate crisis will impact the future trajectory of the global economy. In his influential analysis on the economics of climate change, Stern (2008) argues that without action the cost of climate change will be equivalent to losing 5 percent of global GDP annually. Climate change and economic growth are therefore intertwined. Rising greenhouse gas emissions, increasing atmospheric concentrations, and damage effects will mean the global economy will not operate at capacity, reducing incomes and production possibilities. The climate crisis will hit developing countries hardest. The question is how countries will share the cost of emission abatement necessary to reduce the economic losses from climate change.

One area is *climate adaptation*, the process of adjustment to expected or actual climate effects. Moving forward, the world should determine the adverse effects of climate change and implement appropriate measures to minimize economic damages. Approaches include a carbon tax, energy transition to renewables, and decarbonization—the shift to a low-carbon economy—which are all measured in terms of opportunity cost.

Another area is *climate mitigation*, the effort to stabilize or reduce the levels of GHG in the atmosphere. One option is to decrease the flow of these gases from their sources, such as reducing the demand for fossil fuels in power generation. Another option is to strengthen the natural sinks that absorb greenhouse gases such as forests, oceans, and soil. The objective of climate mitigation is to reduce human interference in the climate system, a goal that requires significant expenditure over multiple generations.

The pandemic and the climate crisis

The spread of infections during a pandemic leads to restrictions on economic activity and travel. Countries close their borders. Populations are confined to their places of residence. This change in behavior, in turn, reduces energy demand, affects energy supply chains, and alters consumption patterns, leading to reductions in both air pollution and GHG. The most prominent drivers of these impacts are household quarantines and mandatory lockdowns (Sovacool et al., 2020). Changes in emissions are not confined to major emitting sources but observed on a global scale. As an example, during the second decade of this century, global CO_2 emissions were rising about one percent annually, with no growth during the year 2019 (Le Quere et al., 2020). With respect to the coronavirus pandemic, daily CO_2 emissions decreased during the months following initial lockdown in 2020, compared with mean levels during the same months in 2019, stemming mostly from a reduction in transportation (Le Quere et al., 2020).

In this context, the short-term impact of the pandemic on GHG depends on the length of shutdown and the reduction in economic activity. The long-term effect depends on lasting changes to global networks, market incentives, and public policy. With government intervention, several initiatives possess high climate impact potential: building efficiency retrofits, clean physical infrastructure, investment in education and training, natural capital investment, and research and development on clean technology (Hepburn et al., 2020). Detecting a change in atmospheric CO_2 concentration related to a pandemic, however, is challenging, "due to the long atmospheric lifetime of CO_2, which makes any perturbation small" (Forster et al., 2020).

Strategies for environmental sustainability

Taken together, the energy, environmental, and climate effects demonstrate the need for *sustainability*, the priority of maintaining resources to meet the needs of the current generation while maintaining the resource base for future generations. In this context, a mix of biodiversity, ecosystem services, energy supply, and climate mitigation will help determine the strength of future economies. Energy, environmental, and climate effects of a pandemic are short-term in nature, but the changes in energy consumption, pollution flows, and climate outcomes require long-term planning with respect to sustainable environmental management. For most countries, a pandemic elicits a response of cooperation. Moving forward, areas of environmental, energy, and behavioral management constitute strategies for a sustainable future (figure 9.8).

Ecological restoration

Assisting the restoration of ecosystems that have been degraded or destroyed serves as an important element for environmental sustainability. This reality holds true for all ecosystems, including freshwater, forests, grasslands, marine, and tundra. Even though these ecosystems differ with respect to species and climate, they all are under threat through industrialization and globalization.

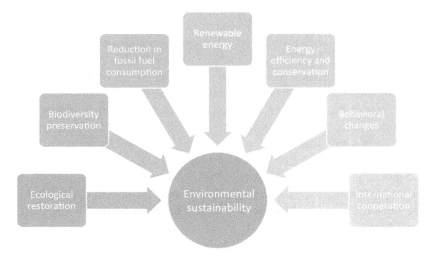

Figure 9.8 Strategies for environmental sustainability.
Source: adapted from Rume and Didar-Ul Islam (2020), Figure 6

Biodiversity preservation

The process of biodiversity preservation involves the maintenance of wildlife and natural resources such as fresh water, grasslands, and forests. Because of the connection between human welfare, economic vitality, and the natural world, biodiversity preservation serves as an important strategy for environmental sustainability. Maintaining biodiversity helps to secure several important ecosystem services, such as disease management, the provision of food, climate regulation, carbon sequestration, purification of air and water, crop pollination, seed dispersal, and the prevention of soil erosion.

Reduction in fossil fuel consumption

The global economy relies on fossil fuels. These combustible organic materials—oil, coal, and natural gas—derive from former plant life and serve as power sources for electricity generation and fuels for buildings, industry, and transportation. Because the combustion of fossil fuels leads to greenhouse gas emissions, including carbon dioxide, methane, and nitrous oxide, long-term atmospheric consequences for humans and the planet depend on the ability of economies to reduce the consumption of fossil fuels.

Renewable energy

The global energy supply includes both *renewable energy* and nonrenewable resources. Renewable energy resources come from natural processes that replenish, including solar and wind. At current levels of global consumption, nonrenewable resources such as coal, oil, and natural gas do not replenish on a human timeframe. Because an increase in the supply of renewables decreases the price, they are becoming more prevalent in global markets. Renewables reduce greenhouse gases, stimulate the green economy, and increase energy security.

Energy efficiency and conservation

Energy efficiency refers to the output produced per unit of energy consumption. Greater energy efficiency means an increase in energy services—including cooking, lighting, cooling, heating, refrigeration, and electricity generation—from each unit of energy consumption. *Energy conservation* leads to the reduction in the total quantity of energy consumption. Economies experience energy conservation when they use energy more efficiently or consume fewer energy services. The long-term benefits of higher levels of energy efficiency and conservation include energy savings, fewer greenhouse gas emissions, economic productivity, less pollution, and energy resource management.

Behavioral changes

The behavioral changes that occur during a pandemic provide a model for the behavioral changes that could contribute to environmental sustainability. A reduction in the carbon footprint, local food production and consumption, public transportation, walking, and bicycling serve as behavioral changes that both contribute to environmental sustainability and hedge against the problem of fracturing global supply chains.

International cooperation

During a pandemic, international cooperation ensures a coordinated response. But international cooperation is also necessary to both maintain environmental resources and meet sustainability goals. In effect, sustainable development serves as a driving force behind the need to balance economic vitality, ecological integrity, and human welfare. The international community may contribute data, information, knowledge, technology, and capital, channel the motivations of industry, and provide incentives for a more sustainable future.

Summary

A pandemic forces countries to implement policy interventions that shut down segments of the economy. When economic activity declines, a decrease in the consumption of fossil fuels occurs, which leads to less pollution. But the pandemic leads to stress on the healthcare system and an increase in the consumption and disposal of personal protective equipment. Taken together, the environmental outcomes are both positive and negative. With respect to climate effects, the world's economic and energy choices impact the flow of greenhouse gases into the atmosphere. This short-run change will not impact the long-term prospects for the climate unless strategies for environmental sustainability—ecological restoration, biodiversity preservation, reduction in fossil fuel consumption, renewable energy, energy efficiency and conservation, behavioral changes, and international cooperation—become permanent characteristics of economies.

Chapter takeaways

LO1   A pandemic impacts the global environment by reducing economic activity, decreasing energy demand, lowering polluting emissions, and reducing the flow of greenhouse gases into the atmosphere.

LO2 A pandemic disrupts energy markets and alters environment outcomes and climate effects.

LO3 A pandemic reduces the demand for energy in different sectors, including fuels, power sources, electricity generation, buildings, industry, and transportation.

LO4 A pandemic reduces the flow of pollution from the economy into the environment by decreasing both industrial activity and distribution.

LO5 A pandemic leads to fewer greenhouse gases because of a decrease in the combustion of fossil fuels. But this outcome does not alter the long-term path of climate change.

LO6 Moving forward, several areas of environmental, energy, and behavioral management constitute strategies for a sustainable future.

Terms and concepts

Absorptive capacity
Climate adaptation
Climate change
Climate mitigation
Climate sensitivity
Decarbonization
Energy conservation
Energy conversion chain
Energy efficiency
Energy innovation
Energy sector
Energy security
Energy system
Energy transition
Fund pollutants
Global pollutant
Greenhouse effect
Greenhouse gases
Integrated assessment model
Local pollutant
Negative externality
Regional pollutant
Renewable energy
Social cost of carbon
Spatial variability
Stock pollutants
Sustainability
Zone of influence

Questions

1. Explain how a pandemic leads to a decline in economic activity. A production process demonstrates how economic resource inputs (factors of production) are transformed into output. How does a pandemic alter the demand for economic resource inputs?

2. During the coronavirus pandemic of 2020, the oil market experienced a decline in price. Why did this outcome occur?

3. Do you believe that a pandemic accelerates the transition from fossil fuels to renewable energy resources? What factors influence the process of energy transition?

4. Is a pandemic likely to create long-term effects with respect to energy supply and demand? In your answer, is there a difference between fossil fuels (coal, natural gas, oil) and renewables (geothermal, hydropower, solar, wind)?

5. Explain the economy/environmental relationship with respect to the flow of raw materials, energy, and ecosystem goods and services from the environment into the economy, and the flow of air and water pollution, solid waste, and waste heat back into the environment. In this model, how does a pandemic fit?

6. Suppose in an urban area a pandemic leads to lower levels of air pollution. The residents decide they value clean air. To ensure a sustained and high level of air quality after the pandemic, what should happen? What is the role of public policy and incentives?

7. Explain the model of the economy and the environment. What forms of pollution flow from the economy to the environment? In your answer, distinguish between local, regional, and global pollutants. Does a pandemic impact these pollutants the same way? Do lower pollution levels provide justification for cities to promote post-pandemic initiatives for walking, cycling, and public transportation?

8. A pandemic leads to disease-related deaths (effect number one). But lower pollution levels lead to fewer pollution-related deaths, especially with cleaner air (effect number two). On a global scale, which effect is larger? What factors impact the result?

9. Why is it easier for researchers to determine the impact of a pandemic on the level of greenhouse gas emissions than changes in atmospheric concentrations of greenhouse gases?

10. Following a pandemic, which strategies for environmental sustainability are most relevant?

References

Abu-Rayash, Azzam, and Dincer, Ibrahim. 2020. "Analysis of the electricity demand trends amidst the Covid-19 coronavirus pandemic," *Energy Research & Social Science*, 68 (October): 101682.

Berman, Jesse, and Ebisu, Keita. 2020. "Changes in U.S. air pollution during the Covid-19 pandemic," *Science of the Total Environment*, 739: 139864.

Dans, Enrique. 2020. "In a post-pandemic world, renewable energy is the only way forward," *Forbes*, May 3. https://www.forbes.com/sites/enriquedans/2020/05/03/in-a-post-pandemic-world-renewable-energy-is-the-only-wayforward/.

Forster, Piers, Forster, Harriet, Evans, Mat, Gidden, Matthew, Jones, Chris, Keller, Christoph, … and Turnock, Steven. 2020. "Current and future global climate impacts resulting from Covid-19." *Nature Climate Change*, 10: 913–919.

Gielen, Dolf, Boshell, Francisco, Saygin, Deger, Bazilian, Morgan, Wagner, Nicholas, and Gorini, Richardo. 2019. "The role of renewable energy in the global energy transformation," *Energy Strategy Reviews*, 24 (April): 38–50.

Hepburn, Cameron, O'Callighan, Brian, Stern, Nicholas, Stiglitz, Joseph, and Zenghilis, Dimitri. 2020. "Will Covid-19 fiscal recovery packages accelerate or retard progress on climate change?" *Oxford Review of Economic Policy*, 36, S1. https://doi.org/10.1093/oxrep/graa015.

Intergovernmental Panel on Climate Change (IPCC). 2018. *Climate Change 2018*. United Nations/IPCC.

International Energy Agency (IEA). 2020a. *Clean Energy Innovation in the Covid-19 Crisis*. Paris: IEA. https://www.iea.org/articles/clean-energy-innovation-in-the-covid-19-crisis.

IEA. 2020b. *Key World Energy Statistics*. Paris: IEA. https://iea.org/reports/key-world-energy-statistics
-2020.

IEA. 2019. *World Economic Outlook*. Paris: IEA. https://www.iea.org/reports/world-energy-outlook-2019.

Irwin, Neil. 2019. "Climate changes' giant impact on the economy: 4 key issues," *The New York Times*,
January 17.

Jefferson, Michael. 2020. "A crude future? Covid-19's challenges for oil demand, supply and prices,"
Energy Research & Social Science, 68 (October): 101669.

Kuzemko, Caroline, Bradshaw, Michael, Bridge, Gavin, Goldthau, Andreas, Jewell, Jessica, Overland,
Indra, ... Westphal, Kirsten. 2020. "Covid-19 and the politics of sustainable energy transition," *Energy
Research & Social Science*, 68 (October): 101685.

Le Quere, Corinne, Jackson, Robert, Jones, Matthew, Smith, Adam, Abernethy, Sam, Andrews, Robbie,
... Peters, Glen. 2020. "Temporary reduction in daily global CO_2 emissions during the Covid-19 forced
confinement." *Nature Climate Change*, 10 (July): 647–653.

Liu, Zhu, Ciais, Philippe, and Schellnhuber, Hans. 2020. "Near-real-time monitoring of global CO_2
emissions reveals the effects of the Covid-19 pandemic," *Nature Communications*, 11: 5172.

Muhammad, Sulaman, Long, Xingle, and Salman, Muhammad. 2020. "Covid-19 pandemic and
environmental pollution: a blessing in disguise?" *Science of the Total Environment*, 728: 138820.

Nordhaus, William. 2019. "Climate change: the ultimate challenge for economics," *American Economic
Review*, 109, 6 (June): 1991–2014.

Rume, Tanjena, and Didar-UI Islam, S.M. 2020. "Environmental effects of Covid-19 pandemic and potential
strategies of sustainability." *Heliyon*, 6(9). doi:10.1016/j.heliyon.2020.e04965.

Sadler, Thomas R. 2020. *Energy Economics: Science, Policy, and Economic Applications*. Lanham,
Maryland: Lexington Books.

Sanchez, Luis, and Stern, David. 2016. "Drivers of industrial and non-industrial greenhouse gas
emissions," *Ecological Economics*, 124 (April): 17–24.

Sovacool, Benjamin, Del Rio, Dylan, and Griffiths, Steve. 2020. "Contextualizing the Covid-19 pandemic
for a carbon-constrained world: insights for sustainability transitions, energy justice, and research
methodology," *Energy Research & Social Science*, 68 (October): 101701.

Stern, Nicholas. 2008. "The economics of climate change." *American Economic Review*, 98, 2 (May): 1–37.

Stern, Nicholas. 2006. "What is the economics of climate change?" *World Economics*, 7, 2 (April–June):
1–10.

Tietenberg, Tom, and Lewis, Lynn. 2018. *Environmental and Natural Resource Economics*, 11th edition.
London: Routledge.

Venter, Zander, Aunan, Kristin, Chowdhury, Sourangsu, and Lelieveld, Jos. 2020. "Covid-19 lockdowns
cause global air pollution declines," *Proceedings of the National Academy of Sciences*, 117, 32 (August):
18984–18990.

Wallace-Wells, David. 2019. "Time to panic," *The New York Times*, February 18.

10 Economics of education

The important role of schools

During a secondary infection wave in the coronavirus pandemic, Germany decided to close bars, concert halls, gyms, restaurants, and theaters in an attempt to slow the spread of disease. But the country decided that schools and daycare centers would remain open. Ireland and France adopted the same approach. In these countries, policymakers took extra precautions to decrease the risk of infection, such as airing classrooms, wearing masks, and splitting playground time. But because of the mounting concern that pandemics could lead to lasting academic and psychological harm to a generation of students, these countries decided to value the educational experience but implement special safeguards. Another reason was the rights of young people to an education. A further reason was the important social consequences on families when schools and daycare centers were closed. With respect to the coronavirus pandemic, medical experts argued that the rate of disease transmission in schools was lower than other institutions, especially among younger children (Eddy, 2020). In addition, infected children tended to have milder symptoms, while air circulation, mask wearing, and social distancing proved to be effective measures. While students and teachers faced the risk of infection, the decision to keep schools open served as a method to balance one set of risks against another. The European Center for Disease Prevention and Control (2020) found that, during the coronavirus pandemic, young people accounted for less than 5 percent of the total cases reported in the European Union, concluding that closing schools would be "unlikely to provide significant additional protection of children's health."

A pandemic highlights the value of education. When the educational process is disrupted, families, schools, and policymakers attempt to minimize social costs. The chapter's thesis is that, when a pandemic disrupts the educational environment, teachers, administrators, and policymakers scramble to maintain quality education. To address this topic, the chapter considers the impact of a pandemic on education and establishes an economic model of education. Using this framework, the chapter analyzes the process of school reopening, alternative models of education, technological advances and innovation, and economic stability in higher education.

The impact of a pandemic on education

During a pandemic, one of the first sets of institutions to close is schools. The motivation for school closures is a reduction in transmissions between students. Nevertheless, the closure of schools leads to economic and social costs. When students are not at school, the average number of daily contacts is less than what would occur during regular school hours. But a reduction in attendance reverberates throughout society, impacting families, communities, and the economy. When students do not attend school full-time, household contacts rise, increasing the potential for the disease to spread in the community. Policymakers must therefore evaluate the tradeoff between slowing the spread of disease and economic and social costs. Decisions about the details of school closures, such as timing and length, must be weighed against conflicting factors such as developmental losses for students, less access to publicly-supported meals for low-income children, and the loss of childcare from primary school systems.

> Education is one of the strongest predictors of the health and wealth of a country's future workers, and the impact of long-term school closure on educational outcomes, future earnings, the health of young people, and future national productivity has not been quantified.
>
> (Viner et al., 2020)

Policy context

To put this policy intervention in context, consider the impact of school closures relative to other measures. Wider interventions such as universal mask wearing and social distancing may possess stronger containing effects, meaning that school closings must be evaluated within the context of an overall shutdown strategy. After school systems close, the risk of them reopening depends on how well societies contain the spread of disease and schools follow public health protocols, including occupancy and hybrid learning. If schools do not follow protocols, they may incubate disease outbreaks, given the fact that younger students may have a harder time with social distancing or wearing masks.

On the demand side, before schools reopen, students experience online education. For the consumption of this service, they must have access to technology, including internet connections and electronic devices. But access to technology varies according to socioeconomic circumstances: in the presence of remote education, students in higher-income brackets on average have better internet connections and access to laptops, tablets, and smart phones. Students also need oversight. Parents or guardians with flexible schedules may work from home, providing guidance and supervision. But parents and guardians with essential responsibilities must continue to work at their places of employment, inhibiting their abilities to provide guidance and supervision. This coordination problem complicates the demand for educational services.

On the supply side, before reopening, teachers must provide online education. The change from a full-time, in-person format to an online model creates challenges: teachers must adapt content and deliver it using technology. With respect to adaptation, teachers use technology to facilitate the process. With respect to delivery, a high learning curve eventually plateaus. Teachers are then able to provide an alternative model of education that differs from the traditional model.

Reopening and disease containment

Schools eventually reopen. But for an effective movement back to traditional education, the disease must be safely contained. Before the production and dissemination of a vaccination, however, this may not be the case. As a result, societies must evaluate the costs and benefits of school reopening in the presence of both uncertainty and the prospect of secondary infection waves. Countries may have national educational policies or decentralized policies. With national mandates, a country-wide educational directive facilitates the process of reopening. With decentralized policies, individual school systems determine how to proceed.

In an uncertain educational environment, some school systems evaluate the costs and benefits of reopening and conclude that full-capacity, full-time, in-person classes are preferable to online learning. Other school systems conclude that online learning should continue. In both cases, the risk of reopening schools is the potential for asymptomatic infections. At the same time, younger people may exhibit higher immunities. For these students, scientific evidence points to a nuanced approach, reopening schools according to the local spread of disease, community characteristics, the age of students, and resources for testing and contact tracing.

Lasting effects

Educational innovations during a pandemic may lead to lasting effects. Teachers may find that the provision of assignments in an online format leads to efficiency gains. Students may find that online learning corresponds to the consumption of technology in other aspects of their lives. Administrators may view the infusion of technology with traditional forms of education as a new hybrid model. A pandemic alters the supply and demand sides of the educational environment in both expected and unexpected ways. Therefore, teachers, school administers, and policymakers must prepare for the challenges that exist when the pandemic subsides, including the infusion of new technology into schools, continuing educational gaps between low-income students and everyone else, and the impact of an economic crisis on funding.

Investment in human capital: a model framework

Individuals influence their potential for lifetime earnings through investment activities. One area of investment is education and training. Education and training play an important role in the development of *human capital*, the ability of a person to produce goods and services. The higher the level of investment in education and training, the more that individuals are able to contribute to the economy. From an economics perspective, a person who pursues a higher education (at a university) or improves their skill set (by enhancing human capital) sacrifices current income in the hope of increasing future earning potential. Throughout the life cycle, individuals with higher levels of education and training tend to have higher incomes. These individuals tend to work more, consume more, and accumulate wealth at a faster rate.

Optimal investment path

In this framework, individuals maximize the present value of their lifetime earnings by allocating their time between work and activities that enhance their human capital. That is, they choose an optimal expenditure path for educational services. An important variable is the ability to learn, considered by economists as the *technological efficiency of education*, a function of both individual effort on the demand side and the provision of educational resources on the supply side. As individual effort and the provision of educational resources rise, the technological efficiency of education increases. Therefore, to the extent that families support students and communities support schools, educational outcomes increase.

The challenge is determining the optimal level of investment in human capital, which depends on *net present value (NPV)*, the difference between the present value of costs and benefits. With respect to human capital, the calculation of *NPV* consists of a comparison between the present value of the cost of a person's education and training with the present value of the benefits of an increase in lifetime earnings. If net benefits exist, additional investment should occur.

External benefits

Like with other markets, the market for education includes supply and demand sides. The supply of education entails school systems, educational facilities, and teachers. The demand for education stems from students seeking to enhance their levels of education. In this framework, several reasons exist for the provision of public education. From an economics perspective, investment in education increases the present value of potential future earnings, as the previous section explains. From a social perspective, educated individuals are more likely to be productive citizens. An additional benefit is the integration of students from different socioeconomic backgrounds, ethnic groups, races, and religions, which contributes to social stability and economic vitality. From an economics perspective, these *external benefits*, benefits accruing to people other than the consumers or producers, justify a substantial subsidy to public education.

In the presence of external benefits, market allocation is too low from society's perspective (figure 10.1). For every level of output, *marginal private benefit (MPB)*, the additional benefit to individuals from consuming another unit, is less than *marginal social benefit (MSB)*, the additional benefit to society. The supply curve equals *marginal social cost (MSC)*, the additional cost to society of supplying one more unit.

The difference between *MSB* and *MPB*, *marginal external benefit (MEB)*, represents the spillover effect:

$$MSB - MPB = MEB \qquad (10.1)$$

In the presence of *MEB*, the optimal number of students (Q_o) exceeds the market level (Q_m), while the optimal price (P_o) exceeds the market price (P_m). At point a, the market equilibrium, inefficiency exists: $MSB > MSC$. At Q_m, the market fails to deliver the optimal level of students. At the efficient point b, MSB equals MSC, satisfying the marginal efficiency condition:

$$MPB + MEB = MSB = MSC \qquad (10.2)$$

To reach Q_o, price must decrease to P_c. At point c, the quantity of education demanded by students equals Q_o, but a lower price does not provide the incentive to provide more education. Therefore, in the presence of external benefits, government intervenes, and the increase in net benefits of the movement from a to b is represented by area abd. With external benefits, government may intervene with a *corrective subsidy*, a payment to either sellers or buyers that reduces the price to buyers. By subsidizing education, government accounts for *MEB*.

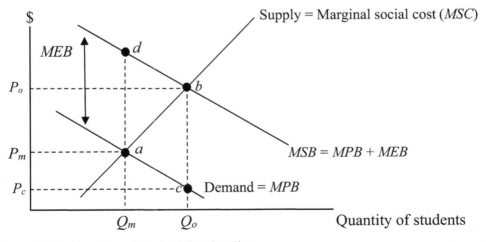

Figure 10.1 External benefits of public education.
Source: author

Reopening schools

Of all the institutions that close during the shutdown interval of a pandemic, few face the same pressure to reopen as schools. For students, a lack of consistent education may lead to developmental harm. Working parents, particularly mothers, worry about having to leave the workforce if their children cannot attend school. But if the risk of infection remains, school districts may hesitate before returning to the full-time, in-person model, instead preparing teachers and students for the provision of a remote-learning experience. Another challenge exists. Even when public health officials deem schools safe from the spread of disease, parents may not share this confidence.

If the disease is not completely eradicated, an important variable is how widespread the disease is in the community. This variable affects how many susceptible students become infected. The potential problem is the presence of asymptomatic cases, when students with no symptoms spread the disease to teachers, school employees, and each other. With these concerns, measures such as mask wearing and physical distancing may persist.

Public health concerns complicate the process of school reopening. One study argues that test frequency is strongly correlated with cumulative infection, concluding that testing every two days for infection coupled with behavioral interventions such as social distancing permits a safe return to schools (Paltiel et al., 2020). But if addressing the developmental challenges, economic concerns, and public health realities is not enough, schools must also ensure student learning. With respect to reopening, several benefits and costs exist. But before addressing these factors, consider the criteria for reopening schools and the education gap.

Criteria for reopening schools

Safety guidelines accompany the process of reopening schools, including testing, the rate of new infections, limited class size, mask wearing, fresh air circulation, and an incremental approach. With community testing capacity, if a higher proportion of people are testing positive for the disease, it is either too soon to reopen schools or public health officials are not testing enough people to adequately measure the spread of disease. With respect to the rate of new infections, the Harvard Global Health Institute proposed a benchmark for reopening schools of fewer than 25 cases per 100,000 people in the community. The World Health Organization proposed a benchmark of a positivity rate of less than 5 percent of all those who are tested over a two-week period (Serkez and Thompson, 2020). As a pandemic subsides, both infections and testing rates change, so school districts should continue with monitoring. Limited class size provides a framework for social distancing and the establishment of cohorts or learning pods that restrict student interaction. Mask-wearing requirements slow the spread of disease and may be linked to testing: if members of a cohort test negative, mask wearing is not mandatory. Fresh air circulation with open windows during warmer months and air filtering during colder months reduces the infectiousness of airborne diseases. With an incremental approach, a percentage of the students initially return to school, while others continue at home with online education. Over time, face-to-face learning accommodates additional students until attendance reaches 100 percent. If students participate in learning pods, the pod quarantines when a student becomes infected, but the entire school does not have to shut down. Taken together, these safety guidelines are necessary for reopening but not sufficient to eliminate the spread of disease among students.

Education gap

A focus on safety guidelines may reopen schools faster than an alternative but may also widen the *education gap* if wealthier school districts reopen before others. The education gap refers to the disparities in performance among different socioeconomic groups. During a pandemic, income levels may determine which workers stay home and which must maintain their positions in the economy as essential workers. Higher incomes correlate with a greater potential to work from home. Income levels also influence which children succeed in a remote learning environment. Students without steady tutoring or internet access may fall behind their higher-income counterparts (Goulas and Megalokonomou, 2020). The communities that may be the first to safely reopen may have a lower prevalence of chronic diseases such as diabetes and heart disease and higher rates of health insurance coverage (Serkez and Thompson, 2020). When reopening schools, these disparities complicate a data-driven approach. As a result, societies should weigh the health risks of reopening schools against the educational benefits for students, making sure to consider the socioeconomic realities of school systems.

Benefits of reopening schools

The benefits of reopening schools include:

- the effectiveness of in-person classes
- positive functions of schools
- safety from disease
- mitigation of risk
- childcare
- meeting mental health needs of students
- adaptive learning opportunities
- protection and safety
- blended learning approaches.

Weeks of lockdown and intermittent access to education create the potential for negative developmental impacts. Interruptions may have lasting effects. Students with lower socioeconomic status may struggle with online learning. Relying on a virtual experience reinforces inequities for students with disabilities, lower incomes, and other marginalized status. Besides education, schools create additional benefits, including health services, meals, and social connections. For many low-income students, schools reduce food insecurity, which improves academic performance, physical health, and mental well-being. When schools operate with a full-time, in-person model, these opportunities especially benefit low-income students. But a pandemic multiplies the number of students who do not get enough to eat, lack connections with friends and teachers, and experience harmful health consequences. With respect to safety, younger people may be less likely to become infected as opposed to older members of the population. This is the case with the coronavirus pandemic of 2020 but not the flu pandemic of 1918. If schools do not cause community outbreaks, reopening provides a service to society. With the mitigation of risk, schools may assign students to pods to minimize interactions, conduct classes outside, educate students on personal hygiene, improve internal air quality, and keep infected students and teachers at home (Eischens, 2020). Schools serve as a method of childcare, which translates into a safe place for students to go while their parents work. Recovering from a pandemic, schools serve as a safe place. Reopening also means the educational system may meet the mental health needs of students. Individuals from marginalized families require particular attention, as their family members are more likely to become infected, lose a job, and suffer from economic repercussions (Darville, 2020). Children from low-income households experience living conditions that make online schooling difficult. By reopening schools, adaptive learning opportunities exist. The acceleration of more creative and motivational structures provide additional methods of providing educational opportunities. When schools reopen, the blended learning approaches that develop during the online period offer more opportunities for teachers to implement their best practices.

Costs of reopening schools

The costs of reopening schools include:

- potential spread of the disease among members of the educational community
- an increase in the reproduction number
- logistical and economic challenges.

While infection rates depend on epidemiological factors and socioeconomic conditions, teachers and students may be vulnerable. If schools reopen while the disease still exists in a community, school infections may follow. The volume of students complicates the practice of social distancing. Reopening schools may increase the reproduction number, the average number of infections tied to a single case. When students are susceptible, exposures strengthen transmission networks. With logistical and economic challenges, school districts that reopen must provide detailed plans for the return of students, clean environments that minimize the spread of disease, and testing. These actions come with costs, requiring government resources (Eischens, 2020).

Educational models during a pandemic

During the shutdown interval in a pandemic, students shelter-in-place. To continue to provide an educational service, schools switch to alternative methods of instruction, including online education. While the initial movement from a traditional in-class model to an alternative model creates the potential for roadblocks, including a lack of knowledge of streaming services, inadequate hardware, teacher training, and student access, the efficiency of alternative forms of education increases through learning and experience. The extent to which school districts minimize efficiency losses helps to determine the success of new educational methods.

Level of education

The impact of a pandemic on education depends on the level under consideration: primary, secondary, or higher education. First, the degree of infectiousness may differ according to age group. Second, education at different levels creates unique challenges and opportunities. Third, education for younger and older students requires different levels of oversight. These factors influence the impact of a pandemic on education.

In the presence of decentralized decision-making, when local school administrators decide when to reopen schools based on epidemiological guidelines, public goals may conflict with the provision of education. Schools that reopen require a sufficient supply of protective equipment, including ventilating systems, sanitizer, masks, testing, tracing, and space for social distancing. In the absence of investment in these safety measures, the disease may reappear, closing schools before the educational process has a chance to build momentum. Depending on the level of education, the decisions of school systems, colleges, and universities impact society at large and the broader economy. If the public sector succeeds in suppressing the disease, schools should implement safety protocols for reopening (Dynarski, 2020).

Primary education

Primary education refers to elementary school. In areas where the disease is under control, an in-class experience is most important for younger children. Elementary school students are the least equipped to learn from online education. But if these children are stunted in their learning process, they may experience developmental problems later in their educational careers. As a practical matter, many younger students struggle with computers, working independently, and maintaining the focus necessary to complete assignments. They need adults in their presence for guidance and assistance. These educational needs have economic implications. During the shutdown interval, affluent families may hire tutors to oversee the educational experience of their children, but most families cannot afford this luxury. Parents may have to reduce work hours or adjust their schedules, hampering economic recovery and aggravating economic inequality. High economic incentives exist for returning younger students to school (Dynarski, 2020).

Secondary education

Secondary education refers to middle school and high school. At this level, the students have a greater potential to learn with online education. Organized and motivated students may use this learning environment to complete their school requirements while creating additional opportunities, including projects and activities. In the absence of oversight, less organized and motivated students may struggle. At the secondary level, an education gap exists. Wealthier school systems and households have the highest potential of maintaining educational quality during the pandemic. Poorer school districts and families do not. Once secondary school students return to an in-person, full-time educational experience, they benefit from structure, including new protocols for classroom space, movement, and methods of interaction. They also benefit from the return to a traditional format, such as traveling to school, returning to the classroom setting, interacting with teachers, lunching with friends, and participating in extra-curricular activities.

Higher education

Higher education refers to the college and university experience. Each fall around the world, millions of students attend institutions of higher education. Most students remain close to home, but some choose to attend institutions in other provinces or countries. Students normally move into crowded residence halls and mix with their friends and colleagues in classrooms, social activities, and cafes. During typical terms, they sit close together in small seminar rooms and large lecture halls, focusing on the learning process. But from an epidemiological perspective, this crowding is risky during a pandemic. When the disease spreads, institutions of higher education may choose to close. When they reopen, they must deal with the potential of secondary waves. The pandemic forces colleges and universities to face tradeoffs regarding the return of students to campus. An optimal provision of education and the best approach to maintain the economic viability of educational institutions involve the offering of all available courses in all formats, but bringing students back to campus may serve as a risk to public health.

Keeping some or all students at home and offering online or hybrid courses contributes to public health but reduces the economic viability of institutions, especially in nonselective schools. Institutions without stable financial backing may lose students to rival institutions in the absence of in-person classes. Alternatively, without the promise of a campus experience, some students choose to take a gap year. If institutions lose revenue from tuition, fees, and room and board, they may eliminate programs, lay off faculty, and lose their position in the educational hierarchy. These outcomes create a *coordination problem*. As a result, coordinated responses serve as a logical decision from an economics perspective as the schools may act in concert while not exposing students to public health risks (Dynarski, 2020).

In regions where the disease is suppressed, institutions of higher education reopen with the most success. In regions where the disease is still present but perceived to be under control, some institutions proceed with no interruption while others experience problems. In the latter case, the disease may still be present in a small percentage of the student population. In schools that do not implement a comprehensive system of testing and tracing, these infected students may mix in classrooms and other events, spreading the disease first among themselves and then to the faculty and community at large. At larger universities, teaching hospitals have the capacity to care for the sick. But at smaller institutions, fewer resources are available to provide cost-effective measures. The traditional university experience of social interaction increases the potential for contagion.

Winner-take-all markets

With higher education, a pandemic creates the conditions for *winner-take-all markets*. In these markets, the best economic performers capture the largest share of market rewards while other competitors are left with less (Frank and Cook, 1995). These outcomes widen economic disparities because a few agents are able to increase the amount of income that would otherwise flow to market suppliers in a more equitable manner. This example applies to the university environment but not primary and secondary schools. On the demand side, learning in an online model provides the opportunity to increase the level of flexibility. For students, the learning process becomes more decentralized. Instead of attending classes at certain times, they may have the flexibility to decide when to view online lectures, complete course assignments, and take examinations. On the supply side, as technology expands the reach of the most able providers, universities may supply their services to larger audiences in a cost-effective manner.

Another feature of a winner-take-all markets is *positive-feedback effects* that create net benefits for suppliers. With internet searches, for example, one company may process the most queries, because the more queries it processes, the more effective is its algorithm. With social media, one company may enjoy the greatest number of users. But with academic instruction, a movement toward a greater level of remote learning occurs slowly, fueled by the need of universities to proceed in a cost-effective manner. But a pandemic amplifies this process, accelerating the transition to remote learning. Although the supply of online instruction may be low before a pandemic, an increase in supply accelerates efficient delivery methods. Over time, remote courses compete for approval and students designate some as superior (Frank, 2020).

In this context, *economies of scale* serve as a driving force, meaning the cost savings from an increase in production. Most of the costs of supplying online courses are fixed. When the number of online students increases, costs per student decline. The cost of creating a lecture for an online platform is the same whether a few students or many students watch it (Frank, 2020).

After the pandemic, educational institutions may find that online learning does not replace the traditional classroom experience but provides an additional option. One reason is the benefits of the traditional education experience mentioned above, including the effectiveness of in-person instruction. When students attend school, they acquire skills that help them in the labor force and strengthen their social networks. Another reason is that not all educational institutions have the resources to provide effective online instruction.

Overall, the forces of supply and demand impact the educational process during a pandemic and lead to lasting effects after the pandemic ends. Technological advances and economies of scale result from alternative models, including remote learning. The most forward-thinking institutions infuse new technology into their offerings. Primary and secondary schools continue to take advantage of efficiency gains while attempting to enhance their traditional academic environments. All institutions grapple with an inequality of outcomes when some students perform better than others. Whether the opportunity for remote learning leads to net benefits therefore depends on the role of the public sector. Addressing the inequality of educational outcomes during the period of transition strengthens the entire educational system.

Educational models

To offer efficient but alternative models of education during a pandemic, three lessons exist. First, schools should differentiate curriculums and classroom environments according to student and age groups. Second, schools should design alternative methods of education specifically for remote and hybrid settings. Third, educational relationships between teachers, students, and parents are the foundation of learning (Dorn et al., 2020). The implication of these lessons is that the provision of education differs according to circumstance. Students who are at risk during remote education, including special-education students, those without technology, children of parents who require childcare, and transition students entering a new phase of education, have a higher urgency to return to a full-time, in-person model than students whose parents do not need a traditional format and students at high risk of infection (Dorn et al., 2020). Three alternative models exist:

- Online education
- Hybrid education
- Safe centers for online learning.

Online education

With online education, teachers provide the educational experience to students in remote locations. They interact with videoconferencing technology. Assignments are posted to internet sites. Teachers mark the assignments remotely, providing feedback when appropriate. This model is characterized by the location of the target population. During a pandemic, online education involves computer-mediated interaction between students and teachers. Online courses provide formal instruction, content, and procedures. The benefits of this model are the continuation of the educational experience and elimination of disease networks in school. But costs exist for families and schools. Families may not have internet access or space for students to study. Schools cannot offer some courses, especially science labs, online. Also, virtual classes lead to lower levels of attendance. In poorer communities, disengagement from the academic process is a problem. Reasons include a lack of an internet connection or computer, care for a sibling, or work. With online learning, some students find the work so tedious that they drop out.

In a pandemic, online education serves as a short-term and cost-effective method of educating students. Online education creates new instructional opportunities, such as links to additional content, methods of problem solving, and examples. Teachers may build current events into their lesson plans. Online instruction that incorporates synchronous and asynchronous networks provides an opportunity for interactive learning.

The outcome is a set of educational materials that conveys information and instruction in multiple ways, often appealing to students more than print materials. It also leads to the potential for the individualization of education when teachers meet the cognitive needs of students. This framework addresses the isolation of online learning and introduces a fluidity of instruction. The problem is that variation exists with respect to the ability of students to learn in online courses. If they have oversight from a parent or mentor, technological support, and a schedule, they have a greater potential to learn. With the allocation of sufficient resources, online education may embody the premise of comprehensive learning. Success with an online format therefore depends on the principles of structure, support, and attentive teaching.

Hybrid education

The hybrid model combines face-to-face learning with online instruction. The idea is to engage students but reduce complexity. New assignments, information, and student exploration may occur remotely while the instruction of new concepts and feedback may occur in person. Designing a remote-learning system with these characteristics requires an understanding of the optimal quantity and mix of online education. While school systems should prioritize face-to-face learning for primary school students, they must determine the optimal number of educational hours per day for students at secondary levels and how many of those hours should occur online. As students mature, they may participate in more asynchronous, self-paced learning and less synchronous, real-time learning. Also changing as students mature are the dynamics of student groups and individual instruction. Older students have a higher capacity to learn remotely. With younger students, educators may limit the number of hours of screen time while instituting more small-group instruction (Dorn et al., 2020).

Safe centers for online learning

This model includes online instruction and space in school. The idea is to provide online education but offer a supervised environment. The school serves as a voluntary resource center as opposed to a compulsory attendance requirement. At the level of primary or secondary education, schools provide classroom space for students who do not have internet access, computers, or supervision at home. At the level of higher education, academic institutions bring a cohort of students to campus so they may participate in the physical experience but take online courses. The benefits of this model are lower levels of population density at school, the ability of teachers to instruct from home, and a method to address the inequality of educational access for low-income students. The drawbacks include an inability to reproduce the traditional educational experience and the problem of small groups trying to learn with less supervision.

Double shifts

During a pandemic, changes in the supply of and demand for educational services depends on the type of education, either traditional or online. Because students shelter-in-place during the shutdown interval, the supply of and demand for traditional education decreases. But the supply of and demand for online education increases. The outcome is a *double shift* when both supply and demand shift in the same example. With double shifts, it is important to consider the impact on equilibrium price and quantity. With a single shift of either supply or demand, the model determines the change in both equilibrium quantity and price. But with a double shift, either the change in price or the change in quantity is indeterminate. For the purpose of simplification, the following examples assume no external effects.

During a pandemic, both the supply of and demand for traditional, in-person education decrease (figure 10.2). When the supply and demand curves shift left from S_1 and D_1 to S_2 and D_2, equilibrium quantity decreases from Q_1 to Q_2. In general, with double shifts, when supply and demand decrease, the change in equilibrium price is indeterminate. But supply and

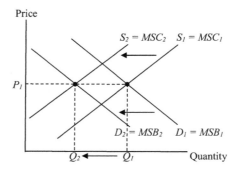

Figure 10.2 The market for traditional, in-person education during a pandemic.

Source: author

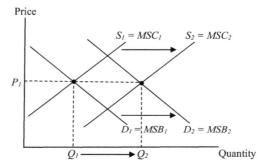

Figure 10.3 The market for online education during a pandemic.

Source: author

demand shift to the left by the same magnitude, so equilibrium price (P_1) remains constant. But the magnitude of the shifts could vary, leading to an indeterminate effect.

During a pandemic, both the supply of and demand for online education increase (figure 10.3). When the supply and demand curves shift right from S_1 and D_1 to S_2 and D_2, equilibrium quantity increases from Q_1 to Q_2. In general, with double shifts, when supply and demand increase, the change in equilibrium price is indeterminate. But in figure 10.3 supply and demand shift to the right by the same magnitude, so equilibrium price (P_1) remains constant.

Technology and innovation

The dynamic between the pandemic, economy, and education challenges society, including the risk of bringing students together before disease eradication, establishing the learning process during online education, and determining the optimal time for reopening. But a pandemic also provides an opportunity to use the educational environment as a laboratory. A pandemic changes the reality of face-to-face learning. Students returning to school may experience a hybrid model. But other changes may occur. In many school systems and institutions of higher learning, students have to register their health status on a daily basis, wear masks, experience quarantine if exposed to the disease, and participate in physical distancing protocols. In other words, the educational experience before a pandemic differs from the educational experience after a pandemic. Several examples of innovation exist, including apps for health, wastewater testing, and powered-up schools. While the purpose of these procedures is innovation, experiments in an educational setting provide examples for society at large.

Apps for health

Colleges and universities have some control over their communities, which include students who are relatively at ease with advancing technology. Their economic models depend on attracting students to campus. But the external spillover from disease transmission means people who are connected to the students, including families, people in the work force, and members of communities, are vulnerable. One example of innovation is the development of *apps for health*, which anonymously track the movement of students. Students who use the app are notified if they come within close proximity of people who are infected. An algorithm in the app assesses the degree of infectiousness of a student at the time of contact. The technology makes this determination by calculating when symptoms first appear. With the algorithm, the app evaluates the level of risk for other students, depending on when they are exposed to infections and the degree to which they are exposed. Students experiencing the highest level of risk first seek a test and then quarantine. To address the privacy issue, the data are kept on personal devices and users determine whether a positive test is shared. As more users participate in the network, information increases, network externalities rise, and the institution may identify potential disease outbreaks more effectively (Richtel, 2020).

Wastewater testing

To reduce disease transmission, educational officials must first identify the presence of the disease in the local student population. During the coronavirus pandemic, one innovation was wastewater testing, an important tool for both detection and stopping the spread of disease. With this extension of technology used for sewage treatment plants, a relatively inexpensive way to detect the disease, samples are taken from wastewater flushed out of residence halls and other campus buildings. When the disease is identified, students who live in the residence hall are given tests. The results determine how to proceed with quarantines. This process of wastewater testing is not meant to replace clinical tests, but to encourage a targeted response (Gluckman, 2020).

Powered-up schools

Referring to the coronavirus pandemic, the educators Emiliana Vegas and Rebeca Winthrop (2020) argue that "It is hard to imagine there will be another moment in history when the central role of education in the economic, social, and political prosperity and stability of nations is so obvious and well understood by the general population." They believe that an opportunity exists to "leapfrog toward powered-up schools," which use technology to provide a strong educational experience at the center of a community and leverage their position among community institutions, families, out-of-school programs, employers and businesses, and health and social agencies (figure 10.4). The idea is to place schools at the center of

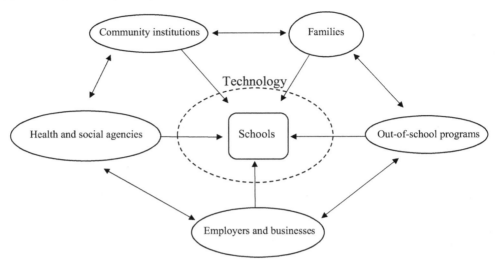

Figure 10.4 Powered-up schools.
Source: adapted from Vegas and Winthrop (2020)

community ecosystems, harnessing innovation for more impactful outcomes. For education systems to emerge from a pandemic in stronger positions, deliberate actions and new technologies must address educational inequality, move innovation to the center of educational models, leverage public support, and galvanize educational allies, including parents, community institutions, and health agencies (Vegas and Winthrop, 2020).

Economic stability in higher education

A pandemic elucidates the challenges of financing systems of higher education. In a taxpayer-funded model, such as in Denmark, France, Germany, Ireland, Norway, and Sweden, students from the European Union do not pay tuition at institutions of higher education. In this framework, a pandemic burdens the public sector by reducing tax revenue, impacting the flow of funds from government to institutions of higher education. But, in the United States, a pandemic highlights the reality that the system of higher education relies on ever-increasing tuition payments from students. In the aftermath of a pandemic, some students resist the return to face-to-face, in-person classes, taking gap years, enrolling in online courses at community colleges, or choosing a part-time schedule. These choices reduce the flow of tuition payments to institutions of higher education, creating additional pressure to increase tuition. In the United States, higher education continues to experience declining enrollment, less support from the public sector, and deferred building maintenance. A pandemic exposes these weaknesses, puts tuition-based institutions of higher education in a precarious economic position, and disproportionately impacts lower-income students. With rising tuition, low-income students may not save enough to pay for school, so they borrow. If they cannot live on the borrowed money, they work, creating a difficult work/school tradeoff. Economic contraction impacts the provision of education. The challenge is to create a stable model for higher education, especially during economic downturns.

Summary

Schools close when a disease outbreak turns into a pandemic. The goal of closing schools is to stop disease transmission among students and teachers. But high economic and social costs result from the process, impacting families, communities, students, and the economy. When students are at home, household contacts rise, childcare responsibilities increase, and school systems implement alternative forms of education, including online and hybrid models. Because education leads to higher levels of human capital and possesses positive external effects, public sectors intervene in the market to increase the level of education. Pandemics disrupt this process through school closures, uncertainty, and an inequality of outcomes that impacts low-income students the most. While online and hybrid education offer alternative models during a pandemic, costs and benefits of reopening schools must be evaluated with respect to primary, secondary, and higher education.

Chapter takeaways

LO1   A pandemic highlights the value of education for economies and society.

LO2   During a pandemic, one of the first sets of institutions to close is schools.

LO3   Individuals influence their potential for lifetime earnings through investment activities. One area of investment is education and training.

LO4   Of all the institutions that close during the shutdown interval of a pandemic, few face the same pressure to reopen as schools.

LO5   Three alternative educational models include online education, hybrid education, and safe centers for online learning.

LO6   Several examples of innovation in the educational environment exist, including apps for health, wastewater testing, and powered-up schools.

LO7   A pandemic elucidates the challenges of financing systems of higher education, especially tuition-based universities.

Terms and concepts

Apps for health
Coordination problem
Corrective subsidy
Double shift
Economies of scale
Education gap
External benefits
Human capital
Marginal external benefit
Marginal private benefit
Marginal social cost
Net present value
Positive-feedback effects

Technological efficiency of education
Winner-take-all markets

Questions

1. For a community, what are the costs and benefits of schools closing their traditional methods of education in favor of alternative methods? How do the characteristics of the pandemic impact the educational process?
2. What are the factors that influence a person's decision to invest in human capital? How does a pandemic alter this calculation?
3. What are the external benefits of education? How should government account for external benefits? Does a pandemic alter this framework?
4. Explain the demand-side and supply-side challenges of online education. How do these factors differ with respect to urban and rural areas, public and private education, and pandemic intervals such as shutdown and recovery?
5. During a pandemic, what happens to the supply of and demand for in-person, full-time education? What happens to the supply of and demand for online education?
6. How does the cost-effective provision of education during a pandemic differ according to primary, secondary, and higher education?
7. What are the costs and benefits of online and hybrid models of education during a pandemic?
8. What are safe centers for online learning? Are these cost-effective and educationally appropriate options for students of all ages? What are the benefits and costs?
9. During a pandemic, why does incentive exist for innovation and technological advance in education? During the coronavirus pandemic, what were some examples of innovation and technological advance in education? What are the costs and benefits of these methods?
10. Consider two model frameworks: a publicly-funded model with free tuition and a tuition-based model with student loans. In a pandemic, which model is more cost-effective?

References

Darville, Sarah. 2020. "Reopening schools is harder than it should be," *The New York Times*, July 26.
Dorn, Emma, Panier, Frederic, Probst, Nina, and Sarakatsannis, Jimmy. 2020. "Back to school: a framework for remote and hybrid learning amid Covid-19," McKinsey & Company, August 31.
Dynarski, Susan. 2020. "Reopening schools, but maybe not in the smartest way," *The New York Times*, August 9.
Eddy, Melissa. 2020. "Why is Europe keeping its schools open, despite new lockdowns?" *The New York Times*, October 29.
Eischens, Rilyn. 2020. "What are the pros and cons of reopening schools this fall?" *Minnesota Reformer*, July 21.
European Center for Disease Prevention and Control. 2020. *Covid-19 in Children and the Role of School Settings in Covid-19 Transmission*. Stockholm: ECDC, August 6.
Frank, Robert. 2020. "Despite hiccups, online courses are here to stay," *The New York Times*, June 7.
Frank, Robert, and Cook, Philip. 1995. *The Winner-Take-All Society*. Glencoe, Illinois: Free Press.
Gluckman, Nell. 2020. "Covid-19 is threatening the in-person semester. Can wastewater testing help save it?" *The Chronicle of Higher Education*, September 1.

Goulas, Sofoklis, and Megalokonomou, Rigissa. 2020. "School attendance during a pandemic," *Economics Letters*, 193 (August): 109275.

Paltiel, A. David, Zheng, Amy, and Walensky, Rochelle. 2020. "Assessment of SARS-CoV-2 screening strategies to permit the safe reopening of college campuses in the United States," *JAMA Network Open*, 3, 7 (July). doi:10.1001/jamanetworkopen.2020.16818.

Richtel, Matt. 2020. "Contract tracing with your phone: it's easier but there are tradeoffs," *The New York Times*, June 3.

Serkez, Yaryna, and Thompson, Stuart. 2020. "Can your child's school reopen?" *The New York Times*, August 23.

Vegas, Emiliana, and Winthrop, Rebecca. 2020. "Beyond reopening schools: how education can emerge stronger than before Covid-19," *Brookings*, September 8.

Viner, Russell, Russell, Simon, Croker, Helen, Packer, Jessica, Ward, Joseph, Stansfield, Claire, … Booy, Robert. 2020. "School closure and management practices during coronavirus outbreaks including Covid-19: a rapid systematic review," *Lancet Child Adolescent Health*, 4: 397-404.

11 Economics of technology and innovation

Learning objectives

After reading this chapter, you will be able to:

LO1 Explain the motivation for innovation during a time of crisis.

LO2 Discuss the process of technological advance, including the stages of invention, innovation, diffusion, and adoption/rejection.

LO3 Contrast theories of economic growth that model technological advance as an exogenous variable and technological advance as an endogenous variable.

LO4 Explain why networks enhance the process of innovation.

LO5 Discuss innovation in a period of transformative change, including technological advances for vaccines and medical care.

LO6 Address why a pandemic may lead to lasting effects with respect to innovation.

Chapter outline

- Innovation in a time of crisis
- The process of technological advance
- Theories of economic growth
- Networks of innovation
- Pandemics, innovation, and transformative change
- Lasting effects
- Summary

Innovation in a time of crisis

A pandemic ravages public health and the economy, impacting industries, businesses, and households. But if history repeats itself, *innovation* emerges from crisis, when necessity fosters creation. One important example occurred after World War II when researchers at drug companies with government support developed new techniques for bringing large quantities of penicillin to the market. In this example, innovation helped to solve a public health problem.

The process of innovation—the application of a new idea or new application of an exist-ing idea—stems from the desire to create new methods, markets, and products. When an exogenous shock strikes, such as a pandemic, the demand for new methods, markets, and products determines the quantity of investment. An economic downturn normally leads to a decrease in investment of all kinds; however, structural competencies, human resources, spe-cialization in high-tech sectors, financial markets, and public-private partnerships may offset a downturn. With the coronavirus pandemic, innovations occurred in both the development of a vaccine and clinical practices in medical care, including advances in diagnoses and tele-medicine. The chapter's thesis is that large-scale disruptions may alter economies, but inno-vation normally occurs. When the crisis subsides, the innovations may lead to lasting effects.

Economists analyze the relationship between innovation and the business cycle. One view is that innovation is cyclical: during economic downturns, firms reduce their level of invest-ment in innovation. Another view is that innovation is counter-cyclical: economic downturns stimulate investment in innovation. Which view is correct? As it stands, research on this relationship finds that, while some firms are persistent in their levels of investment spending on innovation during economic downturns, others are not. Several factors impact the deci-sion, including firm-specific characteristics, stage of development, management attitudes, path-dependent nature of innovation, and industry dynamics such as technological advance, aggregate demand, and profit opportunities. But a crisis creates a "window of opportunity": firms that innovate require human capital, a technology infrastructure, and internal knowl-edge (Filippetti and Archibugi, 2011).

Most innovation occurs in labs, plants, and firms. The firms pay the bills and researchers are compensated with salaries. In modern economies, most innovation occurs in the private sector, but during a pandemic innovation also comes from universities and government labs. In the case of disease outbreaks, history demonstrates that different paths for innovation exist. Private and public sectors often work in tandem to create medical and healthcare solu-tions. This partnership accelerates the pace of innovation. In a pandemic, private organiza-tions, public institutions, and individuals are knit together by a set of incentives that provide opportunity for symbiosis.

To consider these topics, this chapter first discusses the process of technological advance, which includes the stages of invention, innovation, diffusion, and adoption/rejection. This framework highlights three frames of analysis for technological advance: innovation for growth, systems of innovation, and transformative change. Using this framework, the chapter discusses theories of economic growth, networks of innovation, and transformative change. The chapter concludes with a discussion of the potential for lasting effects.

The process of technological advance

Joseph Schumpeter (1934), the prominent Austrian economist, describes economic develop-ment as an historical process of structural change. In Schumpeter's framework, structural change includes three stages: invention, innovation, and diffusion. An economic agent seek-ing profit must innovate. According to Schumpeter (1942), innovation exists at the center of economic growth, the "essence of capitalism," causing periods of *creative destruction*, when innovation as a "process of industrial mutation ... incessantly revolutionizes the economic structure from within, incessantly destroying the old one, incessantly creating a new one."

Stages of technological advance

The process of technological advance includes Schumpeter's three stages of invention, innovation, and diffusion plus a fourth stage of adoption/rejection (figure 11.1).

Each stage serves a specific purpose. "*Invention* is the first occurrence of an idea for a new product or process, while *innovation* is the first attempt to carry it out into practice" (Fagerberg, 2006). Invention involves establishing something new, but innovation (basic, major, or radical) occurs when a new product or process is brought to the marketplace. Even though innovation and invention are linked, a lag may exist between the two. Invention in the lab may occur long before innovation. Also, invention may occur anywhere, but innovation normally occurs in firms that have a culture designed to nurture the practice, including skills, resources, knowledge, and capabilities. Five types of innovation exist: new products, new methods, opening new markets, acquiring new sources of supply, and new industry structure.

While invention and innovation are important, *diffusion* has a greater impact on the economy. What matters for economic growth is the diffusion of an innovation, when imitators realize the profit potential of a new product, method, market, source of supply, or industry structure. Diffusion is the "process in which an innovation is (spread) through certain channels over time among the members of a social system" (Rogers, 2003).

In Schumpeter's (1942) model, the entrepreneur serves as the chief innovator; however, diffusion may occur on the supply side or demand side of the market. On the supply side, when new methods and markets become widespread, diffusion occurs. On the demand side, when consumers purchase a new product, diffusion occurs. In general, diffusion includes both the planned and spontaneous spread of new ideas, but in the context of this chapter, diffusion refers to the intended spread of new products or methods.

After diffusion, a new product or method may be adopted or rejected, depending on market outcomes, network effects, and best practices. If technological change occurs in a linear process, invention flows to innovation, then diffusion, and finally adoption/rejection. But each step may occur in an intermittent manner, starting and stopping in intervals. An invention may proceed to innovation and then stop. An innovation such as a new vaccine may proceed to diffusion but become rejected if it does not lead to the intended outcome. But *rejection* then informs a new round of invention, provides options, demonstrates viability, establishes conditions for *adoption*, and improves the final product. If adoption occurs, it reflects a normal distribution, entailing an increase in new adopters, a peak, and a decline, while the cumulative number of adopters increases and then plateaus (figure 11.2).

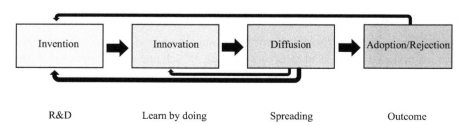

Figure 11.1 Stages of technological advance.
Source: author

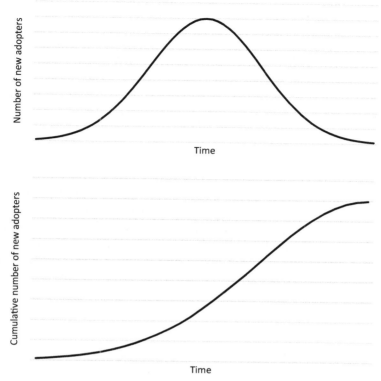

Figure 11.2 Number of new adopters (top) and cumulative number of new adopters (bottom).
Source: author

In each stage, the flow of knowledge is key. To create options, systems of technological advance attract new collaborators. To demonstrate viability, systems of technological advance reduce the risk of research and development, which aids invention. Creating the conditions for adoption of a vaccine during a pandemic, for example, systems of technological advance create strategies for manufacturing and production. Diffusion follows. In the process, early adopters provide knowledge and feedback, while unit costs decline. Widespread consumption of the vaccine then aligns the research process with the needs of the public.

Attributes of innovation

Innovations have different units of analysis. They are not equivalent. While innovations such as trains and electricity grids impact society on a national level, laptops and smart phones spread throughout the global marketplace. Each of these examples increase living standards. But innovations experience different timelines for adoption. The attributes of innovation contribute to their units of analysis, including compatibility, complexity, observability, relative advantage, and trialability. When these attributes appeal to potential adopters, innovations are likely to occur more rapidly (Rogers, 2003).

Compatibility

The concept of *compatibility* means the degree to which an innovation is consistent with the needs of potential adopters. The adopters need to know how the innovation will enhance their production methods, profit margin, or market position. If an innovation requires a large-scale change in the method of production without a corresponding increase in revenue or decrease in cost, then it is likely to be rejected. As a result, innovators must understand both market and business infrastructures and how the innovation will improve a firm's position in a competitive environment.

Complexity

The degree of *complexity* of a product or method means how difficult it is to use. The higher the level of complexity, the slower an innovation will be implemented. In contrast, when an innovation is more intuitive, adopters may implement it in a timelier basis. If a firm increases the pace of innovation, it must balance the cost of new methods or products with the benefit of greater revenue flows. A launch of new methods or products impacts a firm's value chain, requiring more economic data, adjustments in managerial oversight, and new output forecasts.

Observability

The *observability* of an innovation refers to the extent to which potential adopters observe the benefits of the new method or product. After innovation, diffusion spreads the new method or product throughout an industry, but not all potential users adopt. They may wait to assess the cost-effectiveness of the innovation, choosing to observe market outcomes. During a pandemic, the observability attribute serves as an important factor when a vaccine is released. While some people choose to participate in the initial roll-out, others wait and observe.

Relative advantage

The *relative advantage* of a product or method is the degree to which it is perceived as better than the alternative. Potential adopters forecast how the new method or product will enhance their economic position or improve the welfare of potential users. With a new method, firms may consolidate multiple functions, increase productivity, or save time. In the case of a new form of output, an innovative product may increase revenue. With public health, a vaccine may stop the spread of disease, effectively putting an end to a pandemic. Relative advantage, in other words, may occur in different contexts, including better methods for production processes, more choices for consumers, and superior outcomes for society.

Trialability

The *trialability* of an innovation is the degree to which potential adopters may experiment with it. This attribute, crucial for adoption, offers potential users the chance to explore the effects of the innovation. For digital procedures, designers provide beta or demo offerings that enhance the degree of trialability. With vaccines, clinical development includes three steps, when smaller groups receive a trial vaccine, then larger groups receive an updated vaccine that focuses on characteristics such as age or health effects, and finally society receives a vaccine that is tested for safety and efficacy. When a trial product or method replicates the intended outcome, the potential for adoption increases.

Frames of analysis for technological advance

Framings are "interpretations of experience, orderings of present circumstance, and imaginations of future potentialities that create the foundations for policy analysis and action and shape expectations concerning potentials and opportunities" (Schot and Steinmueller, 2018). Framings stem from both historical and contemporary contexts, impacting science, technology, and innovation (STI) policies. These policies arise because of past experiences, present circumstances, and future opportunities.

Practitioners of new ideas connect time periods in the past, present, and future. The framings that result from these connections evolve over time, changing when they cannot adequately interpret existing circumstances. Because they impact economic and social activity, these frames of analysis extend beyond the arena of STI policy, influencing both private enterprise and social behavior. However, because crises such as disease pandemics alter relationships between economic agents, impact market activity, and establish new methods of exchange, previous framings may provide context for technological advance. But contemporary framing must include the consideration of new economic realities that involve the disease pandemic. Schot and Steinmueller (2018) provide a framework of analysis that includes three important framings: innovation for growth, systems of innovation, and transformative change. The third provides a method to consider the impact of a disease pandemic on the process of innovation.

First framing: innovation for growth

The first framing, *innovation for growth*, addresses the impact of science and technological advance on economic prosperity. In the field of economics, economic growth theory, addressed later in the chapter, posits the concept of innovation as either an exogenous or endogenous influence on economic growth. With this first framing, two central features, identified by Kuznets (1973), play a prominent role: improvement in factor productivity and science-based industry.

Following World War II, the role of the nation-state in mobilizing resources became legitimate, especially in the United Kingdom and the United States. A consensus emerged that the nation-state could incentivize research and development, a key aspect of invention, in the private sector. The reason is that industry leaders recognized the contribution of R&D to the modernization of industrial practices and the growth of markets. But innovation involves risk: a new product or method may or may not be adopted. For profitable investments in R&D, commercialization must occur. In effect, the framing for the motivation of invention, inherited from past periods of technological advance, evolves. To profit from invention, a new conception of innovation emerged: "commercialized invention" (Schot and Steinmueller, 2018).

By the late 1950s, a growing understanding of the link between science and the production process encouraged economists such as Solow (1956) to study the relationship between factors of production and the growth in economic output. But the research on the contributions of labor and capital to economic growth did not explain the full impact, leading Solow (1956) to attribute the difference to technological change. Growing interest in this residual led economists to focus on the important role of technological advance.

This research confirmed the link between science and technological advance on one hand and economic activity on the other. But economists questioned whether the market would lead to the socially optimal level of scientific knowledge. An answer in the negative reflected the nature of the market and the challenge of owning or appropriating scientific knowledge. Invention had the features of public goods, both nonrivalrous and nonexclusive, so government support was required. In the 1960s and 1970s, the result was public funding for research for the military, poverty, energy independence, and many other areas (Schot and Steinmueller, 2018).

Second framing: systems of innovation

The second framing, *systems of innovation*, emerged during the 1980s, reflecting globalization, international competition, and inequality of outcomes. This framing grew in response to a level of incompleteness of the first framing, which was subsequently updated to reflect the growing realization of the impact of science on industry. During the 1980s and 1990s, global networks of exchange intensified competition, but low-income countries struggled to close the production and technology gaps. This result called into question the premise of the first framing that invention is a public good available to everyone in the world. In effect, richer countries were developing scientific knowledge and protecting it to gain market share.

This realization led to the reexamination of the linear process of technological advance. First, technological knowledge was not a global public good but possessed characteristics that made it "sticky" or tied to place. Second, the ability to absorb scientific advances depended on absorptive capabilities, which required experience with the scientific process. Third, absorptive capabilities depended on human capital and the culture of entrepreneurship. Fourth, technological advance was path dependent and cumulative. Taken together, these factors suggested that country-level differences in technological advance related to the capacity to innovate, potential to learn, and ability to coordinate the public and private sectors (Schot and Steinmueller, 2018).

In this context, the idea of national systems of innovation emerged, concerned with the application of scientific knowledge to technological advance. But certain characteristics of these national systems were thought to be more efficient than others, including an emphasis on R&D, localized learning, the realization that innovation comes from users, and feedback effects of applied learning. Effective national systems of innovation, in other words, had a national character, reflecting institutional capabilities and policy intervention. Public sector intervention in the second framing addressed a more interactive model of technological advance than the linear depiction in the first framing. The application of knowledge, diversity of organizations, and institutional interactions led to a policy focus that aligned the coordination of different actors in the process of technological advance (Schot and Steinmueller, 2018).

Third framing: transformative change

The third framing, *transformative change*, considers how to use scientific knowledge and technological advance to meet contemporary challenges. New technologies, policies for adaptation, and sustainable consumption patterns require new methods of organization. The challenge for technological advance is to increase economic growth and labor productivity while addressing global environmental problems. With respect to a pandemic, innovation should solve economic, health, and social problems, such as the need for a vaccination.

In a world of global networks and disruptive shocks, investment in the process of innovation determines how well technological advance meets contemporary challenges. The main problem is whether innovation, shepherded by government resources, may address the externalities created by economic growth, including disease pandemics. To date, the degree of international cooperation, national systems of innovation, and budgets for R&D have been insufficient to address global problems that require scientific collaboration and international cooperation.

The framing perspective

The framing perspective implies that technological advance leads to a certain directionality toward a positive outcome. But rejection remains a possibility, especially with the development of a vaccine. In addition, the innovations that emerge during a pandemic, such as remote work and online education, lead to the "creative destruction" or dismantling of previous practices, using Schumpeter's (1942) term. Therefore, the policies and programs from the public sector and methods and strategies from the private sector that attempt to accelerate the process of technological advance during a time of crisis may or may not correspond with social progress during the short run. In the long run, when private sector resources are variable and the public sector matches R&D appropriations with identifiable outcomes, technological advance may improve both health and economic outcomes. But inadequacies during the process of technological advance mean that policies aimed at transformative change should complement the process. Policies include increasing the number of development pathways, coordination between healthcare and the economy, and involving all agents in the process of transformation (Weber and Rohracher, 2012).

Theories of economic growth

The process of innovation is not a new phenomenon. Inherent to human development, innovation characterizes economic activity, labor methods, and technological advance. Even though innovation plays an important role in the growth of economies, economists have not always placed innovation in a prominent role in growth models. Adam Smith (1776), the articulator who created the classical paradigm in the history of economic thought, argues that the division of labor serves as the essential element of the wealth of nations. It results from the expansion of markets. But the expansion of markets is a function of the innovation process. For the classical economists who followed Smith, capital accumulation holds a preeminent role in the study of market performance. Economists now consider innovation as a key driver of economic growth. In particular, they study the factors that encourage firms to innovate. To put this topic in perspective, the following sections discuss technology as an exogenous and endogenous factor.

Technology as an exogenous factor

The *neoclassical growth model* originates in the work of Robert Solow (1956), who posits a long-term relationship between economic growth and capital formation. Aggregate savings, Solow argues, finance an increase in the national capital stock. A high marginal product of capital results from a low capital-to-labor ratio. If a constant fraction of the revenue generated from new capital equipment is saved, investment in additional capital may exceed the amount necessary to equip additional members of the workforce and offset depreciation. The ratio of capital to worker rises and the marginal product of capital falls. In this situation, the savings from new capital decreases to a level equal to depreciation and the amount necessary to equip new workers. The economy reaches a steady state. The implication is that the standard of living is constant. In this framework, technological change is an exogenous phenomenon. Technology serves as an explanatory variable that leads to the aspect of economic growth not explained by capital and labor.

Despite this assessment, the neoclassical growth model's steady state does not lead to a pessimistic forecast about the aggregate economy. In the "medium-run," the capital-to-labor ratio continues to rise and investment in machinery and equipment serves as the driving force behind rising incomes. Policies that encourage savings stimulate economic growth. But in this transitional phase economic growth may still occur if technical knowledge expands. When advances in technology augment labor productivity, an increase in the capital-to-worker ratio may not lead to a decline in the marginal productivity of capital. Higher labor productivity increases the stock of "effective" workers. In the long run, the capital stock increases to keep pace with effective labor force. As a result, capital accumulation serves as the driving force behind economic growth (Grossman and Helpman, 1994).

Technology as an endogenous factor

The idea of technology serving as an endogenous factor stems from Schumpeter (1947), who stresses the important roles of innovation and entrepreneurship in the process of economic growth. In this view, improvements in technology serve as the driving force behind rising living standards. But innovation requires investment by entrepreneurs in the hope of creating a new method or product that has market value. Paul Romer's (1990) analysis demonstrated a flaw in Solow's model: technological advance is endogenous. The process of R&D leads to innovation, which temporarily creates a monopoly of supplying best-practice forms of capital but vanishes when subsequent firms employ better processes.

In the Romer (1990) framework, innovation creates a new type of capital, demanded by the producers of consumption goods. Because the innovating firm may characterize the outcome of R&D with weak uncertainty, the firm weighs the costs and benefits of R&D and chooses an optimal level of spending, which corresponds to the quantity of innovation. In this framework, the innovating process serves as the key to generating endogenous growth

(Verspagen, 2006). However, the entrepreneur is the leader who directs the factors of production in new channels. Improvements in the process of innovation lead to better products, which put the entrepreneur in position to reap higher profits and the economy in position to grow. Feedback effects demonstrate that, as the economy grows, new opportunities for entrepreneurs stimulate innovation, leading other entrepreneurs to bring new ideas to the marketplace (Galindo and Mendez, 2014).

Networks of innovation

As chapter 3 explains, a network is a system of interconnected elements, including nodes or agents and the connections between them. *Innovation networks* exist when collaborative efforts between agents contribute toward the development and creation of new markets, methods, and products. Network attributes from chapter 3 characterize different configurations. Innovation networks often exhibit the attribute of small-worldness, when nodes are not neighbors but may reach each other with a small number of links. Innovation networks may possess a large number of agents, few network fragments, and autonomous entities. Innovation networks may also exhibit high power-law functions, especially in the case of the development of a vaccine, when a small number of agents have many connections and direct a large percentage of the flow of knowledge. This latter case is characterized by a model of *hub firms, O* = {$o_1, o_2, ..., o_n$}, which orchestrate the process of innovation and initiate the creation of value with network members, *N* = {$n_1, n_2, ..., n_n$}, who adopt the methods and products established by the orchestrators (figure 11.3).

As hub firms, the orchestrators facilitate the process of knowledge creation, enhance the mobility of ideas, and leverage competencies in the network. Combining the technologies of the network in new ways requires the identification, assimilation, and accumulation of knowledge. This process creates absorptive capacity at the level of the network, demonstrating learning capacity at the boundary of the firms. The creation of this network identity determines the extent to which information flows (Dhanasai and Parkhe, 2006).

Through market share and previous success, orchestrators gain their position, which they use to gather resources and capabilities. They create value by expanding the size of the market and extract value by increasing their degree of prominence in the network. From the perspective of hub firms, several intentional actions characterize the creation of value, including knowledge mobility, innovation appropriability, and network stability.

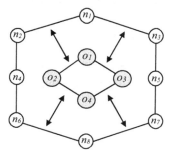

Figure 11.3 Hub firms as orchestrators.
Source: author

Knowledge mobility

The first task for orchestrators in the creation of value is *knowledge mobility*, "the ease with which knowledge is shared, acquired, and deployed within the network" (Dhanasai and Parkhe, 2006). If the knowledge of new methods and products remains locked within an organizational structure, invention, innovation, and network output will not reach their potential. In contrast, if an orchestrator identifies knowledge existing at different points in the network and facilitates the movement of the knowledge to different nodes, learning occurs. An innovation network thrives when the sources of new ideas are shared, the knowledge base is complex, and the rate of exchange is increasing. When knowledge-creating resources flow independently through a network, relative to a hierarchical structure of command, they have greater value. The knowledge-creating resources may be accessed across organization boundaries, combined in unique ways, and unleashed to create new inventions. The problems in one organization may be solved by the solutions of another, but only if knowledge flows between them. Communication channels and exchange forums within and between organizations enhance connections and promote knowledge mobility. As hub firms orchestrate a greater level of knowledge mobility, network innovations increase (Dhanasai and Parkhe, 2006). In this framework, the synergistic effects of networks may replace the large firms posited by Schumpeter (1942) as engines of innovation, especially when knowledge flows across organizational boundaries. "Creative destruction" may occur collectively.

Innovation appropriability

The second task for orchestrators in the creation of value is *innovation appropriability*, the ability of an innovator to capture the profits from an innovation. Copyrights, patents, and trademarks reduce the propensity for unauthorized imitation. Extended to the level of the network, however, appropriability by the orchestrating firms determines the extent to which innovation occurs. A tradeoff exists. When an orchestrator creates value through collaboration, knowledge is shared in the network. When an organization creates value by looking inward and hoarding information, knowledge is not shared in the network. As technology expands, a dynamic process of interaction seeks to find the correct balance of creation, interconnection, and sharing that characterizes a strong network. During transformative periods, such as pandemics, a high variability of outcomes may exist between members of a network with research that leads to innovation and the resulting distribution of benefits. For organizations that are linked in this system, an appropriate distribution of responsibilities and rewards minimizes *free riding*, an important concern in the economics of technology and innovation, which occurs when an organization benefits from the flow of knowledge but does not contribute an appropriate share to the creation of knowledge. In this context, hub orchestrators serve as *triggering entities* that ensure the costs and benefits of network contributors are appropriately distributed (Dhanasai and Parkhe, 2006).

Network stability

The third task for orchestrators in the creation of value, *network stability*, means fostering stable links among network members. Loose connections between members reduce collaboration and risk dissolvability. While firms enter and exit networks in a dynamic process of collaboration and industrial organization, the ability of a network to respond to the challenges of an era depend on the collective knowledge base, research and development, and ability to innovate. These factors benefit from network stability. A weak network is not conducive for the creation of value. But an innovative tension exists. Creatively and loosely designed organizations may be adaptive and agile. However, an erosion of network connections creates instability, which reduces network productivity. This instability may occur in several ways, including isolation, attrition, and migration to other networks, especially if other networks are creating more value or offering better opportunities for collaboration. Hub firms may increase network stability by enhancing the reputation of the network to emerging firms, fortifying reciprocal behavior, and building multiplexity, which means establishing two or more types of connections between network agents (Dhanasai and Parkhe, 2006).

Pandemics, innovation, and transformative change

During a period of transformative change, both strategic and serendipitous alterations to society's methods of operation produce new interactions and outcomes. This transition leads to new ways to supply output. It creates changes in how consumers purchase goods and services. For an economy, it leads to different degrees of product availability, affordability, quality, and reliability. Evolving attitudes toward the marketplace create new methods of organizational structure, such as working from home using telecommunications technology, and new preferences for consumption, such as delivery on demand.

The process of economic transition that leads to transformative change involves a set of alterations to the patterns of market activity, affecting economic resources, supply chains, production methods, patterns of consumption, and public policy. Transition is the time between the introduction of a new set of markets, methods, and products and their growth to an important share of the economy. But technological advance involves conversions and substitutions. New ideas replace old habits. Inefficient methods of delivery are converted into cost-effective practices. Consumers survey a spectrum of new possibilities and make an optimal choice. Examples this century include transitions to digital music, renewable resources, and social networks. Therefore, transitions are complex, cumulative, and multidimensional, spreading from regional to national to international levels. During a pandemic, the challenge is for technological advance in general and innovation in particular to address problems in the economy and systems of public health, including the need for a vaccination, new methods of satisfying demand when people shelter-in-place, and virtual communication when people work from home.

During a crisis, different firms innovate. One category, competitive firms that exhibit the characteristics of dynamic agents, cannot maintain market share without innovation. They upgrade old knowledge, generate new practices, and innovate during all phases of the business cycle. They participate in the process of *creative accumulation* and innovate as a matter of routine (Archibugi et al., 2013). Another category, firms that serve as new innovators, are not members of the industry before the crisis. They take advantage of their opportunity to increase market share, launch new products, and participate in the process of creative destruction, using Schumpeter's (1942) term. With this framework of creative accumulation and creative destruction, technological advances emerged during the coronavirus pandemic, including vaccination and advances in medical care.

Vaccination

Vaccines have the potential to both stop the spread of an infectious disease and eradicate it. But the process of technological advance for the development of a vaccine for infectious diseases averages more than 10 years (Le et al., 2020). The reason is several stages characterize the process, each time-consuming and costly, including academic research, pre-clinical development, clinical trials, building factories, manufacturing, approval, and distribution. Each stage requires economic resources and funding to cover costs (figure 11.4).

Research and clinical trials

Clinical trials, experiments or observations undertaken in clinical research, an important step for the development of a vaccine, almost never work as an initial process. Subsequent behavioral and biomedical research using human participants addresses questions about known interventions and new treatments. Clinical trials generate data, information, and knowledge on the efficacy and safety of potential vaccines, but require a process, including experimental treatments that lead to promising results in the laboratory, trials on humans with safe doses, approval from the overseeing agency in the public sector that a new treatment is effective, and the determination of both costs and long-term effects.

   In the United States, less than 10 percent of the drugs that enter the clinical trial stage are approved by the Food and Drug Administration (Thompson, 2020). The drugs that are not approved may have too many side effects, a lack of effectiveness, or an inability to perform better than existing options. But even with drugs that are approved and adopted, manufacturing and distribution constraints mean some people receive them before others. But after the initial round of vaccinations, researchers determine the effectiveness of the drug and potential costs, including vaccine-induced enhancement, which occurs when suboptimal antibodies bind to a virus and enhance the virus' entry into host cells, leading to replication.

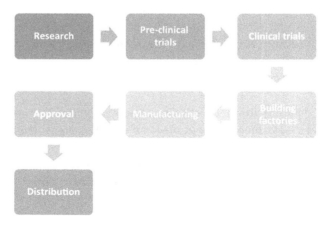

Figure 11.4 Stages of development of a vaccine.
Source: adapted from Thompson (2020)

Research on new technologies has substantial external benefits, but developers may not capture the full value of innovations, so underinvestment may occur. For this reason, incentives from the public sector, including intellectual property, facilitate the process of technological advance. In this context, a vaccine serves the public good. But economic theory posits that competitive markets provide poor incentives to produce public goods: innovators cannot appropriate the benefits of their creation. The creation of a vaccine shares the two properties of public goods, nonrival and nonexclusive. It is nonrival because more people may use it without reducing the ability of others to use it. It is nonexcludable because the provision of the vaccine does not exclude others from using it. Economic efficiency and the full social benefit are achieved when the vaccine is distributed at the optimal price and not the market price.

In January 2020, scientists published the genetic sequence of the novel coronavirus, SARS-CoV-2, that causes the Covid-19 disease, triggering research and development, the beginning of the process of technological advance for the development of a vaccine. The scale of the economic and public health impact of the pandemic drove the development of next-generation technology platforms (viral vectors, recombinant protean, virus-like particle, DNA, RNA). Some vaccine platforms were better suited for demographic characteristics, including age and immunocompromised patients. The first Covid-19 vaccine candidate for human clinical testing began in March 2020, a rapid timeline for the process of innovation (Le et al., 2020).

Collaboration

Oversight from the public sector contributed to the process. At the global level, the Coalition for Epidemic Preparedness Innovations, a global partnership between public, private, civil society, and philanthropic organizations, worked with vaccine developers and public health authorities, maintained an overview of the process of technological advance, monitored vaccine development programs, improved coordination, and encouraged resources and capabilities to flow to their optimal uses. At the country level, public-private partnerships spearheaded the process of technological advance with subsidies providing incentives for exploratory and preclinical research, clinical development, production capacity, and diffusion. Technological advance occurred in the private sector, but projects were also led by academic, nonprofit, and public sector organizations.

The large-scale focus on the development of a vaccine for Covid-19 was unprecedented with respect to scale and speed, a fundamental change from the traditional pathway of vaccine development (Le et al., 2020). Expansion of the paradigm included advances in adaptive and parallel development phases, innovative policies of oversight, and manufacturing capacity. The provision of a vaccine on a global scale required international cooperation and coordination between vaccine developers, governments, policymakers, and public health agencies.

Ethics of distribution

During the coronavirus pandemic, private sector companies, in partnership with the public sector, progressed through the stages of vaccine development, culminating with approval in December 2020, less than one year after scientists published the genetic sequence of the novel coronavirus, SARS-CoV-2, that causes the Covid-19 disease. At the time, with confirmed cases rising in some countries and the initial supply of vaccines limited, a question of distribution emerged: who should initially receive the vaccination? Because of an initial shortage and a desire to both inoculate the masses and stop the disease, the question became the establishment of an objective. Should distribution initially focus on the preservation of human life by vaccinating individuals with serious medical conditions and the elderly or reduce the rate of infection by vaccinating essential workers? The tradeoff between the two choices became an ethical dilemma, guided by the inequities created by the pandemic "from disproportionately high rates of infection and death among poor people and people of color to disparate access to testing, childcare and technology" (Goodnough and Hoffman, 2020).

Focusing on essential workers and reducing the rate of infection became the position of social justice. The essential worker categories in health care, education, maintenance, food preparation and serving, transportation, production, and community services included a high proportion of low-income and minority workers. Ultimately, however, because different definitions of essential workers existed, the choice in countries between preventing deaths and the spread of the disease became one of pragmatic decision-making, because not enough vaccinations initially existed for everyone.

To establish priorities, some states in the U.S. adopted the social vulnerability index from the Centers for Disease Control and Prevention as a method to guide resource allocation. The social vulnerability index uses census variables to help public officials allocate resources to communities impacted by a disaster. The variables include poverty, unemployment, income, education, minority status, and multi-unit housing. During the pandemic, socially vulnerable populations experienced high levels of risk, so the index helped to determine how quickly members of a community needed support.

Medical care

The coronavirus pandemic disrupted systems of clinical care, leading to innovations in virtual care, diagnosis, and therapy. With virtual care, the value of telemedicine, the technology-abled, asynchronous care, increased as a result of the need for medical care, despite private issues and other impediments. During the coronavirus pandemic, clinical care systems expanded their virtual care capabilities, converted an important aspect of their in-person appointments to telemedicine, and addressed a full range of problems, including acute care and the monitoring of chronic diseases. Health clinics and hospitals urged patients to seek virtual care if they had symptoms of Covid-19, rather than appear in person. The benefits of virtual care included access to care without risk of exposure, convenience, the maximization of clinical resources, and interactive improvements over phone calls and email exchange. The costs entailed conversations that may not have presented the same value as in-person visits, the lost social value of face-to-face interaction, and the learning curve for virtual communication for doctors. Overall, education, training, experience, efficiency gains, and resource allocation point to permanent increases in both the supply of and demand for virtual care (Woolliscroft, 2020).

Advances in diagnosis and therapy that occurred during the coronavirus pandemic corresponded with the rapidity of the mapping of the Covid-19 genome, development of therapeutic clinical trials, and instigation of new diagnostic tests. Reliability of new genomic-focused tests reflected the potential presence of a detectible virus. The specificity and sensitivity of the testing apparatus depended on several factors, including technological limitations, the adequacy of sampling, and transportation. Moving forward, technological advance will be leveraged to replace, at least partially, traditional aspects of medical care, including diagnosis and therapy (Woolliscroft, 2020).

Lasting effects

Large-scale crises such as pandemics prompt acts of innovation. The medical system innovates new ways to provide care. Companies adapt to changing market circumstances through the process of technological advance, an example consisting of virtual work models. Households learn to use new methods of communication, consumption, and delivery. Schools systems learn to educate students through distance learning.

   Moving forward, the issue becomes the extent to which the process of technological advance that occurs during a crisis leads to lasting effects. Individuals, companies, and systems of organization could analyze the lessons of technological advance and apply them to periods of relative calm. But not all examples of technological advance that occur during crises offer a blueprint for sustainable methods of innovation. Market circumstances normally do not require large-scale and rapid responses to unpredictable circumstances. Lindsey Lyman (2020), a clinical professor of entrepreneurship at the Chicago Booth School of Business, argues that four tools used to assess economic conditions during a pandemic should become a part of the innovative process. Taken together, the tools provide a framework for creating solutions for upcoming problems.

   First, firms should challenge orthodoxies or pre-existing assumptions concerning business competitors, customers, markets, models, and products. As the marketplace changes, these "truths" may not characterize new market realities. Challenging these assumptions serves as an important input for innovation: a new way of viewing the market motivates the creation of value.

   Second, constraints on methods, capacity, or delivery may accelerate and not inhibit the process of innovation. Firms may not implement new ideas because the process of minimizing risk entails the implementation of established methods and resources. Historical associations and patterns in data may not lead to envisioning new scenarios and pathways for profit. The confrontation of constraints necessitate changes in business models and methods.

   Third, collaboration leads to competitive advantage. High-performing organizations innovate via acquisition or partnership, embracing ideas from external sources. As production processes evolve and become more complex, the acquisition of or partnering with talent accelerates collaboration. This idea of *open-innovation competency*—an innovation process with managed knowledge flows—improves the process of technological advance. Collaboration includes crowdsourcing for new ideas, sponsoring open-innovation competitions, and technology-driven partnerships.

   Fourth, the process of technological advance often moves at a methodical pace because of inefficiency, misaligned incentives, or unnecessary management requirements. While a crisis accelerates the need for new methods, products, and outcomes, sustainable processes of innovation may adopt the preference of speed to match changing economic circumstances, rather than acceptance of previous timelines.

Summary

The process of innovation stems from the desire to create new methods, markets, and products. In the presence of a pandemic, the demand for new outcomes determines the quantity of investment in new methods, markets, and products. The process of technological advance includes invention, innovation, diffusion, and adoption/rejection. The key in each stage is the flow of knowledge. To create options, systems of technological advance attract new collaborators and encourage ideas. Traditionally, the creation of a new idea occurs in the private sector, but, during a pandemic, public funding contributes to the process. Framings, the experiences, circumstances, and imaginations of future possibilities, create the framework for new opportunities. Because they impact economic activity, framings extend beyond the arena of public policy, influence private enterprise and social behavior, and demonstrate the link between technological change and economic growth, networks of innovation, and the conditions for transformative change. While some innovations during a time of crisis lead to lasting effects, firms may implement processes that create sustainable programs of innovation.

Chapter takeaways

LO1   Innovation emerges from crisis, when necessity fosters creation.

LO2   Each stage in the process of technological advance—invention, innovation, diffusion, and adoption/rejection—serves a specific purpose.

LO3   Along with factors of production including labor and capital, innovation contributes to the process of economic growth.

LO4   Innovation networks contribute to technological advance when collaborative efforts between agents contribute to the development and creation of new markets, methods, and products.

LO5   During a period of transformative change, both strategic and serendipitous alterations to society's methods of operation produce new interactions and outcomes.

LO6   Innovations during a pandemic may lead to lasting effects, such as those that provide a model for creating solutions to problems that do not yet exist.

Terms and concepts

Adoption
Compatibility
Complexity
Creative accumulation
Creative destruction
Diffusion
Framings

Free riding
Hub firms
Innovation
Innovation appropriability
Innovation for growth
Innovation networks
Invention
Knowledge mobility
Neoclassical growth model
Network stability
Observability
Open-innovation competency
Rejection
Relative advantage
Systems of innovation
Transformative change
Trialability
Triggering entities

Questions

1. At the firm level, under what circumstances may innovation exhibit counter-cyclical trends?
2. In the process of technological advance, list and describe each stage.
3. In the process of technological advance, what are the factors that determine whether an innovation will be adopted or rejected? If an innovation is rejected, what happens next?
4. List and describe the attributes of innovation. With respect to relative importance, which attributes are more crucial for the process of innovation?
5. Discuss the three framings of innovation. How does the third framing provide context for the impact of a disease pandemic on innovation? To inform your answer, read the article listed in the References section by Schot and Steinmueller (2018).
6. With respect to theories of economic growth, how important is innovation?
7. How might a global network of innovation address public health problems that result from a pandemic more efficiently than a national network of innovation? What economic and technological factors are important?
8. Describe the attributes of the model of innovation networks that includes orchestrating hubs. Do situations exist in which an orchestrating hub consisting of one firm serves as a superior innovation generator than an orchestrating hub of several firms?
9. With respect to the coronavirus pandemic, identify an innovation that addressed an economic or public health problem. What did the innovation address? Where did the innovation emerge? How did the innovation occur? Why was the innovation adopted and not rejected?
10. After a crisis, why do some innovations lead to lasting effects?

References

Archibugi, Daniele, Filippetti, Andrea, and Frenz, Marion. 2013. "Economic crisis and innovation: is destruction prevailing over accumulation?" *Research Policy*, 42, 2 (March): 303-314.

Dhanasai, Charles, and Parkhe, Arvind. 2006. "Orchestrating innovation networks," *The Academy of Management Review*, 31, 3 (July): 659-669.

Fagerberg, J. 2006. "Innovation: a guide to literature," in Fagerberg, J., Mowery, D., and Nelson R. (Eds.). *The Oxford Handbook of Innovation*. Oxford: Oxford University Press, 1-27.

Filippetti, Andrea, and Archibugi, Daniele. 2011. "Innovation in times of crisis: National Systems of Innovation, structure and demand," *Research Policy*, 40, 2 (March): 179-192.

Galindo, Miguel-Angel, and Mendez, Maria. 2014. "Entrepreneurship, economic growth, and innovation: are feedback effects at work?" *Journal of Business Research*, 67: 825-829.

Goodnough, Abby, and Hoffman, Jan. 2020. "Officials agonize over recipients of first vaccines," *The New York Times*, December 6.

Grossman, Gene, and Helpman, Elhanan. 1994. "Endogenous innovation in the theory of growth," *Journal of Economic Perspectives*, 8, 1 (Winter): 23-44.

Kuznets, Simon. 1973. "Modern economic growth: findings and reflections," *American Economic Review*, 63, 3: 247-258.

Le, Tung, Andreadakis, Zacharias, Kumar, Arun, Roman, Raul, Tollefsen, Stig, Saville, Melanie, and Mayhew, Stephen. 2020. "The Covid-19 development landscape," *Nature Reviews Drug Discovery*, 19 (May): 305-306.

Lyman, Lindsey. 2020. "Four ways to ensure innovation continues after the crisis," *Chicago Booth Review*, April 2.

Rogers, Everett. 2003. *Diffusion of Innovations*, 5th Edition. New York: Free Press.

Romer, Paul. 1990. "Human capital and growth: theory and evidence," *Carnegie-Rochester Conference Series on Public Policy*, 32 (Spring): 251-286.

Schot, Johan, and Steinmueller, W. Edward. 2018. "Three frames for innovation policy: R&D, systems of innovation and transformative change," *Research Policy*, 47: 1554-1567.

Schumpeter, Joseph. 1947. "Theoretical problems of economic growth," *Journal of Economic History*, Supplement: 1-9.

Schumpeter, Joseph. 1942. *Capitalism, Socialism, and Democracy*. New York: Harper & Brothers.

Schumpeter, Joseph. 1934. *The Theory of Economic Development: An Inquiry into Profits, Capital, Credit, Interest, and the Business Cycle*. Cambridge, Massachusetts: Harvard University Press.

Smith, Adam. 1776. *An Inquiry into the Nature and Causes of the Wealth of Nations*. Oxford: Clarendon Press.

Solow, Robert. 1956. "A contribution to the theory of economic growth," *The Quarterly Journal of Economics*, 70, 1: 65-94.

Thompson, Stuart. 2020. "How long will a vaccine really take?" *The New York Times*, April 30.

Verspagen, Bart. 2006. "Innovation and economic growth," in Fagerberg, Jan and Mowery, David (Eds.), *The Oxford Handbook of Innovation*. Oxford: Oxford University Press.

Weber, K. Matthias, and Rohracher, Harald. 2012. "Legitimizing research, technology and innovation policies for transformative change: combining insights from innovation systems and multi-level perspective in a comprehensive 'failures' framework." *Research Policy*, 41, 6 (July): 1037-1047.

Woolliscroft, James. 2020. "Innovation in response to the Covid-19 pandemic crisis," *Academic Medicine*, 95, 8 (August): 1140-1142.

12   International economic perspectives

The impact of a pandemic on the global economy

To curb the spread of disease during a pandemic, governing authorities in countries around the world implement lockdown measures, shut down businesses, and reduce economic activity. The results are higher levels of unemployment from a national perspective and less exchange from a global perspective. Firms in the service sector, an important source of economic growth in many economies, experience reductions in economic activity while manufacturing and the volume of global trade also decline. Closing country borders, shuttering workplaces, and limiting distribution in supply chains slow much of the global economy. In the context of the coronavirus pandemic, the International Monetary Fund (2020) calls these interventions the *Great Lockdown*, the extensive measures that reduce disease contagion and save lives. But providing resources and time for healthcare systems to cope with the pandemic leads to a decline in the volume of global economic exchange.

The economic fallout from the Great Lockdown depends on several factors, including the pathway of the pandemic, disruptions in supply, efficacy, and intensity of methods of intervention, changing global market conditions, and behavioral effects. Countries face a catastrophic convergence of health care and economic crises. But the short-term measures that reduce the spread of disease and shutter economies represent an investment in the long-run health of the human population. Over time, as interventions and human behavior bring the disease under control, economies grow while international trade flows, supply chains, and capital markets recover.

When global shocks occur, such as pandemics, the economic outcomes take years to unfold, often spiraling in unpredictable directions. The stock market crash in New York in 1929 contributed to the rise of fascist governments in Europe in the 1930s. In 1997, weakness and interconnection of financial systems caused the Asian Financial Crisis. The mortgage defaults that began in U.S. suburbs in 2007 led to the Great Recession in 2008–2009.

The point is that the global economy is characterized by a web of interconnections. Global economic flows occur in observable patterns, such as exports from one country to others. But higher-order connections make global economic exchange more intricate. This reality, in turn, demonstrates the challenge of identifying global economic outcomes from a disease pandemic. On one hand, economists identify changes in the volume of international trade, the flow of investment, international travel, the delivery of resource inputs in global supply chains, and other measures of international economic activity. The following sections address these variables. On the other hand, economists study changes in the global economy that result from the fracturing or severing of global networks. These factors include the degree of economic interconnection of the global economy, structure of global supply chains, preference for domestic production, and protectionist policies such as tariffs and quotas.

The timeframe is important. In the short term, in global networks, a pandemic shock reduces in quantifiable ways the economic flows of trade, production, and finance. In the long term, several possibilities exist. First, the global economy may return to its pre-existing level of exchange in which the pandemic recession represents a contractionary interval. Second, the global economy may experience a higher level of economic activity. The downturn creates pent-up demand that the recovery interval unleashes. Third, the global economy experiences lower flows of trade, production, and finance. The pandemic recession fractures or severs global supply chains, protectionist policies reduce global interconnections, and the level of international trade declines.

The long-term outcome is an empirical question and subject to investigation. Certain areas of global exchange, such as trade and production, may recover slowly while monetary flows recover quickly. Whatever the eventuality, economic models demonstrate how a pandemic recession impacts economic activity in the short term, but policy prescriptions must acknowledge the possibility of different long-term outcomes. To address these issues, this chapter discusses the factors that impact global economic activity, a pandemic economy tracker, the model of a trading economy, economics of developing countries, and lasting effects from an international perspective.

Factors that impact global economic activity

On a global scale, a pandemic creates public health and economic costs. The crisis in public health requires a reduction in global economic activity. According to the IMF (2020), several factors signal the severity of a global shock, including the nature of the shock, amplification channels, early indicators, and changes in commodity prices.

Nature of the shock

The nature of the shock determines the length and severity of the global economic downturn. During the 1970s, which was a period of both rising prices and unemployment, an increase in the price of oil caused stagflation. In 2008–2009, a period characterized by the subprime mortgage crisis, banks and other lending institutions triggered the Great Recession by issuing high-risk mortgages to borrowers who could not afford them. In 2020, policy interventions that restricted mobility and flattened the epidemic curve, essential to contain the coronavirus pandemic, led to a global economic slowdown. Job losses, a decline in income, a fear of contagion, and uncertainty triggered further economic contraction. These disruptions spread through global economic networks, disrupting the processes of production, distribution, and consumption (IMF, 2020).

Amplification channels

The shock associated with a global pandemic amplifies through familiar channels. One example is financial markets. When shutdown interventions occur, the level of uncertainty increases with respect to financial markets. Because an external shock creates an exogenous impact, models of risk and return have a difficult time forecasting future trends. With an increase in uncertainty and disruptions in economic activity, financial markets establish new asset prices. Investors seek greater liquidity, increasing the cost of borrowing and making the availability of credit relatively scarce. An increase in unemployment leads to loan defaults and foreclosures. In response to an uncertain environment, lenders restrict the supply of credit. Unstable international financial networks exacerbate these disruptions. Economies that rely on external funding experience a decrease in the availability of funds, further straining market conditions. These financial problems contribute to the economic crisis, leading to a convergence of market problems (IMF, 2020).

Early indicators

Early indicators warn of future economic disruptions. Investments in both assets and industrial production decline. The closing of nonessential businesses and the implementation of intervention policies decrease retail sales. Measured on a quarterly basis, economic contraction occurs. Behavioral changes among households lead to a reduction in travel. A decrease in consumer confidence multiplies the initial decline in economic activity. The public health sector reaches capacity, straining the ability to treat those who are sick. Taken together, early indicators warn of upcoming crises and signal to public sectors to mobilize resources (IMF, 2020).

Commodity prices

The deterioration of economic conditions leads to a decline in commodity prices. With a global economic contraction, the prices of commodities such as oil are likely to fall. With this example, two types of markets exist. In the *spot market*, barrels of oil are bought and sold for immediate delivery at a specific location at current market prices. In the *futures market*, contracts that promise a set price for the future delivery of oil are bought and sold. The futures market signals how long the market may experience a relatively lower price. In the oil supply chain, refiners normally purchase oil with futures contracts, either from an exchange or privately negotiated. With this practice, futures markets exist at the center of the oil-pricing system. To establish their positions, speculators use the futures market because it is highly liquid and less vulnerable to distortions. The availability of futures prices enhances the transparency of the market and signals how long commodity prices are expected to remain low.

Pandemic economy tracker

During a pandemic, tracking the global economy reveals both economic trends and the potential for correlation between economic variables. When unemployment rises, changes in gross domestic product and stock market valuations may be indirectly correlated. During a pandemic, households may adjust their expenditure patterns and increase their levels of saving and financial investment, propping up stock prices. According to Chen and Spence (2020), several variables inform a pandemic economy tracker, including mobility and economic performance, speed of intervention, size of the economy, capital markets, and the degree of economic development.

Mobility and economic performance

The loss of mobility relates to changes in economic activity. It is derived from two factors: intervention policies and attitudes toward risk. During a pandemic, when both nonpharmaceutical interventions and attitudes toward risk aversion increase, mobility declines. This outcome reduces economic activity. The relationship between these variables exists for national economies, regions within countries, and time. As countries relax their intervention policies and risk aversion declines, production and consumption increase. Therefore, the countries and regions that apply stronger intervention policies and exhibit greater levels of risk aversion experience larger initial declines in both mobility and economic activity (Chen and Spence, 2020).

Speed of intervention

The more extensive, decisive, and expedient are intervention policies, the slower is the spread of infections. By crushing and containing the disease at the beginning of a pandemic, countries experience larger initial declines in economic activity but minimize losses to the resource base. Choosing less extensive and decisive interventions leads to a tradeoff between public health and the economy. With respect to the coronavirus pandemic, if the length of time is measured in days between the first confirmed infection and the maximum intensity of isolation, the implementation of policy varies between countries. During 2020, New Zealand, Norway, and China reached the maximum intensity of policy strength in less than 30 days, reducing economic losses over time (Chen and Spence, 2020).

Size of the economy

Using business cycle terminology, the contractionary interval is brief for some countries and longer for others. In addition, the intensity of the recessionary period varies between countries. The key to effective navigation is the intensity and speed of intervention policies and the ability of countries to maintain appropriate policy. All else equal, a larger economy and population base create more potential roadblocks to economic recovery, including pandemic fatigue, economic haste, and uncoordinated state responses. Countries may account for these obstacles with comprehensive policies at the national level, but the size of the economy matters.

Capital markets

Intervention policies lead to economic contraction. The reaction of capital markets reveals market expectations. They are forward-looking. In general, capital markets track confirmed cases, changes in economic activity, policy implementation, the development of a vaccine, and technological advance. These factors provide context for investors to judge the potential for future profits. But forward-looking strategies also consider forecasts, pent-up demand, and the prospect of economic recovery. During the shutdown interval, stock markets normally decline, with steeper reductions in economies with more infections. But before economic recovery, stock markets may demonstrate better performance, especially in economies with fewer infections. In this context, however, the optimism may not be consistent with changes in the economy. In addition to speculation, stock market performance depends on the shape of economic recovery. A V-shaped performance, characterized by a steep decline in output and a corresponding rapid recovery, may lead to a swift return to pre-pandemic stock market performance. But an L-shaped pattern, in which an economy contracts and remains at a low level of production for an extended period of time, may lead to an inferior stock market performance.

Developing country status

Subsequent infection waves threaten economic recovery. Unless a country crushes and contains the initial round of infections, additional waves may appear. Compared to first waves, subsequent waves differ with respect to their timeframe, severity, and duration. Second waves, for example, may experience a higher number of peak infections. (A fascinating area of research is to compare epidemic curves for different countries, identifying both the existence and severity of subsequent infection waves, and linking the waves to both policies of intervention and changes in economic activity.) From an international perspective, countries may struggle through subsequent infection waves if they allocate fewer resources to identify, track, and isolate infections. As this chapter discusses, many developing countries exist in this category.

Model of a trading economy

The model of a trading economy by Krugman et al. (2018) demonstrates the impact of economic contraction. It uses several relationships: production possibilities and supply; relative prices and demand; the terms of trade and country welfare; relative supply, relative demand, and global equilibrium; and contraction and the production possibility frontier.

Production possibilities and supply

Assume trade between two countries. Each country produces two forms of output, goods (G) and services (S). Each possesses a *production possibility frontier* (PPF), which demonstrates the maximum level of production, given current economic resources and technology (figure 12.1). If a country operates on the PPF, an efficient level of production occurs. However, a point inside the PPF demonstrates an inefficient use of resources and/or technology. A point outside the PPF is unattainable, given current resources and technology.

Production depends on the ratio of the price of services (P_S) to goods (P_G): P_S/P_G. In the absence of external effects, market power, and other forms of market failure, an efficient economy maximizes the value of output: $P_S Q_S + P_G Q_G$. In figure 12.1, along *isovalue lines*, the value of output is constant:

$$V = P_S Q_S + P_G Q_G \qquad (12.1)$$

But when V increases, the isovalue line shifts away from the origin ($V_2 > V_1 > V_0$). Rearranging the equation yields $Q_G = V/P_G - (P_S/P_G)Q_S$ with P_S/P_G as the slope. The following sections address two cases. In case one, in the presence of full employment, the economy produces at *a*, the point of tangency between PPF and V_1. In case two, when unemployment exists during a pandemic recession, the economy produces on V_0.

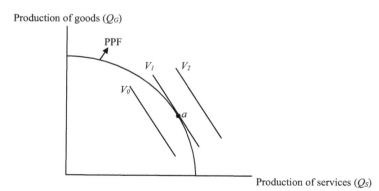

Production of goods (Q_G)

PPF

V_1 V_2

V_0

a

Production of services (Q_S)

Figure 12.1 Production possibility frontier.

Source: author

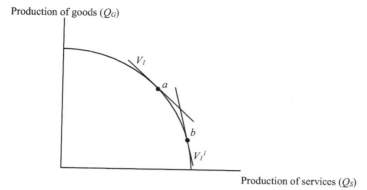

Figure 12.2 A change in relative price impacts supply.

Source: author

Case one: full employment production

A change in relative prices leads to two outcomes. It alters the slope of the isovalue line and determines a new production bundle. Suppose P_S/P_G rises, increasing the slope of V_I. In figure 12.2, the new isovalue line (V_I') moves the production bundle from point *a* to point *b*. As the relative price of services increases, the economy produces more services and fewer goods.

Relative prices and demand

The value of an economy's production equals the value of its consumption:

$$V = P_S Q_S + P_G Q_G = P_S D_S + P_G D_G \tag{12.2}$$

where D_S and D_G represent the consumption of services and goods, respectively. Consumption and production lie on the same isovalue line.

Consumption depends on consumer tastes and preferences, which are represented by *indifference curves* ($I_1, ..., I_n$). Along an indifference curve, the consumption of goods and services leaves consumers equally well off. The assumption is that collective tastes and preferences reflect the tastes and preferences of the typical consumer. Indifference curves demonstrate two concepts. First, tradeoffs between goods and services exist. Greater consumption of one leads to less consumption of the other. Second, the indifference curves that are farther away from the origin correspond to higher levels of satisfaction. More is preferred to less. In figure 12.3, the economy maximizes welfare and consumes at point *c*, where the isovalue line is tangent to I_1. Because the economy produces at point *a* and consumes at point *c*, the economy exports services (measured along the horizontal axis) and imports goods (measured along the vertical axis).

Terms of trade and country welfare

A different *terms of trade*, defined as the price of an item that the economy exports divided by the price of the item the economy imports, alters the welfare effects. While the economy

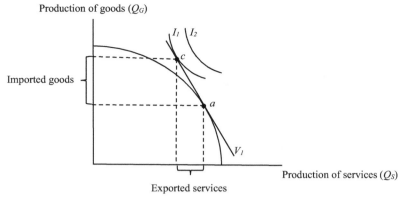

Figure 12.3 Production possibility frontier with trade.

Source: author

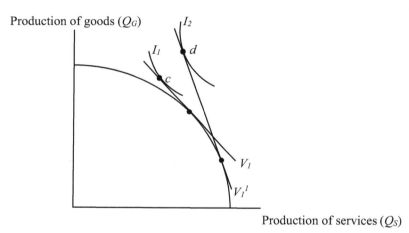

Figure 12.4 Terms of trade alter welfare.

Source: author

is exporting services and importing goods, suppose P_S/P_G increases. This change in relative prices improves the economy's competitive position. In the model, V_1 rotates to V_1^1.
An increase in the terms of trade raises the economy's welfare. In figure 12.4, when P_S/P_G
increases, the economy moves from point *c* to point *d* on a higher indifference curve (I_2).

Global equilibrium

The determination of an equilibrium depends on global relative supply (*RS*) and global relative demand (*RD*). Suppose a home economy and a foreign country. The home economy
exports services and the foreign country exports goods. The production of goods and services by the home country is represented by Q_G and Q_S, respectively. The terms of trade P_S/P_G
applies to the home country. The production of goods and services in the foreign country
is represented by Q_G^* and Q_S^*, respectively. The terms of trade P_G/P_S applies to the foreign

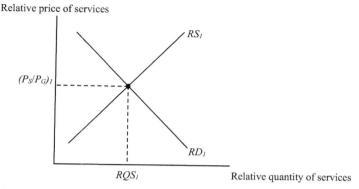

Figure 12.5 Global relative supply and demand.
Source: author

country. In figure 12.5, the global relative supply of and relative demand for services determines both the terms of trade, P_S/P_G, and the relative quantity of services (RQS):

$$Q_S + Q_S^* / Q_G + Q_G^* \qquad (12.3)$$

The *RS* curve slopes upward because an increase in P_S/P_G encourages suppliers to produce
more. The *RD* curve slopes downward because an increase in P_S/P_G encourages consumers to
alter their consumption mix with more goods and less services. The key in the analysis is that
shifts in *RS* may show a bias toward goods or services:

- Rightward shift in *RS*: service-biased growth (more services relative to goods)
- Leftward shift in *RS*: goods-biased growth (more goods relative to services).

Case two: recession during a pandemic

A global recession reduces economic activity but is not evenly distributed. In the model, a
difference between goods and services alters the composition of production.

Contraction and the production possibility frontier

The impact of a contraction depends on its characteristics. During a global recession, one
possibility is that the supply of all forms of output decline equally so that the relative quantity of services to goods remains constant. Another possibility, relevant for a pandemic, is
that a global recession demonstrates *biased contraction* toward goods. That is, the supply of
services may decline, but the supply of goods declines even more. To reflect this outcome,
the PPF in figure 12.6 shifts inward more in one direction (goods) than the other (services).
The economy operates on a lower isovalue line (V_0) and the production bundle moves from
point *a* to point *e*. Biased contraction reduces the production of goods relatively more than
the production of services. A decrease in the supply of a factor of production, labor, in one
area (goods) more than the other area (services) produces biased contraction.

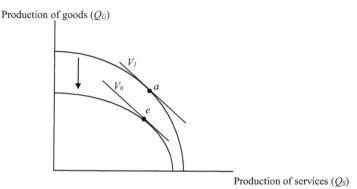

Figure 12.6 Biased contraction.

Source: author

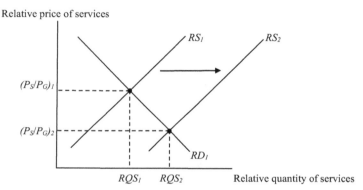

Figure 12.7 Biased contraction and relative supply.

Source: author

Relative supply and the terms of trade

Suppose the home economy experiences biased contraction toward goods, so its production of goods decreases relatively more than its production of services. For the global economy, the production of services relative to goods rises. In figure 12.7, the global relative supply curve shifts to the right from RS_1 to RS_2, decreasing the relative price of services from $(P_S/P_G)_1$ to $(P_S/P_G)_2$ and increasing the relative quantity of services from RQS_1 to RQS_2. This *import-biased contraction* reduces an economy's ability to import goods, which may exacerbate shortages during a pandemic. For an economy in decline, import-biased contraction worsens the terms of trade.

Economics of developing countries

Countries exhibit variation in economic conditions, political structures, and social institutions. It is therefore a challenge to generalize about "richer" and "poorer" countries. Those with larger populations such as China and India experience problems such as administration and national cohesion while benefiting from large markets, diverse resources, and economic diversity. Countries with smaller populations such as Bolivia and Ecuador face limited domestic markets, a smaller labor force, and scarce resources.

The study of *development economics* addresses the efficient allocation of scarce or idle resources and the economic, institutional, and social mechanisms, private and public, necessary to bring about improvements in human well-being. Development economics combines theories and applications from traditional economic analysis with additional approaches that focus on the improvement in the standard of living and quality of life of the majority of the world's population (Todaro and Smith, 2014). A focus on developing economies makes clear that the effects of a global pandemic are not equally distributed.

World Bank income classification

The World Bank, an international financial institution that provides grants and loans, uses data on gross national income per capita in current U.S. dollars to classify economies according to four income groups: high income, upper-middle income, lower-middle income, and low income (table 12.1). Economies in classifications other than high income are considered developing.

Development as a process

The development of an economy from a lower to a higher income classification involves changes in economic activity, national institutions, poverty, social structures, and employment. Development includes the entire process of change, in which a country improves the basic needs of individuals and groups within the system, provides opportunity for greater material well-being, and elevates "an entire society and social system toward a better or more human life" (Todaro and Smith, 2014).

This process of change includes three core values which constitute the meaning of development: freedom, self-esteem, and sustenance. Freedom involves the sense of emancipation from inferior economic conditions and from servitude to institutions and dogmatic beliefs. It entails a greater range of social choices and the minimization of economic constraints. In this context, economic vitality relates to freedom by improving the range of human choices. Self-esteem entails a sense of dignity, self-respect, and worth. While the nature and characteristics of self-esteem may differ between countries, sustainable development goals, highlighted below, demonstrate that greater self-esteem includes access to a cleaner environment, peaceful interactions, and prosperity, universal measures of worth. Sustenance, the ability of a society to meet its basic needs, including food, clothing, shelter, health, and protection, is a function of access to resources, mechanisms of exchange, and effective governance. When sustenance is in short supply, an absolute level of underdevelopment exists. A function of an

Table 12.1 World Bank income classification, 2020

Income classification	Per-capita income	Number of countries
High income	$12,536 - above	83
Upper-middle income	$4,046 - $12,535	56
Lower-middle income	$1,036 - $4,045	50
Low income	$0 - $1,035	29

Source: World Bank, https://www.worldbank.org

economy is to provide the chance for all inhabitants of a country to meet their basic needs, while a function of governing authority is to provide health and protection. Both economic vitality and effective governance are necessary for an improvement in the quality of life. Development creates an economic and social environment in which individuals may expand their opportunities (Todaro and Smith, 2014).

Characteristics of developing countries

Developing countries possess a range of characteristics with economic activity, social structure, language, tradition, history, culture, and political systems. These characteristics provide an illustrative framework, especially when they contrast to the characteristics of developed countries. While the characteristics may differ by degree, they exist as reasons why the status of "developing" persists. Characteristics of developing countries include relatively lower living standards, lower levels of productivity, higher rates of population growth and dependency burden, a greater percentage of work in the informal sector, and dependence and vulnerability in international relations.

Living standards

Relatively lower living standards reflect less freedom, self-esteem, and sustenance, lower average levels of income per capita, higher levels of poverty, less education, inferior housing, higher infant mortality, and lower life expectancy. Across countries, these qualitative and quantitative measures differ with respect to their degrees of significance but may generate a feeling of insecurity. The public sector, for example, may provide housing for migrants to urban areas, but the private sector may not provide employment opportunities. In addition, average income per capita may create "middle-income" status, but higher levels of poverty and infant mortality for members of lower socioeconomic classes may create inferior living conditions. Income gaps between those who benefit from the existing order and those that do not may perpetuate an inequality of outcomes. The magnitude of poverty conditions depends on average per-capita income and income inequality. The greater is the level of inequality, the higher is the incidence of poverty, and the lower is the average standard of living.

Productivity

A *vicious cycle of poverty* entails poor households with few resources and low living standards that exhibit low levels of productivity. Labor productivity as measured by output per worker is relatively low when compared to developed countries. Several reasons exist. Relatively lower labor productivity may result from a lack of complementary resource inputs, especially capital, the machinery and equipment that serve as factors of production. Savings and foreign investment that generate new physical capital purchases and investments in human capital may be inadequate. The institutional influences that enable advances in human and physical capital, such as the implementation of education and training programs, administrative services, banking reforms, and land tenure, may not keep pace with economic requirements. The private sector may not assimilate new methods, processes, and technological advances that enhance worker productivity. Economic arrangements between producers and consumers, the organization of production processes and markets, and the quality of human resources may not exist at levels that enhance the ability of workers to become more productive. Taken together, these factors perpetuate low levels of productivity, which contribute to low living standards and the vicious cycle of poverty.

Population growth

With a world population approaching 8 billion people in 2020, about 85 percent live in developing countries. According to the World Bank, global population growth has declined during this century to a level of about one percent annually. In upcoming decades, almost the entire increase in global population will occur in developing countries. Both birth and infant mortality rates, illustrative of the changes in population, differ between developed and developing countries. With birth rates, a declining trend correlates with labor force participation, particularly among women. Data for crude birth rates, the annual number of live births per 1,000 people, demonstrate a difference between developed and developing countries, although both are declining from 20 births per 1,000 people in 1970 to between 10 and 15 births per 1,000 people in 2018 (figure 12.8).

Infant mortality rates, the number of deaths per 1,000 live births for children under the age of one, signifies the strength of healthcare systems and the availability of healthcare resources. Higher infant mortality rates pressure women to have more children. In addition, higher infant mortality rates signify higher percentages of birth defects, pregnancy complications, injuries, preterm births, and sudden infant death syndrome. Over time, when countries improve their health care systems, increase the availability of resources, and improve human health, infant mortality rates decline. Data on infant mortality rates for high-income and low-income countries signify a major difference, although both are trending downward (figure 12.9).

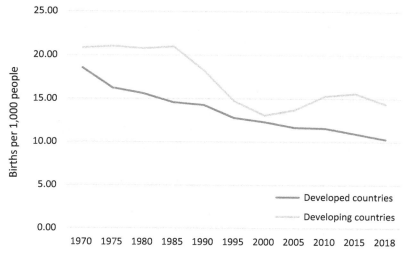

Figure 12.8 Crude birth rates.

Source: author using data from the Federal Reserve Bank of St. Louis, https://fred.stlouisfed.org/series/SPDYNCBRTINHIC

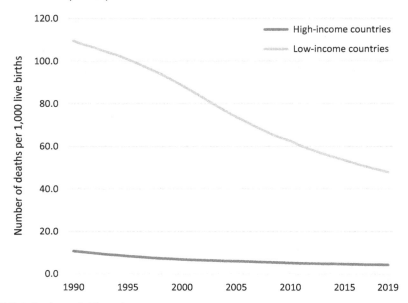

Figure 12.9 Infant mortality rates.

Source: author using data from the Federal Reserve Bank of St. Louis, https://fred.stlouisfed.org/series
/SPDYNIMRTINHIC

Informal sectors

The informal sector is neither monitored nor taxed by government. When compared to developed countries, developing countries possess a higher percentage of informal sector economic
activity. As countries develop, they assimilate individuals from rural areas into cities in the
process of urbanization. They also train workers for employment in expanding markets. But
urbanization and industrialization do not guarantee formal sector opportunities. On the contrary, ineffective or nonexistent social safety nets, limited resources, a lack of opportunity and
human capital, and stagnant formal labor markets persist in developing countries. For large
segments of the working class, this reality leads to both income insecurity and vulnerability.

While economic growth and global interconnection increase the potential for work in the
formal sector, developing countries may struggle to develop formal markets and employment opportunities. An important relationship exists between human capital and the level of
informality. As individuals experience higher levels of education and training and thus have
a greater capacity to produce goods and services, the level of informal work declines. People
who have completed primary and secondary education are less likely to work in informal sectors; however, people living in rural areas are more likely to work in informal sectors. In developing countries, not all informal sector workers are poor, but informal sector employment is
correlated with higher levels of poverty. Moving from informal to formal sector employment
means more economic opportunity, better social protection, and improved working conditions.

International relations

A final factor characterizing developing countries is their unequal position within the global
economic order. Not only is this position perpetuated by high-income countries, networks of

globalization, and international trade, but also the ability of high-income countries to dictate the terms of foreign direct investment, technological advance, and the flow of private capital. In order to advance the needs of developing countries, multinational corporations, governing authorities, international institutions, and regional trade agreements must work proactively to align the interests of developing countries, especially low-income countries, with the rest of the world. Examples of economies moving up in the World Bank's system of income classification, including South Korea and Chile, provide context. These countries improved their systems of education, developed a variety of economic sectors, increased labor market flexibility, encouraged saving and investment, and increased opportunities for foreign direct investment. Countries that transition to high-income status develop and strengthen their domestic markets while integrating into the global economy.

The impact of a pandemic on developing countries

Developing countries are in a difficult position to respond to a global shock. Like developed countries, they suffer from economic contraction, lockdown measures, and rising infections. But lower living standards, lower levels of productivity, higher population growth rates, large informal sectors, and relatively weaker positions in the global economic order constrain the capacity of developing countries to address these problems in a comprehensive manner. As a result, the process of recovery, including economic growth, reductions in morbidity and mortality, and the eradication of the disease, may be intermittent, starting and stopping at intervals. In the absence of an international effort to support low-income countries, permanent reductions in human health, equality, and employment threaten to perpetuate problems of impoverishment.

While developing countries may act to contain the spread of disease, control international travel, close schools, and cancel public events, domestic economic activity may be slow to return to pre-crisis levels. Reasons include large informal sectors and levels of subsistence living, a lack of institutional capacity to help the poor, and limited fiscal support. While some developing countries respond to the pandemic with shutdown interventions, social distancing, and contact tracing, others lack the resources to help the most vulnerable.

Sustainable development goals

The goals of sustainable development, established by the United Nations in 2015 as a collection of interdependent aspirations and made actionable in 2017, are designed as a blueprint for a more sustainable future (figure 12.10). Although a pandemic complicates each goal, the following sections address the impact of a pandemic on three goals: zero hunger, no poverty, and peace. The reader is encouraged to evaluate how a pandemic impacts the other goals.

Food insecurity

In many low-income countries, the risk of food insecurity exists as an ever-present threat. While the drivers of food insecurity vary, reasons include reduced rainfall, drought, conflict, inferior conditions for crops and livestock, and disease outbreaks. A pandemic intensifies the problem, potentially endangering the lives of millions of people. First, a pandemic compounds

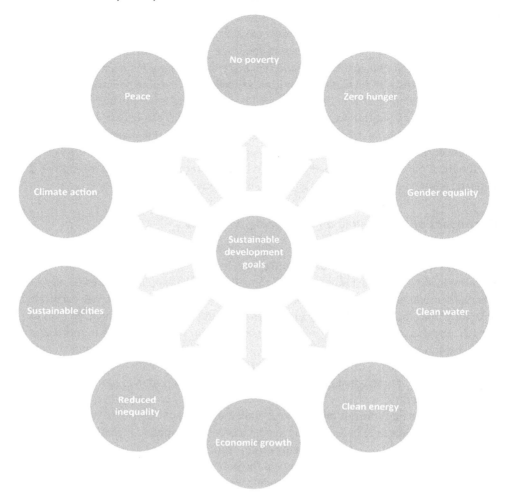

Figure 12.10 Sustainable development goals.

Source: author using information from the United Nations, uno.org/sustainabledevelopment/sustainable
-development-goals/

pre-existing problems. Second, humanitarian relief efforts may not be able to distribute aid. Third, a pandemic complicates the lives of asylum-seekers, migrants, and refugees. Fourth, a pandemic diverts resources from hunger programs to fight the disease.

As food insecurity rises, the pandemic intensifies the inefficiencies and vulnerabilities of the interconnected global food system, severs food supply chains, and shutters markets that produce and distribute food. Localized food shortages raise prices, putting vital food items such as vegetables and meat beyond the reach of many households. As a result, the consequences of a pandemic may increase food insecurity as much or more than the disease itself.

During the coronavirus pandemic, many informal sector workers in developing countries lost their jobs. These workers rely on daily wages for meals. When unemployment rises and informal sector workers have fewer opportunities, they lack a means to subsist. These individuals were not earning enough money to eat, especially when they spent more than half of their income on food. The implication is that, when vulnerable countries implement lockdown measures to slow the spread of disease, interventions are necessary to maintain food security (Sly, 2020).

Poverty

When economies shut down during a pandemic, working hours decline in both formal and informal sectors. While the impact is comparable across countries, the loss of working hours in developing countries burdens people living at the margins of existence. One estimate is that during the coronavirus pandemic 1.6 billion workers in the informal sector, mostly in developing countries and about half of the world's workers, lost their jobs (Sly, 2020). The loss of income for people living close to or in poverty conditions reverses gains that countries make in fighting deprivation. A study by the United Nations (2020) estimates that the economic fallout from the coronavirus pandemic led to an increase in global poverty by half a billion people, or 8 percent of the human population, the first rise in global poverty in 30 years. Extreme poverty, the most severe category, characterized by severe deprivation of basic human needs such as food, shelter, sanitation, clean drinking water, and health, becomes more prevalent during a pandemic. During the coronavirus pandemic, almost 10 percent of the world's population lived in extreme poverty, but the pandemic pushed 100 million more into the category (Lakner et al., 2020). Most of the new people living in extreme poverty were in South Asia, Sub-Saharan Africa, and East Asia and the Pacific.

Conflict

By increasing food insecurity and poverty, a pandemic may establish a pathway to conflict. At the same time, the existence of conflict may weaken a country's capacity to identify and respond to a pandemic, exacerbating the spread of infectious disease. A health emergency becomes worse when it spreads to countries suffering from conflict, fragility, and violence. Conflict may take the form of state repression against individuals or groups, riots not involving the state, interstate conflicts between nations, or civil war. In an economic perspective, the relationship between a large external shock such as a pandemic and conflict reveals three realities. First, in developing countries, environmental resources provide a livelihood for the poor. Second, methods of coping, ingenuity, and resilience do not provide the means for adaptation. Third, structural inequality and relative depravation exacerbate the effects of an external shock.

The pathways between a pandemic and conflict take different forms. A pandemic may lead to the depletion of natural resources as the supply of output in global markets declines. This effect creates resource scarcity with cropland. If the stability of a society is a function of agricultural productivity and food security, resource scarcity could complicate these factors. If mediating characteristics, such as government, markets, public policy, laws, civil society, technology, trade relationships, investment, international organizations, and adaptive capacity are insufficient to address these changes, conflict may result.

If conflict occurs, the possibility of small-scale turmoil evolving into larger-scale violence depends on historical context, pre-existing animosity, inequality, the state of the economy, resource capture—when a decrease in the quality and quantity of environmental resources encourages powerful groups to shift resource distribution in their favor—and ecological marginalization. Wise and Barry (2017) argue that, with respect to a pandemic, conflict may "reduce outbreak surveillance and control capacities, resulting in silent global dissemination; and the potential that infectious outbreaks emerging in areas plagued by civil conflict can generate complex political and security challenges."

The United Nations/World Bank (2018) joint study, *Pathways for Peace: Inclusive Approaches to Preventing Violent Conflict*, provides country-level recommendations to reduce the potential for conflict, which are appropriate during a pandemic. First, conflict sensitivity is important. Countries that experience fragility and violence are particularly vulnerable. An understanding of the causes of these problems and potential solutions provides a framework to address the problem. Second, trust and inclusion matter. Basic services such as education, public health, and safety provide the mechanisms in which individuals interact with government. An equitable delivery of services reduces competition among groups and aids the process of recovery. Third, community engagement and partnerships are important. Working across the peace-economic development-humanitarian aid nexus is crucial in helping unstable countries.

Lasting effects: an international perspective

Impact on globalization

As countries guide their way through a pandemic, decisions about global markets and supply chains hinge upon economic conditions and attitudes toward globalization. On one hand, global interconnection increases both production and living standards. On the other hand, globalization leads to competition, deregulation, inequality, energy consumption, and greenhouse gas emissions. A pandemic shock accelerates, aggravates, and intensifies these global flows and processes. A pandemic may serve as a reason for the world to cooperate or an outcome of a broken globalized system (Fontaine, 2020).

Because a pandemic serves as a major shock, businesses operate in a market with both globalization and anti-globalization sentiments. Economic systems do not operate in a world of disconnection; however, a pandemic highlights the risk of overdependence on global networks. While the interconnectedness of capital, goods, services, data, ideas, and technology produces clear benefits, the creation of new barriers during a pandemic, including export restrictions, travel bans, closed borders, and fractured supply chains alter business conditions and consumer choices. A pandemic leads to the prioritization of national responses and the reinforcement of nationalist arguments. But a pandemic does not lead to the end of globalization. The economic links that produce the goods and services of the modern era, from smart phones to electric vehicles, include many points of connection.

But a pandemic may initiate a transition to alternative models of economic organization. According to Altman (2020), the future trajectory of globalization depends on several factors. First, international flows follow macroeconomic cycles. Economic growth resumes when the pandemic is under control. Second, economic approaches toward supply chains depend on whether businesses seek higher levels of international diversification or domestic self-sufficiency. Third, the fracturing of the global economy leads to calls for more regional economic activity, but this focus depends on the relative influence of economic powers such as the European Union, China, and the United States. Fourth, pandemic-induced technological advances in areas such as telework and e-commerce expand opportunities for global exchange in markets with higher degrees of global integration. Finally, because the process of globalization provides a method for a local disease outbreak to become a pandemic, economic contraction leads to calls for protectionism and opposition to global markets.

These factors demonstrate that a pandemic decreases global economic flows; however, globalization continues to present opportunities. The intensity of trade, for example, may decrease in goods and increase in services. Airline travel may decline, but social networks may expand. Overall, the net change in global economic flows may be modest, depending on the length and scale of the pandemic. Moving forward, pandemics lead to calls for barriers, but solving the crisis requires collaboration and clear information.

Impact on global networks

To reduce the spread of disease, countries restrict travel and economic activity. These interventions decrease exchange in global networks, particularly supply chains. The effect depends on the number of countries implementing restrictions and the duration and severity of shutdown measures. Stricter and shorter interventions minimize economic losses. But the complexity of global supply chains magnifies losses. To minimize this problem in global supply chains, the control of a pandemic requires collaboration and assistance for developing economies (Guan et al., 2020).

A pandemic leads to different policies of disease control and methods of application, including duration (number of months that shutdown measures are in place), spatial spread (quantity of countries affected), and strictness (extent to which transportation and labor capacity decline relative to pre-pandemic levels). As chapter 4 explains, countries may implement targeted or comprehensive shutdown policies, depending on their preferences for prioritizing public health. But they establish these policies for different periods of time.

Global supply chains respond differently to the duration, spatial spread, and strictness of policy interventions. One study found that global supply-chain effects depend first and foremost on the quantity of impacted countries (spatial spread), second on the duration of policy interventions, and finally on the strictness of policy interventions (Guan et al., 2020). In addition, the propagation of supply-chain losses leads to impacts on countries that are not affected by the initial infection wave. For example, when distribution networks cease to operate, all network members experience economic losses, whether or not confirmed cases are rising. With these indirect effects, middle- and low-income countries are most vulnerable. But a tradeoff exists. With global networks, effective containment interventions benefit countries from a public health perspective by slowing the spread of the disease; however, global networks lead to economic losses for those same countries by fracturing supply chains (Guan et al., 2020).

Summary

To curb the spread of disease, governing authorities implement lockdown measures that shut down businesses and reduce economic activity. The results are higher levels of unemployment from a national perspective and less exchange from a global perspective. Several factors signal the severity of a global shock, including the nature of the shock, amplification channels, early indicators, and changes in commodity prices. Tracking the global economy during a pandemic reveals both economic trends and the potential for correlation between economic variables. Several factors provide context for a pandemic economy tracker, including mobility and economic performance, speed of intervention, size of the economy, capital markets, and the degree of economic development. A focus on development economics makes clear that the impact of a global pandemic is not the same for all economies. Characteristics of developing countries include relatively lower living standards, lower levels of productivity, higher rates of population growth and dependency burden, greater percentage of work in the informal sector, and dependence and vulnerability in international relations. A pandemic disrupts economic flows through global networks of exchange but does not eliminate the process of globalization.

Chapter takeaways

LO1   A pandemic impacts the global economy by reducing the production of output, curtailing consumption, and fracturing global supply chains.

LO2   The nature of the pandemic, amplification channels, early indicators, and commodity prices signify the magnitude of pandemic outcomes.

LO3   A pandemic economy tracker reveals that mobility, speed of intervention, size of the economy, capital markets, and developing country status impact the extent to which a pandemic alters an economy.

LO4   The model of a trading economy demonstrates that, when economic contraction occurs, the potential for import-biased contraction makes it even more difficult for the home country to provide the goods that consumers demand.

LO5   The characteristics of developing countries, including lower living standards, lower productivity, higher population growth rates, larger informal sectors, and a lower share of the global economy, make them relatively more susceptible to a pandemic.

LO6   A pandemic may lead to lasting effects on the process of globalization and networks of exchange, depending on the length and severity of the shock.

Terms and concepts

Biased contraction
Development economics
Futures market
Great Lockdown
Import-biased contraction
Indifference curves
Isovalue lines

Production possibility frontier
Spot market
Terms of trade
Vicious cycle of poverty

Questions

1. How does a pandemic impact the global economy? In your answer, be specific with respect to pathways.
2. With a pandemic, how does the nature of the shock and its amplification channel signal its severity?
3. With respect to a pandemic, how do early indicators and changes in commodity prices signal its severity?
4. A pandemic economy tracker includes data for the indicators that reveal changes in the global economy. What indicators best describe changes in the global economy? Why?
5. With a pandemic recession, explain what the following indicators reveal: mobility, speed of intervention, size of the economy, capital markets, and developing country status.
6. In the model of a trading economy, what is the impact of a pandemic on a country's production possibilities? How do relative prices and the terms of trade impact the result?
7. What are the characteristics of developing economies? What unique challenges does a pandemic present?
8. How did the coronavirus pandemic impact the achievement of the sustainable development goals of the United Nations?
9. In developing countries, how did the coronavirus pandemic impact food insecurity, poverty, and the potential for conflict?
10. Does a pandemic lead to lasting effects with respect to the process of globalization and global networks? To answer this question, analyze data on international trade, foreign direct investment, airline travel, and other global indicators.

References

Altman, Steven. 2020. "Will Covid-19 have a lasting impact on globalization?" *Harvard Business Review*, May 20.

Chen, Long, and Spence, Michael. 2020. "Five lessons from tracking the global pandemic economy," *VoxEU*, July 17. https://voxeu.org/article/five-lessons-tracking-global-pandemic-economy.

Fontaine, Richard. 2020. "Globalization will look very different after the coronavirus pandemic," *Foreign Policy*, April 17.

Guan, Dabo, Wang, Daoping, Hallegate, Stephane, Davis, Stephen, Huo, Jingwen, Li, Shuping, … Gong, Peng. 2020. "Global supply chain effects of Covid-19 control measures," *Nature Human Behavior*, 4 (June): 577–587.

International Monetary Fund. 2020. *World Economic Outlook: The Great Lockdown*. Washington D.C.: IMF.

Krugman, Paul, Obstfeld, Maurice, and Melitz, Marc. 2018. *International Economics: Theory and Policy*, 11th edition. New York: Pearson.

Lakner, Christoph, Yonzan, Nishant, Mahler, Daniel, Aguilar, Andres, Wu, Haoyu, and Fleury, Melina. 2020. "Updated estimates of the impact of Covid-19 on global poverty: the effect of new data," *World Bank Blogs*, October 7. https://blogs.worldbank.org/opendata/updated-estimates-immpact-covid-19-global -poverty-effect-new-data.

Sly, Liz. 2020. "Hunger could be more deadly than coronavirus in poorer countries," *The Washington Post*, May 14.

Todaro, Michael, and Smith, Stephen. 2014. *Economic Development*. New York: Pearson.

United Nations. 2020. "Covid-19 fallout could push half a billion people into poverty in developing countries," April 8. https://www.wider.unu.edu/news/press-release-covid-19-fallout-could-push-half -billion-people-poverty-developing-countries.

United Nations and World Bank. 2018. *Pathways for Peace: Inclusive Approaches to Preventing Violent Conflict*. Washington D.C.: World Bank Publications.

Wise, Paul, and Barry, Michele. 2017. "Civil war & the global threat of pandemics," *Daedalus*, 146, 4 (Fall): 71-84.

13   New economic geography

Learning objectives

After reading this chapter, you will be able to:

LO1   Explain that pandemics spread through geographic space in uneven patterns.

LO2   Identify the components of the model of new economic geography, focusing on the importance of transportation costs.

LO3   Discuss themes of economic geography, including globalization, uneven development, and place.

LO4   Analyze applications such as urbanization and pandemic shocks, spatial equilibrium and pandemic costs, and smart cities and pandemic resilience.

LO5   Contrast factor-driven outcomes with network-driven contagion in the context of spatial diffusion.

LO6   Identify appropriate responses to pandemic outcomes for urban and rural areas.

Chapter outline

- Economic geography and pandemic outcomes
- New economic geography: a framework for economists
- Themes of economic geography
- Applications of economic geography
- Spatial diffusion and network-drive contagion
- Responses to pandemic outcomes
- Summary

Economic geography and pandemic outcomes

The coronavirus pandemic first infected people in urban areas and then spread to rural sectors. Urban areas are connected through global networks. People first spread the disease to others during international travel, starting in China, spreading to Europe and North America, and then to the rest of the world. Initially, rural areas experienced lower rates of transmission, but in many countries secondary outbreaks penetrated rural areas while cities managed to control the disease. In the United States, for example, the coronavirus started to spread in urban areas in March 2020. By October 2020, confirmed cases in rural areas were higher (figure 13.1).

If early surges in a pandemic are defined by concentrated outbreaks in cities, subsequent infection waves spread across urban and rural populations. In the United States, when a third infection wave began during the fall of 2020, none of the major hotspots were in large cities (Leatherby, 2020). However, the effects on rural areas were uneven, reflecting the vulnerability of local populations, quality of healthcare services, and policy interventions. In many smaller communities, hospitals struggled with capacity, health officials could not rely on contact tracing, and many businesses had to shutter for an additional period of time, including bars, restaurants, and retail stores.

The field of *economic geography* addresses where economic activity occurs and why. The field is particularly interested in the location of the factors of production. This focus is important for understanding both the structure of economies and the effects of pandemics. With the structure of economies, several examples demonstrate the importance of the topic. One example is regional economic integration. In 1999, the introduction of the European euro and the integration of economies highlighted the need to combine analyses of international economics and regional economics. Another example is urbanization. In 2007, the United Nations estimated that, because of the global movement of people from rural to urban areas, the world's urban inhabitants constituted half of the world's population for the first time in history. A third example is economic development. In the United States, a country with substantial land mass, the overall population density of 36 per square kilometer is lower than China and India, countries with comparable geographic space, which have population densities of 148 per square kilometer and 382 per square kilometer, respectively. A substantial

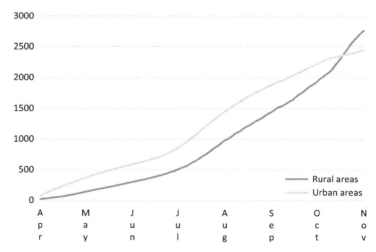

Figure 13.1 Rural and urban coronavirus cases in the United States during 2020−cumulative confirmed cases per 100,000 residents.

Source: author using data from Johns Hopkins University Center for System Science and Engineering, accessed through the United States Department of Agriculture, https://www.ers.usda.gov/covid-19-rural-america/

portion of economic activity occurs on the two coasts with population and economic bases in the northeast U.S. and southern California. A large agricultural sector exists in the Midwest. The question of interest is why this pattern of economic activity developed. In the field of economics, many other interesting examples exist.

With respect to pandemics, they do not spread evenly across economies, socioeconomic characteristics, or geographic space. Chapter 4 argues that the shutdown interval during the pandemic phase leads to an uneven distribution of employment outcomes. Individuals in "nonessential" sectors may experience unemployment at higher rates than other members of the labor force. Chapter 8 argues that members of marginalized communities with pre-existing conditions and less access to health care suffer more from the spread of disease than other members of the population. This chapter argues that pandemics spread unevenly across geographic space, leading to regionally differentiated outcomes. In the case of the coronavirus pandemic, the impacts on health and economic activity serve as examples. Interconnectedness, urbanization, demographics, health expenditure, and interventions influence the spread of disease. But, as this chapter argues, these factors are regionally differentiated.

To address these topics, the chapter first discusses new economic geography as a framework for economists. It then addresses themes of economic geography. The chapter follows with sections on applications of economic geography, spatial diffusion and network-driven contagion, concluding with appropriate responses to pandemic outcomes.

New economic geography: a framework for economists

Known as "new economic geography" after the publication of Paul Krugman's seminal (1991) article, spatial economics addresses why production and economic activity concentrate in geographic space. A circular pattern develops. Businesses locate where workers live and workers want to live where businesses operate. Yet not everyone lives and works in one big city, or even a small number of big cities. In addition, economies do not concentrate the production of each good in specific locations. In contrast, production and human populations spread throughout countries, influenced by urbanization, industrialization, and globalization. To explain this process, an agglomeration force promotes geographical concentration (*centripetal force*) while a dispersion force pushes economic activity away from a geographic center (*centrifugal force*). New economic geography addresses the nature of these forces. What are they? How do they influence the location of economic activity? The answers to these questions may be traced to Krugman's (1991) article on increasing returns and economic geography.

Increasing returns and economic geography

Krugman (1991) develops a simple model that demonstrates how an economy may become differentiated between a production core and an agricultural periphery. This section leaves the mathematics of the model to the interested reader but discusses the important ideas. In the model, two regions exist. Each region has the same number of farmers who exhibit immobility and identical productivity. But manufacturing activity and the manufacturing labor supply are mobile. On the supply side, manufacturers minimize transportation costs, pursue economies of scale, and locate in regions with higher demand for their products. On the demand side, the consumption of output depends on the location of production.

With this model of economic organization, Krugman addresses an important question: why do manufacturing companies concentrate in geographic space, leaving other regions relatively undeveloped? He argues that the core-periphery pattern depends on the share of manufacturing in national income, economies of scale, and transportation costs. But Krugman's important insight is that when manufacturing firms choose a location for production, they hire workers who live and consume in that region. This pattern creates local forward and backward linkages that perpetuate the economic activity.

The conditions that lead to the core-periphery pattern are considered *pecuniary externalities*, which occur when the actions of an economic agent cause a change in market conditions. The presence of imperfect competition provides context. When a competitor takes market share away from a rival, profits decline for the latter but their ability to produce remains. The actions of one firm impact the demand for output of another firm, which is common in many industries. In this case, a pecuniary externality exists that is just as important as innovation spilling over from one firm into an industry. Whereas negative externalities represent market failure, pecuniary externalities occur when a market is working. This distinction is important because pecuniary externalities signify a transfer of welfare from one set of firms to another.

Manufacturing, agriculture, and economies of scale

The model of new economic geography proposes an economy with two sectors, manufacturing and agriculture. Manufacturing is characterized by a modest use of land and increasing returns to scale. Agriculture is characterized by an intensive use of land and constant returns to scale. The distribution of agricultural production depends on the availability of suitable land.

In this framework, the question of interest is where manufacturers choose to locate. Because of the existence of economies of scale, the production of manufacturing output occurs in specific sites. All else equal, the sites are characterized by high levels of demand because locating production near consumers decreases transportation costs. These production hubs then serve other locations by establishing distribution networks. But where will demand exist? Demand for manufacturing output comes from both the agricultural sector and the manufacturing sector. A positive feedback effect emerges: manufacturers locate in large markets but markets will be large where manufacturing occurs.

In an economy with manufactured goods, mass production, distribution networks, and decreasing transportation costs, it is more desirable to live and produce in areas with higher concentrations of manufacturing. Reasons include larger markets and lower costs for buying the output produced in those areas. Over time, these production centers attract more people at the expense of agricultural regions. The process builds upon itself until the entire nonagricultural population concentrates in urban areas.

Geographical concentration

Centripetal and centrifugal forces influence the outcome. According to Krugman (1998), the centripetal forces that keep economic activity in motion around a geographic center include market-size effects, thick labor markets, and pure external economies. A large local market and economies of scale create sites that are conducive for production, support the production of intermediate inputs, and decrease costs for downstream producers. Industrial concentration supports a thick labor market of specialized skills, enhancing the market-clearing potential of the labor market. Local concentration also impacts the creation of external economies that result from information spillovers.

The centrifugal forces that encourage economic activity to expand outward from a geographical center include immobile factors, land rents, and pure external diseconomies. Immobile factors such as natural and land resources push against market concentration because of demand-side reasons (dispersed production leads to some producers locating near dispersed consumers) and supply-side reasons (agricultural production seeks workers in areas of lower population density). Agricultural activity increases land rents and provides incentive for lower population density. Industrial concentration leads to pure external diseconomies in the form of pollution, congestion, and crime.

In the progression of new economic geography, Krugman (1998) argues that market-size effects as a force for greater concentration and immobile factors as a source of less concentration serve as important modeling factors. If location is important for the examination of economic activity, spatial diffusion should enter the modeling framework. These linkage effects are a function of distance and mediated by transportation costs:

> The central thrust of the new economic geography … has been driven by considerations of modelling strategy toward an approach that concentrates on the role of market-size effects in generating linkages that foster geographical concentration, on one side, and the opposing force of immobile factors working against such concentration on the other.
>
> (Krugman, 1998)

Economic development therefore entails a process of economic growth in interlinked spatial structures, which includes production, consumption, and commuter networks. Although the manufacturing sector in many developed economies represents a small percentage of total production, economic concentration suggests that economic geography displays structures of regionalization that match descriptions of urban cores and agricultural peripheries.

Agglomerated and dispersed equilibria

When will economic activity concentrate in one region? When will dispersion occur? Krugman's (1991) model demonstrates that both agglomerated and dispersed equilibria may exist, depending on the value of a key parameter: transportation cost. The model begins with two symmetric regions and two industries: imperfectly competitive and mobile manufacturing and perfectly competitive and immobile agriculture. Three simplifying assumptions exist. The first is farmers that produce agricultural goods are sector-specific, face zero transportation costs, and receive a uniform wage. The second is that workers in manufacturing pursue higher real wages in either region. The third is manufacturing firms enter and exit the industry in response to profits and losses. With these assumptions, it is possible to analyze when diversification (manufacturing dispersed between regions) or agglomeration (core-periphery) occurs. The dynamic aspect is that the pull of the immobile farmers generates the centrifugal force but the linkages in manufacturing generate the centripetal force.

In the model, the difference in real wages depends on the distribution of manufacturing between regions. But that dependence is a function of transportation costs (T). Consider two cases. First, higher levels of T encourage economic stability. Little inter-regional trade exists. Wages depend on the level of local competition. Wages decrease with the number of other workers in the region. Home production is profitable because imports into the region are expensive. This scenario leads to diversification and the dispersion of manufacturing between regions. Second, lower levels of T discourage economic stability. The typical firm sells in both regions. Because the firm has better access to markets in the region with higher population and demand, it may pay higher wages. Workers have better access to consumer goods, so the purchasing power of their wages is higher. But locational instability exists: neither region has comparative advantage.

Between high and low levels of T, two important threshold values exist. A high level of T encourages diversification between regions; however, as T declines from a high level it reaches the sustain point (T_S). Diversification between regions ceases to serve as an equilibrium. When transportation costs decline, producers evaluate opportunities in the other region. As T decreases further, transportation costs reach the break point (T_B), at which the diversified equilibrium breaks down. As transportation costs decrease below T_B, the conditions are sufficient for core-periphery organization (agglomeration). To summarize, the following threshold conditions motivate the establishment of one equilibrium or several equilibria:

- T_S - Sustain point: diversification between regions ceases to serve as an equilibrium
- T_B - Break point: the diversified equilibrium breaks down
- $T_S > T_B$

To put this model in perspective, consider the potential values of T. Transportation costs may (a) exceed T_S, (b) equal T_S, (c) exist between T_S and T_B, (d) equal T_B, or (e) fall below T_B. All else equal, the value of T determines the outcome. In case (a), $T > T_S$, transportation cost is high, a unique equilibrium exists, and workers are evenly divided between the two regions. This equilibrium represents the highest level of diversification and the lowest level of agglomeration. The core-periphery equilibrium does not hold. With (b), $T = T_S$ (transportation cost equals the sustain point), two potential equilibria exist: manufacturing may concentrate in either region. The most interesting case occurs with (c), when transportation cost exists between the two thresholds, $T_B < T < T_S$. Both diversification and agglomeration are possible equilibria. Three stable equilibria exist: one diversified with manufacturing spread between the two regions and two agglomerated equilibria, one in each region. With the three potential equilibria, economic policy and historical influences have a role in determining which equilibrium prevails. With (d), $T = T_B$, two potential equilibria exist with partial concentration of manufacturing in one region or a full concentration of manufacturing in one region. With (e), $T < T_B$, a unique equilibrium exists with the lowest level of diversification, agglomeration in one region, and a stable core-periphery framework.

Application of the model reveals that a decrease in transportation cost increases agglomeration and the movement to the core-periphery configuration. As long as transportation costs are below T_s, the model will not restore the diversified equilibrium (Neary, 2001). The model organizes the economy in spatial structure, creates the potential for multiple equilibria, and leads to the uneven distribution of economic activity between regions. In sum, model configuration depends on transportation cost:

- $T > T_s$: unique equilibrium with the highest level of diversification, workers equally divided between regions, and the absence of a core-periphery configuration
- $T = T_s$: two potential equilibria with manufacturing concentrating in either region
- $T_B < T < T_s$: three potential equilibria with manufacturing spread between the regions and two agglomerated equilibria, one in each region
- $T = T_B$: two potential equilibria with partial concentration of manufacturing in one region or a full concentration of manufacturing in one region
- $T < T_B$: unique equilibrium with the lowest level of diversification, agglomeration in one region, and a stable core-periphery framework.

Bifurcation model

With a division of economic activity, this is called a *bifurcation model* (figure 13.2). In particular, Fujita et al. (1999) call the model a "tomahawk bifurcation." The vertical axis measures the share of the manufacturing labor force (λ) in region one. The horizontal axis measures transportation cost. Solid lines represent stable equilibria. Dotted lines represent unstable equilibria.

If the economy starts at point *a* with the highest transportation cost and an even division of manufacturing between region one and region two, a decrease in T to point *b* unleashes the movement of manufacturing. Between points *b* and *c*, economic forces shift manufacturing work between the two regions, although a possibility remains that the workers are equally distributed. At point *c*, the economy begins a cumulative process in which a concentration of manufacturing in one region creates momentum for more manufacturing in that region. Below point *c*, the economy establishes a core-periphery framework.

In Krugman's (1991) model, two forces promote agglomeration: the instability of a symmetric structure and the core-periphery outcome. First, *backward and demand linkages*

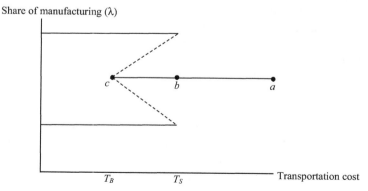

Figure 13.2 Agglomerated and dispersed equilibria.

Source: author using information from Krugman (1998), Figure 1, and Neary (2001), Figure 2

increase the profitability of existing firms when new firms enter the market. The reason is that, when the new firms hire labor in the factor market, the demand for labor increases, promoting in-migration into the region. With an increase in labor demand and labor income, the demand for local output rises, relative to the other region. Second, *forward and cost linkages* lead to market crowding and a decrease in the price index for manufacturing output. The decrease in the price index increases real wages for workers. Higher real wages induce an in-migration of workers to equalize real wages between regions. This increase in labor supply decreases nominal wages, which reduces the cost of production for local manufacturers (Henderson, 2003).

Themes of economic geography

In their book on economic geography, MacKinnon and Cumbers (2019) discuss three main themes. The first theme is globalization, the widening and deepening interconnections among countries, companies, and individuals through all forms of exchange. The process of globalization is manifested through global networks, including production, trade, technology, information, finance, migration, and social connection. The second theme, uneven development, means that some regions or countries are more prosperous and economically influential than others. In geographic space, differences exist with respect to income per capita (demonstrated by World Bank data on country classifications in chapter 12). These differences lead to varying levels of population density and access to healthcare resources. Economic opportunity leads to urbanization but rising living costs lead to de-urbanization. The third theme is place, how areas become interconnected in wider economic processes, and the consequences for their identity, existence, and distinctiveness. Successful urban areas such as San Francisco and London benefit from successive waves of immigration and investment. Rural areas with declining manufacturing bases experience depopulation and a lack of investment.

Perspectives of economic geography

Economic geography builds on these themes, but acknowledges perspectives that include a method of analysis, a systems framework, and spatial representation. First, the method of analysis means exploration of the interconnection between development and the economic landscape. Location is an important concept, referring to the motivations for economic activity to occur in physical space. Networks of globalization increase the scope of analysis beyond Krugman's (1991) two-region model of manufacturing and agriculture. These networks overcome the friction of distance created by transportation cost. With advances in communications and transportation technology, economic actors move goods, services, information, capital, and technology around the world. Second, a systems framework links economic and social forms of organization. Not only do economic agents concentrate in specific regions, but social systems develop in response to this concentration. Third, with spatial representation, *scale* refers to levels of economic activity, starting from the workplace and moving to the local, regional, national, macroregional, and global. These scales of economic activity connect, overlap, and do not exist as mutually exclusive forms.

Connections across space and time

An increase in connection across geographic space occurs because the internet, file shar-ing, and videoconferencing reduce the transaction costs of interconnected systems. These technological advances impact global processes, having accelerated during this century. The flows of technology and information are expediated by *time-space compression*, the reduc-tion of the distance and time required by economic processes, resulting from advances in communication and transportation technologies. An example is the creation of the container ship, which occurred in 1956. Containers filled with goods are loaded onto ships, reducing the cost of loading the goods directly onto ships. This method increases the efficiencies of transportation and distribution as a seamless transfer of containers occurs between ships, trains, and trucks. In addition to altering space and time in economic activity, communication and transportation technologies stretch social relations across time and space in a process called *time-space distanciation*. For example, social media connect business organizations but decouple space and time. This process encourages interaction but does not depend on physical presence. Taken together, these concepts both expediate global flows and strengthen economic networks.

Applications of economic geography

The defining focus of economic geography is the desire to address the concentration of eco-nomic activity and/or population, such as industry clusters, the characteristics of cities, and manufacturing and farm belts. These forms exist because of spatial economics. Economic concentration creates an environment conducive for greater concentration. Applications of the principles of economic geography apply to pandemic shocks, including urbanization, spa-tial equilibrium, and smart cities.

Urbanization and pandemic shocks

Urbanization refers to the movement from rural to urban areas and the methods in which society adapts to the change. Urbanization occurs in the presence of two forces: when countries switch their sectoral composition from agriculture to industry and technological advances in the production of agricultural output releases laborers to move to cities. With these forces, urbanization exists as a transitory process with economic and social implica-tions. In urban areas, workers develop human capital to contribute to the market economy. Businesses increase the demand for labor. Governing authorities enhance social services, such as education, healthcare, and security. This transition requires the development of eco-nomic, social, and political institutions. When complete, the process of urbanization ends with a country having between 60 percent and 90 percent of its inhabitants living in cities, depending on economic development, the public sector, and modern agriculture. On a global scale, migration from rural to urban areas means that a higher percentage of people now live in urban environments (figure 13.3).

Because urbanization exists as a process, it may reverse. In Krugman's (1991) model, four reasons exist. First, as transportation cost decreases, firms may exit the core for lower wage costs and a surplus of labor in the periphery. With less expensive trade, linkage effects do not

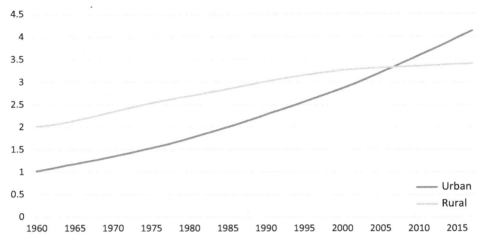

Figure 13.3 Number of people in urban and rural areas in the world (billions).

Source: author using data from Our World in Data, Ourworldindata.org/urbanization#number-of-people -living-in-urban-areas

ensure the core's dominance. Second, manufacturing workers are mobile. If transportation cost falls, manufacturing firms in the periphery may attract workers from the core. Because food costs are relatively lower in the periphery (the core has to import food), firms in the periphery may attract workers (Fujita et al., 1999). Third, congestion may occur in the core. Rising housing prices, commuting, and fixed land for the residential sector may lead to an outflux of workers to the periphery (Henderson, 2003). Fourth, a pandemic spreads disease through areas with higher population density, reducing employment options, increasing the relative price of agricultural output to the core, and providing incentive for workers to move to the periphery.

Spatial equilibrium and pandemic costs

The economic approach to cities applies the concept of *spatial equilibrium* to laborers and businesses. Models of spatial diffusion solve the simultaneous equilibria of regional markets with transportation costs. Locational choices focus on the understanding of the motivations to live in specific areas. The establishment of an urban equilibrium implies that urban amenities, including economic opportunity, cultural attractions, and higher wages offset negative attributes, such as congestion, pollution, and higher housing prices. Because of net benefits, cities attract workers with higher levels of both human capital and productivity that justify the relatively higher wages. In actuality, the development of urban areas reflects numerous choices. The relative attributes of cities matter. Economists assume that the amenities are reflected in linear utility functions, which means the elements of utility related to urban areas are included in the framework:

$$\text{Income} + \text{Amenities} - \text{Housing Costs} - \text{Transportation Costs} \tag{13.1}$$

Holding individual attributes such as income constant, relatively higher housing costs in an urban area are offset by better amenities and/or lower transportation costs (Glaeser, 2007).

The framework is useful to consider pandemics. If pandemic effects vary across geographic space, utility must include the dissatisfaction from pandemic outcomes:

$$\text{Income} + \text{Amenities} - \text{Housing Costs} - \text{Transportation Costs} - \text{Pandemic Costs} \quad (13.2)$$

All else equal, relatively higher pandemic costs in an urban area encourage the flow of workers and businesses to rural areas.

Smart cities and pandemic resilience

To attract residents and improve the quality of life, *smart cities* apply technological advances, sensors, and other methods of observation to gather data for a smart city matrix, including the economy, energy, environment, governance, infrastructure, society, transportation, and pandemic resilience. Each variable includes several indicators (figure 13.4). With an improvement of these indicators, cities move to higher levels of "smartness."

A pandemic impacts all indicators. For example, pandemic resilience depends on shutdown measures, economic support for businesses and households, and the capacity of the infrastructure, especially hospital beds, to handle the crisis. But the pandemic leads to different effects: a decrease in GDP per capita and increases in unemployment and the Gini coefficient; reductions in energy demand and greenhouse gas emissions; an improvement in air quality; political unrest and uncertainty; a lack of emphasis on green space; reductions in

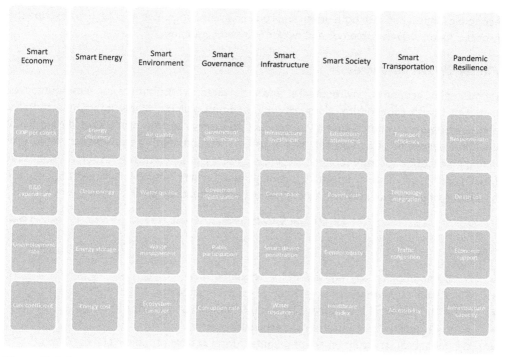

Figure 13.4 Smart city variables and indicators.

Source: Abu-Rayash and Dincer (2020), Figure 3

educational attainment, gender equity, and health, and an increase in the poverty rate; and less traffic congestion. Taken together, the changes lead to a mixed outcome.

Spatial diffusion and network-driven contagion

In epidemiology it is important to identify geographic tendencies that contribute to the spread of disease. In the fourteenth century, the Black Death that swept across Europe killed more than 25 percent of the population. Although human interaction and mobility influenced the trajectory of the plague, on a large geographic scale, a pattern emerged. After the initial outbreak in southern Europe, the pandemic propagated at a speed of a few kilometers per year over the entire continent.

Today many factors influence the spread of disease. Because of network interconnections, patterns emerge. This reality reflects characteristics of the global economy, including modern air transportation with billions of annual passengers and thousands of airports. Because timely interventions may save the lives of thousands of people, understanding the dynamics of global disease transmission serves as an important objective.

Spatial diffusion demonstrates that pandemics spread in global networks, regional sectors, and local areas. But important sites, called hotspots or hubs, defined as areas of origin for the spread of disease, may exist in urban or rural areas. Urbanization makes cities more vulnerable to the spread of disease by increasing population density. At the same time, global networks connect cities through systems of production, trade, and technology. The expansion of economic activity into suburbs and satellite towns in peri-urban zones creates hybrid economic landscapes with both urban and rural characteristics. Two approaches describe the process: factor-driven outcomes and network-driven contagion.

Factor-driven outcomes

Demographic, economic, environmental, and social factors contribute to pandemic outcomes, including health expenditure, air quality, intervention policies, global interconnectedness, and demographic trends. Some cities conduct aggressive testing procedures during initial infection waves but others do not. Higher rates of testing identify transmission rates, providing information for interventions, business closures, and healthcare resources. Kapitsinis (2020) provides a model framework, positing that mortality rates (M_i) between regions i are a function of independent variables that reflect geographic variability:

$$M_i = f\left(D, GI, MM, AQ, IS, SHB, AU, ED, SL, HS\right) \tag{13.3}$$

where

- D = Demographics (average age of the population)
- GI = Global interconnectedness (value of exports per capita)
- MM = Mitigation measures (days between first death and lockdown)
- AQ = Air quality (concentration of particulate matter)
- IS = Industrial structure (share of manufacturing in total economic activity)
- SHB = Size of households/businesses (average number of people living in households and average size of businesses)

- *AU* = Urbanization (number of businesses per 100,000 inhabitants)
- *ED* = Economic dynamism (GDP per capita)
- *SL* = Social life (percentage of people above 65 living in collective living quarters)
- *HS* = Health system (medical doctors and hospital beds per 100,000 inhabitants)

With this model, several hypotheses exist. On a regional basis, higher mortality is expected to correlate with older populations, higher levels of global interconnection, weaker mitigation measures, lower air quality, higher shares of manufacturing, larger households and businesses, higher levels of urbanization, larger degrees of economic dynamism, more people living in collective quarters, and fewer medical doctors and hospital beds. In an empirical investigation of nine countries in the European Union, Kapitsinis (2020) finds varying degrees of significance in the determination of mortality rates, although air pollution, firm size, household size, rate of urbanization, economic dynamism, age of population, share of older people in care homes, health expenditure, mitigation policies, and regional position impact the mortality rate.

Network-driven contagion

The spread of disease is complex, dynamic, and driven by networks. The heterogeneity and multiscale characteristics of the process complicate the understanding of network effects, timelines, and treatments. However, even though a disease may spread on a global scale, *spatiotemporal patterns* that occur in a wide range of natural phenomena may be reduced to wave patterns that spread across geographical space. In the presence of this probabilistic spread through transmission networks, researchers predict the relative arrival time of disease across geographic space (Brockmann and Helbing, 2013). Several questions exist. Where does the disease originate? Where will new infections emerge? When will a pandemic arrive at distant locations? How many global cases will occur? What mitigating factors (economic shutdowns and social interventions) exist? Scientists address these questions with sophisticated and parameter-rich computational simulations, which include demographic, epidemiological, and mobility data.

A study published in *Science* argues that an approach that fuses the predictive power of computational simulations with the conceptual power of diffusion models creates an effective measure of distance (Brockmann and Helbing, 2013). This framework for network-driven contagion demonstrates that patterns of complex structures, such as demographic, economic, environmental, and social factors contributing to pandemic outcomes, may be reduced to "regular, wavelike solutions reminiscent of simple reaction-diffusion systems" (Brockmann and Helbing, 2013). The implications are twofold. First, epidemiological parameters enter the framework separate from the transport-network parameters. Second, global transmission results from a small percentage of network connections. (Within three months of the initial identification of an infected person with Covid-19, in Wuhan, in December 2019, the disease spread throughout the world. A network connection between Wuhan and northern Italy seeded the spread in Europe, while a network connection between Wuhan and the city of Seattle seeded the spread in North America.)

Using a susceptible-infected-recovered framework (chapter two), Brockmann and Helbing (2013) argue that, despite the multiplicity of potential paths, structural complexity of the global transportation network, and redundancy of connections, the spread of disease on a global scale is dominated by the most probable trajectories. That is, a few, initial connections dominate the heterogeneity of a network. As a result, a small fraction of traffic (*effective distance*) is equivalent to a large distance in geographic space. That is, "simple coherent wave fronts," determine the speed and arrival times of the disease at distant sites (Brockmann and Helbing, 2013).

Impact on rural areas

During a pandemic, rural areas may seem immune. When infections and deaths rise in cities, health officials may report fewer rural cases. But that false sense of security becomes a problem when rural areas become susceptible to the spread of disease. Contagion may spread through towns and villages where testing and tracing resources are scarce and families cannot afford to quarantine. As economic shutdown measures reduce economic activity in urban areas, an exodus of workers to rural areas may help to spread the disease. Taken together, rural characteristics, the potential for defiance to national standards, an influx of people from urban areas, and resistance to shutdown measures may create a surge of infections.

In rural areas, several characteristics create an environment for the spread of disease, including a higher average age, lower income levels, weak local economies, large group facilities, employment in nursing homes for the elderly and meat processing plants, fewer hospital beds and protective equipment, and a prevalence of pre-existing health conditions. Shutdown measures in urban areas may initially spare rural sectors. But human connections may increase the number of infections. As the disease upends local economies, towns and villages are vulnerable to job losses because of a lack of a diversified economic base. If a few prominent employers shut down their business operations, a majority of workers in the community may lose their jobs.

With the exception of population density, rural areas may exhibit higher risk factors as a share of the population. Rural areas may have older populations, chronic health conditions, fewer care providers, more uninsured residents, and a greater potential for severe cases. Rural areas may also have large group facilities, including meatpacking plants and nursing homes for the elderly, where the disease may spread. Proper treatment during a pandemic requires a combination of competency and resources that may not be available in all rural hospitals. As a result, rural areas may not have the same access to medical care.

One study addressed the hospital, clinical, and demographic risk factors associated with death in patients with Covid-19. Gupta et al. (2020) argue that data and information on patient characteristics, the availability of treatments, hospital resources, and patient outcomes are needed to inform decisions about resource allocation and capacity constraints in hospitals. This information also provides context to assess the variation of treatments and outcomes across hospitals. Assessing more than two thousand adults with confirmed Covid-19 cases who were admitted to intensive care units in 65 hospitals, the authors find that, after 28 days, 35 percent died, 37 percent were discharged, and 28 percent remained hospitalized. The factors that correlate with death include older age, male designation, higher body mass index, coronary artery disease, active cancer, and liver and kidney dysfunction. But the study also finds that patients admitted into smaller hospitals with fewer than 50 intensive care unit beds were three times more likely to die, compared to patients admitted to larger hospitals. Although the study does not address hospital capacity or staffing, it emphasizes that medical professionals and healthcare systems are crucial for the delivery of critical care, a resource-intensive and laborious process. In rural areas with less access to hospital resources, the inequities of disease become more entrenched.

Impact on urban areas

The process of urbanization intensifies problems in cities, including congestion, pollution, and traffic, but also presents opportunities for economic growth and economies of scale. During a pandemic, policy interventions alleviate these problems but threaten the opportunities. Sheltering-in-place interventions reduce economic activity, traffic, and air pollution. At the same time, economic shutdowns reduce the production of output.

Higher levels of population density make cities more vulnerable to the spread of disease, at least when infections are accelerating. But cities also have the ability to manage the crisis through economic shutdowns. In the short term, a pandemic becomes a crisis of access to urban economies, amenities, and public services, which disproportionately affects the most vulnerable inhabitants of cities. Over the long term, a pandemic highlights the critical role of public sectors in addressing areas of vulnerability, including health care, crisis response, and economic recovery.

The United Nations (2020) argue that shutdown interventions lead to impacts within and beyond urban landscapes. Because urban areas account for the majority of global GDP, a reduction in urban economic activity impacts all sectors of the economy. These urban outcomes lead to an urgent need to transform cities to better cope with future global hazards, including disease pandemics. Not only should cities strengthen their systems of healthcare and housing, but they should build more sustainable and inclusive environments by strengthening the indicators of smart cities addressed earlier in the chapter, including equality, energy efficiency, air quality, government digitization, infrastructure investment, healthcare access, technology integration, economic support, and infrastructure capacity.

Principles for urban areas to become more equitable and sustainable includes governance and public policy. Strengthening policies to address inequality, leadership, and networks within and between cities will increase the level of urban resilience for future shocks. By strengthening the level of interconnection, urban areas may sound warnings, spread information, ensure rapid responses, maintain food supply chains, enhance healthcare facilities, and implement more effective intervention measures for social distancing, quarantines, and masks. The prevention of future pandemics requires transformation in all aspects of urban life, including the provision of adequate and affordable housing, public services, equitable access to healthcare, transparent policy, and economic development strategies for all members of society (United Nations, 2020).

Social vulnerability

The events surrounding the coronavirus pandemic illustrated the world's vulnerability to the global spread of disease. Why was the world so vulnerable? In retrospect, the warnings were clear. In 1994, Laurie Garrett, a Pulitzer-prize winning journalist, using research on virology, medicine, molecular biology, and diseases, documented the potential threat of a pandemic in her book, *The Coming Plague: Newly Emerging Diseases in a World Out of Balance*. In 2018, the Johns Hopkins Center for Health Security gathered U.S. government officials, public health experts, and business leaders to address the potentially devastating economic and social consequences of global threats such as pandemics, issuing a report, "The Characteristics of Pandemic Pathogens," that addressed bacteria, prions, protozoa, and viruses, the latter serving as the real menace (Alexopulos, 2018). Many other warnings existed. But moving forward, the important question is how regions should prepare for future threats.

The emerging field of *vulnerability science* helps to conceptualize circumstances that put people at risk from hazardous events and the conditions that inhibit appropriate responses (Cutter, 2003). Vulnerability science establishes strategies for risk, hazard, and disaster reduction. The field integrates the constructs of hazard, mitigation, resilience, risk, and susceptibility into one framework. It establishes an interactive approach among economic, healthcare, natural, and social systems. Because vulnerability applies to groups, people, places, and systems, spatial solutions serve as important components, especially when evaluating relative degrees of vulnerability between geographic space.

Imbedded in vulnerability science is the necessity of anticipating future shocks, evaluating uncertainty, and modeling potential outcomes. "We need to identify, delineate, and understand those driving forces that increase or decrease vulnerability at all scales" (Cutter, 2003). What makes particular regions vulnerable? How do the processes of globalization, industrialization, and urbanization impact the susceptibility of regions? To answer these questions, the estimation of risk, forecasting of potential losses, establishment of interactive susceptible-infection-recovered models, creation of comparative indicators, visualization of potential responses, and creation of decision-making frameworks serve as important components.

To help regions address emergency events such as disease outbreaks, the Centers for Disease Control and Prevention use the Social Vulnerability Index (SVI). The SVI helps public health officials and policymakers identify communities that require support during and after hazardous events. For the United States, the SVI uses census data and 15 explanatory factors to establish the level of "social vulnerability" of each census tract. The explanatory factors include crowded housing, lack of access to vehicles, and poverty and establish four indicators: housing composition, housing/transportation, race/ethnicity/language, and socioeconomic status. Using these indicators, the framework finds that socially vulnerable populations, which exist in both rural and urban areas, face relatively higher levels of risk during public health emergencies. During the coronavirus pandemic, factors such as pre-existing health conditions and less access to healthcare in urban areas and lower incomes and smaller hospitals in rural areas increased the level of vulnerability.

Responses to pandemic outcomes

By understanding how specific areas are susceptible to the spread of disease, communities may formulate appropriate responses. In urban areas, susceptibility is a function of population density, requiring aggressive intervention measures such as quarantines, social distancing, and sheltering-in-place. In rural areas with lower population densities, these interventions may not be appropriate. Instead, rural interventions should focus on specific members of the population, including the elderly, individuals with poor health, those living in nursing homes, and workers in meatpacking plants and other large facilities. Fewer resources for health care systems and logistical barriers for social services make rural areas particularly vulnerable. Inconsistent internet access means individuals may not rely on telemedicine. Several factors that differ between rural and urban areas are significant in determining uneven mortality rates, including demographics, air quality, household size, urbanization, economic dynamism, and global interconnectedness (Kapitsinis, 2020).

In many developing countries, during the coronavirus pandemic, agricultural output declined due to a decrease in the demand for high-value perishables, women faced additional work in caring for the sick, food insecurity rose, and household income fell. These effects required the establishment of priorities, including the protection of those most affected, maintenance of food systems, and sustenance for rural livelihoods. A disease pandemic focuses the policy discourse around economic and healthcare systems, patterns of urban and rural development, and the livelihoods of the poor.

A pandemic and its outcomes should encourage the implementation of policies that strengthen the institutions of both rural and urban regions. The identification of high-risk areas helps public sectors anticipate and prepare for future shocks. But the management of responses to pandemic outcomes such as lower levels of employment and higher levels of mortality should adapt to changing circumstances, rely on successful experiences, and recognize capacity limits.

The decision of public sectors to address the convergence of economic and health crises through strong containment measures serves as the most effective way to reduce mortality rates. Efficient systems of targeted economic shutdowns and testing, tracking, and quarantining provide the best opportunity to balance public health and economic activity. That is, data on health risks inform decisions about the economy. Taken together, these outcomes demonstrate that urban and rural areas have different vulnerabilities to the spread of disease. Pandemic outcomes are geographically differentiated. Strategies for effective responses should consider the relative weights of all risk factors.

In an article in *Nature*, Bai et al. (2020) argue for cities to develop *networked functional resilience* by "sharing and coordinating disaster risk plans and actions." Clusters of urban-rural networks establish stronger institutions and policies than communities working alone. In the presence of a shock, the network may intervene to provide resources. Geographical proximity provides a useful framework, where cities in regions develop mechanisms of risk prevention to benefit all members.

Summary

The field of economic geography addresses where economic activity occurs and why. The field is particularly interested in the location of factors of production. This focus is important for understanding the structure of economies, but also the effects of pandemics in geographic space. The core-periphery economic structure depends on the share of industry in national income, economies of scale, and transportation costs. When firms choose a location for production, they hire workers who live and consume in that region. This pattern creates local forward and backward linkages that perpetuate economic activity in the region. The centripetal forces that keep economic activity in motion around a geographic center include market-size effects, thick labor markets, and pure external economies. The centrifugal forces that encourage the motion of economic activity to expand outward from a geographical center include immobile factors, land rents, and pure external diseconomies. Urbanization refers to the movement from rural to urban areas and the methods in which society adapts to the change. Urbanization occurs in the presence of two forces: when countries switch their sectoral composition from agriculture to industry and technological advances in the production of agricultural output releases laborers to move to cities. The concept of spatial diffusion demonstrates that pandemics may spread in global networks, regional sectors, and local areas through air travel, trade, commuting, and social connections. Several factors influence the spread of disease and magnify the point of origin, including urbanization and network connections. The process of urbanization makes cities more vulnerable to the spread of disease by increasing population density in specific areas. In rural areas, the spread of disease may exist as a lagged indicator as the disease takes longer to spread through rural populations. But several rural characteristics create an environment susceptible to the spread of disease, including average age of the local population, large group facilities, employment in both nursing homes for the elderly and meat processing plants, and pre-existing health conditions. Because rural and urban areas have different vulnerabilities to the spread of disease, policies should address this reality.

Chapter takeaways

LO1   The field of economic geography addresses where economic activity occurs and why. It is particularly interested in the location of factors of production.

LO2   Production concentrates in geographic space. Businesses locate where workers live and workers want to live where businesses operate.

LO3   Three themes of economic geography include globalization, uneven development, and place.

LO4   Pandemic outcomes are relevant for applications of economic geography, including urbanization, spatial equilibrium, and smart cities.

LO5   For the analysis of spatial diffusion, factor-driven and network-driven approaches differ with respect to their model frameworks, areas of inquiry, and methods of explanation.

LO6   By understanding how areas are susceptible to the spread of disease, communities may formulate appropriate responses.

Terms and concepts

Backward and demand linkages
Bifurcation model
Centrifugal force
Centripetal force
Economic geography
Effective distance
Forward and cost linkages

Networked functional resilience
Pecuniary externalities
Scale
Smart cities
Spatial diffusion
Spatial equilibrium
Spatiotemporal patterns
Time-space compression
Time-space distanciation
Vulnerability science

Questions

1. With respect to economic geography, explain centripetal and centrifugal forces. Why does production concentrate in geographic space?
2. What are the components of the model of new economic geography? Explain the role of transportation cost.
3. With respect to transportation cost, explain how the model of new economic geography argues for economic diversification and agglomeration. What are the roles of the sustain point and the break point?
4. Explain why globalization, uneven development, and place serve as important components of economic geography.
5. Explain the process of urbanization. Why does it occur? What is the implication of urbanization for the potential spread of global diseases?
6. Cities achieve different degrees of smart city status, depending on the indicators. Should the smart city framework include the variable for pandemic resilience? Why?
7. How does a factor-driven model differ from a model of network-driven contagion? What are the models trying to estimate? What are the approaches to estimation?
8. How does a model of social vulnerability identify areas that may experience inferior outcomes from a pandemic?
9. How should policymakers formulate responses to pandemic outcomes in rural areas? What unique characteristics of rural areas impact policy implementation?
10. How should policymakers formulate responses to pandemic outcomes in urban areas? What unique characteristics of urban areas impact policy implementation?

References

Abu-Rayash, Azzam, and Dincer, Ibrahim. 2020. "Analysis of the electricity demand trends amidst the Covid-19 coronavirus pandemic," *Energy Research & Social Science*, 68 (October): 101682.

Alexopulos, Nick. 2018. "Study by Health Security Center identifies characteristics of microorganisms most likely to cause a global pandemic," Center for Health Security, Johns Hopkins Bloomberg School of Public Health, May 10.

Bai, Xuemei, Nagendra, Harini, Shi, Peijun, and Liu, Haiyan. 2020. "Cities: build networks and share plans to emerge stronger from Covid-19," *Nature*, 584 (August): 517-520.

Brockmann, Dirk, and Helbing, Dirk. 2013. "The hidden geometry of complex, network-driven contagion phenomena," *Science*, 342 (December): 1337-1342.

Cutter, Susan. 2003. "The vulnerability of science and the science of vulnerability," *Annals of the Association of American Geographers*, 93, 1: 1–12.

Fujita, Masahisa, Krugman, Paul, and Venables, Anthony. 1999. *The Spatial Economy: Cities, Regions, and International Trade*. Cambridge, Massachusetts: The MIT Press.

Garrett, Laurie. 1994. *The Coming Plague: Newly Emerging Diseases in a World Out of Balance*. New York: Farrar Straus & Giroux.

Glaeser, Edward. 2007. "The Economic Approach to Cities." Harvard Institute of Economic Research, Discussion Paper 2149. Harvard University.

Gupta, Shruti, Hayek, Salim, and Wang, Wei. 2020. "Factors associated with death in critically ill patients with coronavirus disease 2019 in the US," *JAMA Internal Medicine*, July: E1–E12. doi:10.1001/jamainternmed.2020.3596.

Henderson, J. Vernon. 2003. "Urbanization, economic geography, and growth," in Aghion, P. and Durlauf, S. (Eds.), *Handbook of Economic Growth*, Volume 1. New York: North Holland.

Kapitsinis, Nikos. 2020. "The underlying factors of the Covid-19 spatially uneven spread. Initial evidence from regions in nine EU countries," *Regional Science Policy & Practice*, September, 1–19: doi: 10.1111/rsp3.12340.

Krugman, Paul. 1998. "What's new about the new economic geography?" *Oxford Review of Economic Policy*, 14, 2: 7–17.

Krugman, Paul. 1991. "Increasing returns and economic geography," *Journal of Political Economy*, 99, 3: 483–499.

Leatherby, Lauren. 2020. "The worst virus outbreaks in the U.S. are now in rural areas," *The New York Times*, October 22.

MacKinnon, Danny, and Cumbers, Andrew. 2019. *An Introduction to Economic Geography*, 3rd edition. New York: Routledge.

Neary, J. Peter. 2001. "Of hype and hyperbolas: introducing the new economic geography," *Journal of Economic Literature*, 39, 2 (June): 536–561.

United Nations. 2020. *Policy Brief: Covid-19 in an Urban World*. un.org/sites/un2.un.org/files/sg_policy_brief_covid_urban_world_july_2020.pdf.

14 Game theory and mutual interdependence

Learning objectives

After reading this chapter, you will be able to:

LO1 Apply the game theory perspective to pandemic applications.
LO2 Explain why individual decisions may not lead to optimal social outcomes.
LO3 Discuss the principles of both strategic form and extensive form games.
LO4 Determine whether sheltering-in-place orders impact the decision to cooperate.
LO5 Assess the reasons that individuals may cooperate and slow the spread of disease.
LO6 Determine the conditions in which individuals will choose vaccinations.
LO7 Address why risk perception and policy interventions influence human behavior.

Chapter outline

- A game of survival
- Game theory and pandemic outcomes
- Principles of game theory
- Bargaining game
- Donor-recipient game
- Public good game
- Game of risk perception and strategic choice
- Summary

A game of survival

Richard Holden (2020), Professor of Economics at the University of New South Wales, argues that, during a pandemic, we may view individuals as participating in a game of strategic interaction. In the game, members of a target population serve as players. Policymakers establish the rules of the game, including player interaction. Pandemic mediation policies such as sheltering-in-place restrict individuals to their homes and minimize human contact.

In Holden's framework, payoffs exist. Policymakers attempt to minimize the spread of disease. The disease attempts to maximize infections. But the payoff to individuals is more complicated. Individuals attempt to minimize the risk of infection while maintaining economic opportunity. For these individuals, payoffs may change, depending on individual choice, the spread of disease, and the emergence of vaccination.

Policy interventions may lead to cooperation by slowing the spread of disease but involve costs such as economic losses, isolation, and loneliness. For individuals, defecting from the position of isolation, loneliness, and cooperative behavior brings immediate benefits, including interaction and social connection. But defection worsens the position of the population by increasing infections. In this context, an incentive exists for individuals to choose a path that does not produce the optimal social outcome. As a result, the decision to abide by policy interventions exists as a multiplayer version of the game. Individuals may cooperate, experience personal costs, and help society, or defect, reduce personal costs, and impose external costs on the population.

Changes in the decision-making process, especially among individuals and policymakers, have important effects on the outcome of the game. Policymakers may not initially implement strict interventions. Individuals may not abide by policy directives. The disease may spread unevenly throughout a population. Moving forward, policymakers and individuals may choose opposing paths. In this context, it is important to view the game as the potential for disease to exhibit an exponential capacity for growth. In a pandemic, how policymakers establish the rules and how individuals behave determine whether a society "wins" or "loses" the game of survival.

The point is that, during a pandemic, individuals face a series of strategic decisions in unfamiliar situations, including sheltering-in-place and social distancing. Because *game theory*, the study of strategic choice, addresses individual decision making and social outcomes, it offers a method to analyze human behavior during a pandemic. To address this topic, the chapter first discusses game theory, pandemic outcomes, and principles of the field. The chapter then presents several applications that are relevant for pandemics, including a bargaining game, donor-recipient game, public good game, and a game of risk perception and strategic choice.

Game theory and pandemic outcomes

The study of microeconomics is the study of individual aspects of the economy, including consumers and firms, and their interaction with one another. From this perspective, the objective of individuals is to maximize utility. The objective of firms is to maximize profit. But these objectives may be viewed as the maximization of payoffs. The principles of economics guide these payoffs but also determine the context in which the payoffs occur, including the existence of consumption externalities. In the absence of consumption externalities, the consumption of one economic agent does not alter the payoffs of other economic agents. During a pandemic, however, consumption externalities likely exist. When an individual receives a vaccine, for example, the action helps to prevent the spread of disease, creating spillover benefits.

In economics, game theory provides a framework for modeling strategic interaction between decision makers, which may be considered a game with rules, strategies, and payoffs:

- Rules: instructions that dictate choices and outcomes.
- Strategies: options for players in which the outcome depends on both the player's choice and the choices of other participants.
- Payoffs: values assigned to possible outcomes of a game, including monetary, social, and psychological values.

Game theory addresses the outcomes of strategic interaction, focusing on incentives and preferences. This interaction involves rational choice, that is, maximizing behavior, providing a testable hypothesis that asks when rational behavior occurs. Traditional games often assume perfect information and *mutual interdependence*, the idea that the decisions of one player depend on the decisions of others. But in a pandemic, incomplete information may exist with disease characteristics, transmission, and potential outcomes. As a result, the perception of individual payoffs in a pandemic game may differ from the perception of payoffs in a familiar game.

In the presence of a *social dilemma*, game theory serves as a useful tool. A social dilemma exists when noncooperative payoffs exceed cooperative payoffs. That is, individuals receive higher payoffs when they defect from a decision that leads to greater social benefits, no matter the behavior of others. But if most people do not cooperate, everyone is worse off. In contrast, if full cooperation occurs, everyone is better off. One person may decide, for example, not to take a vaccination. If this individual believes everyone else will choose vaccination, the outcome for the individual does not provide incentive for different behavior. But if everyone chooses defection instead of vaccination, the entire population experiences an inferior outcome. In this case, rational choice theory determines that if each self-interested individual chooses the noncooperative route, they are not good predictors of expected future utility. As a result, public policy may guide individuals away from self-interested and competitive outcomes to socially cooperative decision making, especially when the latter creates a large external benefit.

Principles of game theory

Since the publication of the *Theory of Games and Economic Behavior*, by John von Neumann and Oskar Morgenstern (1944), economists and mathematicians have developed the principles of game theory. This influential book develops a game theory framework for applications in many areas of economics, notably strategic decision making. An important idea from the book is that equilibrium occurs when individuals cannot increase their payoffs by altering their strategy. In 1994, John Nash, John Harsanyi, and Reinhard Selten won the Nobel Prize in Economic Sciences for their work on equilibria in noncooperative games. In their research, they demonstrate that, from a social perspective, the outcome of a game may constitute a suboptimal solution.

Game theory in economics

Today, game theory serves as an important tool in economics. The specificity of game theory is the method in which it analyzes a problem. In a book on *Game Theory and Exercises*, Gisele Umbhauer (2016) explains this approach: "Game theory structures an interactive context in a way that helps to find actions–strategies–with specific properties." Building a context as a game serves as an exercise with important applications. Samuelson (2016) offers further description:

> Game theory retains the familiar model of competitive behavior but offers an alterna-
> tive and more general view–containing competitive markets as a limiting case–of how
> models of individual behavior are aggregated to examine more complex phenomena.
> Game theory has subsequently become the standard organizing principle for examining
> interactions between people ...

This instrumental view posits that a model may be used to study interaction. Thus, a game is an approximation of reality, established to include the characteristics of interaction. In fact, an attempt to make a game theory model more realistic does not necessarily improve its predictive power. Actions of cooperation or defection approximate choices that exist in a more complex plane. The point is that the degree of model complexity reflects potential forms of interaction.

Language of game theory

When a choice leads to a higher payoff, a *dominant strategy* exists. This is a strategic decision that is optimal regardless of the decision of the rival. But the outcome of a game may be a *noncooperative solution*, when players do not collaborate, each pursuing their own self-inter-est. A *Nash equilibrium*, named after the mathematician John Nash, serves as an outcome in which players may not improve their position with different choices. In effect, each player makes the best decision possible given the actions of their rivals. This situation establishes an equilibrium because the players do not have the incentive to alter their strategies. In game theory, two common approaches are *strategic form games* and *extensive form games*.

Strategic form games

Strategic form games occur when players choose strategies without knowing the strategies of other players. The game is characterized by potential choices and payoffs. The *action profile* is the collection of actions of all players. Strategic form games use a payoff matrix, informa-tion set, and order of play. The game establishes potential outcomes. This form is common for *simultaneous games*, when players make their strategic decisions at the same time, as opposed to *sequential games*, when players make their decisions in turn. It is important to note that simultaneous games imply the existence of complete information. Players know the payoffs.

Simultaneous move games

A payoff matrix demonstrates a simultaneous move game (figure 14.1). Suppose a player, Yellen, decides whether to make 1 or 2 units of output. At the same time, another player, Powell, faces

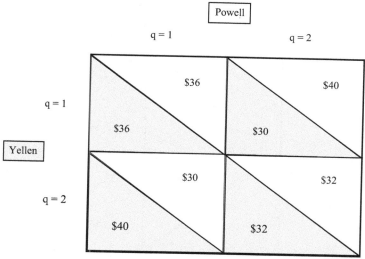

Figure 14.1 Simultaneous move game.
Source: author

the same decision. If Yellen decides to make 2 units, Powell maximizes his payoff by making 2 units. If Yellen decides to make 1 unit, Powell maximizes his payoff by making 2 units. Therefore, regardless of the actions of Yellen, Powell's dominant strategy is to make 2 units. Yellen also has a dominant strategy of making 2 units. With this choice, she maximizes her payoff, regardless of the actions of Powell. A *cooperative solution* occurs in the upper left-hand box when each player agrees to produce 1 unit and receive a payoff of $36. A cooperative solution is an outcome that occurs when each player collaborates with the other. But each player has a dominant strategy of producing 2 units. Therefore, a noncooperative solution serves as the Nash equilibrium. In the lower right-hand box, each player receives a payoff of $32.

Prisoner's dilemma

The most famous version of the simultaneous game is *prisoner's dilemma*. Suppose two suspects, FJ and JJ, are accused of a crime (figure 14.2). The police take them to the station for questioning but place them in different rooms. They cannot collaborate. The police have enough evidence to convict them of resisting arrest, a lesser crime, but suspect them of a more serious crime. Each player must decide whether or not to provide evidence.

The payoffs are established as follows: if a suspect provides evidence but the other does not, the player who provides evidence goes free. The player who does not provide evidence receives a 14-year sentence. If they both provide evidence, they each receive a 7-year sentence (lower right-hand box). If neither provides evidence, they each receive a 1-month sentence for resisting arrest (upper left-hand box). From the perspective of the suspects, what is the best outcome? Clearly, the answer is to provide no evidence. This choice leads to the shortest collective sentencing. But this choice requires collaboration, which the suspects cannot provide.

Consider the actions of FJ, who decides whether or not to provide evidence, but has no control over JJ's decision. FJ knows that JJ has two choices. One, if JJ presents no evidence,

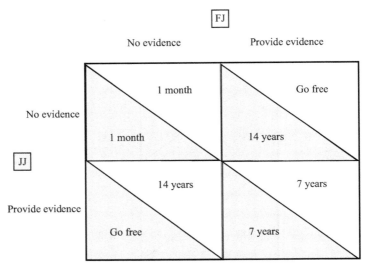

Figure 14.2 Prisoner's dilemma.

Source: author

FJ should provide evidence and go free. Two, if JJ provides evidence, FJ should provide evidence and receive a 7-year sentence rather than a 14-year sentence. A dominant strategy exists: provide evidence. Because this is a symmetric game, JJ has the same dominant strategy. The result is a Nash equilibrium. Both players follow their dominant strategy in a noncooperative solution (lower right-hand box).

Taken together, they would be better off cooperating and withholding evidence. Does this result mean that cooperation never occurs? The answer is no. The suspects may establish a pact ahead of time or trust the other while in separate rooms. But in the prisoner's dilemma, cooperation exists as a beneficial outcome but may be elusive because of the prevailing rules.

In economics, an application is the *duopolists' dilemma*, when competing firms may benefit from cooperation. The problem is the short-term payoff from noncooperative behavior may be higher than from cooperative behavior. By charging a lower price than a rival, for example, a business may initially gain market share. But when the rival also lowers price, payoffs are the same for everyone. In the end, the duopolists would be better off by maintaining a higher price.

Extensive form games

Extensive form games describe the setting with a game tree, a diagram of player choices. At the end of each branch, payoffs exist. Because this form characterizes choices at different moments, it involves sequential games. Players know their previous choices and observe the choices of other players. Information may be perfect or imperfect. Perfect information means all players understand the game structure. When choosing between options, the players are informed about the events that have previously occurred. Imperfect information means the players understand the game structure but may not be informed about previous choices, complicating the link to payoffs. In either case, extensive form games involve sequential moves.

Sequential move games

In sequential move games, arrows represent player decisions. The initial player makes a choice and the other player responds. Payoffs occur at the end of the game. Economists use sequential move games to study many topics, including altruism. Economists normally assume the typical individual makes self-interested decisions. Under what circumstances, therefore, do people behave in altruistic ways? Many examples appear to exist. People volunteer, help others during a pandemic, and donate to charities. However, economists classify some of this behavior as impure altruism or *warm-glow altruism*. People may undertake these actions because it makes them feel good, look good, or experience lower taxes. A sequential move game may determine whether individual behavior leans toward pure altruism, pure self-interest, or somewhere in between.

Ultimatum

A famous sequential move game, *Ultimatum*, assesses the potential for altruism. Suppose two anonymous players, Alpha and Beta (figure 14.3). The first player, Alpha, receives $20 and may give some (call it X) to Beta. Beta must then decide whether to accept or reject Alpha's offer. If Beta accepts, Beta keeps X and Alpha keeps the rest (call it Y). If Beta rejects, neither keeps any money. An equitable offer, for example, would equal $10. If Beta accepts, X = $10 and Y = $10.

In this framework, any offer by Alpha would make Beta better off, even if the offer is small. For example, if money motivates the players and Alpha offers $0.01, Beta should accept. Beta is better off. But the game usually does not work that way. Economists have found that in repeated games the Betas normally reject offers below $3, citing unfairness. The Betas are apparently willing to sacrifice money to make a point. On average, however, the Alphas offer about $6 to avoid rejection, leading to personal gain. The act of giving may be tied to self-interest.

Dictator

As an extension to Ultimatum, *Dictator* simplifies the competing factors of altruism and self-interest. While money is divided between two anonymous players, Alpha makes the only decision. Beta keeps Alpha's offer. The original version of the game provides Alpha with two options: (a) keep $18 and give Beta $2 or (b) keep $10 and give Beta $10. This setup increases the power of measurement. Because Beta has no choice, Beta may not punish selfishness or reward generosity. Anonymity eliminates the potential for personal feelings. What is the

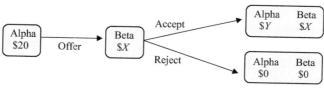

Figure 14.3 Ultimatum.

Source: author

typical result? The results demonstrate that most people, when in the position of Alpha, choose to split the money evenly. Extensions of Dictator allow the Alphas to give any amount of money between $0 and $20, an average which turns out to be $4, signaling a mix of altruism and self-interest.

Forces that may skew the results

First, the potential for *selection bias* may inhibit proper randomization. People that volunteer to participate in experimental games such as Ultimatum and Dictator may be more cooperative than average. Second, the existence of *scrutiny*, when people alter their behavior under observation, may create biased outcomes. Taken together, selection bias and scrutiny challenge the idea of a fair game, requiring repeated games in different settings. Ultimately, people respond to incentives. When properly crafted, incentives may encourage people to make altruistic choices.

Challenges for game theory

With the growth of theoretical and applied forms of game theory, Samuelson (2016) argues that two challenges remain: equilibrium selection and applications.

Equilibrium selection

In game theory, multiple equilibria may exist. This reality holds true with simple games of two players or complicated games with multiple players. But multiple equilibria create a challenging outcome. While a concern is that an application with multiple equilibria may not have a high level of predictive power, Samuelson (2016) provides three responses. First, other models in the field of economics may lead to multiple equilibria, such as poverty traps, liquidity traps, or business cycles. Second, multiple equilibria reflect reality. Sometimes, several potential outcomes exist. Third, empirical applications point the way to a chosen equilibrium. A model may admit multiple equilibria but observed behavior reflects a probable outcome. The choice of equilibrium is reflected in the data. Taken together, these responses demonstrate insight into both model structure and individual behavior. However, identifying an appropriate equilibrium serves as an ongoing challenge in the field of economics (Samuelson, 2016).

Applications

In economics, game theory provides a framework for many applications. Research has yielded theoretical insights and influenced the allocation of resources. Two areas of successful application are auctions and matching. Auctions are mechanisms that establish a process of bidding to determine resource allocation and prices. Because of research in the field of economics, governments routinely auction resources rather than give them away. Businesses may choose to price output using auctions. Advances in the area of the economics of matching have led to students being matched with colleges and applicants being matched with employers. But in other areas, the choice of a game theory framework has not been as successful (Samuelson, 2016). Because pandemic economics is a new field, applications using the game theory framework require additional scholarship. Over time, as research on the pandemic uses a game theory approach, economists will evaluate the merits of this framework. The following sections discuss applications of the game theory approach to pandemic outcomes, including a bargaining game, donor-recipient game, public good game, and a game of risk perception and strategic choice. The most complex model is presented last.

Bargaining game

In the context of the coronavirus pandemic, Professor J. Jobu Babin and his co-authors Marine Foray and Andrew Hussey (2020) address whether loneliness impacts an individual's decision to cooperate. The economists' interest in the issue stems from the fact that, during a pandemic, governments implement sheltering-in-place orders. The objective of these orders is to decrease human contact and the spread of disease. During sheltering-in-place waves, individuals isolate in their residences. From an economics perspective, this policy may disrupt work activity and social interaction. Compared to an office environment, does working at home impact productivity? On one hand, isolation, a lack of human connection, and loneliness may decrease productivity. On the other hand, these same factors may limit distractions and increase productivity. Because the answer to the question has important implications for the future of work, the economists undertake experimental research to provide results.

Spectrum of experimentation

In economics, a large amount of research takes the form of laboratory or natural experiments. Research using experiments has led to a variety of insights in areas such as charity, cost-benefit analysis, discrimination, market mechanisms, and many other topics. The advantage of conducting experiments is that researchers may observe the decision-making process of individuals in the presence of different incentives. In addition, experiments provide a method to establish empirical results for game theory problems. Experiments measure important parameters to test hypotheses. If the hypotheses are rejected, experiments provide information to inform new theories.

According to List (2011), four types of experiments differ with respect to subject, location, and awareness (table 14.1). The subjects may consist of students in an academic setting (standard subjects) or nonstandard subjects that are representative of the general population. The location may consist of a laboratory or a "natural environment," a physical location or online site where people gather. The subjects may or may not be aware that they are participating in an experiment.

Table 14.1 Types of experiments

Type of experiment	Subjects	Location	Awareness
Conventional lab	Standard	Laboratory	Awareness exists
Artefactual field	Non-standard	Laboratory	Awareness exists
Framed field	Non-standard	Natural environment	Awareness exists
Natural field	Non-standard	Natural environment	No awareness

Source: List (2011)

Experimental design

To investigate the impact of sheltering-in-place orders on worker productivity, Babin et al. (2020) design a *natural field experiment* and collect data using methods common in both natural and framed field settings. The economists address two questions, considering that sheltering-in-place orders lead to isolation and loneliness. First, what is the relationship between observable worker characteristics and loneliness? Second, in a labor market setting, what is the relationship between sheltering-in-place orders, loneliness, and cooperative behavior? In an empirical application, the economists analyze the impact on cooperative behavior when states in the U.S. implement shutdown policies in waves. They present several contributions, including an exploration of the labor market during the time of a pandemic, an analysis of the relationship between loneliness and strategic interaction, an assessment of worker profiles as the economy opens and closes, a link between lockdown policies and cooperation, and the use of an online work environment as a proxy for remote work.

Design flow

In a game theory setting, Babin et al. (2020) assess the willingness of participants to cooperate. The payoffs include a flat fee for participation and a potential bonus. The design flow begins with the establishment of online participants. They consent to participate and then proceed to the reporting phase. In the reporting phase, they answer questions on psychometric scales which determine both their degrees of loneliness and willingness to cooperate. They also express whether they are under a sheltering-in-place order. The participants then begin the bargaining phase, in which they play both a *stag hunt game* (discussed below) and a prisoner's dilemma, randomized to eliminate potential bias in the results. High levels of cooperation are expected in the stag hunt game (in the absence of factors such as loneliness or sheltering-in-place orders), whereas cooperation is strictly dominated in prisoner's dilemma. With the latter, players tend not to cooperate.

Consider the stag hunt game. In the original version, players decide whether to hunt a stag or a hare. The stag provides a higher payoff than the hare. To succeed in hunting a stag, the players must cooperate. But individual action may lead to the capture of a hare. In this game, the highest value entails mutual cooperation. In the absence of defection, the maximum payoff is possible. The original stag hunt game serves as a parable for activities in which players pursue different types of coordination. Coordination may lead to higher payoffs but require cooperation. Coordination may also lead to actions with lower payoffs that do not require cooperation. With either possibility, coordinated actions may serve as social norms.

Equilibrium outcomes

In Babin et al. (2020), cooperation leads to higher social gains. Actions are framed as group projects. Participants may cooperate or work alone. The stag hunt framework differs slightly from the framework of prisoner's dilemma. In the latter, the only pure Nash equilibrium is when both players defect, even though cooperation by both players is efficient. But the stag hunt game has two predictions (Nash equilibria): a bad one, which is suboptimal yet safer for each player, and a good one, which is Pareto efficient but risky.

In the stag hunt game, players face a coordination problem. To cooperate, they must first coordinate their behavior. In a remote work environment, participants may not have the confidence or interest in coordinating with others, especially if they feel isolated and lonely. In this context, coordination serves as *social choreography*, a correlating device for equilibrium, rather than a Nash equilibrium based on dominant behavior (Gintis, 2010). While the rules for playing Nash equilibria are stringent, the rules for a correlated equilibrium are a function of the norms of the cultural system. In a costless decision-making process, participants will choose to obey social norms. But in the absence of perfect information or the presence of extenuating circumstances such as a policy of sheltering-in-place, the choice of following social norms is related to factors such as isolation and loneliness. Players may want to cooperate but for some isolation and loneliness influence the decision. In the framework of Babin et al. (2020), payoffs exist for workers *i* and *j* (figure 14.4). For both workers, cooperation leads to higher payoffs. Working alone leads to lower payoffs. Mutual cooperation serves as an efficient equilibrium but mutual exclusion serves as an inefficient equilibrium.

When will participants work alone? Babin et al. (2020) find that, for participants in the stag hunt game, as sheltering-in-place orders extend into subsequent waves, less cooperation exists until the orders are lifted and cooperation rebounds. For participants in the prisoner's dilemma game, cooperation increases as sheltering-in-place orders extend into subsequent waves. The authors conclude that workers under sheltering-in-place orders cooperate less often in the stag hunt bargaining framework when compared to the prisoner's dilemma. While the sheltering-in-place orders do not appear to directly deter cooperation, loneliness is negatively correlated with cooperative behavior strongly in the stag hunt game, even when cooperation provides superior payoffs, but not in the prisoner's dilemma. This conclusion is important because more cooperation leads to higher gains. Because loneliness is an unintended consequence of sheltering-in-place orders, the results of the research of Babin et al. (2020) highlight the tradeoffs involved with pandemic mediation policies.

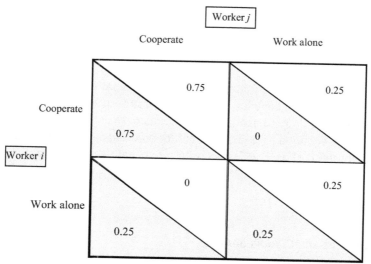

Figure 14.4 Stag hunt game.

Source: Babin et al. (2020)

Donor-recipient game

In a pandemic, individuals decide whether or not to adjust their behavior. These decisions have spillover effects. If individuals avoid contact with others, the population benefits from a reduction in disease transmission. But if individuals do not alter their behavior, the rate of transmission increases. Because game theory provides a framework to address the implication of individual choice, it may assess this interplay between the spread of disease and individual behavior.

Model framework

Karlsson and Rowlett (2020) model a population in which individuals evaluate the merits of behavioral adjustments that slow the spread of disease. Individuals face a choice: either mitigate the spread of disease or not. When they mitigate the spread of disease, they must change their behavior, leading to a "disease dilemma," similar in form to the prisoner's dilemma. They either cooperate with others in the population and minimize the spread of disease or defect and not minimize the spread of disease. With the former choice, society benefits. With the latter choice, society does not benefit. This form of the game is called a *donor-recipient game* when players donate resources to help others. In this version, individuals "donate" their time, effort, and willingness to mitigate the spread of disease for the benefit of society.

Decision matrix and payoffs

Suppose two players, Austin and Claudia, choose to either cooperate with others or defect from the group. Cooperating and mitigating the spread of disease takes the form of social distancing, wearing a mask, and/or sheltering-in-place. Defecting and not mitigating the spread of disease means not changing behavior. Four potential outcomes exist: A and C both defect; A cooperates and C defects; A defects and C cooperates; and A and C both cooperate (figure 14.5).

Mutual defection

If both players defect (lower right-hand box), neither chooses to mitigate the spread of disease. They experience zero benefits; however, they also face zero costs from altering their behavior. That is, they do not have to face the costs of maintaining distance from others, buying a mask and enduring its discomfort, and/or reducing contacts. Karlsson and Rowlett (2020) represent this cost as $-B < 0$. Thus, with zero benefit and zero cost, the payoff $P = 0$.

- Austin's payoff: $P = 0$
- Claudia's payoff: $P = 0$

Austin cooperates and Claudia defects

If Austin cooperates but Claudia defects (upper right-hand box), Austin pays the cost of cooperation ($-B$) but receives a small benefit ($\varepsilon > 0$) by limiting the exposure to disease. Austin's

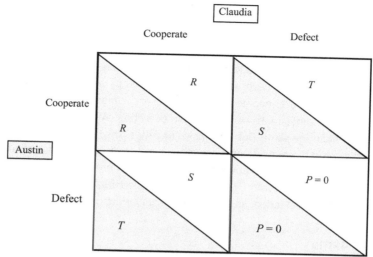

Figure 14.5 Payoff matrix for the donor-recipient game.
Source: adapted from Karlsson and Rowlett (2020), Figure 1

payoff therefore includes costs and benefits: $-B + \varepsilon$. (Karlsson and Rowlett (2020) define S = $-B + \varepsilon < 0$.) The difference between personal and social benefit is important. While Austin experiences a small personal benefit from cooperation, the main benefit of cooperation is external, flowing to others. If Claudia does not cooperate, Claudia faces zero cost but experiences an external benefit (T) from Austin's choice, such that $T > \varepsilon > 0$. Because the benefit to Austin is small and personal, $\varepsilon < B$.

- Austin's payoff: $S = -B + \varepsilon$
- Claudia's payoff: T

Austin defects and Claudia cooperates

If Austin defects and Claudia cooperates (lower left-hand box), Claudia pays the cost of cooperation ($-B$) and receives the small benefit (ε). Austin experiences zero cost and the small external benefit (T) from Claudia's decision.

- Austin's payoff: T
- Claudia's payoff: $S = -B + \varepsilon$

Mutual cooperation

If Austin and Claudia both cooperate (upper left-hand box), they each experience a cost ($-B$) and the maximal benefit ($T + \varepsilon$). As a result, each player receives a payoff equal to $R = T - B + \varepsilon$.

- Austin's payoff: $R = T - B + \varepsilon$
- Claudia's payoff: $R = T - B + \varepsilon$

Network reciprocity

According to Karlsson and Rowlett (2020), this model generalizes to a population game. Each individual decides if they want to mitigate the spread of disease. With a population, two levels of interaction exist. First, everyone may interact, represented by a fully connected graph. Second, some individuals may never interact, represented by a social network. With the latter possibility, the payoffs are modified. If social pressure is high enough, *network reciprocity* exists: cooperation becomes more beneficial than defection. With the matrix framework, the payoffs P and R remain the same. But a variable $N(k)$ alters the payoffs T and S, where k = the average node degree in the network or the average number of connections between nodes. As k increases, the average number of connections increases. Therefore, the new representations add $N(k)$ to S and subtract $N(k)$ from T. As k increases, added pressure encourages cooperation, decreases the payoff for defection, and leads to an equilibrium of mutual cooperation.

Public good game

With many infectious diseases, the choice to obtain a vaccination impacts disease control. Whether or not individuals seek a vaccination impacts the spread of disease. That is, vaccination involves personal and external benefits. But the decision to obtain a vaccine is a function of incentives. When policymakers attempt to achieve an optimal social outcome, more people will choose vaccination compared to when individual self-interest motivates the decision.

Strategic choice

In a vaccination game, Chapman et al. (2012) consider the case of influenza, noting that young people are responsible for most of the transmission, while the elderly experience higher levels of morbidity and mortality. From a social perspective, the optimal strategy is for younger people to assume an important role in the process of vaccination to protect older people. This strategy exists despite the fact that younger people receive a lower personal benefit than older people. This social dilemma fits in a game theory framework. Both individual and group decisions impact the payoffs. The game theory framework predicts how self-interested individuals make private decisions.

In a traditional social dilemma game, such as the donor-recipient game in the previous section, all individuals face the same choice between individual optimization (defection) and group optimization (cooperation). But, as Chapman et al. (2012) explain, a public good game of vaccination provides an important difference: payoffs vary according to age group. As a result, individuals face different decisions. The decision between vaccination and nonvaccination does not map directly into positions of cooperation and defection, respectively. In contrast, vaccination may exist as a perceived benefit for most but not all individuals. Some people may be skeptical of the potential of the vaccination to solve the problem of the disease.

Rules and payoffs

In the vaccination game, Chapman et al. (2012) simulate age-dependent decisions about a vaccination in a laboratory experiment. An epidemiological model both determines the risk of infection and incorporates the potential for herd immunity. As the number of vaccinations increases, the risk of infection decreases. The rules of the game are as follows. To reduce the risk of infection, individuals may choose to receive a vaccination. If they receive the vaccination, they experience a cost. In the laboratory experiment, individuals assume the cost by paying "points." In addition, if they become infected, they lose points. For some individuals, the choice of nonvaccination leads to a higher expected payoff.

Participants are assigned to either young or elderly age groups. The elderly group faces higher costs of infection. Through vaccination, the young group contributes more to herd immunity. Two types of payoffs exist. First, when participants receive compensation based on self-interested behavior and individual point totals, the simulation evaluates behavioral choices. Second, when participants receive compensation based on social behavior and group point totals, the simulation evaluates behavioral choices. The hypothesis is that, in the presence of payoffs for self-interested behavior and individual point totals, fewer participants representing the young age group will choose the vaccination compared to the elderly age group. In contrast, in the presence of payoffs for social behavior and group point totals, more participants representing the young age group will choose vaccination compared to the elderly age group.

Experimental design

In addition to age and payoffs, the experiment in Chapman et al. (2012) focuses on the cost of vaccines, risk of transmission, and severity of the disease. Participants are sorted into groups. Half of the groups represent the young age while the other half represents the elderly. With the payoff conditions, participants begin with the same number of points but gain or lose points according to infection and the cost of vaccination. At the end of the game, a monetary payment corresponds to the number of points remaining. Participants in half of the groups receive payment according to individual points. The other half receives payment according to the average point total for the group. Young players contribute more to herd immunity. Elderly players lose more points through infection. In the experimental design, vaccination creates a higher level of effectiveness in fighting the disease for participants representing the young age group than the elderly age group. The other three variables, cost of vaccines, risk of transmission, and severity of the disease, change according to the stage of the experiment. In early stages, the cost of vaccines is less than in later stages and the severity of disease is lower for participants in the elderly group than in later stages. As additional players choose vaccination, the risk of infection decreases.

Equilibrium outcomes

In this game, Chapman et al. (2012) analyze two types of equilibria. The Nash equilibrium predicts the outcome if participants act in a self-interested manner. It is defined as the number of participants in the young and elderly groups that choose vaccination to maximize individual payoff, beyond which no incentive exists for further vaccination. A *utilitarian equilibrium*, in contrast, represents the group-oriented solution. It is defined as the number of participants in the young and elderly age groups that choose vaccination to maximize the group payoff.

In theory, the Nash equilibrium predicts that more elderly than young choose vaccination. Moreover, the utilitarian equilibrium predicts that more of the young players choose vaccination. The experiment provides confirmation. When groups are paid according to group point totals, more young participants choose vaccination. But when the two equilibria are compared, the utilitarian equilibrium leads to higher point totals for both the elderly and young players and a lower rate of infection for all. Overall, vaccinations for young people provide greater benefits for the elderly. The researchers conclude that, in high-stakes situations, such as pandemics, the overall outcome is "determined by the cumulative effect of individual actions … In these situations, achieving the optimal population outcome necessitates that some individuals act outside of their self-interest" (Chapman et al., 2012).

Game of risk perception and strategic choice

During a pandemic, both the perception of risk and intervention policies influence human behavior. But in a community, uncoordinated actions may lead to changes in human behavior. When control measures relax but infections exist, individuals may re-introduce defensive measures. That is, in order to reduce the risk of infection, they may change their behavior. Depending on the level of infections, an imitation process may spread throughout the community. From the individual perspective, if the perceived risk of infection is large, a choice of fewer contacts will reduce the spread of disease.

In a study that addresses the link between uncoordinated behavioral responses and risk perception, Poletti et al. (2012) use a game theory approach. They argue that the earlier the warnings about the spread of disease, the smaller are the peak prevalence of infections and the number of overall cases.

Model assumptions

In the Poletti et al. (2012) framework, the link between uncoordinated responses and risk perception serves as an important factor in modeling disease transmission. Changes in risky behavior are a function of risk perception of the disease. From the perspective of human activity, the area of interest is the identification of the factors that determine both risk perception and behavioral changes. From the perspective of the disease, these factors lead to changes in the dynamics of infection. A larger perception or risk and more defensive actions may slow the spread of disease. But these changes occur collectively. The researchers ask: in order to reduce the risk of infection, when will people change their behavior? The game theory approach establishes a model of susceptible individuals, focusing on two relationships: (1) behavioral changes that result from the perceived risk of infection and (2) the impact of different levels of infection on risk perception. By taking appropriate defensive measures such as wearing face masks, limiting travel, and avoiding crowded spaces, individuals may reduce the risk of exposure.

The model assumptions involve these factors, adopting a susceptible-infected-recovered framework. The risk of infection applies to susceptible individuals. But both asymptomatic and recovered individuals without symptoms may behave the same as those who are susceptible if they are equally concerned about the risk of exposure. Defensive activities by susceptible, asymptomatic, and recovered individuals may therefore reduce the rate of infection. But the actual rate of disease transmission differs between susceptible, asymptomatic, and recovered individuals.

The model captures the dynamics of defensive behavior. Individual behavior corresponds to strategies with expected payoffs. Behavior is a function of the perceived risk of infection. The framework models this relationship using *imitation dynamics* when each player observes the actions of other players and decides whether or not to imitate their strategy. If the perceived gain is sufficiently large, imitation occurs. If not, imitation does not occur. That is, learning exists as part of the game. Through personal encounters, individuals assess the strategies of others by comparing payoffs. If their payoff increases with the adoption of another strategy, change occurs. The game theory approach therefore captures two processes: dynamics of disease transmission and dynamics of imitation, which differ with respect to a focus on contacts and behavior, respectively.

Transmission process

To model the transmission process, Poletti et al. (2012) place members of the population into five categories. Each represents a fraction of the population:

- S - Susceptible
- I_S - Infective symptomatic
- I_A - Infective asymptomatic
- R_S - Recovered symptomatics
- R_A - Recovered asymptomatics

As a further level of distinction, the individuals in the S, I_S, and I_A categories may alter their behavior or not alter their behavior: $\{S_a, I_{Aa}, R_{Aa}\}$ and $\{S_n, I_{An}, R_{An}\}$. If individuals alter their behavior, they reduce their contacts by a factor q to decrease the potential for infection: $0 \leq q \leq 1$.

Two variables represent the behavioral choices of the two sets:

- b_a - Behavior of individuals in $\{S_a, I_{Aa}, R_{Aa}\}$
- b_n - Behavior of individuals in $\{S_n, I_{An}, R_{An}\}$

Other variables complete the model:

- β_S - Transmission rate for infective symptomatic individuals
- β_A - Transmission rate for infective asymptomatic individuals
- γ - average length of the infectivity period
- p - probability of developing symptoms
- λ - force of infection

The force of infection equals the following:

$$\lambda = \beta_S I_S + \beta_A I_{An} + q\beta_A I_{Aa} \tag{14.1}$$

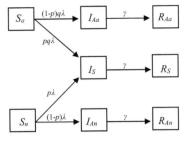

Figure 14.6 Disease transmission and behavioral choice.

Source: adapted from Poletti et al. (2012), Figure 1

which includes transmission from the infective symptomatic ($\beta_S I_S$), transmission from the infective asymptomatic who do not alter their behavior ($\beta_A I_{An}$), and the lower transmission from the infective asymptomatic who alter their behavior ($q \beta_A I_{Aa}$).

Disease transmission differs according to population category (figure 14.6). Starting with those who are susceptible, individuals may either alter their behavior (S_a) and make adjustments such as mask wearing or not alter their behavior (S_n). Based on the characteristics of infection, an individual who chooses to alter behavior becomes either infective asymptomatic (I_{Aa}) or infective symptomatic (I_S). An individual who chooses to not alter behavior may become either infective asymptomatic (I_{An}) or infective symptomatic (I_S). According to the average length of the infectivity period (γ), the individuals become recovered symptomatics (R_S) or recovered asymptomatics (R_A).

The choice of altering behavior or not altering behavior is a function of the perceived outcome, which relates to the risk of infection. The individual may believe that altering behavior will reduce both contacts and the risk of infection. The perceived outcome in turn, is a function of cost-benefit considerations. The individual may decide that the benefit of defensive actions (risk reduction) exceeds the costs (lost income, fewer social connections, isolation). The other possibility may exist. An individual may decide that the benefit of defensive action is too low to outweigh the costs. The latter individual does not alter behavior.

Payoff functions

A *payoff function* exists for individuals who alter their behavior (P_a) and do not alter their behavior (P_n). It depends on the perceived prevalence of disease. The perceived prevalence of disease represents data, information, and knowledge about the risk of infection, characterized by the past number of observed and symptomatic cases. In the Poletti et al. (2012) framework, the perceived prevalence of disease is modeled through a "memory mechanism" (M) that identifies the state of the pandemic in the mind of the individual.

When cases are rising, an individual perceives a higher prevalence of disease. Furthermore, all individuals assume a cost for the risk of infection, which depends linearly on the perceived prevalence of disease. The parameters m_a and m_n relate to the risk of developing symptoms for the individuals who alter their behavior (b_a) and do not alter behavior (b_n), respectively. The risk of developing symptoms is higher for individuals who do not alter their behavior: $m_n > m_a$. The parameter k is the additional cost of altering behavior (lost income, fewer social connections, isolation). The payoff functions for individuals who alter behavior and do not alter behavior are written as follows:

$$P_a = -k - m_a M \tag{14.2}$$

$$P_n = -m_n M \tag{14.3}$$

When interpreting the payoff functions, keep in mind that the risk of developing symptoms is higher for individuals who do not alter their behavior $(m_n > m_a)$. All else equal, when the perceived prevalence of disease (M) is lower, individuals who do not alter their behavior choose the most convenient path. But when the perceived prevalence of disease is higher, altered behavior and reducing the risk of infection provide a better payoff: individuals who alter their behavior have a lower risk of developing symptoms (m_a).

Imitation strategy

After experiencing both the pandemic and the payoffs, individuals may change their strategy. According to Poletti et al. (2012), the rate of changing strategy is proportional to the difference between the payoff functions: $\Delta P = P_n - P_a$ with a proportionality constant ϕ. In a two-strategy game, additional parameters include:

- x - fraction of the population choosing one strategy
- $(1 - x)$ - fraction of the population choosing the other strategy
- $\dot{\omega}$ - rate at which individuals meet

The imitation game is characterized as:

$$\chi = x(1 - x)\phi \Delta P \tag{14.4}$$

When individuals encounter other people with a different strategy, the former group considers the possibility of changing strategy. With respect to the choice, ΔP, the difference between the payoffs, establishes the pattern. As the payoff from altering behavior changes, the individual is more likely to choose to social distance, wear a mask, and/or shelter-in-place. The process of imitation motivates strategy changes. For example, if b_a provides a greater payoff than b_n, some infectives adopting b_n will change to the category of individuals adopting b_a (that is, from I_{An} to I_{Aa}). At the same time, if b_a provides a greater payoff than b_n, some susceptibles will change strategies (for example, from S_n to S_a).

Summary

During a pandemic, individuals face a series of strategic decisions with unfamiliar situations, including sheltering-in-place, social distancing, and working from home. Because game theory addresses individual decision making and social outcomes, it offers a useful method to analyze human behavior during a pandemic. In a game of survival, members of a target population serve as players. Policymakers establish the rules of the game, including player interaction. Individuals attempt to minimize the risk of infection while maintaining economic opportunity. In this context, several game theory applications exist. In a bargaining game, workers under sheltering-in-place orders may cooperate less often in the stag hunt bargaining framework when compared to the prisoner's dilemma. In a donor-recipient game, individuals donate their time, effort, and willingness to mitigate the spread of disease for the benefit of society. In a public good game, more people will choose vaccination when policymakers attempt to achieve an optimal social outcome. In a game of risk perception and strategic choice, from the perspective of the individual, if the perceived risk of infection is large, a choice of fewer contacts will reduce the spread of disease.

Chapter takeaways

LO1 For the analysis of pandemics, game theory provides a useful framework for modeling strategic interaction between decision makers.

LO2 In the game of survival during a pandemic, individuals, policymakers, and the disease serve as the players.

LO3 In game theory, two common approaches are the strategic form game and the extensive form game.

LO4 The bargaining game demonstrates that loneliness may impact an individual's decision to cooperate.

LO5 The donor-recipient game demonstrates that individuals may donate their time, effort, and willingness to mitigate the spread of disease for the benefit of society if they cooperate with policy interventions.

LO6 The public good game demonstrates that when policymakers attempt to achieve an optimal social outcome, more people will choose vaccination compared to when individual self-interest motivates the decision.

LO7 The game of risk perception and strategic choice demonstrates that, if the perceived risk of infection is large, more people will reduce contacts and slow the spread of disease.

Terms and concepts

Action profile
Cooperative solution
Dictator
Dominant strategy
Donor-recipient game
Duopolists' dilemma
Extensive form games
Game theory
Imitation dynamics
Mutual interdependence
Nash equilibrium
Natural field experiment
Network reciprocity

Noncooperative solution
Payoff function
Prisoner's dilemma
Scrutiny
Selection bias
Sequential games
Simultaneous games
Social choreography
Social dilemma
Stag hunt game
Strategic form games
Ultimatum
Utilitarian equilibrium
Warm-glow altruism

Questions

1. Why does game theory provide a useful framework for studying individual behavior dur-ing pandemics? What are some examples?
2. In a game theory framework, discuss the importance of rules, strategies, and payoffs.
3. In a game of survival, how may we view the payoffs of individuals, policymakers, and the disease? What are the costs and benefits of cooperation?
4. How do strategic form games differ from extensive form games?
5. With respect to equilibria, how does the prisoner's dilemma differ from the stag hunt game?
6. Why do experiments provide a useful method of empirical investigation for game theory problems? What different types of experiments exist?
7. Explain the bargaining game in this chapter. What are the rules, strategies, and payoffs? What are the outcomes? With respect to pandemics, what lessons result from the game?
8. Explain the donor-recipient game in this chapter. What are the rules, strategies, and pay-offs? What are the outcomes? With respect to pandemics, what lessons result from the game?
9. Explain the public good game in this chapter. What are the rules, strategies, and payoffs? What are the outcomes? With respect to pandemics, what lessons result from the game?
10. Explain the game of risk perception and strategic choice in this chapter. What are the rules, strategies, and payoffs? What are the outcomes? With respect to pandemics, what lessons result from the game?

References

Babin, J. Jobu, Foray, Marine, and Hussey, Andrew. 2020. "Shelter in place orders, loneliness, and cooperative behavior," Working Paper, Western Illinois University.

Chapman, Gretchen, Li, Meng, Vietri, Jeffrey, Ibuka, Yoko, Thomas, David, Yoon, Haewon, and Galvani, Alison. 2012. "Using game theory to examine incentives in influenza vaccination behavior," *Psychological Science*, 23(9): 1008-1015.

Gintis, Herbert. 2010. "Social norms as choreography," *Politics, Philosophy & Economics*, 9, 3 (August): 251-264.

Holden, Richard. 2020. "Vital signs: a lesson from game theory the coronavirus contrarians ignore," *The Conversation*, April 8. https://theconversation.com/vital-signs-a-lesson-for-game-theory-the-coronavirus-contrarians-ignore-135821.

Karlsson, Carl-Joar, and Rowlett, Julie. 2020. "Decisions and disease: a mechanism for the evolution of cooperation." *Nature Research*, 10: 13113.

List, John. 2011. "Why economists should conduct field experiments and 14 tips for pulling one off," *Journal of Economic Perspectives*, 25, 3 (Summer): 3-16.

Poletti, Piero, Ajelli, Marco, and Merler, Stefano. 2012. "Risk perception and effectiveness of uncoordinated behavioral responses in an emerging epidemic," *Mathematical Biosciences*, 238: 80-89.

Samuelson, Larry. 2016. "Game theory in economics and beyond," *Journal of Economic Perspectives*, 30, 4 (Fall): 107-130.

Umbhauer, Gisele. 2016. *Game Theory and Exercises*. London: Routledge.

von Neumann, John, and Morgenstern, Oskar. 1944. *Theory of Games and Economic Behavior*. Princeton, New York: Princeton University Press.

15   A trail of disruption

Learning objectives

After reading this chapter, you will be able to:

LO1   Explain why the coronavirus pandemic served as a global shock.
LO2   Identify the effects on the economy, health, inequality, environment, education, technology, economic geography, cooperation, policy, and society.
LO3   Analyze changes in the economy, including unemployment effects, digital inter- action, and remote work.
LO4   Discuss the lasting effects on health and inequality, including emergency care and poverty.
LO5   Argue that a pandemic impacts the environment, education, and the process of technological advance.
LO6   Address why a pandemic alters international, spatial, and cooperative outcomes.
LO7   Discuss the importance of policy implementation and social outcomes.

Chapter outline

- Economic loss, social discord, and uncertainty
- A set of pandemic outcomes
- Economic effects
- Health effects and inequality of outcomes
- Effects on the environment, education, and technology
- International, spatial, and cooperative effects
- Policy and social effects
- Summary

Economic loss, social discord, and uncertainty

The novel coronavirus that spread throughout the world during the year 2020 led to an economic collapse and a health crisis. On March 11, 2020, the Director General of the World Health Organization declared Covid-19 as a global pandemic. After that time, economic activity plummeted, unemployment rose, and businesses struggled to operate in an uncertain environment. Meanwhile, the pandemic surged, infecting more than 60,000,000 people and killing more than 1,500,000 by the end of 2020, according to the World Health Organization.

The twin economic and health crises intensified economic and social changes that were already underway. Vulnerable members of the population with pre-existing medical conditions and less access to healthcare experienced relatively larger increases in morbidity and mortality. The working poor were not able to both shelter-in-place and maintain stable incomes. Governments skeptical of cooperation and collective decision-making were slow to fight the spread of disease. The tension between economic integration and isolation persisted.

While the coronavirus pandemic represented a time of disruption, it also led to a period of technological advance, especially with the development of a vaccine, telemedicine, online education, and remote work. The pandemic, in other words, created more future pathways for the implementation of new technology. After the pandemic, whether countries settled into a period of slower economic growth or used the momentum of government intervention, investment in skills and security, and technological advance to accelerate economic prosperity depended on collective action, economic ingenuity, and the willingness to adapt to changing economic circumstances.

While a few countries crushed and contained the disease, multiple infection waves prolonged the crisis. These waves took different shapes, including peaks and valleys, a slow burn, and rising cases. In some hard-hit areas, the disease spread like wildfire through the population, an analogy that became increasingly prevalent. During the first year of Covid-19, essential workers carried out their duties, especially in healthcare, but nonessential employees were forced to work from home. These new economic circumstances altered schedules, productivity, cooperation, isolation, and feelings of loneliness. The circumstances also created an environment for policy interventions to slow the spread of disease, including quarantines, sheltering-in-place, social distancing, and mask wearing. Because of different levels of social cooperation, these interventions experienced mixed results.

Overall, an uncertain environment affected attitudes toward consumption, savings, and investment, the decisions, big and small, that impacted the course of the economy. According Robert J. Shiller (2020), Sterling Professor of Economics at Yale University, "Big events like a pandemic have the potential to leave behind a trail of disruption. They can create social discord, reduce people's willingness to spend and take risks, destroy business momentum and shake confidence in the value of investments." This chapter adopts Shiller's statement as a thesis. The only caveat is that, in historical perspective, pandemics rarely occur. They are widely spaced in time. As a result, whether or not specific pandemic outcomes become lasting effects, rather than short-term disruptions, remains an empirical question and subject to investigation. Mindful of this caveat, the concluding chapter discusses several outcomes from the pandemic, organized according to the structure of the book. The chapter presents a figure with the set of outcomes and then addresses whether the outcomes may lead to lasting effects.

A set of pandemic outcomes

Using the economic approach, this book develops the field of pandemic economics, arguing that a pandemic impacts all aspects of life. It leads to both short-term changes and the

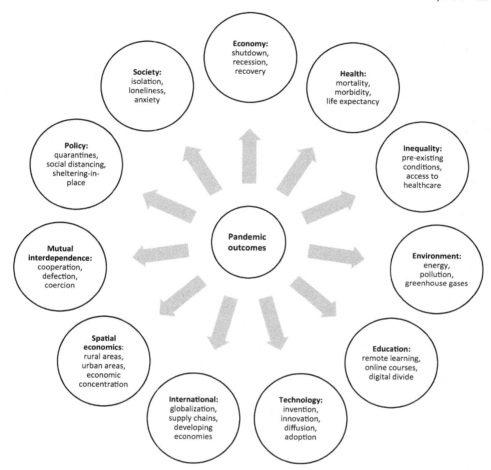

Figure 15.1 Pandemic outcomes.

Source: adapted from Abu-Rayash and Dincer (2020), Figure 4

potential for long-term outcomes (figure 15.1). The analysis reveals the extensive costs of the economic downturn and spread of disease. In many countries the coronavirus pandemic crippled markets, created recessions, and decreased economic activity in multiple sectors, including travel, retail, and aviation. The following sections discuss several effects of the coronavirus pandemic.

Economic effects

Large economic downturns disrupt employment and consumer spending. Because a pandemic-induced economic crisis leads to a service-sector recession, it disproportionately impacts both young people and women. As the economic toll increases, many of these individuals experience shorter work schedules, unemployment, or an exit from the labor market.

Unemployment

Despite policies that provide financial support, many of the unemployed do not receive a sufficient level of aid during shutdown and recession. According to Eurofound (2020), an agency of the European Union that addresses living and working conditions, younger workers experienced some of the largest costs. Compared to older workers, they had less work experience and job security. They were also overrepresented in industries hit hardest by the pandemic, including hospitality, food services, and travel. As a result, they were forced to make difficult adjustments, socially and economically, with declining incomes, cohabitation, internships instead of full-time work, or returning to school (Alderman and Abdul, 2020). The concern was that a prolonged economic downturn early in their careers would lead to higher levels of future joblessness.

Women also faced rising economic and social costs. First, the pandemic impacted sectors of the economy where women hold a majority of jobs, including healthcare, retail, and restaurants. Second, the pandemic reduced government tax receipts and public sector employment. Third, the movement to remote learning and the closing of childcare centers impacted mothers more than fathers (Cohen and Hsu, 2020). These outcomes were both short and long term. They eliminated jobs that women held but also prevented many women from obtaining new jobs. For many individual workers, this disruption reduced both job prospects and lifetime earnings. In addition, inequality in the home impacted inequality in the workplace. The reason was the economic disruption altered the work-life balance for women more than men (Heggeness, 2020). Women were more likely to experience more care responsibilities for both children and the elderly. These losses decreased economic growth rates by reducing the number of experienced and educated workers actively engaged in the economy. The cumulative effect was a rise in financial instability, emotional distress, and a decline in trust in institutions (Eurofound, 2020).

Labor market

During economic recovery, economies recovered most of the jobs that were lost during the downturn. But many positions did not return, even after the dissemination of a vaccine. The reason was that some economic sectors did not return to their pre-pandemic levels of employment. Many jobs were eliminated. In general, a full economic recovery hinges to some extent on the ability of workers at the margins to retrain. Taxi drivers that lose their jobs may have to become electricians. Cooks may have to become software developers. Managers working in sales may have to switch to real estate. For those with transferable skills, transition will occur. But the process proves difficult for low-paid workers in service occupations such as transportation, retail, maintenance, and construction. In other words, the economic recovery may not help all of the workers who have been hurt the most. For those in sectors that experienced a decline in jobs during the coronavirus pandemic, occupations such as restaurant servers, food prep workers, and office clerks occupied positions that transitioned the least into occupations that were growing (Escobari and Yeyati, 2020). The pandemic eliminated many jobs in service areas that required personal interaction but did not require higher levels of education and training. Even more, the pandemic intensified economic dynamics that were already underway, including automation and artificial intelligence, as companies protected their production processes from future shocks. But public policies may provide the incentive for education and training. Work force development serves as an important labor market policy, but especially in the aftermath of major shock. The challenge is to match jobs with skills.

Digital interaction

The economic shutdown triggered by the pandemic led to an increase in demand for digital interaction. Many individuals were sheltering-in-place but needed to continue with their job responsibilities. New technology for group projects, conferences, and meetings replaced previous methods. In many industries, individuals adopted digital tools for the exchange of ideas. As one example, the benefits of digital interaction in academics included the exchange of ideas, temporal and geographical flexibility, and more diverse workspaces (Schwarz et al., 2020). For academics and other sectors, the cost was the loss of social interaction. In addition, digital interaction blurred the boundaries between private and public workspaces and created concerns about cybersecurity. The empirical question moving forward is the extent to which a substitution between digital and physical interaction will continue to occur, especially in industries where digital interaction offers an efficient tool for the work environment.

Remote work

The coronavirus pandemic revealed the difference between employees who must report to work and those who may work from home. Those in the former category, such as healthcare workers and bus drivers, did not experience flexible work environments. But those in the latter category were able to adjust their schedules. The growth of digital interaction allowed businesses to increase their level of remote work. For flexible jobs, this change meant fewer commutes, less time in the office, and more control over the work environment.

Over time, growth of the remote work environment may offer even more benefits. When compared to working at home, working at the office may not create efficiency gains. In addition, office work proposes extra costs for people with disabilities and parents—especially mothers—who benefit from flexible schedules:

> Parents with children at home—whose days are busier than ever—say they're more stressed than nonparents but equally satisfied with working from home ... Mandatory face time has always penalized parents, and even more during lockdown. That helps explain why parents are considerably more likely than people without children to say that working without facetime requirements has improved their productivity, career path, work-life balance, mental health and home life.
>
> (Miller, 2020)

In the presence of these benefits, companies may extend policies for remote work, offering a flexible model with clear expectations about deadlines and performance. The potential economic effects are extensive. Not all workers may return to office buildings, impacting urban real estate. With business districts operating at less-than-full capacity, business ecosystems, including restaurants, grocery stores, bars, public transportation, and retail establishments, may experience a different marketplace. The flow of property taxes to governments may decrease. Businesses competing for office workers may provide more benefits such as wellness breaks, subsidized family care, and time for volunteering. For employees, the flexible schedule may become a basic company offering. Overall, economies molded around the movement of workers from homes to transportation hubs to office buildings may give way to an alternative model that reduces the number of commuting hours per week and provides more flexible hours.

E-commerce

Since the beginning of the century, sales from online shopping have increased; however, changes in the retail industry already underway signaled how the pandemic may permanently alter the market. Many large retail stores began using their spaces as fulfillment centers to process online orders, not as shopping centers. These "dark stores" exist as part of a movement to respond to both online commerce and the demand for faster shipping. The transformation of department stores into fulfillment centers, even in the short term, demonstrates how retailers respond to changing market conditions, the growth of e-commerce, and the increasing irrelevance of traditional shopping centers. The market conditions contributing to the growth in online shopping were apparent long before the coronavirus pandemic. But the decline in economic activity and increase in e-commerce signal the evolution of the retail industry, the infusion of technology, and the permanent shift in how consumers shop. In the retail industry, physical stores will continue to integrate with online businesses. But as shopping centers continue to close, it is unclear how the market will use all of the remaining space during the process of transition (Corkery and Maheshwari, 2020).

Health effects and inequality of outcomes

For individual countries, the magnitude of a crisis is determined by policy interventions, outcomes, and the fragility of the systems in which it attacks. Many countries are vulnerable to a large health shock because they lack the ability to provide healthcare resources for everyone. Countries with unequal access to healthcare resources may struggle in the absence of an effective mechanism of redistribution, as both income and wealth inequality make entire segments of the population more vulnerable during a crisis. Many countries, in other words, do not experience an equitable distribution of the benefits of economic growth, including health outcomes, during "stable" periods of time. During a pandemic, the situation worsens, because economic and social hierarchies become visible. Less affluent members of society experience a disproportionate burden. Those in lower-income classes suffer disproportionately from the spread of disease. Patterns of poor health and economic inequality mean that people at the bottom of the income spectrum are more likely to die during a pandemic.

Health effects

Coronaviruses, first identified in the mid-1960s and named for the spikes that come out of their surfaces, resemble a crown. They form a group of viruses that cause the common cold,

Middle East respiratory syndrome (MERS), and severe acute respiratory syndrome (SARS). They also cause respiratory illnesses. After it passed to humans, the novel coronavirus, named SARS-COV-2, which causes the disease Covid-19, spread during the year 2020 in global transmission networks. Compared to MERS and SARS, Covid-19 was less fatal on a per-capita basis—with a fatality rate around one percent of symptomatic people—but spread on a much wider basis (Basu, 2020).

Long-term health effects

Because human immune systems had not previously experienced the SARS-COV-2 strain, they were unable to stop the negative health outcomes. When people infected with the virus sneezed, coughed, breathed, or talked, they produced respiratory droplets, which passed through the air and potentially infected others. Compared to children, middle-aged and elderly adults, especially those living in long-term care facilities and nursing homes, were at higher risk for illness. But people of all ages with pre-existing medical conditions, including asthma, lung disease, obesity, diabetes, immuno-complications, and kidney or liver disease, had a higher rate of illness from Covid-19. Research and testing revealed that, compared to a simple respiratory virus, Covid-19 was more unpredictable, began with few or no symptoms, and affected the entire body (table 15.1).

Even though most patients recovered and returned to normal health, many demonstrated long-term symptoms, including chest pain, cough, fatigue, fever, headache, joint pain, and muscle pain. Long-term impacts on organs besides the lungs, including the heart and brain, increased the risk of morbidity and mortality. More serious but infrequent complications entailed cardiovascular and respiratory problems, neurological abnormalities including a loss of taste and smell, and psychiatric problems such as anxiety and depression.

Emergency care and telemedicine

With telemedicine, the coronavirus pandemic presented an opportunity for hospitals to decrease the demand for emergency care (Frakt, 2020). From an economics perspective, it is important to consider how to efficiently allocate scarce resources among competing wants. If doctors meet with more patients through telemedicine, fewer emergency room visits

Table 15.1 Symptoms of Covid-19

Target area	Symptom
Brain	Strokes from blood clots or neurological issues
Eyes	Pinkeye
Nose	Loss of smell and taste
Blood	Unexpected blood clotting; attacks the lining of blood vessels
Gastrointestinal	Vomiting and diarrhea
Lungs	Clogs and inflames alveoli, hampering breathing; pulmonary embolism
Heart	Weakens heart muscle; causes dangerous arrhythmias
Kidneys	Damage to structures that filter waste from blood; often require dialysis
Skin	"Covid toes" or fingers; purple rash from the attack on blood vessels
Immune system	Overactive immune response that attacks healthy tissue

Source: Bernstein and Cha (2020)

result, reducing the problem of crowding. During the pandemic, many hospitals established guidelines for when patients should use telemedicine and when they should seek immediate care. Although helpful, this increase in flexibility did not eliminate the problem of hospitals reaching capacity. With respect to beds and protective equipment, secondary infection waves pushed many hospitals beyond their limits. The crowding increased the wait time of patients, which led to adverse health outcomes, lower quality care, higher costs, and longer hospital stays. In these situations, patients with limited digital fluency could not rely on telemedicine.

For context, one study analyzed emergency department wait times in England. Starting in 2004, a policy penalized hospitals if emergency department wait times exceeded four hours for a majority of patients. The study found that the implementation of the policy correlated with an eight-percent reduction in wait times (Gruber et al., 2018). Another study found that longer hospital wait times increased the cost of emergency care (Woodworth and Holmes, 2019). Of course, telemedicine cannot solve problems in emergency departments. But an increase in demand for telemedicine provides a cost-effective option for care.

Inequality of outcomes

During a pandemic, conventional wisdom is that the disease serves as a great equalizer. At first glance, the disease crosses borders and does not discriminate according to income or socioeconomic status. However, because of a higher prevalence of pre-existing medical conditions and less access to healthcare, it disproportionately impacts members of marginalized communities.

Pandemics and inequality

A pandemic reveals pre-existing levels of inequality in a society, whether measured through income, wealth, or access to resources. During a pandemic, inequality exacerbates gaps in healthcare outcomes. In fact, during times of rising inequality, a pandemic may be more likely. The idea is that population growth leads to urbanization, modernization, and globalization. In cities, urban density increases the basic reproduction number. Once the disease is embedded in human carriers, networks of transmission facilitate an outbreak. Inequality then increases morbidity and mortality among the most vulnerable members of society.

Poverty

During a pandemic, the poorest members of society experience a disproportionate burden. Several reasons exist. No matter where they live, the poor have less access to healthcare systems. This outcome is especially problematic in countries where higher out-of-pocket expenses result from noncomprehensive health insurance coverage. Moreover, poorer members of society have lower-paying jobs and a higher propensity for subsistence living conditions. They may lack basic services such as running water and sanitation, which prohibits proper hygiene.

The precarious economic position means the poor may not be able to comply with stay-at-home orders, increasing their exposure. They may not have enough savings or government aid to provide a personal safety net. Essential employees, such as those in meatpacking plants, may not have the option to shelter-in-place. But employees in nonessential forms of work may have the least education and training, putting them at the highest risk for losing their jobs. At the national level, when a vaccine arrives, markets determine distribution. Richer countries that develop the vaccine secure the initial doses. The distribution plan crowds out poorer countries.

Effects on the environment, education, and technology

Environmental outcomes

Given the important role of the economies of China, the European Union, and the United States, the economic shutdown interrupted supply chains and international trade, affecting both upstream suppliers and downstream consumers. The industrial slowdown grounded planes, reduced factory operation, and decreased transportation, distribution, and the consumption of fossil fuels. These outcomes decreased both air pollution and greenhouse gas emissions (Lenzen et al., 2020). This contrast between economic losses and environmental gains reveals the mixed effects of the pandemic. On the one hand, the pandemic highlights the risk of an interconnected global system of exchange, demonstrating the need for global cooperation to fight the spread of disease. On the other hand, the pandemic demonstrates that it is possible to confront a crisis through collaboration, decisive interventions, and lifestyle changes, factors necessary to address the wider climate crisis (Lenzen et al., 2020).

Deforestation

During the pandemic, land grabbers, illegal loggers, and miners took advantage of the distraction to clear large tracts of the Amazonian rainforest with impunity. They cleared land for cattle to graze. The first step after clearing, however, was to set the land ablaze during drier months. This activity led to widespread fires, contributing to the processes of climate change and ecological degradation. The demand for meat came at the expense of environmental quality. In June 2020, when Brazil recorded the world's highest average daily deaths, hundreds of square miles of deforestation occurred (Londono et al., 2020).

Valuing the environment

At the same time of the Brazilian deforestation, urban residents around the world were experiencing cleaner air. The decline in economic activity, so disruptive with respect to employment and production, led to quieter streets where traffic normally flows, cleaner skies where pollution usually exists, and animal sightings. In this context, environmental economists explain that humans establish values for environmental quality, including *use value*, *options value*, and *nonuse value*. Use value applies when individuals use their senses to experience an environmental resource, such as viewing a scenic vista. When pollution obscures the view, the environmental value declines. The individuals, therefore, value cleaner air. Options value exists when people assign value to the future ability to use the environment, such as visiting a national park or beach. Options value reflects willingness to pay to preserve the site, even if it is not being used. Nonuse value refers to the designation of value for a resource that will not be consumed. One type of nonuse value is bequest value, the willingness to pay to preserve a resource for future generations. Another type of nonuse value is existence value, measured by the willingness to pay to maintain an environmental resource over time, such as the Grand Canyon in the United States. Taken together, total willingness to pay equals use value plus options value plus nonuse value (Tietenberg and Lewis, 2018). During the coronavirus pandemic, use value increased when individuals realized they appreciated cleaner skies.

Climate change

The process of climate change, with heat waves, wildfires, hurricanes, and droughts, is locked into the world's ecosystems and cannot be reversed. The burning of fossil fuels and emissions of greenhouse gases increase the average global surface temperature, leading to multiple damage effects. Damages include rising sea levels, lower crop yields, and human displacement. But will the short-term decrease in greenhouse gas emissions resulting from the global recession alter the climate trajectory? All things considered, the most likely answer is no. Even though fewer greenhouse gas emissions are a positive outcome from a climate perspective, it is likely a short-run blip. The rising atmospheric concentration of greenhouse gases means average global temperature will continue to increase.

Educational outcomes

The coronavirus pandemic altered the process of education. Schools opened and closed in an intermittent pattern, depending on the status of the disease. The pressure on teachers and students led to unfamiliar educational outcomes. The digital divide aggravated inequalities. But the instability created a new learning environment, demonstrating adaptability, creativity, resilience, and innovation. The influx of technology into the learning environment, especially teleconferencing, provided more options for teachers and students.

Remote learning

Maintaining the educational experience during a pandemic requires ingenuity from teachers, students, and school systems. Delivering educational content in a remote learning environment increases the demand for guidance, internet access, and technological literacy. During the coronavirus pandemic, several innovations emerged. Many teachers began incorporating the pandemic into different fields of study, including science, social studies, and mathematics, demonstrating that a pandemic impacts all areas of life. Teachers collaborated with lesson plans, creating short lectures and videos that were offered during the period of remote learning. Because of the importance of mental health for student achievement, teachers and counselors learned to recognize warning signs among students, such as missed assignments and a lack of attendance. Educational adaptation included an evaluation of curriculum, methods of collaboration, and assessments of student engagement. Early in the coronavirus pandemic, school systems eased the burden of both grading and homework. But over time it became clear that more students were failing with remote work than during periods of traditional education. Disadvantaged students fared the worst, increasing their risk of long-term disengagement from the educational process.

Budget cuts

During the coronavirus pandemic, tax revenue flowing to government decreased. As a result, public sector funding of institutions of higher education declined. During the coronavirus pandemic, universities increased expenditures for public health measures, testing, student aid, and technology. To meet budget shortfalls, they were forced to cut spending in other areas. Short-term measures such as early retirement incentives and hiring freezes addressed part of the problem, but the economic downturn pushed many schools to consolidate programs, eliminate courses of study, and implement furlough programs. But after the exhaustion of these options, many institutions had to reduce their largest line item, payroll. This action meant laying off faculty and staff. Already facing constraints, the pandemic amplified the financial problems of universities, although institutions with higher endowments weathered the economic downturn more effectively.

Digital divide

When school systems, colleges, and universities sent students home during the coronavirus pandemic, the demand for online education grew. While teleconferencing and network technologies encouraged remote learning, many students were left behind. The reason was the *digital divide*, a lack of internet access and/or electronic devices among lower-income students. This problem occurred in both developed and developing countries. Lacking an internet connection at home, many students sought alternative locations, including parking lots, cafes, and roadside spaces. Even if they had access to cell phones, many of these students could not efficiently complete homework assignments, given the uneven nature of technology.

During the pandemic, millions of students faced these hardships. As a result, educators struggled to make distance education viable. In poorer communities, the problem was particularly difficult. Technological disruptions mixed with inferior health outcomes created an environment for permanent academic setbacks. The question was how to balance online learning with higher levels of anxiety, stress, and tension among students, parents, and teachers. Some school systems created safe spaces for online learning, equipped buses with internet service, or notified students of areas with strong connections. The long-term impact on educational achievement for these vulnerable students remains an important empirical question.

Work effort

In the developing world, the closure of schools forced many children to find work. Because parents may have lost their jobs, families needed money. As a cheap source of labor, children contributing income created more household value than pursuing education, especially in poorer countries without widespread internet connections. The United Nations (2020) estimated that, at the height of the coronavirus pandemic, 192 countries experienced school closures, 1.6 billion students were sent home, 463 million children could not participate in online education, and 24 million dropped out permanently. Millions of these children were drawn into work arrangements such as scavenging for plastic or scrap metal, mining, chopping weeds, and serving as "living statues" who beg for money (Gettleman and Raj, 2020). The increase in work effort from those who were previously attending school eroded the educational progress for millions of students.

Technological advance

Technology companies

During the coronavirus pandemic, the rise of some industries and the fall of others reflected changing market dynamics. Investors struggled to distinguish between temporary and permanent changes. In this economic environment, many technology companies flourished with the growth of cloud computing, social networking, videoconferencing, online education and entertainment, and delivery-on-demand. Several companies allocated a significant amount of resources for growth and expansion into new markets, further developing their platforms and products. During the coronavirus pandemic, the profits of many manufacturers declined, such as those who created clothing specializing in attire for offices. But the profits of other manufacturers grew, including those specializing in household cleaners and detergents. In the marketplace, technology companies occupied a unique position. Many experienced increasing sales during an economic downturn. By adapting to changing conditions and offering new products and services, many technology companies emerged from the pandemic with greater market value.

New technology

During the coronavirus pandemic, new technology was developed in many areas, including disease detection and containment, the provision of healthcare, management of information, and cybersecurity. Many forms of technological advance were global, revealing the interconnected methods of collaboration. But several new applications of existing technology emerged, highlighting the ability of private and public sectors to innovate. One example, digital wristbands, tracked both contacts for tracing and physiological characteristics, offering a way to determine the potential for infection. Second, e-commerce experienced greater market share, especially while individuals were sheltering-in-place. As a third example, the combination of artificial intelligence and online shopping provided a virtual face-to-face experience, such as shopping in a grocery store from home with online purchases. These and other examples demonstrate how a crisis stimulates the process of technological advance.

International, spatial, and cooperative effects

International effects

The coronavirus pandemic marks a transformation in the era of globalization. Economies with extensive global supply chains have become more aware of the risk of single points of failure. That is, fragile supply chains may rely on a single or few sources of production, which makes them vulnerable to external shocks. In this context, firms may, at the behest of their public sectors, invest in domestic systems of production and diversify the supply of resource inputs. Trade wars, technological advance, and global shocks encourage this transition. Over time, firms may pursue more economic integration at the national level. Continent-wide free trade zones may expand. Regional and bilateral connections may emphasize production and exchange, not global interconnection. A focus on the economic losers of the coronavirus pandemic include the workers who suffer from structural unemployment and the businesses that do not adapt to changing circumstances. One response, protectionism, encourages countries to look inward but includes its own costs, including severed supply chains. Another response, globalization, encourages countries to grapple with the challenges of helping workers and growing economies in a world with the potential for major economic disruptions.

> The coronavirus pandemic may mark the end of the post-Cold War era. The enchantment with ever-greater international integration is gone. But it would be folly to replace globalization with the same kind of isolationism and protectionism that has impoverished nations before.
>
> (Fontaine, 2020)

Reconceptualizing the urban

Urbanism involves a city's way of life, including its design and level of economic development. In economics, the idea of a dense city as an incubator for economic and social progress serves as a central theme. The diversity and population density of urban areas creates centers of innovation. A dynamic marketplace and the potential for collaboration counter higher urban living costs. The need to exchange ideas, sell goods and services, and collaborate has always attracted talent and capital to cities. As the theory of new economic geography explains, industries and jobs migrate to urban areas, and workers follow.

The value of urban life

A pandemic challenges this notion. Cities experience disease, the shutdown of restaurants, shops, and museums, and shift to remote work.

> Regardless of whether the high level of infections in cities is due to urban form—including population density, their role as global transport nodes, their specialization in service-oriented work—or other factors, questions have been raised about how we value our present highly urbanized way of life.
>
> (Bailey et al., 2020)

This conceptualization of form impacts both the spatial model of economic concentration and how cities recover from external shocks. For many families, the loss of a job translates into a strain in making house payments. Noneviction policies address this problem. But as apartment vacancies climb and rental prices fall, housing markets adjust. At the same time, when the demand for a remote work environment increases and fewer people commute, priorities change. These outcomes determine market effects with respect to building occupancy, commuting, real estate and rental markets, and urban life. For many cities, a pandemic reduces the supply of tourists, decreasing hotel occupancy rates. This effect leads to a decline in demand for complementary activities, including restaurants, taxis, and theaters. Many small businesses and retailers that rely on the spending of commuters and tourists for their livelihoods close during economic shutdown and may not reopen during economic recovery. A decrease in demand puts downward pressure on prices. It also slows new building construction, including commercial and residential, slowing the construction industry. With vacant space, developers weigh the costs and benefits of turning sales into rentals or restructuring loan obligations. Overall, the extensive economic impacts of a pandemic on urban areas reveal an inequality of outcomes. Higher income households have the financial wherewithal to shelter-in-place. Lower-income households suffer more from economic downturns and disruptions in education, healthcare, and social systems.

Inflection point

This story of economic contraction and human suffering is nothing new. The global history of pandemics, epidemics, and disease outbreaks demonstrates a centuries-old story of hardship, with cities serving as centers of contagion. Economic history reveals that cities recover at different rates, depending on the infectiousness of the disease, policy interventions, and cooperation, although there is nothing fast or inevitable about the process. For urban areas, a pandemic creates an inflection point: the shock exposes systematic problems, raises the question of the feasibility of returning to pre-pandemic patterns of exchange, and reveals ways to improve urban life. With businesses reducing their urban footprint, allowing some employees to work from home, and decreasing their demand for commercial real estate, business districts adjust. Some cities struggle to regenerate, especially those already having difficulty attracting jobs. But others thrive in the new economic environment, adapting to changing conditions, innovating in areas that require new methods of organization, and providing more equitable and affordable opportunities. Certain byproducts of the changing economic dynamic, including an emphasis on repurposing streets as walkways, the creation of more livable space, healthy lifestyles, a reduction in congestion, and clean air, provide momentum to increase living standards. In response to a shock, urban areas have a chance to balance city management, scarce public resources, and quality-of-life improvements. A pandemic demonstrates that human behavior may change. It also reveals, however, that city function favors those with more economic resources. Economic and health crises provide the opportunity to make cities work for everyone.

Cooperation

Populations under collective threat experience pressure to tighten their social norms and punish those who deviate from a cooperative position (Seitz et al., 2020). During periods of major disruption, rules and punishments that discourage free riders are necessary for groups to coordinate their behavior. But cultural characteristics determine how a population responds. Gelfand (2018) explains this concept with *tight-loose theory*. Populations with tight social arrangements have stricter norms and less tolerance for deviation. In contrast, populations with loose social arrangements have weaker norms and more permissive behavior. The degree of tightness of a population is not fixed but a function of historical trends, economic forces, political realities, and social characteristics. A variation in tightness is also related to the extent of collective threats such as warfare, scarcity, and disease. Evolutionary game-theoretic models demonstrate that "differences in normative tightness evolve as a cultural adaptation to threat" (Seitz et al., 2020).

Using the terminology of game theory, as the threat of a pandemic increases, individuals operate in a game of lower payoffs. Pressure increases to choose cooperative outcomes. The implication is that countries with tighter cultural characteristics may be in a better position to limit the spread of disease and number of deaths. These populations experience more cooperation, monitoring, and self-control, critical factors in the presence of a threat. However, "because loose cultures prioritize freedom over rules, they may experience psychological reluctance when tightening is required. The situation is compounded when governmental leaders minimize threat signals" (Seitz et al., 2020).

Policy and social effects

Public policy to fight the pandemic differs between countries due to the public sector's allocation of resources, competence, and foresight. The ability to implement comprehensive systems of testing, tracing, and supported isolation requires enforcement, a realistic timeframe, and cooperation. At the same time, a pandemic creates the opportunity to correct market failures, improve public institutions, and address inequalities. It also threatens to overwhelm economic and social systems. The extent to which a country balances these potential outcomes determines the trajectory of both health and economic effects.

Crises expose fragilities but do not provide obvious solutions. In the absence of a willingness to adapt, countries may experience inferior outcomes. Change, in contrast, requires innovation, effective leadership, and foresight. During the coronavirus pandemic, many of the countries that experienced the most effective processes of economic recovery experienced an activist state and broad trust in government.

Policy effects

The coronavirus pandemic forced countries to implement policy in the absence of full information on the spread of disease. In many countries, the failure of initial containment efforts led to the implementation of nonpharmaceutical interventions. These policies decreased economic activity, restricted travel, and closed schools. Because the world had never experienced the new pathogen spreading in transmission networks, some of the intervention policies were more successful than others. The question became whether the health benefits of the nonpharmaceutical interventions were worth the economic and social costs, including unemployment, business restrictions, and isolation. In a study that measures the health benefits of strict interventions, Hsiang et al. (2020) find that "the deployment of anti-contagion policies ... significantly slowed the pandemic." Without enacting these interventions, millions of more infections would have occurred, reflecting the "timing, intensity and extent of policy deployment ... and the duration for which they have been applied" (Hsiang et al., 2020). Strict policy interventions created substantial health benefits.

Social effects

Birth rates

During a time of recession, uncertainty, and insecurity, many individuals are reluctant to seek commitments. If they lack economic security, they may postpone long-term relationships. As these factors take hold, the birth rate declines. In history, periods of disruption and uncertainty, including wars and pandemics, reveal downturns in birth rates. For countries at population replacement levels, aging demographics and lower birth rates impact economic factors such as the ability to provide a social safety net, employment, and growth rates. While access to birth control and policies toward reproduction affect birth rates, economic conditions impact fertility choices. In modern economies, when the unemployment rate increases, birth rates decline. "A deeper and longer lasting recession will then mean lower lifetime income for some people, which means that some women will not just delay births, but they will decide to have fewer children" (Kearney and Levine, 2020). Ultimately, the extent of a *baby bust* from the coronavirus pandemic is a function of country-specific factors, the length of recession, attitudes toward recovery, and uncertainty. Countries with longer pandemic phases and economic downturns may experience larger declines in birth rates.

Isolation

During a pandemic, societies experience the social cost of isolation, because connections are crucial for human well-being. For many members of society, an increase in anxiety during periods of isolation signal the need for human connection. Isolation impacts public health. Problems emerge, including domestic violence, mental health issues, and substance abuse.

> The substantial changes in our social behavior as a result of this pandemic are clearly far-reaching, but we do not yet know what lingering longer-term public health effects the pandemic may foreshadow. If the rates of social isolation and loneliness remain elevated or increase, such changes are likely to lead to a greater public health burden in the longer term.
>
> (Holt-Lunstad, 2020)

Summary

The coronavirus pandemic led to a health crisis and required governments to implement anti-contagion policies and economic shutdown measures. The policies impacted the spread of infections, number of lives lost, and reductions in economic activity. The pandemic left a trail of disruption. It began with one identified case in December 2019. By December 2020, more than 60,000,000 confirmed cases and over 1,500,000 deaths occurred, according to the World Health Organization. The effects of the pandemic were widespread, including impacts on the economy, policy, society, health, inequality, the environment, education, technology, the international economy, economic geography, and cooperation. In this context, large economic downturns disrupted employment, consumer spending, and production. Many societies were vulnerable to a large health shock because they did not provide universal healthcare coverage. At the same time, many environmental, educational, and technological outcomes led to lower pollution levels and innovation in online education. Policy implementation and social effects differed between countries, largely because of the public sector's allocation of resources, competence, and foresight. While aggressive interventions slowed the spread of disease, they led to social costs with rising levels of isolation, loneliness, and anxiety. Overall, the pandemic created a set of economic, health, and social problems that required a substantial amount of government intervention. Because policy responses varied, some countries were more successful than others in slowing the spread of disease and minimizing economic losses.

Chapter takeaways

LO1   During the coronavirus pandemic, the twin economic and health crises intensified economic and social forces that were already underway.

LO2   A pandemic leads to both short-term changes and outcomes that may not be apparent for a long period of time.

LO3   Because a pandemic-induced economic crisis leads to a service-sector recession, it may disproportionately impact both young people and women.

LO4   Many societies are vulnerable to a large health shock because they lack the ability to provide security to all people during a time of need.

LO5   A pandemic alters environmental outcomes, educational opportunities, and opportunities for technological advance.

LO6   The coronavirus pandemic marked the transformation of the era of globalization, reconceptualized the urban landscape, and encouraged populations under collective threat to tighten their social norms.

LO7   A pandemic creates the opportunity to correct market failures, improve public institutions, and address inequalities, but it also threatens to overwhelm economic and social systems.

Terms and concepts

Baby bust
Digital divide
Nonuse value
Options value
Tight-loose theory
Use value

Questions

1. For specific countries, what is the impact of the coronavirus pandemic on lives lost, infections, production of output, and employment?

2. Why do pandemics leave a trail of disruption? What economic and social costs are in the trail? Which of these costs lead to long-term effects?

3. The book discusses the effects of a pandemic on the economy, policy, society, health, inequality, the environment, education, technology, the international economy, economic geography, and cooperation. Which outcomes are most pronounced?

4. Because of the coronavirus pandemic, did the production of output decrease more in the service sector or goods sector? What is the implication for employment, digital interaction, remote work, and e-commerce?

5. How did the coronavirus pandemic reveal weaknesses in the healthcare system? What changes may enhance the ability of the healthcare system to provide efficient outcomes and address the inequality of access? In the future, what is the role of telemedicine?

6. The coronavirus pandemic led to mixed effects on the environment, including lower levels of pollution and higher levels of hospital waste. How would you characterize the overall environmental impact? In your answer, consider specific pollution flows, changes in greenhouse gas emissions, and the discharge of personal protective equipment.

7. The coronavirus pandemic led to an increase in both the supply of and demand for online courses. During the pandemic, remote education provided a method for schools to educate students. What is the effect of this technology? How should society eliminate the digital divide?

8. What lasting technological advances began during the coronavirus pandemic? How do these advances contribute to the economy?

9. During the coronavirus pandemic, strict intervention policies controlled the disease. They put the economy in a better position to recover. After reviewing country-level epidemic curves and the timeframe for intervention policies, which countries were most successful in stopping the spread of disease and minimizing economic costs?

10. During the coronavirus pandemic, countries shut down large segments of the economy. Business losses were compounded by personal costs, including extended periods of isolation. In retrospect, should public policy have prioritized these economic and personal costs? Explain.

References

Abu-Rayash, Azzam, and Dincer, Ibrahim. 2020. "Analysis of the electricity demand trends amidst the Covid-19 coronavirus pandemic," *Energy Research & Social Science*, 68 (October): 101682.

Alderman, Liz, and Abdul, Geneva. 2020. "Young and jobless in Europe: 'It's been desperate,'" *The New York Times*, October 29.

Bailey, David, Clark, Jennifer, Colombelli, Alessandra, Corradini, Carlo, De Propis, Lisa, Derudder, Ben, … Usai, Stefano. 2020. "Regions in a time of panic," *Regional Studies*, 54, 9: 1163–1174.

Basu, Anirban. 2020. "Estimating the infection fatality rate among symptomatic Covid-19 cases in the United States," *Health Affairs*, May 7. https//doi.org/10.1377/hlthaff.2020.00455.

Bernstein, Lenny, and Cha, Ariana. 2020. "Doctors keep discovering new ways the coronavirus attacks the body," *Washington Post*, May 10.

Cohen, Patricia and Hsu, Tiffany. 2020. "Pandemic could scar a generation of working mothers," *The New York Times*, June 3.

Corkery, Michael, and Maheshwari, Sapna. 2020. "As customers move online, so does the holiday shopping season," *The New York Times*, November 23.

Escobari, Marcela, and Yeyati, Levy. 2020. "Dislocation of labor markets: what policies to mitigate the shock?" *Brookings*, November 17.

Eurofound. 2020. *Living, Working and Covid-19*. Covid-19 Series. Luxembourg: Publications Office of the European Union.

Fontaine, Richard. 2020. "Globalization will look very different after the coronavirus pandemic," *Foreign Affairs*, April 17.

Frakt, Austin. 2020. "Improve emergency care? Pandemic helps point the way," *The New York Times*, November 23.

Gelfand, M. 2018. *Rule Breakers: How Tight and Loose Cultures Wire the World*. New York: Scribner.

Gettleman, Jeffrey, and Raj, Suhasini. 2020. "As Covid-19 closes schools, the world's children go to work," *The New York Times*, September 27.

Gruber, Jonathan, Hoe, Thomas, and Stoye, George. 2018. "Saving lives by tying hands: the unexpected effects of constraining health care providers," National Bureau of Economic Research, Working Paper 24445.

Heggeness, Misty. 2020. "Estimating the immediate impact of the Covid-19 shock on parental attachment to the labor market and the double bind of mothers," *Review of Economics of the Household*, 18 (October): 1053–1078.

Holt-Lunstad, Julianne. 2020. "The double pandemic of social isolation and Covid-19: cross-sector policy must address both," *Health Affairs*, June 22.

Hsiang, Solomon, Allen, Daniel, Annan-Phan, Sebastien, Bell, Kendon, Bolliger, Ian, Chong, Trinetta, … Wu, Tiffany. 2020. "The effect of large-scale anti-contagion policies on the Covid-19 pandemic," *Nature*, 584 (August): 262–267.

Kearney, Melissa, and Levine, Phillip. 2020. "Half a million fewer children? The coming Covid baby bust," *Brookings*, June 15.

Lenzen, Manfred, Malik, Mengyu, Pomponi, Francesco, Sun, Ya-Yen, Wiedmann, Thomas, Faturay, Futu, … Yousefzadeh, Moslem. 2020. "Global socio-economic losses and environmental gains from the coronavirus pandemic," *Plos One*, 15(7): e0235654.

Londono, Ernesto, Andreoni, Manuela, and Casado, Leticia. 2020. "Amazon deforestation soars as pandemic hobbles enforcement," *The New York Times*, June 6.

Miller, Claire. 2020. "The revolution in the way we work," *The New York Times*, August 23.

Schwarz, Marius, Scherrer, Aline, Hohmann, Claudia, Heiberg, Jonas, Brugger, Andri, and Nunez-Jimenez, Alejandro. 2020. "Covid-19 and the academy: it is time for going digital," *Energy Research & Social Science*, 68 (October): 101684.

Seitz, Benjamin, Aktipis, Athena, Buss, David, Alcock, Joe, Bloom, Paul, Gelfand, Michele, … Haselton, Martie. 2020. "The pandemic exposes human nature: 10 evolutionary insights," *PNAS*, 117, 45 (November): 27767-27776.

Shiller, Robert. 2020. "Why we can't foresee the pandemic's long-term effects," *The New York Times*, May 29.

Tietenberg, Tom, and Lewis, Lynne. 2018. *Environmental and Natural Resource Economics*. London: Routledge.

United Nations. 2020. "UNICEF Executive Director Henrietta Fore's remarks at a press conference on new updated guidance on school-related public health measures in the context of Covid-19," September 15. https://unicef.org/press-releases/unicef-executive-director-henrietta-fores-remarks-press-conference -new-updated.

Woodworth, Lindsey, and Holmes, James. 2019. "Just a minute: the effect of emergency department wait on the cost of care," *Economic Inquiry*, 58, 2 (April): 698–716.

INDEX

supply chains 55
supply curve 141
supply shock 2, 92–93
Susceptible, Infected, and Recovered model 24, 29, 36, 284–285
sustain and support 117–120
sustainability 183
sustainable development 185, 241–242
sustain point 254
sustenance 237
Sweden: sustain and support strategy in, 118, 120; higher education in, 204
Swiss cheese model of pandemic defense 67
systems of innovation 214
Syverson, C. 93

Taiwan: crush and contain strategy in, 118; shutdown policies in, 73
Taleb, N. 7
targeted economic shutdown 71–72
targeted lockdown policies 37
tax: corrective, 136
technological advance: process of, 209; stages of, 210–211; economic growth and, 214; lasting effects of, 223–224; technology companies and, 302
technology: education and, 202–203
technologically efficiency of education 192
telemedicine 222, 297–298
terms of trade 233
testing, tracing, and supported isolation 109–110
Thailand 57
Thaler, R. 142
Theory of Games and Economic Behavior 271
therapy 222
Thompson, D. 13
threshold infection probability 38
TIGER model *see* Tracking Indexes for the Global Economic Recover
tight-loose theory 304–305
timeframe: economic recovery and, 116; global networks and, 228
time-space compression 257
time-space distanciation 257
Tooze, A. 2
Toxvaerd, F. 38
Tracking Indexes for the Global Economic Recovery 58
trade agreements 48
tradeoffs 2, 69, 75–78
traffic 263
transformative change 215, 219
transmission potential 52
transportation cost 253–254
trialability 212–213

triggering entities 218
trough 87–88
trust 132
TTSI *see* testing, tracing, and supported isolation
tuberculosis 44

Ultimatum 275
Umbhauer, G. 272
uncertainty: energy trends and, 172; forecasting and, 100; modeling 264; school reopening and, 191
uncoordinated strategy 117
unemployment: European Union, 96; pandemic, 294; United States, 96
United Kingdom: confirmed cases in the, 6; decline in output in the, 58; exports from the, 46; flatten and fight strategy in, 118; health system in the, 144; mobilizing resources in the, 213; nonpharmaceutical interventions in the, 69; preventing joblessness in the, 95; stringency index scores in the, 74
United Nations: estimates of urbanization by the, 250; global poverty study by the, 243; Population Division of the, 179; research on pandemic disruptions by the, 302; research on shutdown interventions by the, 263; study on conflict by the, 244; sustainable development goals of the, 173, 241
United States: clinical trials in the, 220; confirmed cases in the, 6; disease outbreaks in the, 75; economic influence of the, 245; gendered work in the, 73; health system in the, 144; higher education in the, 204; mobilizing resources in the, 213; model of income assistance in the, 80–81, 95; Modern Plague in the, 11; mortgage defaults in the, 228; out-of-pocket healthcare model in the, 145; population density in the, 250; priority for vaccination in the, 222; role of the economy in the, 299; shutdown policy waves, 278; Spanish flu in the, 12; social vulnerability index in the, 264; state governments in the, 73; stringency index scores in the, 74; struggle to contain the disease in the, 120–121; unemployment in the, 95; urban and rural cases in the, 250; willingness to pay in the, 300
universal health care 66, 145, 160
University of California Berkeley 69
University of Cambridge 38–39
University of Chicago 26–27, 93, 142
University of Minnesota 33
University of New South Wales 269